EARLY CHURCH RECORDS OF NEW CASTLE COUNTY

DELAWARE

VOLUME I
1701-1800

F. Edward Wright

WILLOW BEND BOOKS
2007

WILLOW BEND BOOKS
AN IMPRINT OF HERITAGE BOOKS, INC.

Books, CDs, and more—Worldwide

For our listing of thousands of titles see our website
at
www.HeritageBooks.com

Published 2007 by
HERITAGE BOOKS, INC.
Publishing Division
65 East Main Street
Westminster, Maryland 21157-5026

Copyright © 1994 F. Edward Wright

All rights reserved. No part of this book may be reproduced or transmitted in any form or by any means, electronic or mechanical, including photocopying, recording or by any information storage and retrieval system without written permission from the author, except for the inclusion of brief quotations in a review.

International Standard Book Number: 978-1-58549-289-2

CONTENTS

Introduction v

Immanuel Church 1

Welsh Tract Baptist Meeting 77

  New Castle County Quaker Marriages From
    Newark Monthly Meeting 102

      Wilmington Monthly Meeting:
    Births and Deaths 120
    Marriages 147
    Certificates of Removal received 163
    Certificates of Removal sent ... 176

Pencader Presbyterian Church 216

Asbury Methodist Episcopal Church ... 224

St. Peters' Catholic Church 227

Marriage Bonds of New Castle County . 230

Index 265

INTRODUCTION

Volume One of this series covers a number of church registers and other records discussed below. All births through 31 December 1800 were copied, regardless of the date of the baptism. The order of the records usually reflects the order of the "original" from which the transcriber worked. If the date of the baptism was not recorded one can guess that the event might have occurred sometime between the baptisms appearing before and after the given entry. In the case of most denominations the date of baptism usually indicates an approximate date of birth. This does not apply, of course, to the Baptists who baptized as adults. In addition to the church registers we have added other records which will be useful to genealogists, namely, marriage bonds, certificates of removal/letters of dismission and list of church members.

Volume Two is a reprint of the register of Old Swedes Church, taken from the translation by Horace Burr, published by Historical Society of Delaware in 1890, titled, *The Records of Holy Trinity (Old Swedes) Church As Translated By Horace Burr*, as amended by *Catalogue and Errata of The Records of Holy Trinity (Old Swedes) Church*, published by the Society in 1919.

Abbreviations:
MMtg - Monthly Meeting
dau - daughter
co. - county
Phila - Philadelphia
Wit: witness
hd - hundred

OLD SWEDES CHURCH

Among the original colony of Swedes who settled in Delaware and built Fort Christina in 1638 was Rev. Reorus Torkillus, who established religious worship in the fort, the first meeting-place for Christians on the

Delaware, and there it was continued until the church at Tinicum was erected in 1646. Crane Hook Church is said to have been built in 1667, probably by the united efforts of the Dutch congregation and the Swedes. It was used for public worship until the "Old Swedes' Church" was built in 1698 on the present site. Lutheran in denomination the church was the religious center for not only the Swedes but English and persons of various ethnicity and religious affiliation, as evidenced by the names of those who were baptized, married or buried. Eventually Swedish ministers were replaced by English ministers under cordial circumstances.

In using the records keep in mind the words of the translator, Horace Burr.

> "I have not attempted to render the old Swedish in which these records were written, into modern book English, but have made a very literal translation, following the style of the writer ... It would seem that the names of persons not Swedes have been spelt as they would sound to the Swedish ear, and many of them very differently from their proper English orthography."

> "The Bondê or agricultural population of Sweden has not sirnames at the time of the emigration, nor have they even now. The oldest son takes the father's name, as for instance, Johan the son of Johan, would be Johan Johansson, and all the other sons, Peter, Carl, etc., would be Peter Johansson, in English, Johnsson; and the daughters take dotter, as Brita Johansdotter.

> "After their settlement here among English and other nationalities, who had already adopted sirnames for all classes, the father's name naturally became the family name, but the peculiarity of spelling with two s' continued for a long time, and Paulsson

was the correct spelling until a quite recent date."[1]

He and others cite various derivations of the Swedish names, e.g., Didriksson became Derickson or Richardsson and Poulson became Paulsson Justasson became Justis or Justice.

From January, 1773 the records were written in English. Mr. Burr omitted the names of witnesses and sponsors. Burials were also omitted "after the coming of Mr. Acrelius, as they would add to the size of the work, and are of less importance than births, baptisms and marriages." We look forward to the time when these are translated and published.[2]

SOCIETY OF FRIENDS (QUAKERS)

Friends began settling on the east side of the Brandywine in New Castle County around 1682. It was named the Newark Meeting and was continued until 1754. In 1705 a meeting house was built in New Castle which declined in membership until it was finally discontinued in 1758. Its members then attended the meeting at Wilmington. A Monthly Meeting was held in New Castle in 1686. In 1687 this meeting decided that it was "more convenient for the present that the meeting be held twice on the other side of the Brandywine and the third which will be the Quarterly Meeting at New Castle." From 1689 to 1704 the Monthly meeting seems to have been "held at Valentine Hollingsworth's and other Friends' houses," and was called Newark Monthly Meeting. The last monthly meeting held at Newark was in 1707. It was generally held at Centre though sometimes at Kennett, from that date until 1760, when its name was changed to the Kennett Monthly Meeting.

The Wilmington Preparative Meeting was established in 1739. A Wilmington Monthly Meeting was established in 1750 by Chester (Concord) Quarterly Meeting out of Kennett

Monthly Meeting. It was in 1750 that the records begin. Wilmington Monthly Meeting included the particular meetings of Wilmington and New Castle at that time.

Records: Contained here are all the known records of Wilmington Monthly Meeting; the earlier Newark Monthly Meeting marriages are include insofar as one of the parties was from New Castle County. Copies of the records are found at Friends Historical Library of Swarthmore College, Swarthmore, Pennsylvania.

ANGLICANS (PROTESTANT EPISCOPAL)

See also Old Swedes' Church which became Holy Trinity Church.

The Emanuel Protestant Episcopal Church of New Castle was established in 1704. Rev. George Ross was sent by the Society for the Propagation of the Gospel in Foreign Parts as its first minister in 1705. In 1728 the pew holders were Richard Halliwell, Joseph Wood, John Strand, Samuel Kirk, Thomas Dakeyne, John Land, Peter Jaquett, Cornelius Kettle, Richard Grafton, William Read, Samuel Lowman, Yeates & Custis, Zophar Eaton, John Wallace, Thos. Gassel, Richard Reynolds, Peter Hance, James Sykes and John Cann. The records have been taken from Thomas Holcomb's works.[3]

St. Ann's was the earliest organized congregation in the southern portion of New Castle County. It was organized before 1704. The Anglican church at St. Georges was founded by Welsh families prior to 1707. In 1720 land was granted in Mill Creek Hundred for the use of St. James' Church. There are no known early registers surviving for any of these churches.

BAPTISTS

We have abstracted the records based on the published works, *Records of The Welsh Tract*

Baptist Meeting, Pencader Hundred, New Castle County, Delaware, 1701-1828. In Two Parts, published by the Historical Society of Delaware, Wilmington, 1904.

It was early in the 18th century that William Penn granted to David Evans and William Davis 30,000 acres of land to be divided and deeded to settlers from South Wales, some of whom had at that time settled in Radnor Township, Chester County, Penn. This grant, ever after known as "The Welsh Tract," is located partly in Pencader Hundred, New Castle County, Delaware and partly in Cecil County, Maryland. About one-fourth of the tract lay in Maryland. Thomas Griffith, their first minister, came from Pembroke and Carmarthenshire, South Wales in 1701, and soon after erected a long meeting house in which they worshiped until another structure was built in 1746. The original records for several years were kept in the Welsh language, afterwards in English.

Appearing in the minutes is this account of their arrival in this country:
"In the year 1701 some of us who were members of the churches of Jesus Christ in the countys of Pembroke and Caermarthen, South Wales in Great Britain, professing believers baptism; laying on of hands, election, and final perseverance in grace, were moved and encouraged in ... to come to Penn. Our number was sixteen, we sailed from Milford-haven in the month of June, 1701, in a ship named James and Mary and landed in Philadelphia 8 Sep following. Rec. [Received] by the congregation meeting in Philadelphia and Pennypack who held the same faith with us excepting the ordinance of laying on of hands on every particular members ...After our arrival during which time it pleased God to add to our number about 20 members, in which time we, and many other Welsh people purchased a tract of land in New Castle Co, on Delaware called Welsh tract, in the year

1703 we began to get our living out of it, and to set our meetings in order and build a place of worship, which was commonly known by the name of the Baptist meeting house by the Iron-hill."

Records: The records of the Welsh Tract Baptist Church were transcribed by Henry C. Conrad, Librarian, Wilmington, Del., October 1904.

The First Baptist Church of Wilmington, was established in 1785. We have no indication of the existence of these records prior to 1800. Bethel Baptist Church of New Castle Hundred was begun ca. 1786.

PRESBYTERIANS

The First Presbyterian Church of Wilmington took its beginning in 1737 when land was purchased. Three years later a church was erected at the present corner of 10th and Market Streets today. Rev. Robert Cathcart preached there every fourth Sunday until his death. The Second Presbyterian Church was formed by members from the First Church in 1774 with Rev. Joseph Smith as pastor. The name was changed to Christiana Church in 1787.

The only Presbyterian registers that we have for the 18th century are those of Pencader Presbyterian Church of Glasgow. According to J. Thomas Scharf, the Presbyterians of the Welsh Tract were constituted a church as early as 1710.[4] Rev. David Evans, son of David Evans, one of the grantees of the Welsh Tract, was the first pastor. Other ministers: Thomas Evans (1720-1743); Timothy Griffith (1743-1754); Alexander McDowell (1767-1773); Samuel Eakin (1776-1783); and Thomas Smith (1783-1801).[5]

Other Presbyterian churches founded in the 1700s include the following: Old Drawyers Presbyterian Church (ca. 1710); Presbyterian Church on Pigeon Run (ca. 1730); White Clay

Presbyterian Church (ca. 1721) in Mill Creek Hundred; Presbyterian Congregation of Head of Christiana Church (1708); Christiana Presbyterian Church (1730-1738) in White Clay Creek Hundred; Lower Brandywine Presbyterian Church in Pencader Hundred (ca. 1720); St. George's Presbyterian Church (early 1700s); Red Clay Creek Presbyterian Church (1722); Forest Presbyterian Church (1742).

METHODISTS

The Asbury Methodist Episcopal Church of Wilmington began in 1766 with the sermon by Captain Webb, a British army officer near what is now the corner of King and 8th Streets. The original members were John Thelwell and Deborah his daughter, Henry Colesburg, Betsy Colesburg, Sarah Colesburg, John Miller, Thomas Webster, William Wood, J. Jaquet, George Whitsill, David Ford, James Belt, Patience Erwin and Sarah Wood. The church was completed in 1789. There are no known 18th century records extant.

Other Methodist churches which were established in the late 1700s include the following: White's Chapel in Appoquinimink Hundred, Dickerson's Chapel near Dexter's Corner and Bethel Church (Cloud's Chapel).

ROMAN CATHOLICS

There were few Catholics in New Castle prior to 1800. Those who were here would have sought the ministering of the Jesuits of Old Bohemia in Cecil County, Maryland, or St. Joseph's of Philadelphia.

The records of St. Peter's of Wilmington appear just prior to 1800. After the French Revolution, and the Negro insurrection in St. Domingo, some distinguished French Catholic families settled in the Wilmington area.

MARRIAGE BONDS

These were bonds are held in the collections of the Genealogical Society of Pennsylvania, Vol. 246, Phila. In 1910 Gilbert Cope deposited them with the Genealogical Society and made the following comments,

> "When the county seat of New Castle County, Delaware, was removed from New Castle to Wilmington a great many of the old papers were placed in the attic of the new court house without any attempt to make them available for examination. About the only person who seemed to take much interest in them was Amos C. Brinton, the aged janitor of the building. He assorted them to some extent and picked out all the marriage license bonds noticed by him, and these he called my attention to in 1892. ... I went to Wilmington on the 26th of the same month and brought home the papers, which I put into twelve folio volumes. Before returning them I made a list of them for my own use.
>
> "An examination of the numbers preserved for the different years (see page 221) will show that these form but a small part of those originally issued. For some reason not ascertained there are a considerable number from Sussex and a few from Kent County, and this suggests that some from New Castle may have gone astray elsewhere, but it is feared that these have shared the fate of other of the New Castle records, notably from the office of Register of Wills. The records of the Old Swedes' Church show that licenses for marriage were issued much earlier than the date of the oldest bond preserved.
>
> "Those of early date specify the residence and occupations of the parties but after 1800 these facts are generally omitted. Much carelessness is also

manifested in filling up these bonds.. When given in the bonds the residences will appear in the following pages, but the names of sureties and witnesses are mostly omitted after 1790. Gilbert Cope, West Chester, Pa. 1-15-1910."

End Notes

1. *The Records of Holy Trinity (Old Swedes) Church As Translated By Horace Burr*, as amended by *Catalogue and Errata of The Records of Holy Trinity (Old Swedes) Church*, published by the Society in 1919. See "PREFATORY REMARKS," pp. 3-8.

2. Records for burials of Old Swedes for the period, 1713-1765 were published by the Historical Society of Delaware in 1953.

3. Thomas Holcomb, Early Ecclesiastical Affairs In New Castle, Del. And History Of Immanuel Church, pp. 179-254.

4. J. Thomas Scharf, History of Delaware, p.955. Much of the information on the founding of churches in New Castle County was drawn from this source.

5. *Ibid.*, p. 955. The registers for the 1796 - 1800 are for marriages and baptisms performed by Rev. William Chealy. It is unclear why Scharff gives the minister's name for this period as Thomas Smith.

BIBLIOGRAPHY

Burr, Horace. *The Records of Holy Trinity (Old Swedes) Church As Translated By Horace Burr*, as amended by *Catalogue and Errata of The Records of Holy Trinity (Old Swedes) Church*, published by the Society in 1919.

Bicentennial Committee, Edward P. Bartlett. *Friends in Wilmington 1738-1938*. (copy at Historical Society of Delaware).

Colburn, Dorothy. *Old Drawyers. The First Presbyterian Church in St. Georges Hundred*. Odessa, Del (1989).

Craig, Peter Stebbins. *The 1693 Census of the Swedes On The Delaware, Family Histories of the Swedish Lutheran Church Members Residing in Pennsylvania, Delaware, West New Jersey and Cecil County, Maryland, 1638-1693*. Winter Park, FL: SAG Publications, (1993).

Descendants of Early Welsh Tract Families, Newark Delaware. Typed from handwritten manuscript, author unknown.

Eckert, Jack, Ed., *Guide to the Records of Philadelphia Yearly Meeting*. Haverford College, Records Committee of Philadelphia Yearly Meeting and Swarthmore College (1989).

Holcomb, Thomas. *Sketch of Early Ecclesiastical Affairs in New Castle, Delaware, and History of Immanuel Church*. Written By Request Of the Church Club, of Delaware. (1890).

Michener, Ezra. *A Retrospect of Early Quakerism*. Philadelphia (1860).

Rightmyer, Nelson Waite. *The Anglican Church in Delaware*. Philadelphia: The Church Historical Society (1947).

Scharf, J. Thomas. *History of Delaware. 1609 - 1888*. Westminster, Maryland: Family Line Publications (1991). With revised index by Historical Society of Delaware.

Springer, Courtland B. and Ruth L. Springer. "Burial Records, 1713-1756, Holy Trinity (Old Swedes) Church," *Delaware History*, vol. 5: p. 270; vol. 6: p.53, 140, 233, 307. Wilmington: Historical Society of Delaware (1953), 38 pp.

Two Hundredth Anniversary. First and Central Presbyterian Church of Wilmington, Del., Inc. 1737 - 1937. Published by the church (1937). The appendix contains a list of interments in the Old Church Cemetery.

Zepley, Frank R. *The Churches of Delaware*. Wilmington, DE (1947).

Inventory of Church Records of Delaware. Prepared by the Historical Records Survey, W.P.A. 1937.

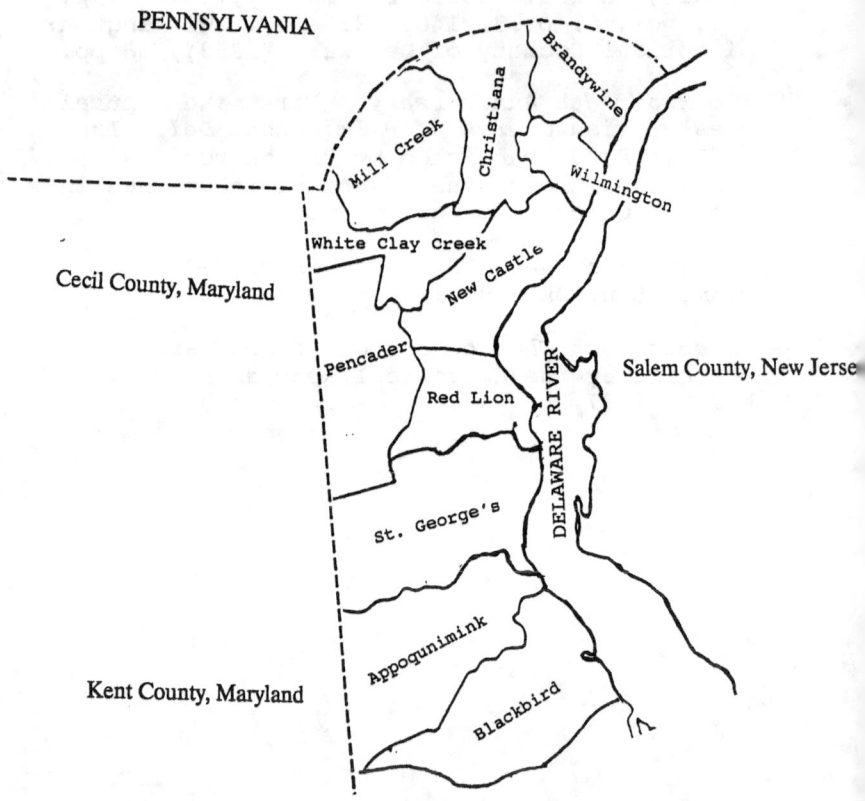

WARDENS OF IMMANUEL CHURCH.

Richard Halliwell,	1710.	Alexander Harvey,	1767.
James Robinson,	1710.	John Stockton,	1784.
John Land,	1715.	Joseph Tatlow.	1784.
Edward Jennings,	1715.	Thomas Aiken,	1786.
John Earl,	1715.	John Wethered,	1786.
James Sykes,	1718.	Joseph Tatlow,	1787.
William Read,	1720.	Matthew Pearce,	1790.
James Merriwether,	1721.	John Stockton,	1790.
Richard Grafton,	1722.	William Lees,	1795.
James Sykes,	1729.	Joseph Tatlow,	1796.
James Merriwether,	1729.	William Clay,	1797.
Jehu Curtis,	1730.	Thomas Bond,	1798.
Richard Grafton,	1731.	Michael King,	1800.
William Read,	1731.	Kensey Johns,	1802.
Henry Gonne,	1734.	Michael King,	1803.
Nicholas Jaquett,	1739.	Thomas Bond,	1806.
John Vangezell,	1745.	Henry Colesberry,	1808.
Jehu Curtis,	1752.	William T. Read,	1820.
John Stoop,	1752.	James Booth,	1824.
Richard McWilliam,	1753.	Evan H. Thomas,	1833.
Jacob Grantham,	1753.	William T. Read,	1838.
William Till,	1759.	James Rogers,	1855.
John Stoop,	1759.	John D. Bird,	1855.
Richard McWilliam,	1761.	William T. Read,	1856.
John Vangezell.	1762.	George B. Rodney,	1856.
Joseph Enos,	1762.	Alfred C. Nowland,	1873.
William Sluby,	1766.	John McFarlin,	1884.
		Michael King,	1888.

PARISH REGISTER.

A Register of Christenings in the Parish of Emmanuel Church at New Castle, from Mr. Rosse's entering upon the cure of the said Parish, which was the 29th August, 1714.

Adult, Lydia Reed, daughter of George Reed, of White Clay Creek, October 17, 1714.

Infant, John Rosse, son of George Rosse, minister to New Castle, October 21, 1714.

Adult, Ruth Gumbly, daughter of John Gumbly, of Duck Creek, October 31, 1714.

Infant, Mary, daughter of Ephraim Aug. Herman, November 27, 1714.

Infant, Catharine, daughter of Richard Clarke, November 29, 1714.

Child, Elizabeth Cole, daughter of Edward Cole, January 5, 1714-15.

Child, Ann, daughter of Edward Cole, January 5, 1714-15.

Adult, William Smith, son of John Smith, January 9 1714-15.

Infant, Martha, daughter of ————, January 16. 1714-15.

Infant, William, son of Thomas Guey, January 25, 1714-15.

Infant, Elizabeth Young, daughter of Christopher Young, January 25, 1714-15.

Adult, Sarah Nash, daughter of ———— Nash, January 30, 1714-15.

Infant, Sarah, daughter of Edward Jennings, April 3, 1715.

Infant, John, son of ————————, of White Clay Creek, April 10, 1715.

Adult, Rebecca Land, wife of John Land, April 17, 1715.

IMMANUEL CHURCH
BAPTISMS.

Infant, Ellis, daughter of George Peterson, of Swanwick, May 1, 1715.

Infant, John, son of —————— ————, May 1, 1715.

Infant, Priscilla, daughter of James Robison, of White Clay Creek, May 8, 1715.

Infant, Lucas, son of ——————————, of St. George's Tract, June 5, 1715.

Infant, Alexander Fraser, son of Alexander Fraser, of Christeen Bridge, June 12, 1715.

Child, Abraham Fiere, son of Philip Fiere, of Coristogoe, August 22, 1715.

Infant, James, son of Morgan Morgan, of White Clay Creek, September —, 1715.

Infant, William Empson, son of Ebenezer Empson, Brandywine Creek, September 20, 1715.

Infant, William, son of William MacDaniel, of White Clay Creek, September 23, 1715.

Infant, John, son of George Reed, of White Clay Creek, September 23, 1715.

Infant, Sibylla, daughter of John French, October 3, 1715.

Infant, Benjamin, son of Thomas Ogle, of White Clay Creek, November 20, 1715.

Infant, Mary Hore, daughter of John Hore, February 8, 1715-16.

Infant, John, son of John Cann, of White Clay Creek, February 26, 1715-16.

Infant, Nathaniel, son of James Sykes, New Castle neighborhood, May 9, 1716.

Infant, Margaret, daughter of Jacob Rogers, June 18, 1716.

Infant, Sarah, daughter of Powel Garison, June 18, 1716.

Infant, Joseph, son of John Land, June 27, 1716.

Infant, John, son of John Erle, August 5, 1716.

Infant, Margaret, daughter of Cornelius Kettle, August 10, 1716.

Infant, Elleanor, daughter of Peter Jaquet, of Swanwick, August 14, 1716.

Infant, Anne, daughter of Peter Johnston, August 19, 1716.

BAPTISMS.

Infant, Mary, daughter of Gunning Bedford, August 25, 1716,

Infant, Henry, son of Nicolas Bishop, September 3, 1716.

Infant, William, son of ———— ————, September 9, 1716.

Adult, Edward, son of Edward Green, September 23, 1716.

Adult, Susanna, daughter of John Gumblee, September 26, 1716.

Infant, Eneas, son of George Rosse, October 17th, (nat 17th September,) 1716.

Infant, John, son of Nicolas Calender, January 2, 1716-17.

Infant, Elizabeth, daughter of Nicolas Calender, January 2, 1716-17.

Infant, Joanna, daughter of Edward Robison, January 6, 1716-17.

Adult, Stephen Hollingsworth, of White Clay Creek, February 17, 1716-17.

Infant, Mary, daughter of John Stoops, March 31, 1717.

Infant, Rebecca, daughter of Peter Johnson, September 18, 1717.

Infant, Stephen, son of James Sykes, of Christeen Creek, December 26, 1717.

Infant, Rowland Monroe, son of John Monroe, December 27, 1717.

Adult, Mary, daughter of ———— Maxwell, ———— —, 1717.

Infant, Margaret, daughter of ———— Rogers, of New Castle County ———— —, 1717.

Infant, Peter, son of Peter Jaquet of Swanwick, April 14, 1718.

Infant, Adam, son of Robert Marley, October 12, 1718.

Infant, Charles Gookin, son of Richard Birmingham, December —, 1718.

Infant, Ann Mary, daughter of William Shappon, December 26, 1718.

Infant, William, son of William Reed, May —, 1719.

Infant, John, son of Peter Hanson, May 31, 1719.

IMMANUEL CHURCH
BAPTISMS.

Infant, Anne, daughter of George Rosse, August 14, 1719.

Infant, Mary, daughter of Gunning Bedford, September —, 1719.

Infant, William, son of Samuel Lowman, September 24, 1719.

Infant, Nicolas, son of Packer Adams, December 20, 1719.

Infant, Jonathan, son ot Ebenezer Empson, December 21, 1719.

Infant, Avice, daughter of John French, January 22, 1719-20.

Infant, Susanna, daughter of William Read, June 22, 1722.

Child, James, son of Peter Alricks, August 1, 1723.

Infant, Ann, daughter of Peter Alricks, August 1, 1723.

Adult, Joseph Fox, September 11, 1723.

Infant, Katharine, daughter of William Reed, September 29, 1723.

Infant, Mary, daughter of Capt. William Battell, October —, 1723.

Infant, Mary, daughter of Richard and Hannah Grafton, October 10, born September 4th, preceding, 1727.

Alice, daughter of Jacobus Peterson and Elizabeth, born April 17, 1734.

Jane, daughter of Jacobus and Elizabeth Peterson, born March 11, 1736.

Susanna, daughter of Jacobus and Elizabeth Peterson, born November 6, 1743.

Elizabeth, daughter of Richard McWilliam, born May 19, 1749.

Richard, son of Richard McWilliam, born October 9, 1754.

William, son of Richard McWilliam, born September 4, 1757.

Stephen, son of Richard and Margaret McWilliam, born November —, 1759.

Christenings in the Parish of New Castle, by Aeneas Ross, missionary from the 1st day of October, Anno Domini, 1758.

Isabella, danghter of Mark and Elizabeth Cowen, November 14, 1758.

EARLY CHURCH RECORDS OF NEW CASTLE COUNTY
BAPTISMS.

David, son of Elizabeth McLaughlin, November 14th, aged 17 months, 4 days.

John, son of William and Jane Armor, November 14, 1758, aged 4 months.

John, son of Jacob Ross and Jane, his wife, October 31, 1758, aged 2 weeks.

Elizabeth, daughter of John McGhee and Margaret, his wife, January 22, 1759, aged 2 days.

Richard, son of William and Sarah Peterson, January 23, 1759, aged 11 days.

Elizabeth, daughter of John and Isabell Armstrong, March 26, 1759, aged 4 days.

James, son of David Anderson and Jane, his wife, April 19, 1759, aged 4 months, 10 days.

John Tub, May 16, 1759, aged 2 years and 7 months.

Margaret, daughter of Robert Lloyd and Mary Ann, his wife, May 18, 1759, aged 2 months.

Mary, daughter of Jeroboam Robison and Elizabeth, his wife, May 24, 1759, aged 5 years, 3 months.

Rhenere, son of John Gilbert and Eliza, his wife, May 24, 1759, aged 1 year, 10 months.

James, son of Joseph Enos and Jane, his wife, May 25, 1759, aged 5 months, 8 days.

Susannah, daughter of Stephen Enos and Rebecca, his wife, January 16, 1759, aged 6 weeks.

Judith, daughter of John and Alice Stoop, June 9, 1759, aged 10 days.

Hannah, daughter of John and Eliza Eves, June 10, 1759, aged 9 years, 6 months, 24 days.

Jane, daughter of John and Eliza Eves, June 10, 1759, aged 7 years, 9 months, 26 days.

John, son of John and Eliza Eves, June 10, 1759, aged two years, 4 months, 10 days.

James, son of James and Sicily McConnoghee, was baptized the 3d of June, 1759, aged 3 months, 9 days.

Adult, James Burns, the 12th day of June, 1759, aged 21 years, 4 days.

IMMANUEL CHURCH
BAPTISMS.

Samuel, son of William and Charity Land, 25th June, 1759, aged 1 year and 5 days.

John, son of John and Jane Gordon of Penn's Neck, June 8, 1759, aged 2 months, 25 days.

Grace, daughter of John and Elizabeth Carne, August 12, 1759, aged 2 years, 1 month, 6 days.

Ann, daughter of Slator Clay and Ann, his wife, August 12, 1759, aged 6 weeks.

Elizabeth, daughter of George and Alice James, September 27, 1759, aged 6 years and 6 months.

Ann, daughter of George and Alice James, September 27, 1759, aged 2 months and 18 days.

Hannah, daughter of William and Mary Davers, October 1, 1759, aged 1 day.

Peter, son of Daniel and Mary Worms, October 30, 1759, aged 4 years and 10 months.

Elizabeth, daughter of Daniel and Mary Worms, October 30, 1759, aged 2 years and 1 month.

William, son of John and Catharine Cope, October 30, 1759, aged 3 years and 2 months.

Mary, daughter of John and Catharine Cope, October 30, 1759, aged 1 year and 1 month.

Elizabeth, daughter of James and Rachel Harris, October 30, 1759, aged 1 week.

Mary, daughter of Catharine Butler, October 30, 1759, aged 1 year and 11 months.

Elizabeth Polson, daughter of Susannah Minor, October 30, 1759, aged 4 years and 10 months.

Ann, daughter of Adam and Rosanna Marley, November 14, 1759, aged 3 years and 2 months.

Samuel, son of Adam and Rosanna Marley, November 14, 1759, aged 6 weeks and 3 days.

Thomas, son of Isaac and Margaret Adams, November 14, 1759, aged 1 year and 9 months.

William, son of George and Mary Patten, November 15, 1759, aged 5 months and 19 days.

Jennet, daughter of John and Eleanor Reynolds, November 23, 1759, aged 2 weeks and 4 days.

EARLY CHURCH RECORDS OF NEW CASTLE COUNTY
BAPTISMS.

Catharine, daughter of John and Mary Griner, December 8, 1759, aged 9 weeks and 5 days.

John, son of Philip and Margaret McBride, December 16, 1759, aged 1 month and 1 day.

John, son of Thomas and Rose Hamilton, December 16, 1759, aged 6 months.

Ann, daughter of Alexander and Elizabeth Harvey, December 17, 1769, aged 2 weeks and 2 days.

Mary, daughter of James and Mary Eves, January 30, 1760, aged 2 months and 5 days.

Ann, daughter of Israel and Agnus Stalcop, February 18, 1760, aged 1 day.

Adult, James, a negro and slave of Mr. Cornelius Garrettson, February 24, 1760.

Philim, son of Philim and Catharine McCampbell, March 3, 1760, aged 2 months and 2 days.

Sarah, daughter of John and Isabell Armstrong, May 1, 1760, aged 5 days.

William, son of John and Elizabeth Carne, May 4, 1760, aged 3 months and 20 days.

Mary, daughter of Philip and Mary Vanleurenigh, May 11, 1760, aged 5½ months.

Zacharias, son of Philip and Mary Vanleurenigh, May 11, 1760, 2 months and 7 days.

Ann, daughter of John and Margaret Patterson, May 14, 1760, aged 3 months.

Elizabeth, daughter of Elizabeth McLaughlin, May 14, 1760 aged 3 months.

Mary, daughter of Robert and Mary Scott, May 19, 1760, aged 7 months and 5 days.

William, son of George and Eleanor Shugal, June 30, 1760, aged 13 months.

Sarah, daughter of John and Elizabeth Eves, June 13, 1760, aged 6 days.

Ibred, daughter of Anthony and Frances Frenantz, June 13, 1760, aged 9 months.

Mary, daughter of Miles and Susanna Dalton, August 4, 1760, aged 13 months.

IMMANUEL CHURCH
BAPTISMS.

Margaret, daughter of James and Ann Moffet, August 31, 1760, aged 6 weeks.

Mary, daughter of William and Mary Allen, August 31, 1760, aged 19 months.

Mary, daughter of John and Margaret Barnes, August 31, 1760, aged 18 months.

William, son of William and Ann Hall, September 3, 1760, aged 4 years and 10 months.

Sarah, daughter of William and Annie Hall, September 3, 1760, aged 4 months.

James, son of Patrick and Elizabeth Leadan, October 5, 1760, aged 7 weeks and 3 days.

Martha, daughter of Mathias and Elizabeth ———— October, 7, 1760, aged 3 years and 2 months.

Henry, son of Swen Colesberry and Ann, his wife, May 10, 1761, aged 8 months and 27 days.

Robert, son of Robert and Mary McMun, May 30, 1761, aged 6 months and 8 days.

James, son of Jacob and Jane Ross, March 8, 1761, aged 1 year, 1 month.

Rebecca, daughter of Jacob and Rachel Janvier, May 30, 1761, aged 9 months and 12 days.

Elizabeth, daughter of Slater and Ann Clay, August 16, 1761, aged 1 year and 25 days.

William, son of Slater and Ann Clay, August 16, 1761, aged 3 weeks.

Mary, daughter of James and Mary Lansley, September 4, 1761, aged 1 month.

John, son of James and Cicely McConogee, September, 5, 1761, aged 10 months and 25 days.

Joseph, son of James and Sarah Wilson, November 10, 1761, aged 5 months, 20 days.

Samuel Bradford, November 10, 1761, aged 18 years.

John, son of John and Mary Patterson, —— 1762, aged 1 month.

Hannah, wife of Peter Morton, November 28, 1761, aged 27 years.

BAPTISMS.

Margaret, daughter of Peter and Hannah Morton, November 28, 1761, aged 6 years, 10 months.

Sarah, daughter of Peter and Hannah Morton, November 28, 1761, aged 4 years, 4 months.

John, son of Peter and Hannah Morton, November 28, 1761, aged 9 months.

Elizabeth, daughter of David and Ann Bush, November 30, 1761, aged 4 years, 5 months.

Sarah, daughter of David and Ann Bush, November 30, 1761, aged 1 year and 7 months.

Hance Miller, son of Nathaniel Hance, December 31, 1761, aged 2 months and 7 days.

Alexander, son of Alexander and Elizabeth Harvey, January 13, 1762, aged 3 weeks.

William, son of James and Jane Millikin, January 27, 1762, aged 4 weeks and 4 days.

Eliakim, son of Eliakim and Mary Stoop, March 20, 1762, aged 6 years, 1 month and 9 days.

Judith, daughter of Christopher and Sarah Stoop, March 20, 1762, aged ————.

John, son of Leonard and Elizabeth Stoop, March 20, 1762, aged 12 years, 11 months.

Jeremiah, son of Leonard and Elizabeth Stoop, March 20, 1762, aged 9 years.

Elizabeth, daughter of Leonard and Elizabeth Stoop, March 20, 1762, aged 6 years, 7 months.

Sarah, daughter of Leonard and Elizabeth Stoop, March 20, 1764, aged 4 years, 1 month.

James, son of William and Mary White, April 15, 1762, aged 6 months.

William, son of Morris and Mary McNemara, April 28, 1762, aged 1 year, 18 days.

Thomas, son of Thomas and Sarah Morton, May 5, 1762, aged 4 months, 4 days.

Cornelia, daughter of John, Jr. and Alice Stoop, May 6, 1762, aged 4 months, 25 days.

Margaret, daughter of Donald and Ann Drummond, May 9, 1782, aged 2 weeks.

James, son of William and Mary Davers, May 15, 1762, aged 8 weeks.

Elizabeth, daughter of James and Mary Eves, May 17, 1762, aged 3 months, 17 days.

Elizabeth, daughter of John and Elizabeth Eves, May 24, 1762, aged 1 month, 24 days.

Frances, daughter of James and Ann Readin, May 29, 1762, aged 5 weeks.

Alexander, son of Alexander and Mary Cummings, ———— — 1762, aged 3 months and 12 days.

Alice, daughter of William and Sarah Sutton of Newport, February 1756, aged 2 weeks.

Sarah, daughter of William and Sarah Sutton, of Newport, September 1760, aged 2 months and 7 days.

Mary, daughter of William and Sarah Sutton, of Newport, August 8, 1762, aged 2 months and 8 days.

William, son of John and Jane Sutton, of Newport, August 20, 1762, aged 4 months, 25 days.

Isaac, son of George and Ann Peterson, of Newport, October 11, 1762, aged 5 years, 7 months and 10 days.

Jennet, daughter of Mary McMullen, of Newport, September 1, 1762, aged 6 weeks.

Ann, daughter of Thomas and Ann Kenton, ———— — ———— aged 8 months.

Margaret, daughter of John and Margaret Gillalan, November 1, 1762, aged 4 days.

Jane, daughter of Bartholomew and Bridget McGuire, November 1, 1762, aged 2 months, 11 days.

John, son of Doherty and Rebecca Allen, September 19, 1762, aged 7 months, 5 days.

Margaret, daughter of William and Mary Allen, of Newport, September 19, 1762, aged 1 month, 1 day.

Stephen, son of Joseph and Jane Enos, February 26, 1763, aged 6 weeks, 5 days.

Araminta, daughter of William and Jane Hazlett, February 26, 1763, aged 10 weeks.

Elizabeth, daughter of Jacob and Mary Morton, February 27, 1763, aged 2 months and 4 days.

EARLY CHURCH RECORDS OF NEW CASTLE COUNTY
BAPTISMS.

Sarah, daughter of Swen and Ann Colesberry, May 1, 1763, aged 4 months, 2 weeks.

Sarah, daughter of Charles and Elizabeth Burk, May 3, 1763, aged 10 months.

Ann, daughter of Charles and Ann Springer, February, 1761, aged 1 month.

Thomas, son of Charles and Ann Springer, June 25, 1763, aged 4 months, 6 days.

John Ramsey, son of Alex. and Mary Cummings, March 17, 1763, aged 2 months, 15 days.

William, son of James and Jane Milliken, July 21, 1763, aged 5 months, 7 days.

David, son of James and Cicily McConoly, July 31, 1763, aged 6 weeks, 4 days.

Elizabeth, daughter of John and Mary Smith, May 21, 1763.

Mary, daughter of Daniel and Mary Worms, August 18, 1763, aged 4 months, 3 days.

Andrew, son of John and Mary Neil, July 20, 1763, aged 1 month, 2 days. Born at sea.

Elizabeth, daughter of Mark and Elizabeth Cowen, November 13, 1763, aged 3 years, 7 months and 5 days.

Isabell, daughter of Mark and Elizabeth Cowen, November 13, 1763, aged 1 year, 4 months.

Catharine, daughter of Francis and Susannah McCauley, December 10, 1763, aged 9 months.

John, son of George and Gertrude Read, ——.

Levy, son of Jacob and Catharine Colesberry, January 6, 1764, aged 6 weeks.

William, son of John and Chloe Elliott, January 30, 1764, aged 4 weeks.

Elizabeth, daughter of Henry and Unity Law, February 15, 1764, aged 6 years, 9 months.

Thomas, son of Henry and Unity Law, February 15, 1764, aged 2 years, 4 months.

George, son of Alex. and Elizabeth Harvey, February 25, 1764, aged 2 weeks.

Mary, daughter of Abraham and —— Short, June 15, 1764, aged 6 months, 18 days.

IMMANUEL CHURCH
BAPTISMS.

Ann, daughter of Thomas and Sarah Morton, March 14, 1764, aged 3 months, 5 days.

Samuel, son of William and Jane Armor, January 6, 1765, aged 5 months, 2 days.

Elizabeth, daughter of John and Eleanor Reynolds, September 27, 1764, aged 6 weeks, 5 days.

Mary, daughter of William and Jane Hazlett, January 26, 1765, aged 2 months, 9 days.

George, son of George and Phyllis Culp, February 16, 1765, aged 4 weeks, 2 days.

Nicholas, son of Nicholas and Sarah Fitzgerald, December 30, 1764, aged 5 days.

Richard, son of Theodore Maurice, Esq., ——.

Mary and Jane, twin daughters of Robert Phillips, March 21, 1765, aged 2 days.

Mary, daughter of John and Jane Reece, April 27, 1765, aged 4 weeks, 4 days.

Hannah, daughter of James and Ann Readen, April 27, 1765, aged 4 months, 12 days.

James, son of James and Eleanor Massy, May 14, 1765, aged 3 months, 23 days.

William and James, twin sons of John and Susannah Cinoll, March 13, 1765, aged 2 days.

Eleanor, daughter of John and Mary Post, April 10, 1765, aged 1 year, 9 months.

Ann, daughter of John and Abia Macelroy, June 4, 1765, aged 2 months.

Margaret, daughter or Adam and Mary Dyel, July 9, 1765, aged 5 months, 17 days.

Samuel, son of Samuel and Elizabeth Skelton, August 17, 1765, aged 7 weeks.

John, son of James and Catharine Johnston, August 12, 1765, aged 9 days.

Cathrine Margaret, daughter of John and Margaret Patterson, August 19, 1765, aged 2 months.

John, son of Patrick and Susannah Holland, May 23, 1765.

Jacob, son of Margaret McCormick, August 20, 1765, aged 13 months.

BAPTISMS.

Mary, daughter of James and Cicily McConoly, December 19, 1765, aged 2 months, 2 days.

Josiah, son of William and Sarah Anderson, February 22, 1766, aged 6 months.

Joseph, son of David and Jane Anderson, May 14, 1766, aged 8 months.

Elizabeth, daughter of Felix and Bridget McCugn, May 23, 1766, aged 6 months, 10 days.

Henry, son of Jacob and Catharine Colesberry, June 11, 1766, aged 7 weeks.

Cornelius, son of John and Elizabeth Hinsay, June, 1766.

Isaiah, son of Flora Miller, a free negro woman, September, 1766, aged 1 month.

Rachel, daughter of Joseph and Mary Tatlow, July 20, 1766, aged 8 weeks, 3 days.

Margaret, daughter of James and Jane Rudden, August 17, 1766, aged 1 year, 2 months.

Margaret, daughter of Solomon and Lydia Springer, August 23, 1766, aged 4 months, 10 days.

Thomas, son of George and Isabell Bullock, September 1, 1766, aged 4 months, 19 days.

Margaret, daughter of John and Chloe Elliott, September 27, 1766, aged 1 month, 11 days.

James, son of James and Elizabeth Wardlow, November 14, 1766, aged 6 months.

Edward, son of Edward Gibson and Cathrine Conly, November 22, 1766, aged 8 months.

Mary, daughter of John and Mary Mackee, October 22, 1766, aged 9 months.

Fanny, daughter of Patrick and Fanny Dougherty, October 2, 1766, ———— ————.

Edward, son of John and Sarah Macum, August 15, 1766, aged 10 months, 6 days.

Hugh, son of Robert and Mary Mukelhuron, November 23, 1766, aged 8 weeks.

Elizabeth, daughter of John and Martha McNamee, September 10, 1766, aged 8 years, 1 month.

BAPTISMS.

Jane, daughter of John and Martha McNamee, September 10, 1766, aged 8 years, 1 month, twin.

Ann, daughter of John and Martha McNamee, September 10, 1766, aged 5 years, 7 months.

John, son of John and Martha McNamee, September 10, 1766, aged 4 years, 3 weeks.

William, son of John and Martha McNamee, September 10, 1766, aged 1 year, 10 months.

James, son of Samuel and Margaret Mcginnis, December 11, 1766, aged 3 months, 7 days.

Elizabeth, daughter of Alex and Elizabeth Harvey, February — 1767, aged 5 weeks.

Prudence, daughter of Patrick and Mary Hughs, March 17, 1767, aged————— —.

Ann, daughter of James and Mary Campbell, March 25, 1767, aged 1 year, 6 months, 16 days.

Mary, daughter of James and Mary Campbell, March 25, 1767, aged 9 and 2 weeks.

Frances, daughter of William and Jane Hazlett, May 8, 1767, aged 1 month, 13 days.

Edward, son of Peter and Rosanna Dimpsey, May 8, 1767, aged 6 days.

John, son of Robert and Jane Phillips, May 14, 1767, aged 7 weeks.

David and John, twins of Hugh and Jane Martin, May 17, 1767, aged 9 months, 9 days.

Ann, daughter of William and Mary Lewis, April 27, 1767, aged 9 years, 10 months.

Rachel, daughter of William and Mary Lewis, April 27, 1767, aged 7 years, 2 months, 2 days.

Lucretia, daughter of Joshua and Rebecca Story, August 10, 1767, aged 6 months.

Henry, son of Matthias and Ann Morton, August 10, 1767, aged 10 months, 27 days.

John, son of William and Charity Land, September 17, 1767, aged 2 years, 8 months, 16 days.

Joseph, son of William and Charity Land, September 17, 1767, aged 5 months, 27 days.

EARLY CHURCH RECORDS OF NEW CASTLE COUNTY
BAPTISMS.

Isaac, son of John and Susannah Kirk, September 19, 1767, aged 3 months.

Elizabeth, daughter of Thomas and Margaret Shepherd, November 15, 1767, aged 7 months.

Reuben, son of John and Susannah Collins, January 30, 1767

Elizabeth, daughter of Samuel and Cathrine Bradford, March, 31, 1768, aged 7 weeks.

John, son of John and Cathrine Cann, February 10, 1769, aged 3 months, 5 days.

Susannah, daughter of Robert and Cathrine Walker, October 31, 1767, aged 1 year, 5 months, 6 days.

Mary, daughter of James and Susannah Enos, July 24, 1769, aged 1 month, 5 days.

John, son of Andrew and Elizabeth Hutton, July 24, 1769, aged 1 year, 5 months, 17 days.

Susannah, daughter of John and Cathrine Gilbert, March 5, 1769, aged 9 months, 5 days.

David, son of John and Mary Post, May 15, 1769, aged 1 year, 2 months, 14 days.

Elizabeth, daughter of Sampson and Ann Smith, May 15, 1769, aged 5 months, 19 days.

George, son of Robert and Jane Phillips, July 29, 1769, aged 2 months, 27 days.

William, son of Patrick and Mary McLaughlin, February 2, 1772, aged 11 months, 20 days.

Hugh, son of Edward and Judith Sweeney, December 31, 1769, aged 6 weeks and 5 days.

Sarah, daughter of Robert and Mary McGhee, November 15, 1769, aged 1 year, 2 months, 23 days.

John, son of George and Phyllis Culp, November 26, 1769, aged 10 months, 28 days.

Mary, daughter of Matthias and Sarah Homan, August 24, 1769, aged 5 months, 16 days.

Mary, daughter of James and Sarah Campbell, September 13, 1769, aged 5 months, 3 days.

Ruth, daughter of David and Jane Anderson, November 14, 1769, aged 9 months, 12 days.

IMMANUEL CHURCH
BAPTISMS.

Sarah, daughter of David and Jane Anderson, November 14, 1764, aged 2 years.

John, son of Thomas and Ann Holsen, September 18, 1769, aged 6 months, 28 days.

William, son of William and Ann Copeland, October 11, 1769, aged 5 months, 22 days.

Magdalene, daughter of Michael and Magdalene Livingston, October 29, 1769, aged 6 months, 11 days.

George, son of John and Mary Williams, November 15, 1769, aged 1 year, 7 months, 10 days.

Mary, daughter of Robert and Mary McMun, February 22, 1770, aged 5 months, 14 days.

Elizabeth, daughter of Knight and Rhoda Gilborn, of Dragon Neck, November 16, 1769, aged 6 months, 2 days.

Mary, daughter of John and Cathrine Grimes, May 14, 1770, aged 3 months, 12 days.

Susannah, daughter of John and Cloe Elliott, April 14, 1769, aged 1 month, 7 days.

Rebecca, daughter of John and Ann Toppin, October 30, 1769 ——.

Ann, daughter of Samuel and Elizabeth Skelton, January 17, 1768, aged 3 months, 2 weeks.

Elizabeth, daughter of Charles and Ann McCreden, April 9, 1768, aged 3 months, 20 days.

Isaac, son of Jacob and Cathrine Colesberry, January 30, 1769, aged 3 months, 20 days.

Elizabeth, daughter of Morris and Mary McCreden, April 9, 1768, aged 1 year, 6 months, 5 days.

Mary, daughter of Jacob and Ann Cathrine Colesberry, March 31, 1774, aged 2 months.

James, son of John Stafford, February 10, 1770, aged 10 months and 7 days.

George, son of Joseph and Cathrine Clark, March 31, 1770, aged 3 months, 16 days.

Elizabeth, daughter of Isaac and Ann Justis, April 18, 1770, aged 4 months, 4 days.

Thomas, son of Thomas and Elizabeth Darbyshire, April 2, 1774, aged 5 weeks, 1 day.

EARLY CHURCH RECORDS OF NEW CASTLE COUNTY
BAPTISMS.

William Sanky, son of Abraham and Bridget Sadler, May 17, 1771, aged 1 year, 11 days.

Grantham, son of Morton and Dorcas Morton, August 24, 1771, aged 2 weeks.

Margaret, daughter of Thomas and Lucretia Turner, August 26, 1771, aged 3 months, 17 days.

Mary, daughter of Samuel and Mary Hoey, October 27, 1771, aged 4 weeks, 5 days.

Sarah, daughter of Thomas and ——— Morton, November 12, 1771, aged ———.

Sarah, daughter of William and ——— Post, November 12, 1771, aged——— and 9 days.

Elizabeth, daughter of Joseph and Sarah Garretson, November 14, 1771, aged 11 months.

William, son of Knight and Rudy Gilbert, November 15, 1771, aged 8 months.

Henry, son of John and Susannah Kirk, March 17, 1772, aged 5 months, 7 days.

Rebecca, daughter of Thomas and Ann Hinton, September 11, 1771, aged 8 months.

Thomas, son of Henry and Sarah White, September 11, 1771, aged 3 years, 5 months, 19 days.

John, son of Henry and Sarah White, September 11, 1771, aged 1 year, 6 months, 15 days.

Martha, daughter of Wm. and Jane Flemin, September 11, 1771, aged 1 year, 6 months, 29 days.

Christiana, daughter of Samson and Ann Smith, July 25, 1772, aged 1 month.

Jane, daughter of Robert and Jane Watson, September 7, 1772, aged 7 months, 5 days.

Rebecca, daughter of Nathaniel and Cathrine Sappington, September 4, 1772, aged 7 weeks, 4 days.

George, son of William and Mary Robbins, September 8, 1772, aged 1 year, 4 months.

Robinson, son of Andrew and Margaret Polson, October 1, 1772, aged 2 months, 5 days.

Christina, daughter of Matthias and Ann Morton, October 10, 1772, aged 13 months, 10 days.

IMMANUEL CHURCH
BAPTISMS.

Henry, son of Andrew and Mary Morton, October 10, 1772, aged 1 year, 4 months, 26 days.

Joshua, son of Samuel and Margaret Pickin, October 10, 1772, aged 6 months, 21 days.

Neil, son of Neil and Eleanor Gillespy, December 27, 1772, aged 4 weeks.

Ann, daughter of Patrick and Sarah Dougherty, December 27, 1772, aged 3 months, 2 weeks.

Ann Cathrine, daughter of Joseph and Mary Tatlow, January 14, 1772, aged 2 months, 27 days.

Margaret and William, twins of John and Ann Hamilton, near White Clay Creek, May 2, 1773, aged 8 days.

Margaret, daughter of Joseph and Jane Reaper, May 14, 1773, aged 11 months.

Mary, daughter of Abraham and Hannah Garrettson, May 14, 1773, aged 8 months, 11 days.

Phœbe, daughter of John and Cathrine Cann, of White Clay Creek, April 5, 1773, aged 1 month, 11 days.

David, son of David and Agnes Lewis, of White Clay Creek, April 5, 1773, aged 8 months, 28 days.

Barnabas, son of Andrew and Bridget Murphey, July 23, 1769, aged 6 months, 23 days.

Sophia Catharina, daughter of Frederick and Catharina Wilderson, May 27, 1770, aged 3 months, 16 days.

Sarah, daughter of William and Ann Owens, May 27, 1770, aged 10 months, 11 days.

William, son of Hugh and Margaret Connoway, August 26, 1772, aged 3 weeks, 1 day. Born at sea.

Jennet, daughter of Robert and Martha McFarland, August 28, 1772, aged 2 years.

Thomas, son of James and Eleanor Ross, June 6, 1773, aged 6 years, 4 months.

Ann, daughter of James and Eleanor Ross, June 6, 1773, aged 3 years, 10 months.

James, son of James and Eleanor Ross, June 6, 1773, aged 1 year, 1 month, 14 days.

John, son of William and Sarah McCauley, June 8, 1773, aged 1 year, 2 months, 22 days.

EARLY CHURCH RECORDS OF NEW CASTLE COUNTY
BAPTISMS.

Eleanor, daughter of Michael and Hannah Brannel, July 18, 1773, aged 4 months, 27 days.

Ann Catharine, daughter of John and Mary Post, January 24, 1771, aged 8 months, 6 days.

Elizabeth, daughter of Michael and Magdalene Livingston, June 24, 1772, aged 9 months, 8 days.

Mary, daughter of Gustavus and Jane Grimes, June 24, 1772, aged 1 year, 2 days.

Elizabeth, daughter of John and Mary Martin, June 24, 1772, aged 1 year, 5 months, 15 days.

John, son of Philip and Catharine Clem, June 24, 1772, aged 5 years, 5 months, 4 days.

Elizabeth, daughter of John and Catharine Symmonds, June 24, 1772, aged 6 weeks, 5 days.

Elizabeth, daughter of Edward and Ruth McCreden, June 24, 1772, aged 1 year, 3 months.

Phœbe, daughter of John and Catharine Cann, April 5, 1773, aged 1 month, 11 days.

David, son of David and Agnes Lewis, April 5, 1773, aged 9 months.

Thomas, son of Thomas and Sarah Cumberland, —— 1774, aged 4 years.

Agnes, wife of Jacob Morton, August 2, 1778, aged 21 years, 5 months.

David, son of James and Rebekah Stephenson, September 21, 1778, aged 6 years, 1 month.

George, son of James and Rebekah Stephenson, September 21, 1778, aged 3 years, 9 months.

Stephen, son of James and Rebekah Stephenson, September 21, 1778, aged 3 months, 1 day.

David, son of Mordacai and Elizabeth Thompson, September 21, 1778, aged 2 years, 11 months.

Fanny, daughter of John and Sarah Harp, May 6, 1781, aged 1 month.

John, son of George and Patience Kirk, April 11, 1781, aged 3 weeks.

William, son of Thomas and Mary White, April 11, 1781, aged 7 weeks.

IMMANUEL CHURCH
BAPTISMS.

John, son of Samuel and Barbara Shaugh, May 9, 1781, aged 7 years.

Margaret, daughter of Robert and Barbara Johnston, May 9, 1781, aged 6 weeks.

Elizabeth, daughter of Samuel and Mary Enos, August 25, 1781, aged 3 months.

Rebecca, Maffett, June 13, 1773, at St. James' Church, aged 6 years, 7 months.

Jacob, son of Jacob and Mary Morton, July 28, 1773, aged 7 months.

Ann, daughter of John and Lydia Palmer, August 8, 1773, aged 3 years, 7 months.

Ann, daughter of John and Ann McLaughlin, August 8, 1773, aged 3 years, 3 months.

Mary, daughter of John and Ann McLaughlin, August 8, 1773, aged 1 year, 7 months.

Mary, daughter of Philip and Bridget Aclawery, August 8, 1773, aged 4 weeks.

Jane, daughter of David and Mary Cader, August 8, 1773, aged 2 months.

Ann Catharine, daughter of John and Mary Post, January 24, 1771, aged 8 months.

Mary, daughter of William and Margaret Shepherd, February 16, 1774, aged 9 months.

Catharine, daughter of Peter and Abiah Peterson, November 5, 1774, aged 2 years and 3 months.

Cornelius, son of Cornelius and Rachel Floyd, November 5, 1774, aged 8 years, 5 months.

Rebekah, daughter of Henry and Sarah White, November 5, 1774, aged 3 weeks.

Mary Ann, daughter of Daniel and Ann Smith, November 7, 1774, aged 4 weeks.

Elizabeth, daughter of Nathaniel and Sarah Gillespy, November 24, 1774, aged 4 months.

Thomas, son of William and Eliza Johnston, April 1, 1775, aged 6 months, 19 days.

Elizabeth, daughter of James and Margaret Welsh, of Brandywine Hundred, May 7, 1775, aged 3 months.

EARLY CHURCH RECORDS OF NEW CASTLE COUNTY
BAPTISMS.

Jacob, son of Edward and Ruth McCreden, October 5, 1777, aged 5 years, two months.

Samuel, son of Matthew and Ann Overton, August 8, 1778, aged 5 years, 6 months.

Ann, daughter of Matthew and Ann Overton, August 8, 1778, aged 9 months, 28 days.

Thomas, son of William and Martha Cumberland, June 25, 1780, aged 1 year, 8 months.

Susanna, daughter of Charles and Agnes Johnston, June 25, 1780, aged 3 months.

Thomas, son of John and Sarah Lyons, of Christeene Bridge, March 10, 1776, aged 1 year, 1 month.

John, son of John and Sarah Lyons, September 16, 1781, aged 1 year, 1 month.

David, son of John and Mary Harp, December 12, 1784.

John, son of Stephen and Mary Gilbert, December 18, 1784.

John and Maria, children of Philip and Maria Francis, February 10, 1785.

John Kenie and Joseph and William Craig, February 21, 1785.

Sarah, daughter of Jas. and Elizabeth McWay, March 1, 1785.

Fidelia, daughter of Kensey and Ann Johns, March 27, 1785.

James and Robert, sons of James and Ann Martin, April 30, 1785.

Ann Tobin, July 20, 1785.

Ann McClay, July, 24, 1785.

Chambers Vansant and William King, August 10, 1785.

John Farren, an infant, September 6, 1785.

William, son of Elrich and Rachel Fenister, September 14, 1785.

Margaret Carr, an infant, December 15, 1786.

Thomas Aithren, January 4, 1786.

Maria Ellis, daughter of Jas. Horatio and Anna Watmough, February 15, 1786.

Peter Abraham, son of Rev. Lawrence Gerilius, August 9, 1786.

Alexander Ewing, August 20, 1786.

Michael Dougherty, August 23, 1786.

Mary, daughter of the Rev. James Wilmer, September 12, 1786.

IMMANUEL CHURCH
BAPTISMS.

Catherine, daughter of Stephen Gilbert, September 13, 1786.

Sarah Williams, October, 19, 1786.

John Kirk, November 23, 1786.

David and Catherine King, infants, January 26, 1788.

A register of Christenings in the Parish of Emanuel Church from Mr. Clay's entering upon the cure of said Parish commencing March 24, 1788.

George, son of Joseph and Ann Enos, March 28, 1788.

Isaac, son of James and Rachel Cann, April 6, 1788, aged 14 years, 9 months and 21 days.

Jane, daughter of James and Rachel Cann, April 6, 1788, aged 9 years, 6 months, 11 days.

Elizabeth, daugter of James and Rachel Cann, April 9, 1788, 5years, 1 month, and 9 days.

Ann, daughter of James and Rachel Cann, April 6, 1788, aged 1 year, and 3 weeks,

John, son of William Cann, April 6, 1788, aged 2 years, 2 months, and 8 days,

Mary, daughter of Joseph and Susannah Israel, May 26, 1788, aged 6 years, 2 months and 3 weeks.

Elizabeth, daughter of Joseph and Susannah Israel, May 26, 1788, aged 5 years, 2 months and 2 weeks.

William Pusey, son of Joseph and Susannah Israel, May 26, 1788, aged 3 years, 7 months and 1 week.

Rebecca, daughter of Joseph and Susannah Israel, May 26, 1788, aged 1 year, 2 weeks and 5 days.

Sarah, daughter of John and Phœbe Ewen, June 29, 1788.

Henry, son of Matthew and Mary Pearce, July 13, 1788.

George, son of George and Mary Read, July 13, 1788.

Elizabeth, daughter of Stephen and Sarah Gilbert, September 12, 1788, aged 8 months.

Sarah, daughter of John and Catharine Vansant, October 5, 1788, aged 1 year and 11 months.

John, son of John and Martha Downs, October 16, 1788, aged 9 months, 3 days.

Thomas, son of Barney and Sarah McClay, December 4, 1788, died same day.

EARLY CHURCH RECORDS OF NEW CASTLE COUNTY
BAPTISMS.

Ann, daughter of Henry and Elizabeth McTouch, January 18, 1789, aged 4 years, 1 month and 3 weeks.

Sarah, daughter of Henry and Elizabeth McTouch, January 18, 1789, aged 1 year and 4 months.

John, son of Thomas and Hannah Williams, January 18, 1789 aged 6 weeks.

George King, son of John and Catharine Vansant, January, 18, 1789, aged 3 weeks, 3 days.

Rachel, daughter of David and Rebecca Harp, January, 11, 1789.

Joseph, son of ———Housman, Sunday, February, 15, 1789.

Susannah, daughter of Joseph and Susannah Israel, April 19, 1789, aged 3 weeeks.

James and Jacob, sons of James and Rebecca Carter, May 12, 1789, aged 3 and 6 years, respectively.

Margaret Hanna, an adult, May, 20, 1789.

Ann, daughter of R. Hall, June 7, 1789, aged 3 months.

Isaac, son of John and Elizabeth Jaquet, June 13, 1789, aged 3 years and 7 months.

Christiana, daughter of John and Elizabeth Jaquet, June 13, 1789, aged 2 months.

At St. James' Church, Ann, daughter of Jas. and Ann Raysford, August 23, 1789, aged 4 months.

Sarah, daughter of Eleanor McLean, August 25, 1789, aged 4 months.

At St. James' Church, Joseph, an infant son of ——— and Sarah Garrison, aged 3 months, September 6, 1789.

Sarah, daughter of Mrs. Eliza Esham, November 4, 1789, aged 4 years.

Mary, daughter of ———Furnanes, April, 10, 1790.

Mary, daughter of Stephen and Sarah Gilbert, May 2, 1790, aged 9 months.

Esther, daughter of Richard and Rebecca McWilliams, Sunday evening, May 9, 1790, aged 4 years, on 12th last December.

Mary, daughter of James and Ann Booth, Sunday evening, May 9, 1790, aged 4 years, 2 months and 12 days.

George Clay, son of James and Ann Booth, May 9, 1790, aged 2 years and 4 months.

IMMANUEL CHURCH
BAPTISMS.

James, son of James and Ann Booth, May 9, 1790, aged 5 months, 12 days.

George, a negro boy, May 9, 1790. He belongs to James Booth.

Gunning Bedford, son of Matthew and Mary Pearce, June 20, 1790.

David and George, sons of Adam and Mary Burchard, aged 5 and 2 years respectively.

Harriet Cordelia, daughter of John and Mary Wethered, July 4, 1790, aged 13 months.

Margaret, daughter of Alexander and Jane Read, August 1, 1790, aged 6 months.

Alice, daughter of Patrick and Mary McCormick, August 6, 1790, aged 1 day.

Joseph, son of Thomas and Mary Aiken, August 11, 1790, born June 6, 1787.

William Derby, son of Thomas and Mary Aiken, August 11, 1790, born July 23, 1790.

Hannah, daughter of Thomas and Mary Aiken, August 11, 1790, born July 23, 1790.

John, son of John and Elizabeth Dayson, September 5, 1790, aged 4 months, at St. James'.

Mary, daughter of Joshua and Rebecca Pusey, October 11, 1790, aged 6 years.

Martha, daughter of Joshua and Rebecca Pusey, October 11, 1790, aged 2 years.

Abigail Israel, daughter of Joshua and Rebecca Pusey, October 11, 1790, aged 1 year.

William, son of John and Mary Kearns, March 10, 1791, aged 1 year.

Margaret, daughter of John and Margaret Laugherty, March 25, 1791, aged 5 months.

Sarah, daughter of William and Elizabeth Lees, April, 1791, aged 3 months.

Elizabeth, daughter of Samuel and Eleanor Jackson, May 22, 1791, aged 4 months.

Susannah, daughter of John and Susannah Alice, August 7, 1791, at St. James' Church.

EARLY CHURCH RECORDS OF NEW CASTLE COUNTY
BAPTISMS.

Alexander, son of Alexander and Sarah Leiper, September 17, 1791, aged 3 months.

John, son of Joseph and Ann Enos, September 28, 1791, aged 2 years, 6 months.

Mary, daughter of Joseph and Ann Enos September 28, 1791, aged 1 year and 2 months.

Henrietta Jane, daughter of Barney McClay and wife, November 1, 1791, aged 1 year.

Rebecca, daughter of Stephen and Sarah Gilbert, November 20, 1791, aged 5 months.

Araminta, a girl that lives with Mrs. Latham, December 18, 1791, aged 15 years.

Elizabeth, daughter of George and Elizabeth King, February 11, 1792, aged 3 years.

George, son of George and Elizabeth King, February 11, 1792, aged 1 year, 4 months.

Anna Gertrude, daughter of Matthew and Mary Pearce, May 6, 1792, aged 4 months.

John, son of Alexander and ―― Read, May 30, 1792, aged 10 weeks.

Moore, son of James and Eleanor Wilson, June 3, 1792, aged 2 months.

John, son of John and Mary Kearnes, ―― 1792.

Abigail, daughter of Joseph and Susannah Israel, July 19, 1792, aged 7 months.

Latitia, daughter of Israel and Hannah Israel, July 19, 1792, aged 4 years.

Elizabeth, daughter of Thomas and Hester Magens, July 24, 1792, aged 3 weeks.

Ann, daughter of James and Ann Booth, July 29, 1792, aged 9 months.

William Bond, son of William and Elizabeth Lees, July 29, aged 2 months.

Rosanna and Robert, children of Barney McClay's widow, August 8, 1792.

Kensey, son of Kensey and Ann Johns, September 8, 1792, aged ――.

BAPTISMS.

William Thompson, son of George and Mary Read, December 16, 1792.

Sarah, daughter of Michael and Ann King, April 7, 1793, aged 1 year and 9 months.

Thomas, son of Patrick and Mary Grant, May 13, 1793, aged 5 months.

John, son of John and Ann Yeates, May 16, 1793, aged 3 weeks.

Joseph, son of Joseph and Susannah Israel, May 18, 1793, aged 1 month.

Agnes and Elizabeth, daughters of Nicholas and Ann Cashety, June 22, 1793, aged 10 and 5 years, respectively.

Ann, daughter of Dennis and Ann McGuire, January 30, 1794, aged 4 years.

Thomas, son of Michael and Ann King, April 13, 1794, aged 8 months.

John, son of Stephen and Sarah Gilbert, June 29, 1794, aged 2 months.

Mary, daughter of Matthew and Mary Pearce, July 17, 1794, aged 2 months.

George, son of James and Ann Booth, August 3, 1794, aged 8 months.

Elizabeth, aged 9 years, 3 months, John, aged 6 years, James, aged 2 years and 8 months, children of widow McCormick, August 10, 1794.

Margaret, daughter of John and Mary Alexander, August 10, 1794, aged 2 years.

Rafello James, son of James and Eleanor Ferrie, August 18, 1794, aged 4 months.

Mary, daughter of Thomas and Mary Smith, August 18, 1794, aged 2 months.

George, son of James and Ann McGranahan, August 28, 1794, aged 8 months.

George Latimer, son of Joseph and Susannah Israel, October 29, 1794, aged 6 weeks.

Ann Catharine, daughter of George and Mary Read, February 1, 1795, aged 3 months.

EARLY CHURCH RECORDS OF NEW CASTLE COUNTY
BAPTISMS.

Elizabeth, daughter of Thomas and Mary Aicken, February 8, 1795, aged 1 month.

Mary, daughter of James and Eleanor McDowell, July 5, 1795, aged 6 months.

Hester Cox, daughter of Rev. Joseph and Mary Clarkson, July 19, 1795, infant.

Maria, daughter of William and Mary Spotswood, August 29, 1795, aged 6 weeks,

Rachel Miller, daughter of Stephen and Mary Gilbert, September 13, 1795, aged 3 months.

Eleanor, daughter of Samuel and Eleanor Jackson, October 1795, aged 8 months.

William, son of John and Mary Caulk, November 23, 1795, ——.

William, son of James and Sarah Carpenter, December 25, 1795, aged 4 months.

Elizabeth, daughter of Gasper, and —— Smith, March 9, 1796, aged 1 year.

John, son of John and Mary Zimmerman, June 27, 1796, aged 2 weeks.

Elizabeth, daughter of James and Ann Booth, August 28, 1796, aged 4 months, 8 days.

William Shepherd, an infant, August 31, 1796.

Hugh Alexander Mullin, August 31, 1796, aged 2 years, 5 months.

Elizabeth, daughter of Joseph and Mary Tatlow, September 11, 1796, aged 7 weeks.

John, son of Kensey and Ann Johns, October 13, 1796, aged 3 months.

David, son of Michael and Ann King, November 13, 1796, aged 6 months.

Mary, daughter of James and Mary McKinley, December 3, 1796, aged 1 year, 3 months.

Sarah, aged 16 years, 10 months; Mary, aged 14 years, 10 months; Elizabeth, aged 10 years, 5 months; Hester, aged 6 years, and Deborah, aged 3 years, all daughters of the widow Nessbitt, March 19, 1797.

Joseph, an infant son of Mr. and Mrs. All, May 4, 1797.

IMMANUEL CHURCH
BAPTISMS.

Jacob, son of Mr. and Mrs Corke(Caulk?) June 19, 1797, aged 11 years.

John, infant son of Mr. and Mrs. Aicken, June 25, 1797.

Lydia Corke (Caulk?) an adult, July 25, 1797.

James, aged 9 years, Oliver, aged 7 years, Elizabeth, aged 1 year, children of above named Lydia, July 25, 1797.

Martha Dowdle, infant October 2, 1797.

Sarah and Deborah, infant daughters of Joseph and Mary Israel, October 17, 1797.

Henry, son of Matthew and Mary Pearce, October 29, 1797, aged 1 year, 2 months.

George, son of William and Anne Read, October 29, 1797, aged 4 months.

James Rudolph Vining, October 29, 1797, aged 4 months.

George Carpenter, an infant, October 29, 1797.

Harriet Rumsey, daughter of Rev. Joseph and Mary Clarkson, November 26, 1797, infant.

Ann Shepherd, an infant, January 21, 1798.

Eleanor, an infant, August 11, 1798.

Margaret, daughter of Samuel Israel, August 11, 1798.

Sarah Corke, an infant, August 12, 1798.

William, aged 5 years and Elizabeth aged 3 years, children of Mr. Andrews, December 7, 1798.

John, son of Michael King, February 3, 1799, aged 9 months.

Jane, daughter of William Spotswood, March 31, 1799, aged 2 years.

William, son of Matthew and Mary Pearce, June 23, 1799, aged 4 months.

John Meredith, son of John and Mary Read, June 23, 1799, aged 2 years.

William Clay, August 7, 1799, aged 3 years.

William, son of James and Ann Booth, August 7, 1799, aged 4 months.

Vandyke, son of Kensey and Ann Johns, August 25, 1799, aged 8 months.

Glevs Corke, September 8, 1799, aged 8 months.

Stephen, son of Stephen and Mary Gilbert, October 13, 1799, aged 9 months.

EARLY CHURCH RECORDS OF NEW CASTLE COUNTY
BAPTISMS.

Mary Springer, an infant, November 3, 1799.

Eliza Jane, daughter of James and ———McCullough, November 10, 1799, aged 11 months.

Isaac Grantham, son of Joseph and Susannah Israel, December 15, 1799, aged 4 weeks.

Elizabeth, aged 6 years and Maria, infant, January 24, 1800.

Margaret Spotswood, an infant, January 27, 1800.

John, infant son of William and Sarah Marshall, April, 13, 1800.

Ann, daughter of Robert and Elizabeth Dowdle, June 8, 1800, aged 3 months.

Lydia, daughter of John and Dorcas Hall, June 29, 1800, aged 2 years, 4 months.

John, son of John and Dorcas Hall, June 29, 1800, aged 4 months.

Elizabeth and Mary, aged 3 years, and 1 year, respectively, daughters of John and Mary Zimmerman.

James Sykes, son of Mr. and Mrs. Rumsey of Wilmington, August 10, 1800, aged 6 weeks.

Sarah, daughter of Abraham and Elizabeth Eves, September 10, 1800, aged 1 year, 6 months.

Grantham, son of Nicholas and Mary Vandyke, September 15, 1800, aged 6 months.

Margaret Meredith, daughter of John and Mary Read, September 19, 1800, aged 4 months.

Charles, son of George and Mary Read, September 19, 1800, aged 3 months.

James, son of James and Ann McAnnis, October 4, 1800, aged 5 months.

Hannah Ball, daughter of Peter and Hannah Springer, November 2, 1800, at St. James' Church, aged 1 year and 9 months.

Ann, daughter of James and Mary Bowman, November 9, 1800, aged 13 months.

William McKnight, July 12, 1801, aged 16 months.

Ann Jane Stone, August 16, 1801, aged 1 year, 8 months.

Mary, daughter of James and Elizabeth Gaston, August 30, 1801, aged 10 months.

IMMANUEL CHURCH
BAPTISMS.

James Ross, son of ———— Foote, November 15, 1801, at St. James' Church.

Mary and Martha, daughters of James and Mary Elliot November 19, 1801, aged 2 years and 3 months.

David McCormick, son of Thomas and Phœbe Singleton, December 29, 1801, aged 1 year, 4 months.

Robert, son of John and Elizabeth Gillman, March 9, 1802, aged 2 months.

Esther, daughter of Joseph and Susannah Israel, March 21, 1802, aged 3 weeks

Lewis, son of Jeremiah and Mary Springer, April 11, 1802, aged 5 months.

William Archibald, son of William and ———— Read, May 25, 1802, aged 19 months.

Robert Blackwell, son of Joseph and Mary Clarkson, June 1, 1802, aged 4 months.

Benjamin Howell, an adult, September 13, 1802.

Isabella, daughter of John and Catharine Campbell, October 31, 1802, aged 4 weeks.

Henry and John, sons of John and Ann Marshall, November 14, 1802, aged 3 years and 7 weeks respectively.

William Stewart, son of Robert and Martha Rogers, November 29, 1802, aged 4 months.

Philippa Miller and Margaret, daughter of Benj. and Rachel Howell, January 2, 1803, aged 2 years and 10 months, and 10 months, respectively.

Washington, son of James and Lucinda Hartley, January 16, aged 3 months.

Francis McClellan, an infant, May 1, 1803.

Margaret, daughter of John and Jane Fulton, July 2, 1803, aged 5 months.

Elizabeth, daughter of John and Martha Tibby, July 17, 1803, aged 7 months.

Sarah Ann, daughter of Thomas and Louisa Clarke, July 17, 1803, aged 8 months.

Michael, son of Michael and Ann King, July 24, 1803, aged 9 months.

Robert Dowdle, July 24, 1803, aged 13 months.

EARLY CHURCH RECORDS OF NEW CASTLE COUNTY
BAPTISMS.

John, son of Henry and Mary Rowen, July 31, 1803, aged 15 months.

Christopher Springer, an infant, August 14, 1803.

John, son of John and Judith Gilpin, September 30, 1803, aged 8 months.

Lydia and Margaret, daughters of ———— ————, September 30, 1803.

Joseph, son of Peter and Hannah Springer, October 23, 1803, aged 2 years, 6 months.

Sarah, daughter of Matthias and Margery Warner, October 23, 1803, aged 2 years and 5 months.

Eleanor, daughter of Matthias and Margery Warner, October 23, 1803, aged 7 months.

James Lefevre, son of Jeremiah and Susannah Bowman, October 23, 1803, aged 3 months.

John Dickinson, son of George and Mary Read, December 25, 1803, aged 11 months.

Mary, daughter of Richard and Margaret McConnell, January 22, 1804, aged 2 years, 2 months.

John, son of John and Agnes Stewart, January 22, 1804, aged 5 months.

William, son of Thomas and Eleanor Magens, February 29, 1804, aged 5 months.

Mary and Rebecca, daughters of Patrick and Sarah McMullen, May 25, 1804, aged 5 years, 4 months, and 2 years respectively.

Sarah Bowen, an adult, May 25, 1804.

William Reynolds, son of John and Margaret Foote, June 24, 1804, aged 7 months.

Isabella Ann, daughter of Jeremiah and Mary Springer, August 4, 1804, aged 3 months.

Catharine Hamilton, September 29, 1804, aged 11 months.

Mary, daughter of John and Mary Brown, November 2, 1804, aged 4 years.

Rachel Ann, daughter of John and Rebecca Gardner, November 2, 1804, aged 14 months.

John, son of James and Mary Gardner, November 2, 1804, aged 14 months.

IMMANUEL CHURCH
BAPTISMS.

Margaret, daughter of John and Catharine Brannon, February 22, 1805, aged 13 months.

Hannah, daughter of Joseph and Mary Israel, March 17, 1805, aged 3 weeks.

Joseph Israel, son of William and Lydia Massey, March 17, 1805.

Mary Ann, daughter of David and Margaret Virtue, March 24, 1805, aged 1 year.

Thomas, son of Thomas and Sarah Miles, April 15, 1805, aged 3 months.

Elizabeth, daughter of Stephen and Mary Magner, April 15, 1805, aged 6 months.

Mary Jane, daughter of John and Mary Bowman, July 28, 1805, aged 4 years.

John Janvier, son of John and Mary Bowman, July 28, 1805, aged 2 years, 3 months.

Jeremiah, son of Jeremiah and Susannah Bowman, August 11, 1805, aged 5 months.

Mary Ann, daughter of Abraham and Elizabeth Eves, August 25, 1805, aged 4 years, 4 months.

Spencer, son of Abraham and Elizabeth Eves, August 25, 1805, aged 1 year, 11 months.

Margaretta Jane, daughter of Abraham and Elizabeth Eves, August 25, 1805, aged 6 months.

George, son of Benjamin Springer, September 15, 1805, aged 13 years, 4 months.

Charles, son of Benjamin Springer, September 15, 1805, aged 9 years, 10 months.

Andrew, son of Benjamin Springer, September 15, 1805, aged 7 years, 9 months.

Benjamin, son of Benjamin Springer, September 15, 1805, aged 6 years, 2 months.

Caleb, son of Benjamin Springer, September 15, 1805, aged 3 years, 5 months.

Jane, daughter of Benjamin Springer, September 15, 1805, aged 11 years, 7 months.

Lydia, daughter of Benjamin Springer, September 15, 1805, aged 1 year, 9 months.

EARLY CHURCH RECORDS OF NEW CASTLE COUNTY
BAPTISMS.

Joseph, Ball, son of Thomas and Ann Rice, December, 1805, aged 6 years.

Ann Ball, daughter of Thomas and Ann Rice, December, 1805, aged 1 year.

Stephen, son of Stephen and Sarah Gilbert, December 22, 1805, aged 9 months.

James, son of John and Ann Marshall, October 6, 1805, aged 2 months.

Mary, daughter of Matthew Meek, November 14, 1805, aged 14 years.

William and James, sons of John and Elizabeth Aull, March 9, 1806, aged 12 and 2 years, respectively.

John, son of John and Mary Charleson, March 29, 1806, aged 6 months.

Jane, daughter of Richard and Margaret McConnell, April 6, 1806, aged 16 months.

Henry Meredith, son of John and Mary Read, born October 31, 1802.

Margaret Meredith, daughter of John and Mary Read, born April 7, 1806.

Sarah Ann, daughter of William and Sarah Thomson, May 18, 1806, aged 3 years.

Catharine Rebecca, daughter of William and Sarah Thomson, May 18, 1806, aged 1 year, 1 month.

Edward, son of Harding and Rebecca Williams, June 1, 1806, aged 4 years, 6 months.

Matilda, daughter of Harding and Rebecca Williams, June 1, 1806, aged 2 years, 6 months.

Charles, son of Harding and Rebecca Williams, June 1, 1806, aged 9 months.

Henry, son of Henry and —— Rowen, June 1, 1806, aged 2 years, 4 months.

Mary, daughter of Henry and —— Rowen, June 1, 1806, aged 4 weeks.

Elizabeth, daughter of Thomas and Ann Chesterman, June 10, 1806, aged 4 months.

William Hamilton, son of John and Bridget Hamilton, July 9, 1806, aged 9 months.

IMMANUEL CHURCH
BAPTISMS.

Mary Gertrude, daughter of George and Mary Read, July 13, 1806, aged 12 months.

Robert, son of John and Mary McGill, July 13, 1806, aged 6 months.

David, son of John and Elizabeth Foote, September 14, ——

Aaron, son of John and Dorcas Hall, September 28, 1806, aged 4 years, 6 months.

William Thomas, son of John and Dorcas Hall, September 28, 1806, aged 1 year, 1 month.

Thomas, son of Susannah Devers, February 21, 1807, aged 14 years, 2 months.

John, son of Susannah Devers, February, 21, 1807, aged 12 years, 5 months.

William, son of Samuel and Ann Crooks, February 27, 1807, aged 3 months.

Margaret, an infant, was baptized, aged 4 months, June 25, 1807.

Catharine, an infant, aged 1 year and 10 months.

An infant son of Joseph and Susannah Israel, September 15, 1807.

George, son of Jeremiah and Susannah Bowman, January 3, 1808, aged 9 months.

George, son of John and Mary West, February 13, 1808, aged 3 years.

William, son of John and Mary West, February 13, 1808, aged 9 months.

James and Mary McConnell, March 6, 1808, aged 9 months and 2 years, respectively.

William and Jane McCollian, March 6, 1808.

Susannah Anderson, an infant, April 3, 1808.

Ann Booth, daughter of Curtis and Elizabeth Clay, August 7th, at St. James' Church, aged 1 year.

Joseph, son of Michael and Mary King, August 10, 1808, aged 3 years, 7 months.

Ann, daughter of Michael and Mary King, August 10, 1808, aged 1 year.

John Penton, adult, August 10, aged 25 years.

EARLY CHURCH RECORDS OF NEW CASTLE COUNTY
BAPTISMS.

Richard McWilliam, son of Bankson and Hester Taylor, August 20, 1808, aged 10 months, 3 weeks.

Samuel, son of Abraham and Elizabeth Eves, August 20, aged 9 months.

Rebecca, daughter of Benjamin and Louisa Marley, August 20, aged 8 months, 2 weeks.

Mary Ann, daughter of Edward and Susannah Sturgeon, August 28, aged 2 years, 2 months.

Margaret Letitia, daughter of Edward and Susannah Sturgeon, August 28, aged 8 months.

John, son of Thomas and Margaret Kidd, September 11, 1808, aged 5 years, 10 months.

James, son of Martha Leonard, October 24, 1808, aged 4 years.

Rosy, daughter of Elizabeth Dowdle, October 24, 1808, aged 3 weeks.

Jane, daughter of John and Martha Tibby, October 30, 1808, aged 4 years.

William, son of John and Martha Tibby, October 30, 1808, aged 2 years.

Robert, son of John and Elizabeth Aull, November 20, 1808, aged 1 year, 4 months.

Joseph, son of James and Ann Booth, February 19, 1809, aged 8 years.

James, son of James and Maria Rogers, February 19, 1809, aged 1 year.

Hester, daughter of Thomas and Ann Ross, March 22, 1809, aged 1 year.

Benjamin, son of John and —— Foote, May 21, 1809, aged 7 months.

William, son of James and Hannah Welsh, July 29, aged 2 weeks.

Samuel Devear, son of Samuel and Martha Davis, August 3, 1809, aged 10 months.

Mary Eliza, daughter of Jeremiah and Susannah Bowman, September 17, 1809, aged 9 months.

William, son of William and Eleanor Clungeon, April 9, 1810, aged 3 years, 8 months.

IMMANUEL CHURCH
BAPTISMS.

Sarah Ann, daughter of William and Eleanor Clungeon, April 9, 1810, aged 11 months.

Margaret Charlotte, daughter of John and Dorcas Hail, May 27, 1810, aged 2 years.

Margaret, daughter of John and Elizabeth Gillmore, May 27, 1810, aged 2 years.

Mary, Elizabeth, Susannah, Rachel Saunders and Sally Ann, daughters of Samuel and Martha Davis, July 17, 1810, aged 11 years, 8 years, 6 years, and 3 months, respectively.

John, son of Penelope French, July 22, 1810, aged 7 months.

Susannah, daughter of Thomas and Ann Ross, August 5, 1810, aged 4 months.

Hannah, daughter of Benjamin and Louisa Marley, September 5, 1810, aged 1 year.

Thos. Knox, son of Edward and Susannah Sturgeon, September 16, 1810, aged 1 year.

Agnes Emmeline, daughter of Margaret Kidd, October 28, 1810, aged 4 months.

Curtis, son of Curtis and Elizabeth Clay, April, 1811, aged 1 year, 9 months.

Catharine, daughter of Curtis and Elizabeth Clay, April, 1811, aged 2 months.

Mary Ann Murray, daughter of George and Louisa Read, May 6, 1811, aged 3 months.

Charles, son of John and Mary Colgan, June 2, 1811, aged 4 weeks.

Ingeber Lefevre, daughter of Jeremiah and Susannah Bowman, September 15, 1811, aged 6 months.

George Jackson, son of Adam and Teresa Snyver, October 1, 1812, aged 18 months.

Jane, daughter of Adam and Teresa Snyver, October 1, 1812, aged 3 years.

Mary, Susannah and Hannah, daughters of James and Isabella Ball, October 25, 1812, aged 8 years, 5 years, and 2 years, respectively.

Ann Booth, daughter of Jeremiah and Susannah Bowman, May 16, 1813, aged 4 months.

BAPTISMS.

Henry, son of Cæsar and Abigail Handy, (colored) May 30, 1813, aged 11 months.

Philip Fatio, son of Philip and Mary Ann Sendin, July 4, 1813, aged 6 months.

John, Washington, Eliza and Thomas, children of James and Sarah Hilton, October 3, 1813, aged 11 years, 8 years, 4 years, and 10 months, respectively.

Mary Ann, daughter of Thomas and Ann Ross, June 21, 1814, aged 17 months.

James, son of John and Mary Colgan, December 25, 1814, aged 6 months.

John, son of John and Mary Harp, December 25, 1814, aged 2 years.

Ann Jane, daughter of John and Mary Harp, December 25, 1814, aged 2 years.

Rebecca Eleanor, daughter of John and Mary Harp, December 25, 1814, aged 2 years.

James Washington, son of James and Isabella Ball, May 24, 1815, aged 6 months.

Margaret, daughter of Mary Smith, June 11, 1815, aged 6 years, 10 months.

Catharine, daughter of Elizabeth Gilman, June 11, 1815, aged 4 years, 10 months.

Mary, daughter of George and Rebecca White, June 11, 1815, aged 4 years, 5 months.

Frances Burrows, daughter of Thomas and Elizabeth McGuire, June 11, 1815, aged 5 months.

Thomas, son of Thomas and Ann Ross, June 11, 1815, aged 4 months.

Sarah Johns, an adult, June 25, 1815.

Mary and Elizabeth, daughters of Peter and Mary McGowen, July 27, 1815. (Twins.)

Emma Wood and Ellen Lohra, twins, daughters of Curtis and Elizabeth Clay, August 14, 1815, aged 17 months.

Kensey Johns, an adult, August 27, 1815.

George Read, son of George and Louisa Read, September 28, 1815, born October 10, 1812.

BAPTISMS.

Louisa Gertrude, daughter of George and Louisa Read, September 28, 1815, born December 1, 1814.

Anne Sword, daughter of Ann and Levi Hollingsworth, September 28, 1815, born December 3, 1812.

Mary Evans, daughter of Ann and Levi Hollingsworth, September 28, 1815, born June 15, 1814.

Thomas Hyatt, son of John and Ann Tatlow, November 23, 1815, born July 28, 1802.

Mary Janvier, daughter of John and Ann Tatlow, November 23, 1815, born November 4, 1804.

Joseph, son of John and Ann Tatlow, November 23, 1815, born December 27, 1814.

Elizabeth Corbit, an adult, November 26, 1815.

MARRIAGES.

"A Register of Marriages in Emmanuel Church at New Castle from Mr. Rosse's entering the cure of the said Church which was (Secundo) the 29th of August, 1714-15."

License. Thomas Parke and Sarah Mahan, October 24, 1714.

Banns. Morgan Rygan and Lydia Reed, November 2, 1714.

Banns. Ambrose Lunden and Bridget Stalcope of White Clay Creek, January 6, 1714-15.

License. Thomas John and Susanna Welsh of the Welsh Tract, January 27, 1714-15.

License. Robert Gordon and Mary French, February 17, 1714-15.

Banns. Peter Clawson and Walbert Unster of Christeen, May 12, 1715.

Banns. William Stone and Hannah Hays, May 15, 1715.

License. Thomas French and Susanna Parradee, both of Kent county, were married in the Church in the said county, June 19, 1715.

Banns. Thomas Falconer and Mary Catharina Fara, June 30, 1715.

MARRIAGES.

Banns. John Hendrickhame and Mary Hodges, July 2, 1715.

Banns. Richard Davis and Jane Fara, both of Coristogo, August 22, 1715.

Banns. Cornelius Kettle, and Gartwieth Waxford, September 21, 1715.

Banns. John Danilla and Elizabeth Haly, both of Appoquinimink, September 22, 1715.

Banns. William Guest and Jane Wainsford, both of White Clay Creek, October 10, 1715.

License. Edward Millson of Christeen and Catherin Pierce, of Concord, November 13, 1715.

License. Jacobus Williams Neering and Mary Garland, Novembar 18, 1715.

Banns. Bryan MacDaniel and Katherine Robison, both of White Clay Creek, December 8, 1715.

Banns. Christopher Hollins and Elizabeth Brewster, both of White Clay Creek, December 8, 1715.

Banns. Nicholas Wansford and Elizabeth Boucher, both of White Clay Creek, December 12th, 1715.

Banns. William Cane and Jane Lewis, both of White Clay Creek, May 1, 1716.

Banns. Robert Marley and Margaret Hykie, both of Swanwicke, May 3, 1716.

Banns. Israel Robison and Lydia Rygan, both of White Clay Creek, May 10, 1716.

Banns. John Harris and Mary Mohaer, May 15, 1716.

License. Samuel Lowman and Letitia Wood, June 14, 1716.

Banns. William Cleany and Mary Springer, July 31, 1716.

License. George MacCall and Ann Yeates, August 9, 1716.

License. Baldwin Johnson and Jane Dyer, October 25, 1716.

Banns. Jeremiah Larkins and Penelope Brown, October 29, 1716.

Banns. Edward Green and Mary Bowen, November 1, 1716.

IMMANUEL CHURCH
MARRIAGES.

Banns. Joshua Robinson and Mary Champion, December 11, 1716.

Banns. Robert Street and Sarah Win, December 12, 1716.

License. Stephen Hollingsworth and Ann Robinson, February 18, 1716-17.

License. Jeremiah Ball and Mary Ogle, married at St. James' Church, October 10, 1717.

License. Matthew Fulton and Ellenor Williams, at Appoquinimink Church, November 25, 1717.

License. James Gordon and Ann French, November 28, 1717.

Banns. Hugh Matthews and Elizabeth Webb, December 27, 1717.

License. Thomas Fleming and Susanna Gumby, January 21, 1717-18.

License. William Battle and Parnel French, June 19, 1718.

License. Ralph Thompson and Ann Hicks, September 23, 1718.

Banns. William Richardson and Mary MacCordice, September 23, 1718.

Banns. Evan David and Ann Ball, October 24, 1718.

Banns. John Jones and Christiana Poulson, November 5, 1718.

Banns. Henry Bradley and Kathrine Lewis, November 13, 1718.

License. John Smith and Elizabeth Leuden, November 18, 1718.

License. Thomas John and Hannah Green, January 13, 1718-19.

License. James Ganeau and Jane Owen, April 15, 1719.

Banns. James Jones and Elizabeth LeGarr, October 13, 1719.

Banns. William Johnston and Hanna Emly, February 2, 1719-20.

Banns. William Jenkin and Susannah ———, February 25, 1719-20.

Banns. John Harris and Esther Cole, April 19, 1720.

EARLY CHURCH RECORDS OF NEW CASTLE COUNTY
MARRIAGES.

License. Richard Grafton and Elizabeth Brewster, June 4, 1721.

License. Richard Grafton, merchant, and Hannah Chetham daughter of Edward Chetham chirurgeon late of Maryland, October 17, 1726.

License. Richard Edwards and Martha Askew, July 28, 1723.

Banns. Daniel MacDaniel and Margaret Ferrel, August 1, 1723.

Banns. George Jeffreys and ——— Nowell, August 25, 1723.

License. John Rall and Lydia Read, August 28, 1723.

License. Thomas Barber and Eleanor Peterson, August 30, 1723.

License. Fabius Tourson and Mary Shappon, November 5, 1723.

License. Richard McWilliam and Mary Curtis, daughter of Jehu Curtis, Esq., August 20, 1748.

License. Richard McWilliam and Margaret Shaw, daughter of William Shaw, Esq., May 18, 1753.

"A Register of Marriage, in the Parish of New Castle, on Delaware, by Aeneas Ross, Missionary from ye 1st day of October, 1758, to ———."

License. Forgus Smith and Elizabeth McCay, October 20, 1758.

Banns. John Stowe and Cathrine Hyers, of Salem County, October 30, 1758.

License. William Preston and Esther Jones, November 7, 1758.

License. Israel Stalcop and Agnes Means, November 21, 1758.

Banns. George Micklebright and Kathrine Moring, December 5, 1758.

License. John Douglas and Mary Smith, widow, February 15, 1759.

License. William Carr and Elizabeth Few, March 10, 1759.

License. William Quigely and Mary Ryall, February 22, 1759.

IMMANUEL CHURCH
MARRIAGES.

License. John Parkinton and Margery Downing, widow, March 23, 1759.

License. William Ford and Lowas Wilson, May 14, 1759.

Banns. John Kelley and Ann Maddox, widow, June 4, 1759.

License. Malcum McNaught and Mary Younger, June 5. 1759.

License. James Henderson and Hannah Cartman, June 14, 1759.

License. William Goforth and Ann Furguson, October 5, 1759.

Banns. Anthony Bushong of New Port, and Cathrine ————, November 6, 1759.

License. Lewis Morgan and Elizabeth Grimes, November 16, 1759.

License. Jacob Janvier and Rachel Tatlow, November 23, 1759.

N. B. The first marriage of Gov. Hamilton's, License in New Castle.

Banns. John Stephenson and Eleanor Johnson, widow of Wilmington, November 27, 1759.

License. Samuel Janvier and Elizabeth Tatlow, November 27, 1759.

License. Dougherty Allen and Rebecca Gillan, November 28, 1759.

License. John McKnight and Rosannah Jordan, January 10, 1760.

License. Samuel Moore and Martha Williams, February 7, 1760.

Banns. John Cunningham and Catharine Morrison, widow, April 16, 1760.

Banns. Morris McNamara and Mary Gardner, May 2, 1760.

Banns. Timothy Williams and Susannah Minor, May 14, 1760.

License. Robert Lindsey and Elizabeth McLaughlin, May 19, 1760.

License. Thomas Lambson and Mary Dunlap, of Penn's Neck, of West Jersey, May 22, 1760.

EARLY CHURCH RECORDS OF NEW CASTLE COUNTY
MARRIAGES.

License. William Gray and Jane Porter, May 29, 1760.

Banns. Benjamin Imlay and Hannah Curley, of Penn's Neck, July 3, 1760.

Banns. James Readin and Ann Keane, October 1, 1760.

License. Charles Hunter, of Maryland, and Sarah Brown, October 2, 1760.

License. John Small and Sarah Moore, October 16, 1760.

Banns. Arthur Roston and Rebecca Kinkead, October 23, 1760.

License. James Kinkead and Rosanna Hollan, October 23, 1760.

License. John Eckles and Alice James, widow, October 27, 1760.

License. James Lapsley and Mary McFarland, October 28, 1760.

License. Andrew Rider, of Maryland, and Rachel Whitten, November 15, 1760.

License. Jacob Colesberry and Ann Cathrine Gravenroot, January 20, 1761.

Banns. William White and Mary Doran, January 26, 1761.

License. Henry Spencer and Rebecca Hainis, January 30, 1761.

Banns. James Hall and Charity Hall, of White Clay Creek, February 2, 1761.

License. Benjamin Crocket and Cathrine Peterson, February 10, 1761.

License. Michael Butler and Barbara Malcom, of Penn's Neck, February 20, 1761.

License. William Thompson and Jane Evans, March 5, 1761.

Banns. David Rodgers and Ann Anderson, March 23, 1761.

License. Thomas Williams and Elizabeth Gillyard, April 5, 1761.

License. Morris McCredden and Mary Pratt, April 21, 1761.

License. Israel Springer and Cathrine Springer, April 21, 1761.

IMMANUEL CHURCH
MARRIAGES.

License. John Williams and Hannah Golden, April 21, 1761.

License. Ephhraim McCoy and Elizabeth Donnald, May 11, 1761.

Banns. Felix McCowen and Bridget Birk, May 13, 1761.

License. William Currie and Elizabeth Yeates, widow, May 19, 1761.

License. Samuel Evans and Grace Rickets, May 26, 1761.

License. Joseph Parks and Ann Sinclair, May 27, 1761.

License. Peter Hance and Mary Ogle, July 30, 1761.

License. William Taylor and Jane Frankland, of Bohemia Manor, August 11, 1761.

License. Griffith Thomas and Rachel Hance, August 20, 1761.

License. Jacob Morton and Mary Whitely, August 25, 1761.

License. James Lathim and Elizabeth Yates, October 22, 1761.

Banns. Robert Robertson and Agnus Colley, of Chester County, November 16, 1761.

License. Joseph Miller and Margaret Sharp, October 15, 1761.

License. Stephen Harland and Mary Carter, of Chester County, December 2, 1761.

Banns. Griffith Williams and Deborah Curfy, of Cecil County, December 11, 1761.

Banns. John Post and Susannah Vandevir, December 31, 1761.

Banns. Richard Gay and Isabell Davis, January 24, 1762.

License. Thomas Carson and Mary Smith, January 28, 1762.

License. William McKinney and Elizabeth Bratchey, January 28, 1762.

License. James Clark and Mary Ramsay, April 22, 1762.

Banns. Richard Thomas and Catharine Scot, June 1, 1762.

License. Benjamin Howell and Sarah Gibbs, June 3, 1762.

License. John Hendry and Jane Kennedy, June 24, 1762.

License. John Berry and Elizabeth Dickey, June 26, 1762

EARLY CHURCH RECORDS OF NEW CASTLE COUNTY
MARRIAGES.

License. Abraham Nanna and Hannah Clements, July 14, 1762.

License. Laughlin McNeil and Lucy Granger, July 28, 1762.

License. Stephen Parr and Mary Davis, September 14, 1762.

License. Robert McCulley and Jane Robinson, December 9, 1762.

Banns. William Sanders and Mary Acten of Penn's Neck, December 30, 1762.

License. George Read and Gertrude Till, widow, January 11, 1763.

License. Thomas Turner and Lucretia Gravenroot, February 10, 1763.

License. Tobias Casperson and Catharine Macum, of Penn's Neck, March 6, 1763.

License. David Moody and Jennet Eakin, March 11, 1763.

License. Thomas Davis and Mary Howell, both of Maryland, April 1, 1763.

Banns. Samuel Barker and Margaret Greenfield, April 25, 1763.

License. Samuel Currie and Jane Corson, May 11, 1763.

License. Jacob Springer and Catharine Springer, April 27, 1763.

Banns. John Palmer and Lydia McLoglin, March 20, 1763.

Banns. John Sweeney and Eleanor Plowright, April, 1763.

Banns. William Walker and Elizabeth Kirkland, widow, —— 1763.

License. Archibald Hall and Mary McDead, both of Christiana Hundred, July 2, 1763.

License. Samuel McGinnis and Margaret Canady, August 22, 1763.

Banns. William Brown and Susannah Macormet, September 28, 1763.

Banns. Arthur Veail and Sarah Hall, August 14, 1763.

Banns. Thomas Robinson and Jane Young, September 3, 1763.

License. Robert Stewart and Isabella Huston, October 17, 1763.

IMMANUEL CHURCH
MARRIAGES.

License. David Miskimmon of Lancaster County, and Rachel Ferie, October 24, 1763.

License. Capt. Jonathan Robinson, of Wilmington, and Mary Morris, November 9, 1763.

License. William Burrough of New Castle County, and Elizabeth Young, November 14, 1763.

License. John Moore of Chester County and Eleanor King, November 16, 1763.

License. Autre McKibbin of Cumberland County, Pa. and Jane Howe, November 19, 1763.

License. Joseph Park and Rachel Dawson of Chester County, November 30, 1763.

License. Edward Karlin and Elizabeth McLaughlin, January 10, 1764.

License. Robert Furniss and Eleanor Martin, widow, January 1, 1764.

License. John Wood and Agnes McWhorter, March 15, 1764.

License. John Clark and Mary Read, April 2, 1764.

License. John Garrettson and Mary Elder, April 10, 1764.

License. Thomas Flannagan and Catharine Creelin, May 14, 1764.

License. George Spencer and Mary Jubart, June 21, 1764.

License. Joseph Dolby and Christian Flough, April 18, 1764.

License. Samuel Skelton and Elizabeth Reynolds, May 31, 1764.

License. David Beard and Sarah Eaton of Salem County, June 25, 1764.

License. Henry Dorrel and Elizabeth Kent of Salem County, August 2, 1764.

License. Matthew Scott and Jane Spires, September 27, 1764.

License. Thomas Newlin and Joanna Prior, September 27, 1764.

License. Giles Lambson and Elizabeth Darby, October 1, 1764.

License. John Passmore and Abagail Whitely, widow, September 17, 1764.

License. Robert Bell and Jane Minor, October 17, 1764.

License. Joseph Gilpin and Elizabeth Read, widow, November 7, 1764.

EARLY CHURCH RECORDS OF NEW CASTLE COUNTY
MARRIAGES.

License. Zebulon Beaston and Ann Hughs, November 15, 1764.

Banns. Andrew Hutton and Eliza McCormeck, —— 1764.

License. John Hewes and Martha Hardin, December 20, 1764.

License. Patrick Culbertson and Isabella McClintock, December 25, 1764.

License, Joseph Haffry and Hester Dushane, January 10, 1764.

License. John Lewden and Margaret Crughton, January 29, 1765.

License. John Short and Mary Elliott February 6, 1765.

License. Cornelius Lafferty and Mage McLaughlin, March 7, 1765.

License. William Pyke and Elizabeth Crawford, January 16, 1765.

License. Stephen Lewis, of Pencader Hundred and Agnus Coburn, January 17, 1765.

License. Samuel Watson and Rachel Short, April 10, 1765.

License. William Black and Ann Reynolds, April 16, 1765.

License. Samuel Veal and Christian Cheeck, April 22, 1765.

License. Benjamin Devan and Eleanor Hance, April 22, 1765.

License. James Macdonald and Mary Macdonald, May 2, 1765.

License. William Shedford and Cathrine Post, May 5, 1765.

License. Joseph Ford and Mary Woodrow, May 8, 1765.

Banns. David Caldwell and Elizabeth Ledener, May 14, 1765.

Banns. Samuel Post and Rachel Allen, June 3, 1765.

License. Samuel Rowan and Ann Garrison, June 11, 1765.

License. Robert Rankin and Martha Latimor, June 13, 1765.

Banns. Joseph Howell and Margaret McCullough, June 18, 1765.

IMMANUEL CHURCH
MARRIAGES.

49

Banns. John Hameson and Eliza Carlit, June — 1765.

License. Cullender Garretson and Cathrine Beech, July 10, 1765.

License. Samuel Slizer and Ann Glascow, July 18, 1765.

License. John Jones and Mary Bolton, July 30, 1765.

License. Philip Rice and Abigail Poppins, June 22, 1765.

Banns. John Smith and Jane Davis, July 3, 1765

Banns. George McFee and Ann Preston, July 4. 1765.

License. Robert McIlheran and Mary Donald, August 8, 1765.

Banns Alexander McCart and Eleanor Mossman, July 1765.

Banns. George Allcorn and Ann Clarke, July 1765.

Banns. Henry Gibson and Lena Worms, August 20, 1765.

License. Alexander Ferris and Jennet James, September 5, 1765.

License. Henry Brackin and Jane Moore, October 31, 1765.

License. Gustavus Grimes and Jane Conn, October 30, 1765.

License. John White and Hannah John, November 22, 1765.

Banns. Samuel Harris and Mary McCormet, December 18, 1765.

Banns. Edward McCreden and Ruth Wetherlee, December 24, 1765.

Banns. Solomon Springer and Lydia Husbands, December 26, 1765.

Banns. John Morgan and Mary Phenix, January 2, 1766.

License. James Peery and Elizabeth Donald, December 31, 1765.

Banns. Joshua Story and Rebecca Stoop, January 2, 1766.

License. Robert Bryan and Rebecca Webster, January 2, 1766,

Banns, John Willis and Deborah Thetford, February 1766.

License. John A. Payne and Elizabeth Harris, March 25, 1766.

License. Jeremiah Cloud and Esther Harry, of Chester county, June 16, 1766.

EARLY CHURCH RECORDS OF NEW CASTLE COUNTY
MARRIAGES.

License. Matthew Robinson and Alice Gray, June 26, 1766.

License James Gibson and Mary Fuller, July 3, 1766.

License. James Townsley and Margaret McDill, July 8, 1766.

Banns. Hance Scheer and Frances Patterson, July 24, 1766.

License. Hugh Martin and Jane Thompson, February 25, 1766.

License. David Lewis and Agnes Abrahams, September 9, 1766.

Banns. Archibald MacChess and Cathrine White, October 23, 1766.

Banns. William Bilderback and Ann Macum, October 26, 1766.

License. Nathan Oldham and Elizabeth Giles, November 18, 1766.

License. Abraham Vannemon and Rebecca Dougherty, November 20, 1766.

License. James Boyd and Sarah Janvier, November 27, 1766.

License. Thomas Janvier and Jane Clark, April 2, 1766.

License. Benjamin Whitten and Sarah Hughes, March 24, 1767.

License. John Elliott and Mary Shaw, April 3, 1767.

License. Shadrack Larew and Mary Lewis, May 9, 1767.

License. John Long and Rebecca Wright, May 30, 1767.

Banns. John Test and Mary Cowing, December, 1768.

Banns. Samuel Harris and Mary McCormick, December, 1768.

Banns. Edward McCreden and Ruth Wetherbee, December, 1768.

Banns. John Wood and Lettice Jones, December, 1768.

Banns. John McKay and Ruth Musgrove, —— 1768.

License. Moses Ladley and Mary Alexander, widow, March 28, 1759.

License. Henry Reily and Mary Dannalah of Christiana, July 26, 1769.

Banns. David Cangleton and Sarah Jones, March, 1769.

IMMANUEL CHURCH
MARRIAGES. 51

Banns. James Campbell and Sally Smith, March, 1769.
Banns. Samuel Hamilton and Mary Lewis, March, 1769.
Banns. Erasmus Kent and Mary Kilcriss, —— 1769.
Banns. John Stalcup and Caty Phi!zgera!d, April, 1769.
Banns. Matthew Clark and Cicily Karlan, —— 1769.
Banns. Hugh Robeson and Margaret McLum, —— 1769.
Banns. William Thompson and Ann Webb, —— 1769.
Banns. James Ellis and Elizabeth McCaffdeed, —— 1769.
Banns. Jonathan Alexander and Sarah Macum, —— 1770.
Banns. Giles Yourason and Elizabeth Marshall, —— 1770.
Banns. Samuel Picken and Margaret Moore, ——1770.
Banns. Thomas Hamilton and Rosanna Laragan, —— 1770.
Banns. David Davis and Mary McNeelie, —— 1770.
Banns. Francis Dunlop and Abagail Davis, of Penn's Neck, September 3, 1771.
License. William Hemphill and Elizabeth Allison, of Christiana Hundred, May 22, 1770.
Banns. Erick Philpot and Ann Lamson, of Penn's Neck, March 15, 1772.
Banns. Thomas Williams and Sarah Kinkead, March 24, 1772.
Banns. John Holland and Lydia Crawford, of Pencader Hundred, 1771.
Banns. Morris Singer and Eleanor Welsh, in 1773.
Banns. Jacob White and Elizabeth Martin, in 1771.
Banns. William Steel and Jennet Hamell, November 10, 1772.
Banns. John Kenedy and Ann Scot of New London, June, 1773.
Banns. William Dennis and Isabella Laughlin, December 1, 1772.
License. William Weeir and Sarah David, August 8, 1771.
License. Neal Gillespie and Eleanor Dougherty, August 21, 1771.
License. James Creed and Susannah Hutton, August 1, 1771.

EARLY CHURCH RECORDS OF NEW CASTLE COUNTY
MARRIAGES.

License. Frederick Hill and Rachel Cannon, December 18, 1771.

License. John Lloyd and Elizabeth Pedrick of Salem County, N. J., September 9, 1771.

License. Joseph Elliott, Jr., and Mary Elliott of Brandywine Hundred, November 14, 1770.

License. Fergus McVeey and Mary Connor, December 8, 1770.

License. James Lefever and Ingeber Blackburn, July 4, 1771.

License. William Aiken and Elizabeth Kirk, June 26, 1771.

License. Thomas Carney, Jr. and Mary Harris of Salem County, May 14, 1771.

License. Isaac Cannon and Lydia Cannon, January 23, 1771.

License. Morton Morton and Dorcas Jacquet, widow, February 6, 1770.

License. Wm. Gil Johnson of Penn's Neck, N. J., and Jane Standley, June 30, 1770.

License. Hugh Steel of St. George's Hundred and Elizabeth Hance, September 11, 1771.

License. Samuel Campbell and Margaret Patterson, widow, November 20, 1771.

License. Humphries Green and Susannah Grubb, February 9, 1771.

License. George McLaughlin and Elizabeth Jones of Cumberland County, N. J., June 5, 1772.

License. Capt. Paul Cox and Ann Stewart, widow, both of Philadelphia, July 3, 1772.

License. John Miller of Red Lion Hundred and ———, March 27, 1772.

License. William Hazlett and Elizabeth Hume, widow, January 21, 1772.

License. John Cunningham and Eleanor Wiley, spinster, both of East Fallowfield, Chester County, September 28, 1772.

License. Capt Thomas Rawlings and Margaret Giffin, both of Wilmington, October 3, 1772.

License. James Conway and Christiana Cazier, of St. Georges' Hundred, October, 3, 1772.

License. John Robinson and Catharine Surmizer, both of New London, October 29, 1770.

IMMANUEL CHURCH
MARRIAGES.

License. Charles Fogg, Jr., Tanner and Priscilla Bowen, of Salem County, November, 5, 1772.

Banns. Samuel Gibson and Martha Thompson———— 1773.

License. Isaac Cannon, of Red Lion Hundred, and Susannah Devan, January, 27, 1773.

License. Jonathan Wilson of St. Georges' Hundred, and Mary Skeer, of Cecil County, Md., February 4, 1773.

License. William McCarter, of Christiana Hundred, and Eleanor Slater, of same place, February 18, 1773.

License. John Jaquet and Frances Belveal, February 24, 1773.

License. Hugh Bradley and Margaret Bradley, both of Red Lion Hundred, May 15, 1773.

License. David Justis and Hannah Tatlow, May 20, 1773.

License. Patrick McCormick and Margaret Dougherty, June 10, 1773.

License. Edward Dougherty and Elizabeth Bellieu, both of Red Lion Hundred, March 11, 1773.

License. Edward Booram and Mary Goforth, both of Red Lion Hundred, March, 31, 1773.

License. George Adams and Jane McCurdy, both of Pencader Hundred, April 1, 1772.

License. Thomas Gillespie and Frances Bellew, May 14, 1772.

License. Alexander Porter and Lydia Woodward, of Christiana Hundred, May 2, 1772.

License. Simon Marshall, of Salem County, and Jane Dunn, of Fin's Point, June 6, 1772.

License. Moses McKnight and Mary Barker, May 9, 1773.

License. John Kettle, husbandman, and Mary Silsbee, spinster November 9, 1772.

Banns. George Johnson and Mary Bryan, June 22, 1773.

License. John Ball and Agnes Ferguson, both of Mill Creek Hundred, July 29, 1773.

Banns. Joshua Castello and Mary Hill, widow, August 1, 1773.

Banns. Robert Woods and Elizabeth Anderson, Aug. 5, 1773.

Banns. Thomas Nodes and Hannah Thompson— 1773.

Banns. Samuel Jordan and Sarah Stilley— 1773.

EARLY CHURCH RECORDS OF NEW CASTLE COUNTY
MARRIAGES.

Banns. David Britchard and Mary Ruthe, 1773.

License. Valentine Dodds and Ann Dunning, both of Red Lion Hundred, December 30, 1773.

License. Abraham Short and Priscilla Stevens, November 3, 1773.

License. John Lyon and Sarah Williams, September 15, 1774.

License. James Welsh and Margaret Armstrong, April 16, 1774.

License. Joshua Jamison and Ann Caldwell, September 27, 1774.

License. Robert Coney and Eliza Allen, April 22, 1774.

License. Samuel Allison and Mary Burch, September 28, 1774.

License. Henry Fiver and Barbara Smith, October 27, 1774.

License. William Nicholson and Eliza McCuffin, November 14, 1774.

License. David Jenkins and Ann Floyd, November 22, 1774.

License. Thomas Pusey and Elizabeth Stewart, October 19, 1774.

License. John Lewden and Martha Wollaston, December 15, 1774.

License. John Enos and Rebecca Moore, February 9, 1775.

Banns. John Crahsuer, of Brandywine Hundred, and Hannah Fossen, May 13, 1775.

License. James Hazley and Mary Vansant, October 24, 1774.

License. William Robinson and Sarah Sergeant, March 13, 1775.

License. William Hezlet and Mary Ladly, widow, March 24, 1775.

License. Jonas Walraven and Eliza White, March 29, 1775.

Banns. Henry Clark and Dorcas Hinton, May 16, 1775.

Banns. John Lewis and Jane Hitherington, May 18, 1775.

License. Peter Kuhn and Elizabeth Keppele, both of Philadelphia, May 22, 1775.

IMMANUEL CHURCH
MARRIAGES. 55

License. Charles Stewart and Mary Barr, both of White Clay Creek Hundred, December 3, 1774.

License. James Garretson and Elizabeth Morton, April 6, 1774.

Banns. William Kilty and Esther Burrows, October 17, 1775.

License. Capt. Thomas Holland and Joanna Ross, October 13, 1775.

Banns. Benjamin Woodden and Sarah Lambson, September 5, 1781.

License. Stephen Thackrey and Elizabeth Humphreys, widow, of Penn's Neck, N. J., September 19, 1781.

License. Benjamin Worthington and Margaret Ross, June 24, 1784.

License. Benjamin Gregory and Margaret Gray, September 23, 1784.

License. James Booth and Ann Clay, May 5, 1785.

Banns. Joseph Balley and Frances Branson, August 10, 1785.

——— Daniel McManamy and Mary McKee, July 2, 1778.

Archibald Croxon and Margaret Walker, July 6, 1778.

William Berry and Jane Marshall, widow, of Penn's Neck, N. J., July 4, 1778.

License. Richard Asby and Jane Burns, December 9, 1784.

License. John Grimes and Mary Toland, December 20, 1784.

License. John Smales and Catherine Grant, December 22, 1784.

License. David Ambler and Mary Kelch, from Jersey, March 19, 1785.

License. Ashbury Tobin and Catharine Hart, February 2, 1786.

License. John Brannan and Jane Crocket, March 9, 1786.

License. Philip Reading and Mary Noxon, at Middletown, April 20, 1786.

License. Joseph Janvier and Sara Wall, March 11, 1786.

License. Benjamin Worrell and Mary Thompson, July 27, 1786.

EARLY CHURCH RECORDS OF NEW CASTLE COUNTY
MARRIAGES.

License. John Diss and Catherine Cavender, August 8, 1786.

Banns. Joseph Lowe and Mary Peterson, of Jersey, August 9, 1786.

Banns. Michael Levenstein and Catherine Wilderson, January 23, 1788.

——— Henry Duff and Jane Greares, negroes, January 27, 1788.

Banns. Francis Laverdy and Margaret White, January 26, 1788.

License. Jeremiah Springer and Mary Reece, March 12, 1788.

License. Adam Close and Jane Farrell, April 17, 1788.

License. John Kean and Margaret Forrest, August 4, 1788.

License. William Holliday and Elizabeth Cail, September 29, 1788.

License. John Dixon and Margaret McMullen, December 16, 1788.

License. James Armstrong and Joanna Holland, January 29, 1789.

License. John Taylor and Sarah Williams, March 13, 1789.

License. Robert Milligan and Sarah Jones, April 9, 1789.

——— Samuel Rowen and Elizabeth Thomas, May 25, 1789.

License. Henry Johnston, free negro man, and Hannah Rickards, negro, belonging to Mrs. Sarah Cantwell, June 9, 1789.

License. John Patterson and Rebecca McElwee, June 17, 1789.

License. John Toppin and Rebecca Johnston, June 18, 1789.

License. John Donnell and Isabella Lummis, July 12, 1789.

Banns. Christopher Armstrong and Lydia Miller, October 28, 1789.

License. John Hall and Lucretia Rees, November 25, 1789.

License. Thomas Lollar and Eleanor Post, December 31, 1789.

IMMANUEL CHURCH
MARRIAGES.

License. Francis Kitely and Margaret Underwood, January 28, 1790.

License. London, a negro man, belonging to Kensey Johns, Esq., and Hannah, a negro woman, belonging to Geo. Read, Jr., Esq., were married by consent of their masters, March 4, 1790.

License. Samuel Jackson, a free negro, and Eleanor, a negro, belonging to Mary Clay, March 11, 1790.

License. John Yeates and Ann Bonner, March 15. 1790.

Banns. George Moore and Sarah Jenkins, May 6, 1790.

License. James Martin and Ann Mitchell, June 8, 1790.

License. Dennis McGuire and Ann Morton, July 29, 1790.

License. George Dougherty and Mary Collins, August 31, 1790.

License. William Spotswood and Mary Ann McAvoy, September 1, 1790.

License. John Murphy and Annie Fitzgerald, two free blacks, September 12, 1790.

License. William Massey and Abigail Israel, October 11, 1790.

License. Asaph Vansant and Mary McMullen, November 2, 1790.

License. William Davis and Rachel Truax, December 2, 1790.

License. John Hancock and Ann Saunders, December 8, 1790.

License. James Clark and Elizabeth Gunn, December 9, 1790.

License. Patrick Morrison and Susannah Beach, February 1, 1791.

License. Stephen Pike and Eleanor Rainy, February 9, 1791.

License. Samuel Armstrong and Ann Robinson, April 18. 1791.

License. George Stroud and Rachel Reece, June 9, 1791.

License. George Medford and Elizabeth Latham, December 18, 1791.

License. John Toland and Ann Blankford, December 26, 1791.

MARRIAGES.

License. Patrick Grant and Mary Rumsey, January 16, 1792.

License. Robert VnJoy, a free black, and Dinah, a slave of Stuart Thompson, February 16, 1792.

License. Francis Haughey and Sarah Thomson, July 1, 1792.

License. John Alexander and Mary McCormick, July 19, 1792.

License. Peter Stidham and Elizabeth Williams, September 16, 1792.

License. Patrick McGinnis and Eleanor Cobine, October 13, 1792.

License. Thomas Walker and Ann Goodfellow, November —, 1792.

License. Benjamin Pearce and Margaret David, November 12, 1792.

License. Abraham Eves and Elizabeth Spencer, February 28, 1793.

License. Benjamin McLean and Mary Dunwoody, June 12, 1793.

License. John Stuckey and Margaret Muckleherron, July 11, 1793.

License. Charles Thomas and Breta Johnson, August 17, 1793.

License. John Mitchell and Jane Stewart, September 6, 1793.

License. John Instons and Anna Eliza Beners, September 23, 1793.

License. Benoni Bird and Sidney Dyet, February 5, 1794.

George Lewis, a free black, and Dorcas, a slave to Gunning Bedford, October 30, 1794.

License. Patrick McFudgon and Rosanna McDade, March 10, 1794.

Joseph and Elizabeth, free blacks, November 12, 1794.

William, a free black, and Margaret, slave to John Crow, November 28, 1794.

Geo. Rodney and Alice, free blacks, December 5, 1794.

Isaiah and Annis, free blacks, January 1, 1795.

IMMANUEL CHURCH
MARRIAGES.

License. Thomas Titus and Dorcas Rowen, February 27, 1795.

License. Thomas Thompson and Ann Kennedy, June 25, 1795.

Richard, slave to Robert Aiken, and Margaret, slave to Dr. McMechen, August 23, 1795.

License. John Zimmerman and Mary Watt, September 10, 1795.

License. John Macglathry and Margaret Howk, November 13, 1795.

License. Samuel Rowen and Elizabeth Penton, November 22, 1795.

Abraham Rumsey and Ann Spencer, free blacks, February 26, 1796.

William, a free black, and Hannah, a slave, March 12, 1796.

License. James Creed, Jr., and Susannah Vangezell, March 31, 1796.

License. John Young and Elizabeth Logan, May 19, 1796.

License. Richard Anderson and Elizabeth David, August 16, 1796.

License. John Murphy and Hellena Martins, August 18, 1796.

Tobias and Sarah, blacks, both slaves, September 3, 1796.

License. William Clay and Sarah McWilliams, September 7, 1796.

License. Josiah Peirce and Sarah Newton, September, 10, 1796.

License. David Aiken and Anna Derrick, September 29, 1796.

License. John Bryan and Mary Darby, October 13, 1796.

Jonas, a slave of James Booth and Violet, slave of Nicholas Vandyke, November —, 1796.

James, a black man belonging to the Governor, and Sarah, a free mulatto, December, 1796.

License. John Hendrickson, Jr., and Elizabeth Springer, April 18, 1797.

License. Joseph Way and Ann Bond Webb, September 6, 1797.

EARLY CHURCH RECORDS OF NEW CASTLE COUNTY
MARRIAGES.

License. Lancaster Lifthall and Hannah Webb, November 19, 1797.

Charles and Cotter, negroes, January 4, 1798.

License. Robert Rowen and Elizabeth Bevard, February 6, 1798.

License. Thomas Campbell and Eleanor McGee, March 2, 1798.

License. Erasmus Jackson and Elizabeth Eves McCullough, March 4, 1798.

License. William Clarke and Elizabeth Baldwin, April 21, 1798.

License. John Tatlow and Ann Aiken, May 19, 1798.

License. Robert Connel and Mary Rothwell, October 9, 1798.

License. Samuel Toppin and Hannah Garretson, December 18, 1798.

Christopher and Annis, black people, January 31, 1799.

License. Joseph Swany and Martha Wood, April 1, 1799.

License. Thomas Justis and Mary Wollaston, June 2, 1799.

License. John Bowman and Mary Janvier, June 30, 1799.

License. Capt. George Lockyer and Ann McWilliam, July 11, 1799.

License. Charles Hair and Eliza Ann Wann, July 14, 1799.

License. Edward Jack and Sarah Freel, August 30, 1799.

License. Robert Shields and Ann Stidham, January 3, 1800.

License. Joseph Leger d'Happart and Elizabeth Thomson, April 24, 1800.

License. William Clark and Mary Springer, May 1, 1800.

License. George Ruth and Sarah James, May 15, 1800.

License. John Landers and Catharine Doorsh, May 16, 1800.

License. James Toland and Ann Williams, May 25, 1800.

License. John Clark and Margaret Galaha, August 5, 1800.

License. Joseph Warner and Mary Thompson Firth, August 7, 1800.

License. John Bulles and Charlotte Jane Rumsey, August 10, 1800.

IMMANUEL CHURCH
MARRIAGES.

License. Lancaster Lightall and Mary Ball, August 10, 1800.
Henry and Grace, blacks, October 2, 1800.
License. George Giles and Elizabeth Devenshire, September 22, 1800.
License. Robert White and Mary Ternall, October 21, 1800.
License. Jeremiah Bowman and Susannah Lefevre, October 30, 1800.
License. Thomas F. Williams and Esther Swann, July 31, 1801.
License. William Thompson and Sarah Clay, June 1, 1802.
License. William Patterson and Elizabeth Small, August 5, 1802.
License. John Brady and Margarat Brady, August 5, 1802.
License. Curtis Clay, Jr., and Elizabeth Lohra, September 21, 1802.
License. Thomas Springer and Margaret Well, December 7, 1802.
License. Neal Martin and Margaret Henderson, May 15, 1803.
License. Barney McBride and Rose Daniels, February 2, 1804.
License. John Morrison and Elizabeth Madicar, February 21, 1804.
License. Benjamin Parker and Sarah Passmore, June 9, 1804.
License. James Linch and Eleanor Whiteside, June 11, 1804.
License. John Reiemanand and Isabella Williams, October 2, 1804.
License. Francis Sword and Maria Miller, October 7, 1804.
License. Anthony Creshen and Eliza Riggs, November 2, 1804.
License. James Johnston and Mary Elliot, March 7, 1805.
License. Arch'd McLannand and Mary Matthews, April 15, 1805.
License. James Garretson and Joanna Matthews, May 23, 1805.

EARLY CHURCH RECORDS OF NEW CASTLE COUNTY
MARRIAGES.

License. Richard Phepoc and Elizabeth Hartung, June 29, 1805.

License. Hugh Ferguson and Rebecca Downing, February 20, 1806.

License. George Vanzant and Margaret Sullivan, March 28, 1806.

License. James Stroud and Hannah Springer, May 29, 1806.

License. John Reece and Susannah Hogmore, July 24, 1806.

License. James Curlet and Ann McKinley, August 7, 1806.

License. Capt. Bankson Taylor and Hester McWilliam, October 16, 1806.

License. Thomas Miles and Eleanor Shepherd, January 9, 1807.

License. Benjamin Marley and Louisa Clark, February 17, 1807.

License. Charles Allen and Jane Armstrong, February 19, 1807.

License. James Rogers and Mary Booth, April 16, 1807.

License. Thomas Ross and Ann McGuire, June 25, 1807.

License. Justis Wilson and Sarah Reece, March 22, 1808.

License. James Welsh and Agnes Hannah, September 1, 1808.

License. Archibald McMullen and Mary Sterratt, October 28, 1808.

License. William G. Tilghman and Anna Polk, December 13, 1808.

License. John Colgan and Mary McDowell, May 16, 1809.

License. Benjamin Mendenhall and Rebecca Seal, August 19, 1809.

License. David Sample and Elizabeth Walker, August 31, 1809.

License. William Orim and Mary Castalow, October 6, 1809.

License. Spenser Price and Rebecca McKinley, December 24, 1809.

License. John Wiley and Elizabeth McKinsey, January 10, 1810.

License. George Read, Jr. and Louisa Dorsey, April 19, 1810.

IMMANUEL CHURCH
MARRIAGES. 63

License. Lewis Nicholas and Margaret Brown, July 7, 1810.
License. Thomas Middleton and Joanna Mason, July 20, 1811.
License. Levi Hollingsworth and Ann Dorsey, February 13, 1812.
License. Howard Ogle and Charlotte Moore, April 27, 1812.
License. James Pattersbey and Jane McFinley, May 13, 1812.
License. Zacariah Smith and Margaret McKinley, May 28, 1812.
License. Allen McLane and Catharine Read, June 18, 1812.
License. Joseph Marich and Margaret Stone, September 16, 1813.
License. Nehemiah Delaplain and Lavinia Springer, January 1, 1814.
License. Ebenoner Greenough and Abigail Israel, March 5, 1814.
License. Joseph Grimes and Ann Adams, April 1, 1814.
License. John Lawler and Ellen McDowell, April 7, 1814.
License. James Hamilton and Elizabeth Shirley, April 18, 1814.
License. James Rich and Mary Merrit. September 18, 1814.
License. Adam Rowen and —— Broadfoot, January 29, 1815.
License. Samuel Barr and Elizabeth Bird March 21, 1815.
License. John Stroud and Elizabeth Walker. April 6, 1815.
License. Joshua Burrows and Eliza Ann Kidd, August 17, 1815.
License. John Dunn and Sarah Aysen, September 14, 1815.
License. Joshua Deputy and Ann Richards, November 2, 1815.
License. John Pink and Ann Edgar, December 4, 1815.
License. John Mason and Mary Foster, December 29, 1815.
License. William Sheley and Maria Derby, February 8, 1816.
License. Enoch Hugg and Margaret Walker, January 30, 1817.
License. Charles Lisle and Eliza Bennet, January 30, 1817.
License. John Ritchie and Martha Foster, February 15, 1817.

EARLY CHURCH RECORDS OF NEW CASTLE COUNTY
MARRIAGES.

License. Matthew Newkirk and Jane R. Stroud, May 1, 1817.

License. David Ross and Margaret Hukill, May 22, 1817.

License. William Guthrie and Maria Magens, June 19, 1817.

License. Barge Vanderslice and Maria Herring, October 1, 1817.

License. John Shepherd and Sarah Barker, January 19, 1818.

License. Joseph Reece and Mary Holland, June 4, 1818.

License. John McConnister and Penny McConnell, October 6, 1818.

License. James R. Corrington and Jane Springer, November 5, 1818.

License. John Jamison and Rebecca Philips, November 6, 1818.

License. Edward Croft and Alice Frazer, January 6, 1819.

License. James Booth, Jr. and Hannah W. Rogers, June 1, 1819.

License. Garrett Lewis and Elizabeth James, June 10, 1819.

License. John Lynam and Mary Long, November 23, 1820.

License. Henry Colesberry and Hester Bowman, December 11, 1820.

License. David Justis and Maria Springer, February 19, 1821.

License. Benjamin Willis and Sarah Rechisson, May 17, 1821.

License. Joseph Rozell and Margaret Clark, May 22, 1821.

License. Alexander Henry and Eliza Boyd, May 30, 1821.

License. James Davis and Jane Mullen, September 8, 1821.

Richard Rosthill and Mary Ann Robinson, November 17, 1821.

License. Nicholas Coleman and Susannah Allcorn, December 6, 1821.

License. John Foote and Margaret Poulson, May 15, 1823.

License. Thomas Challenger and Sarah Price, June 10, 1823.

License. Timothy Temple and Henrietta Canston, January 29, 1824.

License. John King and Catharine Owen, March 4, 1824.

REGISTER OF BURIALS.

"A Register of Burials in Immanuel Church and Churchyard at New Castle upon Delaware, begun in May, 1716."

In the Churchyard, Mary MacFarlan was buried the 15th May, 1716.

Within the Church, John Frogg was buried the 12th February, 1716-17.

In the Churchyard, Charles Gookin Barninghame, a child, was buried the 20th September, 1717.

In the Churchyard, Hannah, wife of Richard Grafton of New Castle, was buried the 16th January, dyed 13 eodem mense, 1728-29.

In the Churchyard, Elizabeth, daughter of Richard McWilliam, November 17, 1749.

In the Churchyard, Mary, wife of Richard McWilliam, dyed 6th, buried 9th May, 1751.

Zachariah Van Luveneigh, February, 1789.

Catharine Bradford, February, 1789.

John Ewing, April 17, 1789.

James Carter, May 14, 1789.

Ann Clay, June 16, 1789.

Christiana, infant daughter of John and Elizabeth Jaquet, June 17, 1789.

Doctor Elliott, on Sunday, July 26, 1789.

Mrs. Hall, on July 30, 1789.

Sarah McCormick, on September 2, 1789.

Mrs. Lackey, on November, 1789.

Mary Eves, on Sunday, December 20, 1789.

Mrs. Janvier, on Tuesday, December 28, 1790.

—— Nesbitt, an infant, April, 1790.

Ann Stockton, on April 16, 1790.

Mrs. Bird, on June 10, 1790.

BURIALS.

Mrs. King, on April 28, 1791.
Mrs. Till, May, 1791.
Charles Gofton, August 7, 1791.
John Blanford, October 1, 1791.
—— Sutton, February, 1792.
John Bond, August 7, 1794.
Mrs. Thevin, a French lady, on August 22, 1796.
Mrs. Spencer, on August 28, 1796.
Mrs. Pearce, June, 1803.
Mr. Matthews, August 1, 1803.
John Aicken, August 12, 1803.
Henry Rowen's child, on August 19, 1803.
Mrs. Hall's child, on September 7, 1803.
William Aull, on September 15, 1803.
Mrs. Armstrong, on October 16, 1803.
Mrs. Tanner, on October 23, 1803.
Mrs. King's child, January 10, 1804.
Mrs. ——, a foreign lady, May 25, 1804.
Mrs. Eves, June 8, 1804.
Jacob Colesberry's child, August 23, 1804.
Rachel Taylor, September 20, 1804.
Mr. Cork's child, September 25, 1804.
Jacob Peterson's child, September 25, 1804.
Mrs. Sutton, June 2, 1805.
Carpenter's mate on board the ship Louisiana, July 28, 1805.
Stephen Gilbert, May 4, 1806.
Elizabeth Bush, June 5, 1806.
William Hazlett, November 12, 1806.
Mrs. Sarah Colesberry, December, 1806.
John Jaquett, March 15, 1807.
Sarah Thompson, July 10, 1807.
Mrs. Jones, July 10, 1807.
Joseph Israel, December, 1808.
Joseph Tatlow, February, 1808.
Mrs. Aicken, August 30, 1809.
Gertrude Vangezell, March 27, 1810.
Dorcas Hall, September 4, 1810.
Thomas Magens, Jr., April 26, 1810.

John Hall, of St. James' Church, April 26, 1811.
Thomas Magens, 1819.
Nicholas Vandyke, Jr., June 23, 1820.
Thomas King, 1821.
Joseph Ball, at St. James' Church, July 26, 1822.
Rebecca McWilliam, February 3, 1822.
Sarah King, February 12, 1822.
John Stockton, October 29, 1822.
Jacob Welsh, November 16, 1822.
John D. Eves, July 30, 1823.
Isaac Grantham, August 1, 1823.
Martha Howley, a child, September 5, 1823.
Mary Ann Babcock, October 6, 1823.
Mrs. Mary King, October 7, 1823.
John Springer, October 8, 1823.

SOME INSCRIPTIONS UPON OLD TOMBS IN IMMANUEL CHURCH-YARD.

There are several vaults, and while these in some cases contain the remains of many, there is rarely more than one inscription on each, which is probably to the first buried in the vault; and as the entries of deaths in the parish register are so imperfect, there is no record whatever of the burials of very many who rest in the Church-yard.

The Rev. George Ross and his son, Rev. Aeneas Ross, were buried in the Church, but there is no record to show it, and so there is none of William Read, Richard Halliwell, Richard Grafton, Richard McWilliam and other leading men in the Church in early times.

"Traveller what do you inquire. Known our friend Hercules Coutts was born in Montrose in Great Britian. Thence he came to this Colony at New Castle. In the discharge of his duties he was indefatigable; in temper, forbearing; in manner, courteous.

In this country he filled many trusts, civil as well as military. He yielded to a premature fate of fever and running dysentery, the 30th day of September, Anno Domini 1707." Translated from the Latin.

"Reader since minutes Fly in Hast
Improve ye Present As thy Last.

Underneath this marble Lyes ye Body of Elizabeth, wife of Richard Grafton of this City, and Daughter of ——— White, of Waterford in ye Kingdom of Ireland. She dyed, September ye 5, 1725, aged 60 years."

"Here Lyes the Body of Jane, wife of William Read, late Sheriff of this county, with the Remains of three of their Children who died in their Infancy. She was born in London, of the ancient creditable Family of Spauldings. Many were her examplary virtues. Her Temper meek and carriage obliging, Strict Chastity, Prudent economy, Piety without Ostentation, and Hospitality without Grudging. Her Grateful Loving Husband caus'd to hew and here to place this lasting monument of real conjugal Affection. Obiit 5 Julii M. D. C. C. XXXII. Anus Aetatis XXXVI."

"Memor virtutum Johannae, conjugis, honesto genere natae, hoc sepulchri monumentum Maritus, Georgius Ross, Evangelii Praeco, extruendum curavit. Anno acquievit illa aetatis trigesimo septimo. 29th September, 1726. Dixet ei Jesus quisquis vivit et credit in me non morietur in eternum.
Calcanda semel via lethi."

"In memory of Ann, the wife of Zach Van Leu-enigh, who departed this life, December 27, A. D. 1749, aged 22 years.

"Under this stone are buried the remains of the Reverend Walter Hackett, who, while a Missionary, discharged, with great success, the duties of the Pastoral office at Appoquinimy about five years. He was born in Frasersburg, in Bampf, a province of Scotland, and was descended from the ancient and respectable family of Hackett. His life was blameless; in spirit, meek; in office, faithful; in labors, abundant. He died lamented by many good, but by none more than his beloved wife, who is pleased to erect to the memory of her worthy husband this sepulchral monument. He died, March 7, 1733, aged 33 years." Translated from the Latin.

"To the memory of Jehu Curtis, Esquire, Late Speaker of the Assembly; A Judge of the Supreme Court; Treasurer and Trustee of the Loan Office, who departed this Life, November 18, 1753, aged 61 years.

> If to be Prudent in Council
> Upright in Judgment,
> Faithful in Trust,
> Give value to the Publick Man;
> If to be Sincere in Friendship,
> Affectionate to Relations,
> And Kind to all around him,
> Makes the Private Man amiable
> Thy death, O Curtis,
> As a general Loss
> Long shall be lamented."

This epitaph was written by Dr. Benjamin Franklin.

"Beneath this marble is deposited the Body of Mary, the wife of Richard McWilliams, and Daughter of Jehu Curtis, Esq., together with Elizabeth, their only child, who died 16 November, 1749, at the age of 3 months and 28 days.

In her did conspicuously shine all the Divine and Amiable virtues of the Human Soul. Piety without Ostentation, Humility without Affectation, unbounded Charity, Filial Duty, Conjugal Love and Affection, Maternal tenderness and Indulgence but with economy, and beloved when living and in death lamented. Obiit 6 Maii Anno Domini 1757, Aetatis 24. Dixet Jesus qui credit in me etiams mortuis fuerit vir and quisquis vivit et credit in me moreitur in aeturnum.

EARLY CHURCH RECORDS OF NEW CASTLE COUNTY
INSCRIPTIONS.

"In memory of Edward Howts who died the 25th day of January, 1743, aged 28 years.

>Death thou hast conquered me
>I by thy darts am slain;
>But Christ shall conquer thee
>And I shall rise again."

"In memory of Catharine, daughter of Peter and Elizabeth Jaquett, of Long Hook, who departed this life the 15th day of August, 1774, aged 9 years."

"In memory of John Jaquett, who died the 1st day of September, 1754, aged 51 years."

"In memory of Peter Jaquett, of Long Hook, who departed this life the 29th day of October, 1772, aged 54 years."

"In memory of Elizabeth Jaquett, wife of Peter Jaquett, of Long Hook, who departed this life the 31st day of January, 1801."

"Here lyeth the Body of Mathew Usker, who departed this life the 7th of October, 1753."

"Mary Eves, Born November 19, 1724, Died January 4, 1768."

"Sacred to the memory of Ann Catharine Yeates, whose mortal part lies here deposited until the Resurrection of the Just. Adorned with every virtue that refines the Human Soul and elevates it to divine.

She departed this life, February 3, 1772, aged 48 years, in the full assurance of a most Glorious Eternity, deservedly lamented by all that knew her, to whom the sweetness of her temper rendered her particularly endearing, especially to her Husband and Children, whose loss is irreparable.

>Death has conquered her,
>She by his dart is slain,
>But Christ will conquer him
>And she will rise again."

"In memory of John Yeates, who departed this life, February 14, 1795, aged 73 years."

"In memory of Mr. John stoop, late Warden of Emmanuel Church, at New Castle. In which station he behaved himself with integrity and Honor, who departed this life the 12th day of December, 1771, aged 74."

"In memory of Mrs. Mary McKean, the wife of Thomas McKean, Esquire, who departed this life on the 12th day of March, 1773, aged 28 years.

 Fair was her form, serene her mind,
  Her Heart and Hopes were fixed on high;
 Her Hand beneficent and kind
  Oft wip'd the Tear from Sorrows Eye,
 The sweets of friendship softened care,
  Love, Peace and Joy her Soul Profest;
 Meekness perfumed each rising Prayer
  And every rising Prayer was Blest.
 In Heaven we trust her sainted spirit sings
  Glad Hallelujahs to the King of Kings."

"Here lieth the body of Jehu Clay, son of Slater Clay, who departed this life the 29th of July, 1757, aged 18 months."

"In memory of Jehu Clay, Jr., who died February 5 1758, aged 6 months."

"To the memory of Slater Clay, who departed this life February 20th, 1767, aged 55 years."

"In memory of Ann Clay, who departed this life June 14, 1789, aged 66 years."

"In memory of Mary Van Bebber, who departed this life September 18, 1780, aged 78 years."

"In memory of Thomas Clay, who departed this life September 6, 1793, aged 40 years."

"In memory of John Bond, who departed this life 6th August, 1794, aged 52 years."

"In memory of William Clay, who departed this life the 25th September, 1797, aged 36 years.
    'How lov'd, how valued once, avails thee not,
      To whom related or by whom begot,
    A heap of dust alone remains of thee,
      'Tis all thou art, and all the proud shall be.' "

"In memory of William, the son of George and Ruth Garland, who departed this life January 6, 1777, aged 3 years and 11 months.
    When I was young Christ called me home,
      My soul to leave this frame,
    And in the dust my body must
      Till the last day remain."

"In memory of Catharine Bradford, who departed this life February the 25, 1788, aged 45 years."

"In memory of Mary Ross, who departed this life April 30, 1784, aged 24 years."

"In memory of Rebecca McWilliam, who departed this life October 5, 1798, aged 16 years."

"In memory of Rebecca Lockyer, who departed this life May 9, 1801, aged 26 days."

"In memory of Dorothy, wife of John Hall, who departed this life July 28, 1789, in the 40th year of her age."

"In memory of John Hall, who departed this life July 4, A. D., 1810, aged 71 years."

"In memory of Richard Harrison, Obt. October, 1798, aged 17 years and 8 months."

"In memory of Ann Jane Stone, daughter of Guy and Dorothea Stone, who departed this life August 17, 1801, aged 1 year, 9 months and 3 days.

"In memory of Elizabeth, wife of Samuel Rowen, who departed this life October 9, 1793, aged 26 years and 6 months."

"In memory of Elizabeth, wife of Samuel Rowen, who departed this life August 11, 1806, aged 50 years."

"In memory of John, son of Henry and Mary Rowen, who died August 19, 1803, aged 1 year and 3 months."

"This monumental marble, inscribed to the memory of Gunning Bedford, Esquire, late Governor of the State of Delaware, who departed this life September XXX, M.D.C.C.VII, and lies here interred. His afflicted widow devotes, to discriminate the cold and silent repository of the remains of a much loved and sincerely lamented husband. Endeared to all that knew him by the amiable qualities of the heart, in his life, high in the esteem of the wise, the good and the patriotic; in his death, lamented by every friend to merit, truth and virtue.
'So he dies but soon revives, death over him
No power shall long usurp.'"

"George Read born, A. D., 1732,
Died 21st September, 1798.
Member of the Congress of the Revolution.
The Convention that framed the Constitution of the United States,
and of
The first Senate under it.
Judge of admiralty,
President and Chief Justice of Delaware
and
A signer of the Declaration of Independence."

"Gertrude, wife of George Read, and daughter of the Rev'd George Ross."

"In memory of James LeFevre, who departed this life January 18, 1787."

Here lyeth interred the Body of Mrs. Mary Reynolds, who departed this life on the 29th day of December 1777, aged 53 years. 7 months and 7 days,
    To that fond frame which here quite breathless lays
    The humble Marble weeping orphans raise
    Fain from oblivious clay cold hands to save
    Thy honour'd name and snatch it from the Grave.

"Here lies the Body of Ann, wife of John Stockton, who departed this life the 15th of April 1790, aged 45 years."

"In memory of Erasmus Jackson a native of Ireland, who departed this life March 18, 1800, aged 33 years.
Also Elizabeth, wife of Erasmus Jackson, daughter of James and Jane McCullough, who departed this life July 1, A. D. 1818, in the 42nd year of her age."

"In memory of Ann, second wife of William Armstrong, who departed this life October 16, 1803 in the 38th year of her age."

"In memory of William Aull, who departed this life September 13, 1803, aged 41 years.
    Frail man attend and view this grave
    In prime of life death conquered me
    The rich, the poor, the great, the slave
    Is hastening to Eternity.
    Since death is sure and life is vain
    Oh! haste to gain the heavenly prize
    Ah! don't delay in Christ to gain
    You then shall in his image rise."

"Sacred to the memory of Robert Wiley, who departed this life the 4th day of June 1801, aged 21 years, 6 months and 27 days.
> View this monument ye young and careless
> And boast no more of to-morrow."

"Sacred to the memory of David Bush, M. D. who departed this life July 3, 1801, in the 38th year of his age."

"Sacred to the memory of Capt. John Ewer Sword, who departed this life January 21, A. D. 1801. Anno Aetatis 45."

"In memory of Van Dyke Johns, who departed this life the 13, February 1801, aged 12 years, 3 months and 10 days,"

"In memory of Joseph Tatlow, Esquire, who departed this life January 26, 1808, aged 67 years."

"Here lies deposited the mortal remains of Joseph Israel, Esq., who departed this life, universally regretted, December 15, 1807, in the 54th year of his age. This marble cannot delineate his many virtues of which the hearts of his affectionate widow and children retain an indelible record, nor the benevolence which in the breasts of his numerous friends and acquaintances will long be remembered.
> 'Log'd in the Grand Lodge of the Sky
> He lives with God no more to die."

"In memory of John Bird, Esq., who departed this life April 12, 1810, aged 41; also his wife Elizabeth Van Leurcnigh died February 1848, aged 75 years."

"This tomb is erected to perpetuate the memory of Susanna Israel, relict of Joseph Israel, Esquire. She departed this life June 20, 1817, in the 52nd year of her age leaving a numerous family of children to lament a most affectionate mother."

"In memory of Nicholas VanDyke, Esq., late a Senator of

the United States from Delaware. He died May 21, 1826, in the 56th year of his age. Faithful and conscientious in the discharge of the varied duties of his private and public life his memory is revered as a relative and friend, his loss deplored as an honest and eminent statesman; and also of Mary VanDyke, relict of Nicholas VanDyke, who was born June 13, 1768, died May 4, 1831, in the 63rd year of her age."

"In memory of Kensey Johns, Chief Justice and afterwards Chancellor of the State of Delaware. Born June 14, 1759, died December 21, 1848; and Nancy, his wife, born August 9, 1768, died October 21, 1839."

"Here are deposited the remains of James Booth, late Chief Justice of the Court of Common Pleas of the State of Delaware. He was born the 6th February, 1753, and died 3d February 1828—Ann Booth, wife of James Booth, Chief Justice Court of Common Pleas, Born July 2, 1759, died May 10, 1846—James Booth, Chief Justice of the State of Delaware and for more than 30 years a warden of Immanuel Church. Born November 21, 1789, died March 29, 1855—Hannah W. Booth, wife of James Booth Chief Justice of the State of Delaware. Born June 4, 1797, died September 8, 1857."

"John Stockton, born 1755, died October 29, 1822. An officer of the Revolution.

John Stockton, Mid U. S. N., wounded in the Battle of Lake Ontario, May 28. Died at Kingston, Canada May 30, 1813, aged 26 years.

Thomas Stockton, born April 1, 1781, elected Governor of the State of Delaware, November 12, 1844, died March 2, 1846."

"In memory of James R. Black, one of the Judges of the Superior Court of the State of Delaware who was born on the 14th day of May 1785, and departed this life in the Christian hope of a blissful immortality, on the 3d day of September 1839. In the hearts of his fellow-citizens is engraven an epitaph more honourable to his memory than the hand of the warmest affection could inscribe upon this marble."

WELSH TRACT BAPTIST MEETING

Extracted from *The Welsh Tract Baptist Meeting, Pencader Hundred, New Castle County, Delaware, 1701-1828.* In Two Parts. [Extracting up through 1800]

Names of the members who first came over
Year 1701
Thomas Griffith, "minister"
Griffith Nicolas
Evan Edmond
John Edward
Elizeus (Elisha) Thomas
Enoch Morgan
Righart (Richard) David
Elizabeth Griffith
Lewis Edmond
Mary John
Mary Thomas
Elizabeth Griffith
Shonnet (Jennet) David
Margaret Matheas
Shonnet (Jennet) Morris
James David

Added to during the year and a half we abode at Pennepek
1701 Rees Ryddarch
1702 Catharine Ryddarch
Easther Thomas
Thomas Morris
Hugh Morris
Peter Chamberlain
Mary Chamberlain, Junior
Mary Sorensee
Magdalen Morgan
Henry David
Elizabeth David
Samuel Griffiths
Richard Seruy
Rebecca Marpole
John Grinwater
Edward Edwards
John James
Mary Thomas
Thomas John
Judith Griffith
Mary John, Jun
Thomas Thomas

After our removal down to New Castle County in the 1703 were added to the church by a letter from Wales:
1703 Thomas John
1708 Rebecca John
By Baptism:
John Wild
Thomas Wild
James James
Sarah James
Shuan (Jaen) Morgan
Samuel Wild
Mary Nicholas
Richard Boen
David Thomas
Mary Bentley
Jaen Edwards

In the year 1709 were added by letter from a church in Pembroke shire: (Samuel John, Minister)
John Devonallt

Mary Devonallt
Lewis Philip
Catharine Edward

From East Jersey
Philip Truax
Elizabeth Tilton

By a letter from
Pennepek
David Miles
Alce Miles

In the year 1710 were added to us by letters from the following churches in Wales, as follows:
From Rydwilin
1710 (John Jenkins, pastor)
Lewis Philip
Rees David (Deacon)
Thomas Evan
Thomas Edmond
Arthur Edward
Eleanor Philip
Susanna David
Mary Wallis

From Kilcam.
Samuel John, Past.
John Philip (Elder)
John Jenkin (afterwards Minister of Philadelphia)
John Harry
John Boulton
Richard Edward
Eleanor Philip
Mary William
Elizabeth Harry
Susanna Owen
Mary Bowen
Elizabeth John

From Lantivy.
1710 (James James, past.)
John Griffith (Elder)
Rees Jones
Hugh Evan
Samuel Evan
David Lewis
Rachel Griffith
Easther John
Mary Evan

From Langenych (Morgan Jones, Minister)
Hugh David (afterward Minister of the Great Valley)
Anthony Mathew
Simon Mathew
Simon Butler
Arthur Melchor
Hannah Melchor
Margaret David

From Lanwennarth
1711 (Timothy Lewis, pastor)
Joseph James

Added by Baptism
1711 Thomas Rees
Thomas David
Margaret Evan
Sarah Emson
Rachel Thomas
Daniel Rees
William Thomas
John Thomas
Martha Thomas
John Evans
Lydia Evans

Added by Letter from Pennepek in 1712
1712 Nicholas Stephen
Mary Stephen
John Paine

Elizabeth Paine

By Letters from Pennepek in 1713
1713 John Eaton
Juan Eaton
Joseph Eaton
Gwenllian Eaton
George Eaton
Mary Eaton

1713 From Lantivy (James James, pastor)
Elias Thomas
Thomas Evans
Ann Thomas

From Pembrokshire (Samuel John, Pastor)
Philip Rees

In 1714 were added to us by Baptism,
John Bentley
James James, Jun.
Eleanor David
Mary Thomas
Ann Thomas
David John
Richard Lewis
Sarah Nicholas
Mary Lewis

1714 By letter from Philadelphia (Abel Morgan, past.)
Benjamin Griffith
Emly Davis
Catherine Hollinsworth

1714 From Cohansey by letter: (Timothy Brooks, pastor), John Miller, Joanna Miller

In the year 1715 were added:
By letter from Shiregar (Pennsylvania): Mary Robinet
By Baptism: Thomas James (aged 16), John Jones, Richard Witten
By letter from Rydivilim: (John Jenkin, pastor), Griffith Thomas

In 1716 were added by baptism: Elizabeth John (Jenkin Jones's sister), David Davis, Thomas Richard and wife, and Mary Prys (Price)

In 1717, added by letter from Pennepek: Cornelius Vansant, Richard Herbert
And the same year by baptism
Sarah Herbert

Philip Truax dismembers Jan. 6, 1721-2. Neglecting to come to church meeting for several years, neglecting his business to the hurt of his family and creditors and other.

A large confession of faith put forth by upwards of a hundred congregations, holding believers, baptism, election and final perseverance was translated to Welsh by Abel Morgan (minister of the gospel in Philadelphia) to which was added, an article relative to Laying on of hands; Singing Psalms; and Church covenants; this confession (after being read and thoroughly considered at our quarterly meeting, Feb 4, 1716) was signed: Thomas Gryffyth, Elizous Thomas, Enoch Morgan, Shon Gryffyth, Shon Phylips, James James, Joseph Eton, Rhys Dafydd, Shon Doufnallt, Anthony Mathew, Dafydd Thomas, Thomas Shonn or Cryn, Thomas Shonn Rhys, Hugh Morys, Shon Efans, Shons Etton, Elias Thomas, Thomas Weild, Samuel Weild, John Pain, Thomas Rhichart, Edward Edwards, Thomas Edmond, William Thomas, Simon Mathou, Simon Butler, Thomas Efan, Thomas Moris, Elrhys Jones, Shonn Jones, Rhichart Whitin, Samuel Efans, Shon Butler, Richart Goary, Shon James, Shon Grinwator, Rhichart Dafydd, Samuel Gryffyth, Owen Thomas, Shoncin Shon, James James, Thomas James, Shonn Thomas, Dafydd Shon, Abel Nigolas, Arthyr Edward, Gryfyth Thomas, Shon Milor, Benjamin Gryfyth, Cornolius Fomsand, Richart Harbert, Shion Harry, Shioni Boulter, Phylip Trywax, Thomas Dafydd, Hugh Efan, Dafydd Thomas, Shion William, Samuell Philip, Thomas Rhys, ---, Daniol Rhys, Philip Rhys, Dafydd Lewis, Dafydd Efan, Shion Dafydd, David Davis, John Holinswoth, Garls Milor, William Denn, ---, John Evans.

1712 Morgan John, Danioll James, Phillip James
1719 Hugh Lewis, Richartt Lewis, Griffydd Lewis, William Truax, Thomas Jones, Choffry Bontley, John Stoutt, William Truax, Thomas Hodchoson, Richart Barow, Thomas David, Philip David, Barnott Young, Cornolius Truax.
1720 Philipp Duglass, Joshuia Dugless
1720 Joshua Edward
1722 Thomas Harry
1724 William Parson, Rinall Howell, Thomas James
1724 Lewis Jones
1724 Thomas Bowan
1725 Nathaniel Wilds, John Rentfro

1726 John James, Griffyth Nicholas
1726 Joseph Thomas, Moris Howel, Thomas Jenkin,
   Francis Boulton, Stephen Holinsworth
Augt 1727 William Evan
1727 James Howell
Epril [April] Richart Thomas
1728 Stephen David, Simon Parson
Aug 1728 William Hugh, David Harry
Sep 1 1728 Aboll James, Lewis Jorman
Dec 1728 Benjamin Underwood
Sep 7 John Bowen
1729 William Griffith
Jan 1729 David Davis
Oct 4 1730 James Hiatt

Names of the women who signed (1716):
Elizabeth Gryffyth, Mary Thomas, Shunan Morgan,
Rachel Gryffyth, Sara James, Guoullian Etton,
Suusana Dafydd, Mary Dofnallt, Robecca Shonn,
Ann Shonn, Mary Walis, Elinor Moris, Lidia
Efans, Shan Mathow, Mary Wiliana, Mary Etton,
Mary Thomas, Mary Weild Ros, Elizabeth Pain,
Elizabeth Rhys, Shywan Rhichart, Shan Edwards,
Mary Prys, Elizabeth Thomas, Mary Edmund, Ann
Rhichart, Ann Buttler, Ann Efan, Hana Shon,
Elinor Thomas, Ann Lewis, Mary Lewis, Sarah
Nigolas, Joanna Milor, Mary Robinot, Cathoring
Holinsworth, Elizabeth Tilton, Sara Harbort,
Sara Curd, Mary Bontler, Emlom Dafis, Rachel
Thomas, Estor Thomas, Estor Shon, Mary Shoncins,
Margaret William, Lyns Edmond, Elizabeth Harry,
Elizabeth Shion, Elizabeth Truwax, Martha Dafis,
Als Mils, Elonor Phylip, Mary Rhys, Margaret
Moris, Shusan Etton, Susana Dafydd, Elizabeth
Dafydd, Mary Thomas, Mary James, Cathring
Thomas, Margaret Robinott, Elonor Griffyth,
Hanah Philip, ---, Sara Milchor.
1712 Mary Jones, Sarah James, Sara Griffith
1719 Margaret James, Cathrin Lewis, Sarah
Edward, Jann Edward, Margaret James, Rebekah
Truax, Ann Pirce, Chathoring Roos, Rachol Milos,
Mary Truax, Elizabeth David, Abigal Thager,
Elinor Jones, Widow Forman, ---.

1720 Elizabeth Thomas, Sarah Thomas, Phebeh
   Bruor, Jane Miles, Lidia Osboorn, Cathoring
   Evan Harry

1722 Elizabeth Milchor, Mary Edwards, Mary Harry, Mary Nicholas
1723 Osboorns Dater, Janott Davis
1724 Elizabeth Roger, Mary Howol, Lottie Bowon
1725 Susanah William, Margaret Rontfro, Sarah James
1726 Elizabeth Thomas, Jane Howol, Rebeka Jenkin
1727 Elinor Johns, Mary Lewis
1728 Sarah Jenkin
1728 Epril Elizabeth Jones, Gownllian Hugh
Aug 1728 Marey Hugh, Margaret Edward, Mary John, Hary Howell, Mary Underwood
Sep 1728 Sarah Edward, Margaret Forman
1728 Jane Evans, Elizabeth Edward, Elizabeth Evan
1729 Elanor Stephen
1729 Elanor Jenkin
1729 Mary Nicholas
1739 Sara Barrow, Rachel Bomish, Mary Jones.

- - - - -

Sep 4, 1731, William Nicholas recd. from Wales.
June 3, 1732, Thomas Underwood bapt.
Sep 6, 1732, John Jones bapt.
Sep 30, 1732, Mary Jones bapt.
Nov 5, 1732, Hugh Jones bapt.
Nov 5, 1732, Thomas Jones bapt.

DEATHS

N.B. The first column denotes the year: the second, the month: the third, the day of the month.

1701/6/10 Jan'th Dafydd wife of Richard Dafydd
1701/11/12 Catherin Rhyddarch
1707/10 - Rees Rhyddarch
1706 John Edward
1710/10/26 Lewis Philip (Deacon)
1712/3/20 Nicolas Stephen
1712 William Mirick
1713/5 Jamos Jones
1713/8 Mary John wife of Hary John
1710 Dafydd Miles
1714/6/20 Arthyr Milchor
1714/1/- Thomas Efan
1715/2/- John Wild
1715/3/22 Mary Stephen
1715/5/- Rebecka Edward
1715/2/24 Lewis Phillip
1717/3/- John Etton

1717/10/- Juan Eatton
1717/11/- Samuel
 Philips
1718/1/22 Mary Bowen
1718/3/6 John Philips
1718/7/26 Edward
 Edwards
1718/9/30 John
 William
1718/11/5 Elizabeth
 Truax, Daniel
 Howlands wife.
1719/1/10 Elizabeth
 Rees, Daniel Rees
 wife.
1719/2/16 Richard
 Dafydd
1719/7/5 John Thomas
1719/8/- Joana Miller
1720/4/27 Thomas
 John, Iron hill
1721/2/10 Sarah James
1721/6/2/ Mary Evans,
 wife of John
 Evans, Junr.
1721/8/- Mary Wallis
1721/9/1/John
 Greemwator
1721/11/11 Jane
 Edwards
1721/9/- Elizabeth
 Griffith
1722/6/- John
 Wolinsworth
1722/7/5/Arthyr
 Edward
1724/6/6/Garlls Miles
1725/6/25/Thomas
 Griffith (minister
 of the Gospel)
1726/7/23/Thomas
 John, Cristeen
17269/27/Aboll
 Nicholas

1726/10/9/Griffith
 Nicholas
1726 11/11/Joshua
 Duglas
1727/1/-/Richart
 Lewis
1727/2/20/Emling
 Davis
1727/11/10/Rachel
 Miles
1727/11/26/Samuel
 Griffith
1727/11/29/Lidia
 Osborn
1728/12/-/Elizabeth
 Lewis
1729/3/-/John Boulton
1729/7/7/Lewis Jones
1730/20/1/Hugh Lewis
1730/6/-/Cornelius
 Truax
1729//William Truax
1730/9/1/Elisha
 Thomas (Paster)
1730/9/-/John Paine
1730/9/27/Elinor
 Philips
1730/10/13/Susanna
 David
1730/11/10/Griffith
 Lewis
1731/9/-/Dyws Edmond
1731/11/-/Thomas
 Moris
1731/11/24/Perry
 Thomas
1732//Leffis Bowen,
 died Nov 1732
1732//Sarah Vanholan
 died Nov 1732.
1732//Thomas Jenkins
1732//Elizabeth Davis

Case of Martha David - put out of the church
Mar. 4, 1732.

REMOVED TO OTHER MEETING HOUSES

Translation from Welsh in to English by Revd. W. F. D. Lewis.

To the Pennepack meeting house, Peter Chamberlin, Mary Chamberlin, Mary Chamberlin, Jr., Thomas Morris and Janett Morris.

To the Mysyfodd (Radnor) meeting house, Hugh David (Minister), Margaret Dafydd (David), James Dafydd, Richard Edwards.

To the Philadelphia meeting house, Judith Morgan, 1717.

To the Gwynedd meeting house Barnett Young.

To the Gwynedd meeting house Benjamin Gryffyd (Griffith).

Joseph Eatton, George Eatton, Gwen Eatton, Mary Eatton, Simon Mathew, Jane Mathew, Anthony Mathew, Daniel Rhys (Rees), Ann Rhys (Rees), Simon Butler and Ann Butler, all of them to Gwyneed meeting house 1721.

Ann Lewis to the Great Valley meeting house.

Thomas Rees and his wife Elizabeth Rees to the Gwynedd Meeting house 1722.

Katherine Hollinsworth to the Philadelphia meeting house 1722.

Margaret James and Margaret Robinet to the Cranddiwen meeting house.

Jenkin John and his wife Hannah John to the Philadelphia meeting house by letter May 2, 1726 and Elizabeth Melchor.

Stephen Hollinsworth to the Phila, Jan 6, 1727.

Cheffrs (Iefferies) Bently to Cranddiwen.

Elinor (Eleanor) Stephen to the Philadelphia meeting house Aug 3, 1727.

Philip David to the Great Valley meeting house April 1730.

THOSE WHO WERE EXCOMMUNICATED

1714 Magdalen Morgan - Unseemly dress, neglected church meeting.

Joseph James, his associates are godless men, spends his time with loud talkers and in the midst of disorderly nights...

1714 Evan Edmunds and Catherine keeping company too often and too unseemly ...

1716 - Griffith Nicholas - brook his promise which he had made relative to a matter of

business between him and brother Thomas John from Bryn.
1717 Richard Lewis - kept unseemly company with his neighbour's wife.
1717 John Pain - gross conduct and disobeying rules of the church; repented in 1723.
1720 - Richard Seary - falsely accused this congregation of a charge.
1721 - Philip Truax for reasons given earlier.
1723 Mary Rees, married a man in opposition to the advice of her Christian brethren and of her natural father; also has broken her marriage vows with her other husband because neither she nor we know but he is yet alive.
1724 - Thomas Jones and Elinor his wife - improper conduct towards each other.
Abigail Thatcher, lying.

- - - - -

Jacob John restored May 5, 1770.
John Evans, Esq., bapt. June 20, 1770.
Oct 6, Martha Griffith received.
Nov 3, 1770, Rev John Sutton received.
Nov 3, 1771, David Miles and Levy Dungan taken into communion. Same day John Boggs bapt. and received into full communion.
May 2, 1772, Enoch Morgan, Jr. bapt.; also Joseph Griffith restored Sep 1772, and John Thomas bapt.
Dec 5, 1773. Evan Jenkin received from Philadelphia Church.

Abel Morgan bapt. March 31, 1733, died 1785, pastor of church at Middletown for many years.
John Harry bapt. Sep 1, 1733. Feremia Rees same day.
David James and his wife Elinor recd. by letter from Mountgomarin Nov 3, 1733.
William Lewis bapt. Aug 3, 1734.
Jeremiah Rowell bapt. Aug 31, 1734.
Evan Rees and John Watson and John Cockerel bapt. Aug 2, 1735. The same day William Rees received from Mountgymru. Thomas John and Zacharies Thomas bapt. Oct 4, 1735.
Thomas Money bapt. 1835.
Edward Milos bapt. Oct 2, 1736.
Nathaniel Evan bapt. Oct 2, 1736.

John Jones bapt. Dec 4, 1736.
John Thomas recd. June 4, 1737 from Great Valley.
March 31, 1739 John Morgan and Benjamin Jones bapt.
Oliver Alison bapt. 1739.
John Griffith bapt. Aug 4, 1739.
David Thomas and Enoch Morgan bapt. May 3, 1740.
Thomas Howell restored.
Moris Thomas and Lewis Thomas bapt. July 5, 1740.
Jacob Jones bapt. Aug 2, 1740.
Jacob Jones restored May 5, 1770.
Walter Downe recd. from church at Brandywine Aug 2, 1740.
John Goforth and Moris Howell bapt. Oct 4, 1740.
James Jones and James James bapt. May 2, 1741.
Enoch Davis recd. from Philadelphia Aug 1, 1741.
Daniel John bapt. Sep 14, 1742.
Died Nov 1748 James Pearson bapt. Oct 2, 1742.
Joseph Brown bapt. Aug 6, 1743.
Rees Jones Doctor bapt. Sep 30, 1743.
John Hughes recd. Dec 31, 1743 from church on P.D. [Pee Dee] in South Carolina. Excommunicated July 1747.
Joseph Bedome bapt. Oct 6, 1744
Thomas Farr bapt. July 7, 1745, removed by a letter to another church May 1776.
Edward Vizey bapt. Aug 2, 1746. The same day was the two sons of David Rees bapt.: Thomas and John and also John James at the same time.
Sep 6, 1746 was William Starkey bapt.
Jonathan David restored Sep 6, 1746.
Daniel Griffith recd. from Mountgomry by letter dated April 30, 1748.
Daniel David recd. from Wales Nov 4, 1749.
Rev. Mr. Griffith Jones recd. from Wales Jan 2, 1750.
Morgan Jones bapt. May 6, 1750.
Stephen Cantwell bapt. Aug 3, 1750.
June 1, 1751 William Bukingham recd. from church of Brandywine.
Nicolas Paine bapt. May 2, 1752.
Thomas McKim recd. Aug 2, 1752, being bapt. two weeks before at Brandywine by Rev. Bonham.
Also at the same time was Thomas Edmund recd. from church of Mountgomrey.

Jonathan Joly living in Quine Anns County in Mariland bapt. May 18, 1753 and added to the church.
Alixander McKim bapt. Oct 19, 1752.
Jonathan Davis bapt. April 6, 1754.
Isaic Lewis recd. from Montgomry April 6, 1754.
Hugh Glasford bapt. May 9, 1754.
Thomas Davis son of David Davis bapt. Aug 9, 1754.
Ebenezer Howel restored 1756.
Abel Davis bapt. Aug 3, 1755.
David Hugh bapt. Sep 5, 1755.
William James bapt. April 2, 1756.
John Hall bapt. at the same time.
John Morgan and James Williams added, one from the Great Valley, the other from Montgomrey July 3, 1757.
Thomas Robinson and David John, Morgan Johns son were bapt. May 6, 1758. John Davis, David Davis his son of --- was bapt. May 6, 1758.
Thomas James, Esq. restored April 5, 1761.
John Jones, the Rev Mr. Griffith Jones, his son, bapt. Oct 4, 1761 and added to the church.
Zachria Jones bapt. Oct 6, 1764.
John Buckingham bapt. Aug 3, 1765.
Joseph Griffith and Isaac Hugh bapt. Oct 5, 1765.
John McCormick bapt. Nov 2, 1765.
Joseph Garner rec'd., Dec 1, 1765 from the Church in Phila.
John Townsend bapt. May 24, 1766.
Joseph Price bapt. Oct 4, 1767.
John Davis bapt. Nov 1, 1767.
William Buckingham, Junior bapt. Oct 1, 1768.
John Bowen recd. March 5, 1769 by letter from Vinsent.
Aug 4, 1769 James Mundel recd. from the Church at Brandywine.

Mary Howel, Mary Underwood, Sarah Edward, Margaret Forman, Jane Evans, Elizabeth Edward now James, Elizabeth Evan, Eleanor Jenkin, Mary Nicholas, Sarah Barrow, Rachel Bemish, Mary Jones, Mary Nicholas, Elinor James, Sarah Devenald, Rachel Devenald, Mary Devenald bapt. Aug 31, 1734.
Mary Howell, Martha William, Mary Devonald, Hannah Devonald, bapt. Nov 2, 1734.

Martha Rogers bapt. Nov 30, 1734.
Sarah Hary [bapt.?] Sep 1733.
Jane Hyatt and Mary Watson bapt. Aug 2, 1735.
Elizabeth Jones bapt. Oct 4, 1735.
Jan 31, 1736, Then was Mary Lewis now Mary Smith, she was, Aug 1, 1731, excommunicated, but restored now upon her repentance.
April 30, 1736, Then was Elizabeth Owen (Thomas) baptized April 30, 1736, Then was Sarah and Mary Jones baptized June 5, 1736, Then was Sarah Thomas and Elizabeth Jones baptized Mary Miles was bapt. Oct 2, 1736.
Ann Jones bapt. Sep 3, 1737.
Hannah Roos bapt. Aug 5, 1738.
Rachel Alison bapt. May 5, 1739.
Martha Richards recd. from Wales Aug 4, 1739.
Rachel Griffith and Elenor James bapt. Aug 4, 1739.
Sara Evans bapt. July 5, 1740.
Baptized Aug 2, 1740: Lettice Douglass, Annie Jones, Mary Hugh, Judith Devonald, Elizabeth Jones.
Elizabeth James recd. from Great Valley Aug 2, 1740.
Margaret John.
Lydia Go Forth bapt. Oct 4, 1740.
Susannah Jones
Mary Jones
Elizabeth Heath bapt. May 2, 1741.
Margaret Howel bapt. Apr 3, 1742.
Ann Gill bapt. July 31, 1742.
Mary Rothwell bapt. April 3, 1743.
Mary Price recd. June 4, 1743 [who was for some time earlier in communion among the Presbyterians.]
Hannah Eynon recd. from church of Brandywine Aug 6, 1743.
Abigel Childs bapt. Sep 3, 1743.
Sarah Jones wife of Dr. Jones bapt. Sep 30, 1743.
Ann Welsh alias Bush bapt. June 2, 1744.
Mary Evans alias Obarne bapt. Aug 7, 1744.
Mary Cantrel alias Thomas bapt. Oct 6, 1744.
Margaret Howel, Rynal Howels daughter bapt. March 2, 1745.
Died May 5, 1750 Ann Thomas, Thomas Thomas [h]is daughter was bapt. Apr 6, 1745 [sic].

Died April 25 1750 Mrs. Cottman bapt. Oct 5, 1745. The same time was Margaret Buckingham bapt.
Aug 2, 1746, was Ann Elizabeth Vezey bapt.
Oct 4, 1746, Then was Mary the eldest daughter of Howel James baptized.
1748 Dec 3. Jane Rowland wife of David Rowland bapt.
Dec 2, 1749, Then was Elizabeth Buchun recd. from church of Brandywine.
Jun 1, 1751 Jane Buckingham recd. from Brandywine.
Aug 1751 Mary Jonson recd. from Wales.
At the same time was Magdalen Morgan. Alias Cox restored.
Then was baptized the following persons in Kent County by the ministry of Rev. Mr. Jones: Rachel Davis, Deborah Evans, Hanah Rees and Hester Rees, Aug 2, 1752.
Then recd. from church at Montgomery, Mary Edmund.
At the same time Sarah McKim recd.
Catharine Dope and Godmah Heyet bapt. April 18, 1753, by Mr. Jones in Kent County.
Magdalen Towson living in Kent bapt. by Mr. Jones Sep 1753.
Rachel and Sarah Hugh, daughters of William Hugh and also Hannah Buckingham, daughter of William Buckingham, bapt. May 9, 1754.
Phebe Hugh bapt. Aug 3, 1755.
June 1752 bapt: Mary Thomas (Thomas Thomas daughter) and Hana Oborne and Rachel Oborne.
July 13, 1752 Margaret Murfey and Mary Joley bapt. by Mr. Jones in Kent.
Nov 7, 1752 Mary Juney a daughter of Mr. Owen Thomas bapt.
Elizabeth Rockhold living in Baltimore bapt. by Mr. Jones Aug 1755.
Widow Smith, daughter of Zachria Buchen bapt. Oct 19, 1753.
Cathrin Wattson bapt. Aug 4, 1754.
Elizabeth Owen added by letter from church at Talrahobin, June 7, 1755.
Sep 2, 1755 was three of John Garets daughters bapt.: Ann Robinson, Elizabeth Robinson and Sarah.
Sarah James wife of William James bapt. April 2, 1756.

Ruth Buckingham bapt. June 4, 1746.
Weize Evans bapt. Aug 3, 1756.
Mary Morgan wife of John Morgan recd. from Great Valley July 3, 1757.
Sarah Milles wife of David Milles bapt. Sep 3, 1757.
Hannah Davis wife of David Davis of Chester County near Conestoga, recd. March 3, 1759. She was bapt. and hands laid on her by a sevenday minister about 30 years before.
Jane Williams, James Williams wife bapt. Aug 4, 1759.
Elenor Davis, Daniel Davis wife of Kent bapt. Oct 6, 1759.
Susana Lewis now Susana Wattson recd. from church of Philadelphia, July 6, 1760.
Hannah Bonham recd. Aug 3, 1760 from church of Kingswood.
Famer Edwards now James recd. July 5, 1761 from church at Philadelphia.
Hannah M. Conell alias Blind Hannah and Deborah Davis, daughter of David Davis, living near Conestoga, bapt. Aug 1, 1761.
Mary Rogers bapt. Oct 4, 1761.
Jane Thomas, wife of Thomas Thomas bapt. July 2, 1763.
Mary Lewis, wife of Isaiah Lewis and her sister Johanna Jones wife of Zachrias Jones bapt. Nov 3, 1769.
Sarah Smith daughter of Lewis Morgan bapt. Aug 31, 1765. The next meeting she was dismissed to one of our churches in Carolina.
Hanah Hugh wife of Hall Hugh and Mrs. Pritchard, John Pritchards wife, bapt. Oct 5, 1765.
Hannah McCormick wife of John McCormick and Mary Roberts bapt. Nov 2, 1765.
Mary Price, Mary Griffith and Hanah Jones bapt. Oct 4, 1767.
Sarah Oborne bapt. Oct 5, 1768.
Sarah Osborne bapt. Nov 5, 1768.
Jane Bowen recd. March 5, 1769 from Vingent.
Hester Davis recd. from the church of Baltimore July 2, 1769.
Aug 4, 1769 Margaret Mundel recd. from church of Brandywine.
1769 Sarah Oborn bapt.
John Bowen recd. from Vinsent or the Valley church

Nov 3, 1770, Ruth Sutton recd. from Hopewell.
Aug 31, 1771, Mary Eynow and Ann Murrain bapt.
Oct 5, Ann Glasford and Sarah Morgan and
  Elizabeth bapt.
Nov 3, 1771, Rachel Morgan and Sarah Thomas
  bapt.
At the same was Levy Dungan's and his wife and
  William Magachlin's wife taken into
  communion, both living in Kent County.
Nov 30, 1771, Mary Jones wife of John Jones
  bapt.
Elizabeth Edwards, a cousin of Mr. James, bapt.
  Jan 4, 1772.
Jane wife of William Buckinham, junior, bapt.
  March 1, 1772.
May 2, 1772, Enoch Morgan, Junior, bapt.
At the same time was Joseph Griffith restored.
May 23, 1772, Hannah Boggs, wife of John Boggs
  bapt.
At the same time was Clark, a widow near Duck
  Creek bapt.
July 1772, Ann Bowen wife of Thomas Bowen bapt.
At the same time Mary Branan she served her time
  at Mr. James, bapt.
Elizabeth Tompson bapt, June 1774.
Judith Hendrickson bapt. 1774 She had lived some
  time earlier at David Hughes, London Track.
Isaac Lewis bapt. Nov 1, 1775, in his 17th year.
April 6, 1776, James Jones, Junior, recd. At the
  same time Samuel Woodbridge and Sarah his
  wife recd. from Philadelphia Church.
May 24, 1777, John Maguire.
Oct 4, 1777, John Tayler bapt.
Feb 28, 1778, Samuel Morgan recd. from church at
  Diffical, Fairfax County in Virginia.
Nov 1, John James bapt.
July 1, 1780, Jane wife of John Taylor bapt.
Aug 5, 1780, Sarah Jones, now Patton, bapt.
Aug 27, Gwentlian Dunsmore and Hester Jones
  bapt.
At the same time was Kezia Carlile and Mary
  Richchy recd. from Philadelphia Church.
1780, bapt. Samuel Griffith, Mary Griffith from
  Kent.
At the same time John Price and John Patton and
  Rachel Scotton, bapt. by John Sutton at
  Cowmarsh.

Feb 3 1781, Samuel Davis recd. from Philadelphia Church.
At the same time his daughter Elizabeth Davis bapt.
March 3, 1781, Kezia Lewis daughter of Isaiah Lewis bapt.
1780, Sarah Davis wife of Abel Davis bapt.
April 1781, Joanna Jones restored.
May 6, 1781, Thomas William and Lettis Woods and Susanna James bapt.
Last day of June 1781, Samuel Jones and Elizabeth Pringle bapt.
Sep 1, 1781, Deboroh Eynon and Dorcas Armitage bapt.
Oct 7, 1781, Mary Pasmore alias Evans, bapt.
Margaret Knarsborough recd. April 6, 1782.
Jun 1, 1782, James William bapt.
Aug 3, Thomas Prindle a member of New York Church recd.
Aug 3, 1782, Robert Shields bapt.
Aug 31, 1782, John Stow recd. from Philadelphia church.
Oct 1782. Elizabeth Lewis, wife of John Lewis bapt.
April 1784, Andrew Edge and Sarah his wife recd. from Philadelphia Church.
May 1784, Andrew Morton and Rachel his wife and Susana Morton, recd.
Oct 1, 1785, Judith Hendrickson restored.
Nov 6, 1785, James Griffith bapt, in his 17th year and at the same time Ephraim Stoops and Elizabeth Tompson, the younger bapt.
Jan 1, 1786, Ebenezer Morton and Patience Morton his wife and Cornelia Stoops wife of Ephraim Stoops, bapt.
June 4, 1786, Joseph Boggs and Abigal Morton and a young girl called Anne Hamilton, bapt.
July 1, 1786, Isaac Eaton and Thomas Smith bapt.
Aug 5, 1786, Margaret Goteer bapt.
Sep 1786, Amelia McSpaven recd. from Wilmington.
Apr 1, 1787, Fanney Ruffee Forgeston and Elisabeth Kimble recd. by bapt.
May 6, 1787, Ann Morton recd. by bapt.
Since June 3, 1787, til year of 1793 there have been added to this church by baptism, by men: John Price, Robert McMullin, Frederick Hare, John Rudolph, John Kimble, John Miles, Isaac Hill, John Cornish, Noble Bolden, Sharp

Grantam, William Price, Francis Guttier,
Andrew Harvey, Joseph Carman, Benjamin
Charles, Joseph Flood, Eaesar Richardson, Wm.
Vert, John Boggs, Jun., Hackey McGowen,
Rudolph Mitchell, James Champion, Jacob
Bryan, Andrew Walker, Jacob Till, Peter
Richardson, David Henderson, Anthony Porter,
Nicolas Quinn.
Of Women: Sarah Williams, Annie Morton, Nancy
McGowin, Sarah Griffith, Flora Champion,
Dorcas Price, Jane Bowen, A. Morton, Mrs.
Wiley, Rebecca Miles, Seney Griffith, Eleanor
Townsend, Mary Post, Jane Reynolds, Margaret
Simpers, Phillis Grantam, Sarah Stoops,
Rebecca Vert, Sarah Pierce, Margaret Smith,
Agnes Thomson, Sarah Morton, Nancy Davy,
Katharine Griffith, Sarah Cooch, Anne
Crawford, Margaret Welch, Mary Walker,
Elizabeth Black, Sarah Kimble, Hannah Flood,
Margaret Gosboro, Anne Averite, Savannah
Waters, Eleanor Delany, Rebecca Ozier, Sarah
Price, Eliz'th Grantam, Elizth Quinn, Rebecca
---, Hannah Mitchell, Mary Rutter, Susanna
Griffith, Hanna Death, Anne Welch, Mary
Rudolph, Elizth. Mitchell, Mary Flinn, Hannah
Johnson, Jane Wates, Phebe ---, Katharine
Harwood, Elizabeth Miller, Mrs. Hughes, Mary
Ruze, Susanna Dushane, Sarah Porter, Sarah
Morton.
Recd. by letter Mary Jones.
Mary Boldon bapt. Nov 2, 1793.
April 5, 1794, Michael Bryan, Margaret Minough &
  (Mary Stewart recd. by bapt. April 16)
May 3 Elizabeth Cooley and Jane Connoway bapt.
Margaret Conoway bapt. 1798.

BURIALS
Philip Nicholas bur. Sep 9, 1733.
William Peerson bur. Jan 31, 1734.
David Thomas bur. May 6, 1734.
Cornelius Vansant bur. May 9, 1734.
John Dovenal, Elder, bur. Mar 9, 1735.
Joanna Richard bur. Aug 28, 1735.
Ann John bur. Oct 29, 1735, aged 48.
John Griffith, Elder, bur. Nov 12, 1735, age 80.
Lydia Evans bur. Dec 25, 1735.
Thomas Richard bur. July 1, 1736, age 82.
Nathaniel Wild bur. ---.

Elias Thomas bur. Jan 10, 1738, age 70.
Elizabeth Pain bur. April 22, 1738.
John Evans, Elder, bur. April 16, 1738.
Rev. Mr. Enoch Morgan, minister of the gospel, died March 25, 1740, age 64.
John Evans bur. April 28, 1740.
Mary Jones bur. April 7, 1740.
Rees Jones, Elder, bur. Nov 25, 1739.
Phillip Rees, died in South Carolina, Oct 1739.
Rees David, Deacon, bur. Jan 1740.
Catherine Thomas bur. May 25, 1741.
Mary Thomas bur. July 26, 1742.
Thomas Hutchinson died Oct 1741.
Richard Whitten, Ruling Elder, bur. Jan 1742.
William Nichlas bur. April 18, 1743.
Mary Davis, wife of David Davis, teaching elder, bur. July 24, 1743.
Sarah Underwood bur. Aug 8, 1743.
Hugh Marice bur. Nov 19, 1743.
Mary Thomas, widow of Elisha Thomas, teaching elder, died Aug 24, 1744.
Margaret John bur. Sep 22, 1744.
Catherine Lewis bur. Nov 1746.
Ann Clement bur. Dec 1746.
Joseph Browne bur. March 1, 1747.
Mary Oborn, Joseph Oborn's wife, died Dec 20, 1767.
William Thomas died in winter day and month not known the 1760.
David Davis, minister, died Aug 19, 1769.
Thomas Griffith, Ruling Elder, died.
Zachariah Thomas, a young minister, died.
Richard Thomas, Ruling Elder, died.
Mary Edmond, wife of Thomas Edmond, died.
John Watson, Deacon, died Nov 12, 1755, aged 45.
James James died Feb 1755.
Hester Jones, died.
Dr. Jones [h]is wife died.
Dr. Jones died.
Benjamin Underwood died.
Hugh Evans, Deacon, died.
Caterine, wife of Hughe Evans, died.
John Thomas, Ruling Elder, died.
Elenor, wife of Jorgan Jones, died.
Lewis Thomas, Deacon, died May 10, 1761 in his 40th year.
John David of White Oak Swamp, died.
Mr. Griffith Jones, minister, died.

Thomas Edmond died.
Sarah wife of William James died.
Reinald Howell, Ruling Elder, and his wife died.
Margaret wife of Edward Miles died.
Thomas David and Stephan died.
Jane Thomas wife of Thomas Thomas died.
Ann Robinson died.
Mary wife of J. Oborn died Dec 20, 1767.
Zachariah Jones died.
William Thomas died Jan 1769.
Mr. David Davis, our worthy minister, died Aug 19, 1769.
Thomas John died Sep 1770.
Sarah Miles wife of Edward Miles, died Jan 29, 1771, age 54.
Edward Miles died a few months after her.
Margaret Williams wife of David Williams died in the Fall of 1771.
Rachel Davis, Mr. Davisis widow, died Nov 1, 1771, age 78.
Choice wife of John Townsend, died Jan 26, 1772, age 35.
Joseph Griffith died Sep 9, in his 40th year, 1773.
Jenet Jones, widow of Griffith Jones, B. M., died Oct 25, 1773, age 68. (Griffith Jones was a Baptist minister from Wales.)
Elizabeth Lemon wife of Jacob Lemon, died Jun 26, 1774, age 39.
James Williams died July 21, 1774, age 63.
Sarah Oborn died Aug 14, 1774, age 35.
Mary Thomas died Sep 9, 1774, age 51. She was Lewis Thomasis widow and lived a widow near 14 years.
Mary Branen died April 11, 1775, age 23.
Mary Clark died July 13, 1775, age 64.
Isaac Lewis died Jun 20, 1776, aged 18 years; he lived at Jos. Prices, was his wife's nephew.
Hannah Bonham died Aug 22, 1776.
Daniel Griffith died Jan 19, 1777, age about 76.
Mary Jones, John Jonesis widow, died Feb 2, 1777. aged ---.
Catherine Reese died Feb 26, 1777, age about 80.
Hannah Eynow died May 21, 1777, in her 55th year.
William Eynon died Oct 10, 1777, a member of 48 years.
Mary Rogers died April 22, 1778.

Jacob John died Sep 22, 1778, age 58.
Elizabeth John died 4 days after the disease of her husband John John, age 56.
Jane widow of James William died March 1779, age about 70.
Hannah Davis, widow of David Davis, died April 1779. "They did live toward Canistoaga."
Thomas James, Esq., died Dec 28, 1779, age 82, bapt. 1715.
Evan Jenkin died Jun 16, 1780 age about 64.
July 23, 1781, Hannah Connolly died age about 57.
Rachel Griffith died Jun 12, 1782, had been a widow 33 years.
Jane wife of John Bowen died Oct 21, 1783, age 84.
April 14, 1785, William James died age about 85.
May 26, 1786, James John died.
June 3, 1786, Elizabeth Kehoon died.
Sometime in the beginning of the year 1786 Mary Cann an ancient member of this church died, supposedly above 90 years of age.
Andrew Edge died Oct 15, 1786, in his 51st year.
June 3, 1787, Susanna John, widow of James John, died age 70.
Isiah Lewis, Deacon, died Aug 1787.
John Bowen died 1789.
Abel Davis died 1790.
Andrew Walker died 1791.
Robert Shields, deacon, died 1792.
Hannah Boggs, Elizabeth Edwards, Kezia Carlisle, Sarah Griffith, Mrs. Wiley, Katharine Harwood, died between June 3, 1787 and the year 1793.
Margaret Hinsey and Sarah Edge died Feb 1799.
June 9, 1733, Esther Thomas excluded ... for carrying her grand daughters to the presbyterians to be sprinkled contrary unto the will of their father and mother while alive, which then were dead ... Same day Susannah William excluded.
Oct 5, 1735 William Hugh excluded for his obstinacy.
Jan 31, 1736 Rachel Bemish excluded for she reported she was with child by John Evan's man ... .

April 3, 1736 Elinor Griffith excluded - married to another husband and that while her first husband was alive.
[same day?] James James, Junior excluded for absenting from the church and other.
Feb 3, 1744/5 Jonathan Davis excluded, for marrying disorderly and without consent of his father and other.
Aug 3, 1746 Sarah Evan disowned for drunkenness and falsehoods.
Daniel John disowned for drunkenness, fornication.
William Lewis disowned for drunkenness, using unlawful means to find money by casting up figures. Executed May 4, 1760.
Jacob Johns, for drinking to excess and speaking untruths. Jan 1766.
John Jones disowned.
Joseph Griffith disowned for heinous crimes contrary to the moral law. Oct 4, 1769.
Elizabeth Pritchard disowned for swearing and cursing, not bridling her tongue... Feb 6, 1773.
Joanna Jones disowned for fornication. March 6, 1773.
Mary Eynon disowned for fornication. April 4, 1773.
Hanah Magachlin disowned for fornication. Jan 5, 1777.
John Macwire disowned for breach of covenant with the church. May 3, 1778.
Mary Price disowned for false accusation, Feb 1781.
Judith Hendrickson disowned for marrying another woman's husband and living with him as a wife, Jun 3, 1781.
Dr. John Thomas disowned for fornication, Feb 1782.
Hugh Glasford disowned for his refractory conduct in leaving the church ...
Catherine Bigum disowned for breach of Covenant with the church and drunkenness. April 3, 1783.
Dec 2, 1786, Benjamin Jones, formerly of Kent County, disowned for his long absence in a disorderly way and had reason to believe he lived several years in adultery and had some

children by a woman even in his wife's life time.

Thomas John recommended to care of church at Phila, Sep 8, 1733.

Francis Maybery admitted from church at Meedletown, 1733.

Richard Herbert and Sarah Herbert recommended to church of Philadelphia, May 4, 1734.

Stephen David recommended to church of Philadelphia by letter May 13, 1734.

Eleanor Moris recommended to Church in Great Valley, Jun 1, 1735.

Stephen David is returned and recommended to us by church in Philadelphia, June 1, 1735.

Sarah Mitcher now Sarah James is removed to Carolina and recommended to church at Charles Town, South Carolina.

Elanor Nicholas and Mary Nicholas recommended by church in the Great Valley, June 12, 1736.

Francis Boulten removed and recommended to church in Great Valley.

Our Brothren and sisters whose names are as followeth Abel Morgan, teaching elder (Abel Morgan is returned), James James, Ryuling Elder, Thomas Evan Deacon, Daniel James, John Harry, Junior, Richard Barrow, Mary James, Mary Wilds, Sarah Harry, Samuel Miles, Thomas Harry, Thomas Money, Annie Evan, Elizabeth Harry, Margaret William, John Harry, Jeremiah Rowel, Nathyaniel Evan, Sarah James, Eleanor Jenkin, Mary Rowel, Sarah Barrow, are removed to Carolina and recommended by letter to the church of Christ in Charles Town or elsewhere in South Carolina or they might constitute themselves into a church, from us Nov 1735.

Thomas John is returned and recommended from church in Philadelphia, Jan 8, 1736/7.

Samuel Evan and his wife Mary Ann Evan recommended to our Christian friends on Pedee in South Carolina. April 30, 1737.

Recommended to care of Christian friends on Pedee in South Carolina: Daniel Devonald, Phillip James, Abol James, Catherine Harry, Elinor James, Thomas James, David James, Simon Pirsons, Elizabeth James, Mary Hugh, David Harry, Mary Boulton, Elizabeth Jones. Nov 4, 1737.

John Jones and wife Ann Jones recommended to
Christian friends on Pedee in South Carolina,
March 11, 1738.
Thomas Edmund and his wife Mary Edmund
recommended to church of Christ in Mountgumw
May 15, 1738.
Ales Thomas and Jane David and Mary Dovenald
recommended to Christian friends on Peedee in
South Carolina, Nov 3, 1739.
Martha Rogers recommended to Great Valley, March
1, 1740.
John Bowen dismissed to church in the Great
Valley, Dec 6, 1740.
John Jones, Phillip Douglass, Oliver Alison and
Walter Down, Elizabeth Jones, Lettis Douglas,
Rachel Alison, Rachel Downs, recommended to
sister church on Pee Dee River in South
Carolina Nov 1, 1741.
Letter of dismission for Sarah Morton from
Church of Christ at Salem in Jersey. Sep 15,
1787.
Signers of the church covenant in 1710: Thomas
Griffith, Elisha Thomas, Enoch Morgan, James
James, Evan Edmond, Griffith Nicholas, Edward
Edwards, Richard Owen, Hugh David, John
Griffith, John Philips, Antony Matthew, Rees
David, Thomas Evans, Thomas Edmond, Thomas
Morris, Arthur Milcher, Jenkin Jones, John
Bolton, John Edward, Hugh Morris, Thomas
Wild, Samuel Wild, Thomas John, Thomas John,
Lewis Philip, John Devonald, Samuel Griffith,
David Thomas, Rees Jones, in all 30. And
Mary Wallace, Elinor John, Elinor Morris,
Hanah Milcher, Mary David, Jane James,
Elizabeth John, Luce Edmond, Joan Morgan,
Rebeka Edward, Caterine Edward, Rebeka John,
in all 12.
In attendance at business meeting March 31,
1770: Thos. James, Esq., Morris Thomas,
Willm. Eynon, Dan'l Griffith, Ja's Jones,
Willm, Buckingham, David Evans, Isaiah Lewis,
Hugh Glasford, Thos. Rhoads, Abel Davine,
Willm. Buckingham, Jun., Jno. Buckingham,
Jo's Price, Jacob Lemmon, James Mundel, John
McCormack, Thos. John, Jno. Davis.
Recd. of Joseph Oborn sum of six pounds being
the rent of the Plantation he rents from the

Baptist Church at the foot of the Ironhill, Nov 3, 1770.

Feb 2, 1778 - reference to decease of wife of Edward Miles.

July 6 1771, Mary McCutchion bapt.

May 3, 1794 Brothers Ebenezer Morton and Frederic Hire appointed to meet at Francis Goteers house to endeavor to bring about a reconciliation between Hackey McGowin and Andrew Henry.

To enquire about some things alleged against Rebecca, a black woman a member with us who lives at Mr. Fishers.

Aug 2, 1794 Mary Camble attended according to the request of the Church.

Hackey McGowen requests dismission for himself and for his wife Nancy.

Dec 6, 1794 Mary Richardson bapt.

Feb 28, 1795 Sarah Davis applied for letter of recommendation to Church of Philadelphia.

Amilia Mack-Sparan requested dismission to Church of Phila.

Hannah Cooch and Ann Mcgowin requested dismissions.

May 2, 1795 Fransiney Kinkey bapt.

Uneasiness subsists between Robert McMullen and Mary Mackmullen.

Uneasiness subsists between Noble Boldon and his wife.

John Vaughan recommended from church of Brandywine.

Dec 5, 1795 Joseph Watkins and Amelia McSparran received in Philadelphia Baptist Church - dismissed.

Sarah Davis deceased and John Cornish both members of this church - 2 dead.

March 5, 1796. John Bounds received from Broad Creek Church.

April 2, 1796. Joseph Carman requested dismission on account of his intention of traveling and settling in some part of the back country.

Dec 3, 1797. Peter, a black man, has a daughter living with David Henderson in Virginia and desires to have sent home to him. John Bounds and Rebecca Griffith desire letters of recommendation.

April 1, 1797. Complaints against Elizabeth Smith and Margaret Simpers.
Andrew Harvey lately removed from among us.
Oct 6, 1798. Dispute between Francis Gottier and John Kean.
Jan 4, 1799. Disagreement between Benjamin Stoops and his wife Sarah.
Aug 3, 1799. James Williams presented a letter of dismission from Philadelphia Church.
Jan 4, 1800. Revd. Gideon Ferral and Mary his wife have presented a letter of dismission from the Church of Bryn Zion Baptist Church.
Elizabeth Grantham, a black woman, has removed to Philadelphia and requests a letter of dismission.
Oct 4, 1800 A committee was appointed to deal with Elizabeth Smith, Benjamin Stoop, Robert McMullin and Mary Moony for neglecting meetings.

NEW CASTLE COUNTY QUAKER MARRIAGES FROM NEWARK MONTHLY MEETING

Most of the Quaker families of the Newark Monthly Meeting were residents of Pennsylvania although a significant number, of course, lived in New Castle County, Delaware. Only those marriages have been included here in which one of the parties was from New Castle County or on the Delmarva Peninsula. A complete coverage of the records of New Monthly Meeting will be included in the forthcoming publication of church records of Chester County, Pennsylvania. The first few entries below are marriages performed in Ireland, being recorded in the Newark Monthly Meeting records, presumably pertaining to families which settled in the verge of the Newark Monthly Meeting. The date in each case is the date of marriage. Information on births, deaths and other data pertaining to these families will be covered in the Chester County church series.

John Hoopes of Lurgan Parish of Shankill and County of Ardmagh and Ruth Webb of the parish of Sego and county afsd. 22-8-1687 at meeting house at Ballhagen.

William Dixson and Isabell Rea, both in parish of Sego and county of Ardmagh. 4-5-1683 at the house of Roger Webb, parish of Sego and county of Ardmagh.

Timothy Kirk, parish of Shankill and Kathern Robson parish of Sego and county of Ardmagh. 17-3-1776 at the house of Marke Wright, parish of Shankill and county of Ardmagh.

Valentine Hollingsworth, parish of Sego, county of Ardmagh and Anne Calvert of same parish. 12-4-1672 at house of Marke Wright in parish of Shankill.

Fransis Hobson of Drunilly, parish of Lougnall and county of Ardmagh and Mary Harding of Lissacurran in the parish of Sharbill and county afsd. 29-11-1694 at the meeting place at Ann Webbs.

George Harland in parish of Donnaghlony, county of Down and Elizabeth Duck of Lurgan, parish of Sharbell and county of Ardmagh. 27-9-1678 at house of Marke Wright.

Henry Hollingsworth of Pennsylvania, county of New Castle in America and Lydia Atkinson, parish of Sefoe and county of Ardmagh in Ireland. 22-6-1688 at meeting house at John Robinson's.

Thomas Conway, parish of Lisbourn and county of Antrim and Mary Hollingsworth, parish of Sefo and county of Ardmagh. 28-4-1682 at house of Francis Robson.

Stephen Lewis son of late John Lewis of county of New Castle and Rabucah Hussey, daughter of Jedediah Hussy of City of New Castle afsd. 10-9-1726 at New Castle.

Joseph Hadley son of Simon Hadley, county of New Castle and Emey Gregg, daughter of John Gregg, county afsd. 25-8-1721 at Center meeting house.

George Dixon son of William Dixon, dec'd., of Christiana Hundred, New Castle County, and Ann Chandler, daughter of Swithin Chandler in Burmingham, Chester County. 29-10-1725 at Center.

Nathan Hussey of New Castle County, New Castle Hundred and Ann Garritson, widow. 16-3-1720 at meeting house in New Castle.

John Dickson of Mill creek Hundred, New Castle County, and Sarah Hollingsth. of Christian Hundred, afsd. county. 29-8-1724 at Center meeting house.

Tho: Hollingsworth of Christiana Hundred, New Castle County, and Judith Lampley, afsd. hundred. 28-12-1723.

William Gregg, New Castle County, Christiana Hundred, and Margery Kinkey of Cecil County, Maryland. 29-7-1725 at Center.

Enoch Hollingsworth son of Saml. Hollingsworth of Burmingham, Chester County, and Joanna Crowley of New Castle County. 23-10-1725.

John Nichols son of Thomas Nichols, dec'd., and Mary Nichols, widow of Christiana Hundred, New Castle County, and Charity Chandler, daughter of Swithin and Ann Chandler of Bermingham of Chester County. 1-3-1728.

John Pasmore, Junr., of Kennett Twp., Chester County, and Elizabeth Harris of Mill Creek Hundred of New Castle County. 18-3-1727.

George Robinson of Cecil County, Maryland, son of George Robinson of Newark, New Castle County, and Mary Mackay, daughter of Robert Mackay of Cecil County afsd. 14-2-1726 at meeting house at Nottingham.

John White of Nottingham Twp., Chester County, husbandman, son of William White of New Castle County, wheelwright, dec'd., and Mary Job, daughter of Andrew Job of afsd. twp., yeoman. 31-8-1717 at Nottingham meeting house.

Robert Cain of Londongrove Twp., Chester County, and Ann Dixson of Mill Creek Hundred, New Castle County. 26-9-1730 at house of William Cox, Mill Creek Hundred.

Jacob Chandler, son of Swithin Chandler and Ann his wife of Burmingham, Chester County, yeoman, and Martha Greave, daughter of Samuel and Sarah his wife at Christiana Hundred, New Castle County, spinster. 3-7-1730 at Center meeting house.

John Day, son of John Day, Chester County, and Ann Hussey, daughter of John Hussey, New Castle County. 11-9-1730 at New Castle.

Joseph Hollingsworth of Christiana Hundred, New Castle County, and Martha Haughton of afsd. hundred and county. 23-2-1730 at Center meeting house.

Alphonsus Kirk of Christiana Hundred, New Castle County, carpenter, son of Alphonsus Kirk and Abigail his wife of afsd. county and Mary Nicols, daughter of Mary Nichols, widow. 14-3-1730 at Center meeting house.

Peter Hunter of Middletown, Chester County, tanner, and Esther Beason, New Castle County, Brandywine Hundred, widow. 15-2-1730 at Newark meeting house.

John Garritson son of Garret Garritson, New Castle County, and Margret Colinder, daughter of Nicholas Colinder, late of county afsd. 8-10-1727 at New Castle.

Thomas Dickson of Mill Creek Hundred, New Castle County, and Hannah Hadly, daughter of Simon Hadly of Mill Creek Hundred. 25-8-1727 at New Garden meeting house.

Thomas Gregg, son of John Gregg of Christiana Hundred, New Castle County, and Dinah Harlan, daughter of Michael Harlan Twp. of London Grove, Chester Co. 10-2-1729 at New Garden mtg. house.

Jacob Hollingsworth of Christiana Hundred, New Castle County, yeoman, and Rachel Chandler of Burmingham, Chester County, spinster. 23-2-1729 at Center meeting house.

John Greave of Christiana Hundred, New Castle County, and Jane Chandler of twp. of Burmingham, Chester County. 2-8-1733 at Center meeting house.

John Hurford of Aston, Chester County, yeoman, and Esther Hunter, New Castle County, widow. 5-10-1733 meeting house at Newark.

Thomas Jacob of Chester County, and Mary Robinson of New Castle County. 13-8-1710 at house of Volentine Hollingsworth, New Castle County.

Thomas Jacob, Cecil County, Maryland, and Anne Mankin, widow of Chester County. 27-12-1733/4 at Center meeting house.

Isaac Cook of twp. of London Grove, Chester County, yeoman, and Mary Houston of Christiana Hundred, New Castle County. 22-3-1734.

Elikim Hussey of town of New Castle, and Eliz: Burroughs of town of New Castle. 31-8-1734 at New Castle.

John Richardson, Jun. of New Castle County, near Christiana Hundred, and Ann Ashton of George Creek of said county. 7-7-1704 at house of Robert Ashton.

Thomas Hays of Marlborough Twp., Chester County, and Mary Kirk of Christiana Hundred, New Castle County, widow. 11-10-1734 at Kennett meeting house.

Henery Green of Mill Creek Hundred, New Castle County, and Betty Hollingsworth, daughter of Samuel Hollingsworth of Burmingham Twp., Chester County. 1-11-1734/5 at Center meeting house.

Christopher Willson of New Castle County, and Esther Woodward of Chester County, Thornbury Twp. 22-8-1719 at Concord meeting house.

John Morgan, Caln Twp., Chester County, and Lydia Babb of Brandywine Hundred, New Castle County. 17-10-1735 at Newark meeting house.

James Green of Mill Creek Hundred, New Castle County, and Mary Harry, Kennett Twp, Chester County. 9-2-1735 at Kennett meeting house.

John Garretson, late of Hockessin of New Castle County, and Content Hussey of the same place. 5-9-1736 at Hockessin.

Christopher Hussey, late of Hockessin, New Castle County, and Ann Garretson of same place. 5-9-1737 at Hockessin meeting.

John Swett and Content Maul, both of Willing Town [Wilmington], New Castle County. 11-3-1738 at Willing Town.

James Pryor of Kennet, Chester County, yeoman, and Elizabeth Philips, New Castle County. 27-9-1734 at Center meeting house.

Richard Carson and Ann James of Willing, New Castle County. 19-8-1738 at Willing Town.

Jonathan Greave of Christiana Hundred, in New Castle County, and Sarah Chandler of same place. 14-9-1730 at Center meeting house.

Allexander Seaton of the borough of Wilmington, Christiana Hundred, New Castle County, and Rebecah Robinson of Newark in Brandywine Hundred in said county. 2-2-1740 at Newark.

Swithin Chandler, Jr. of Christiana Hundred, New Castle County, and Ann Willson of same place. 21-9-1739 at Center.

Richard Woodward of West Bradford Twp., Chester County, yeoman, and Susannah Cureton of New Castle County. 29-9-1739 at Bradford meeting house.

Samuel Gregg of Christiana Hundred, New Castle County, and Ann Robertson of same place. 22-2-1737.

Joseph Peters of the borough of Wilmington, in Christiana Hundred, New Castle County, and son of Thos. Peters of City of Philadelphia, and Rebecah Richardson, daughter of John and Ann Richardson of Christiana Hundred. 13-2-1741 at Wilmington.

Zachariah Farries of the borough of Wilmington, Christiana Hundred, New Castle County, tanner, and Elizth. Scott of same place. 13-6-1741 at Wilmington.

John Standfield, New Castle County, and Hannah Dixson, Mill Creek Hundred, county afsd., widow. 13-8-1742 at Hockessin meeting house.

Joseph Gregg of Christiana Hundred, New Castle County, and Hannah Beason of Brandywine Hundred, New Castle County. 4-10-1735.

James Robertson of the borough of Wilmington, New Castle County, and Elenor West of the same place. 22-5-1742 at Wilmington Meeting.

John Dennis of Christiana Hundred, New Castle County, and Mary Slater of same place. 14-5-1742.

Joseph Dixson of Christiana Hundred, New Castle County, and Esther Philips of same place. 22-7-1742 at center meeting house.

William Phillips of Christiana Hundred, New Castle County, yeoman, and Mary Roberts of Kennett in Chester County. 26-3-1742.

James Phillips of Mill Creek Hundred, New Castle County, and Ruth Dickson of same place. 27-3-1741 at Hockessin Meeting.

Benjamin Hance of borough of Wilmington, Christiana Hundred, New Castle County, and Sarah Woodward of same place. 11-1-1741 at Wilmington Meeting.

Thomas Chandler, Junr. of Christiana Hundred, New Castle County, yeoman, and Elizabeth Gibson of Burmingham, Chester County. 23-1-1742.

Isaac Nickols of Christiana Hundred, New Castle County, wheelwright, and Margery Cox of Mill Creek Hundred, county afsd. 26-3-1742 at Hockessin Meeting.

John Dixson of Mill creek Hundred, New Castle County, yeoman, and Rebecah Cox of same place. 26-3-1742 at Hockessin meeting house.

Daniel Nickels of Mill creek Hundred of New Castle County and Sarah Dixson of same place. 13-2-1743 at Hockessin Meeting.

Thomas Willson, Jr., and Ann Dixson Jr. of Christiana Hundred, New Castle County. 28-7-1743 at Center meeting house.

Richard Carson and Martha Rumford, both of borough of Wilmington, New Castle County. 15-7-1743 at Wilmington Meeting.

John Stapler and Hannah West, both of borough of Wilmington. 22-10-1743 at Wilmington Meeting.

John Clark of Kennett Twp., Chester County, yeoman, and Ann Young of Christiana Hundred. 13-2-1743 at Center meeting house.

John Kirk son of Jacob Kirk, late of Lancaster County, Pennsylvania, and Ann Woleston, daughter of Jereh. Woleston of New Castle County. 7-3-1744 at Wilmington Meeting.

William Ferrell of Christiana Hundred, New Castle County, and Martha Cox of Mill Creek Hundred, county afsd. 26-7-1744 at Hockessin meeting house.

John Hammer of Germantown Twp., Philadelphia County, and Jean Stanfield, borough of Wilmington, New Castle County. 11-8-1744 at Wilmington Meeting.

William Kirk of West Nottingham, Chester County, and Mary Robinson of Christiana Hundred, New Castle County. 19-10-1745 at Wilmington Meeting.

Joseph Mendenhall, son of Joseph and Ruth Mendenhall of Kennett, Chester County, and Rachel Robinson, daughter of Joseph and Elizabeth Robinson of Christiana Hundred, New Castle County. 21-3-1747 at Wilmington meeting house.

Elikim Garretson, New Castle County, and Lydia Walter, Chester County. 25-9-1747 at Hockessin meeting house.

Robert Beeby of Wilmington, New Castle County, and Jean Elwall of same place. 15-1-1743/4 at Wilmington meeting house.

Isaac Mendenhall of Kennett Twp., Chester County, yeoman, and Martha Robinson of

Christiana Hundred. 31-8-1745 at Wilmington meeting house.

Adam Kirk of Christiana Hundred, New Castle County, yeoman, and Phebe Mendenhall, Kennett Twp., Chester County. 14-9-1744 at Kennett meeting house.

Hercules Young of East Marlborough, Chester County, yeoman, and Sarah Phillips, daughter of James Phillips of Christiana Hundred, New Castle County. 17-3-1745 at Center Meeting.

William Marshall of Mill Creek Hundred, New Castle County, and Rebecah Dixson, hundred and county afsd. 28-3-1746 at Hockessin meeting house.

Thomas Wilson of Christiana Hundred, New Castle County, yeoman, and Esther Wilson of Christiana Hundred. 16-7-1744 at Center meeting house.

Oliver Canby and Elizabeth Shipley, daughter of William Shipley, both of borough of Wilmington, New Castle County. 22-9-1744 at Wilmington Meeting.

Samuel Curle, son of Richard Curle of Mill Creek Hundred, New Castle County, dec'd., and Hannah Hadley, daughter of Joseph Hadley of Mill Creek Hundred. 26-8-1748 at Hockessin Meeting.

Isaac Minshall of borough of Wilmington, New Castle County, bricklayer, son of Isaac Minshall of Providence, dec'd., and Lydia Ellis, daughter of Evan Ellis, dec'd. 6-4-1745 at Wilmington Meeting.

William Whiteside of Wilmington, New Castle County, and Susanna Hill of county afsd. 12-4-1746 at New Castle Meeting.

Joseph Webb of City of Philadelphia, house carpenter, and Edith Way, daughter of Joseph Way of borough of Wilmington, New Castle County. 29-3-1746 at Wilmington Meeting.

John Wilson of Christiana Hundred, New Castle County, and Abigail Harlan of Kennett Twp., Chester County. 29-9-1744 at Kennett meeting house.

Joseph Underwood of Christiana Hundred, New Castle County, and Hannah Shortledge of same place. 17-2-1745 at Center Meeting.

Thomas Underwood of Christiana Hundred, New Castle County, widower, and Sarah Keeler of hundred and county afsd., widow. 24-10-1746 at Center Meeting.

Francis Way of West Bradford, Chester County, yeoman, and Mary Dawes of Wilmington, New Castle County. 17-8-1745 at Wilmington meeting house.

Joseph Nichols, Christiana Hundred, New Castle County, yeoman, and Sarah Ellis of borough of Wilmington. 23-11-1745/6 at Wilmington Meeting.

Thomas Chandler of Christiana Hundred, New Castle County, widower, and Ann Hicklin of Brandywine Hundred. 23-10-1747 at Center Meeting.

John Dawes of Christiana Hundred, New Castle County, and Elizabeth Sell, county afsd. in borough of Wilmington. 21-4-1744 at Wilmington Meeting.

Wilmington Farson of Duck Creek in Kent County and Jane Beeby of Wilmington, New Castle County. 2-2-1749 at Wilmington meeting house.

Isaac Dixson, son of John Dixson, dec'd., of Mill Creek Hundred, and Ann Nichols, daughter of Thomas Nichols of Christiana Hundred, New Castle County. 13-2-1748 at Hockessin.

Benjamin Barrat, son of Benjamin Barrat of Kent County, and Elizabeth Hogg, daughter of George Hogg, late of town and county of New Castle, dec'd. 8-6-1749 at meeting at town of New Castle.

David Ogden, Christiana Hundred, New Castle County, carpenter, and Zabiah Wolliston, daughter of William Wolliston of county afsd. 16-12-1748/9 at Wilmington Meeting.

Samuel Milner, son of James Milner, late of Christiana Hundred, New Castle County, and Elizabeth Robinson, daughter of Elizabeth Babb of Brandywine Hundred, county afsd. 14-4-1749 at meeting house in Brandywine Hundred.

Samuel Levis of Kennett, Chester County, and Elizabeth Gregg of Mill Creek Hundred, New Castle County. 6-7-1749 at Kennett Meeting.

Joseph West of borough of Wilmington, New Castle County, and Hannah Andrew of afsd. borough. 19-8-1749, at Wilmington Meeting.

Thomas Chandler, Jun. of Burmingham Twp., Chester County, yeoman, and Hannah Wilson of Christiana Hundred, New Castle County. 15-9-1749 at Center Meeting.

Joseph Buckingham, son of John Buckingham, Senr., of Mill Creek Hundred, New Castle County, and Deborah Dixson, daughter of Thomas Dixson of the same place. 15-9-1749 at Hockessin.

Joseph Hill, Junr., town and county of New Castle, cordwainer, and Judith Wood, daughter of Nathan Wood of Wilmington. 23-9-1749 at Wilmington Meeting.

William Wood, son of Thomas Wood, late of Chester County, dec'd. and Mary his wife, and Margarett Holland, daughter of Thomas and Margarett Holland of Prince George's County, Maryland, dec'd. 6-10-1749 at London Grove meeting house.

Joshua Byrne of borough of Wilmington, New Castle County, son of Daniel and Rebeccah Byrne, Philadelphia County, and Ruth Woodcock, daughter of Robert and Rachaell Woodcock, of borough of Wilmington. 15-1-1749/50 at Wilmington Meeting.

Benjamin Chandlee of Nottingham, Chester County, and Mary Folwell, borough of Wilmington, New Castle County. 19-2-1750 at Wilmington Meeting.

Adam Redd of Christiana Hundred, New Castle County, and Miriam Chandler of county and hundred afsd. 23-3-1759.

Nicholas Robinson, son of Francis Robinson and Elizabeth of borough of Wilmington, New Castle County, and Mary Hicklin, daughter of William and Dinah Hicklin of Brandywine Hundred, county afsd. 22-3-1750 at Center Meeting.

Daniel Gest of Christiana Hundred, New Castle County, cordwainer, and Hannah Mendenhall of Kennett Twp., Chester County. 23-3-1750 at Kennett meeting house.

Herman Gregg of Christiana Hundred, New Castle County, and Mary Dixon, daughter of Henry Dixon, of Mill Creek Hundred, dec'd. 17-8-1750. Hockessin.

Jozabad Lodge of Darby Twp., Chester County, and Katharine Strange, Christiana Hundred, New Castle County. 16-11-1750/1 at Center meeting house.

Joshua Johnson of London Grove, Chester County, and Elizabeth England, relict of John England of White Clay Creek, New Castle County. 10-2-1751 at Hockessin.

Daniel Byrnes, borough of Wilmington, New Castle County, son of Daniel and Rebecca Byrnes of Whitpane, Philadelphia County, and Dinah Hicklin, daughter of William and Dinah Hicklin, of Brandywine Hundred, New Castle County. 27-9-1751 at Center.

William Tate, son of George Tate of Christiana Hundred, New Castle County, and Martha Dixon, daughter of Henry Dixon of Mill Creek Hundred, New Castle County. 17-1-1753 (new style) at Hockessin.

Thomas Harlan, son of Thomas Harlan, and Mary his wife, late of Kennett Twp., Chester County, dec'd., and Mary Baldwin, daughter of John Baldwin, late of Christiana Hundred, New Castle County, dec'd., and Elizabeth his wife. 19-9-1753 at Kennett.

Charles Goss of East Marlborough, Chester County, son of Charles Goss of Nottingham, dec'd., county afsd. and Grace Dixon, daughter of John Dixon, dec'd and Sarah his wife of Mill creek Hundred, New Castle County. 21-11-1753.

Thomas Hollingsworth of Christiana Hundred, New Castle County, yeoman, and Jane Smith of hundred and county afsd. 20-11-1754 at Center.

William Pugh of East Nottingham, Chester County, and Sarah Chandler, daughter of Jacob Chandler, dec'd., of Christian Hundred, New Castle County. 13-3-1755 at East Nottingham.

Caleb Seal, Christiana Hundred, New Castle County, son of William Seal, and Lydia Temple, daughter of William Temple of Kennett Twp., Chester County. 13-4-1755 at Kennett meeting house.

Caleb Peirce, twp. of East marlborough, Chester County, and Hannah Greave of Christiana Hundred, New Castle County. 22-10-1755 at Kennett meeting house.

Samuel Hanson, son of Timothy Hanson, late of Little Creek, Kent County, Delaware, dec'd., and Sarah Levis, daughter of William Levis, late of Kennett, Chester County, dec'd. 19-11-1755 at Kennett meeting house.

William Gregg of Mill Creek Hundred, New Castle County, son of William Gregg, dec'd., and Ann Dixon of same hundred and county, daughter of John Dixon, dec'd. 19-11-1755 at Hockessin meeting house.

Jeremiah Wollaston, New Castle County, yeoman, and Catharine Robinson of New Castle County. 21-9-1756 at Newark meeting house.

David Pusey, son of Caleb Pusey, dec'd., of East Marlborough, Chester County, and Sarah Dixon, daughter of John Dixon, dec'd., of Mill Creek Hundred, New Castle County. 7-7-1756.

Thomas Hanson of Little Creek Hundred, Kent County, son of Timothy Hanson, late of same place, dec'd., and Mary Levis of Kennett, Chester County, daughter of William Levis, late of county afsd., dec'd. 22-9-1756 at Kennett meeting house.

John Wilson, son of Thomas Wilson of White Clay Creek Hundred, New Castle County, and Sarah Prew, daughter of Caleb Prew, late of Kennett Twp., Chester County. 27-10-1756 at Center meeting house.

William Underwood, son of Joseph Underwood, New Castle County, and Elizabeth Dixon, daughter of William Dixon, New Castle County. 27-4-1757 at Center meeting house.

Adam Redd of Christiana Hundred, New Castle County, and Ann Mendenhall, Kennett Twp., Chester County. 19-4-1758 at Kennett meeting house.

William Allen, son of John Allen of London Grove Twp., Chester County, and Sarah Grave, daughter of John Greave of Christian Hundred, New Castle County. 24-5-1758 at Center.

Samuel Clark, son of William Clark of West Bradford Twp., of Chester County, yeoman, and Abigail Shortledge of Christiana Hundred, New Castle County, daughter of James Shortledge, late of West Bradford, Chester County. 30-11-1758 at West Bradford meeting house.

Solomon Dixon, son of Henry and Ruth Dixon, dec'd., of Mill Creek Hundred, New Castle County, and Sarah Pryor, daughter of James and Elizabeth Pryor, daughter of James and Elizabeth Pryor of New Garden Twp., Chester County. 30 Nov 1758 at New Garden meeting house.

Christopher Wilson of Christiana Hundred, New Castle County, yeoman, and Dinah Gregg, Chester County, Kennett Twp. 20-12-1758 at Center meeting house.

Jacob Wilson of White Clay Creek Hundred, New Castle County, son of Thomas Wilson and Mary Wilson, dec'd., of county afsd. and Betty Gregg, daughter of Samuel and Ann Gregg of Christiana Hundred, New Castle County. 29-10-1760 at Center meeting house.

James Wilson of Christiana Hundred, New Castle County, and Emy Gregg, Chester County, Kennett Twp. 30-12-1761 at Center meeting house.

Samuel Grubb of Brandywine Hundred, New Castle County, yeoman, and Lydia Baker of Christiana Hundred, New Castle County. 15-1-1762 at Center meeting house.

George Harlan, son of George Harlan, late of Kennett, dec'd., Chester County, and Margery Baker, daughter of Joshua Baker of Christiana Hundred, New Castle County. 21-4-1762 at Center.

Gideon Gilpin, son of Joseph and Mary Gilpin of Christiana Hundred, New Castle County, and Sarah Gregg, daughter of Samuel and Ann Gregg of same place. 1-12-1762 at Center meeting house.

William Walter, son of William Walter of Concord, Chester County, and Betty Hicklin, daughter of William Hicklin of Brandywine Hundred, New Castle County. 2-12-1762 at Center meeting house.

William Tate of Mill Creek Hundred, New Castle County, and Ann Dixson of same place. 28-12-1763 at Hockessin meeting house.

Mordecai Hayes of East Marlborough, Chester County, and Ann Greave, daughter of John Greave and Jane his wife, New Castle County. 18-4-1764 at Center meeting house.

George Taylor of West Marlborough, Chester County, and Hannah Phillips of Christiana Hundred, New Castle County. 23-5-1764 at Center meeting house.

John Pyle, son of John Pyle of Kennett of Chester County, and Judith Hollingsworth, daughter of Thomas Hollingsworth of Christiana Hundred, New Castle County. 9-4-1765 at center meeting house.

Christopher Hollingsworth, son of Thomas Hollingsworth, dec'd., of Christiana Hundred, New Castle County, and Elizabeth Chandler, daughter of Thomas Chandler, hundred and county afsd. 24-4-1769 at Center meeting house.

Amor Hollingsworth, son of Thomas Hollingsworth, dec'd., Christian Hundred, New Castle County, and Mary Chandler, daughter of Jacob Chandler, dec'd., hundred and county afsd. 26-2-1766 at Center meeting house.

Benjamin Reynolds, son of Thomas Reynolds, and Elizabeth his wife, both dec'd., of Upper Chichester, Chester County, and Sarah Baker, daughter of Joshua Baker, dec'd., and Margery his wife of Christiana Hundred, New Castle County. 23-4-1766 at Center.

Joseph Pennock of Christiana Hundred, New Castle County, and Jane Wilson of New Garden, Chester County. 25-3-1767 at Hockessin meeting house.

Robert Phillips of Mill Creek Hundred, New Castle County, and Katharine Dixon of New Garden, Chester County. 22-4-1767 at Hockessin meeting house.

Joshua Baker, widower, of Christiana Hundred, New Castle County, and Allice Pennock, widow, East Marlborough Twp., Chester County. 30-3-1768 at Center meeting house.

John Shortledge of Christiana Hundred, son of James Shortledge, dec'd., and Phebe Chandler, daughter of Swithin Chandler, hundred and county afsd. 1-3-1769 at Center meeting house.

Blakeston Janney of Loudoun County, Virginia, and Mary Nichols of Christiana Hundred, New Castle County. 22-3-1769 at Center meeting house.

Abraham Gregg, son of William Gregg of Christiana Hundred, New Castle County, dec'd., and Mary Heald, daughter of Jacob Heald, hundred and county, afsd. 29-3-1769 at Hockessin meeting house.

William Cherry of Christiana Hundred, New Castle County, and Charity Nichols of same place. 26-4-1769 at Hockessin Meeting.

Joshua Green of Mill Creek Hundred, New Castle County, and Susanna Jordan of same place. 24-5-1769 at Hockessin meeting house.

John Grubb, son of William Grubb, of Brandywine Hundred, New Castle County, and Hannah Gilpin, daughter of Joseph Gilpin of Christian Hundred, New Castle County. 23-11-1769 at Center.

Christopher Chandler, son of Swithin and Ann Chandler of Christiana Hundred, New Castle County, yeoman, and Prudence Grubb, daughter of Samuel Grubb, late of Chester County, dec'd. 27-12-1769.

William Hicklen of Brandywine Hundred, New Castle County, and Jane Greave of Christiana Hundred, New Castle County. 1-11-1769 at Center meeting house.

Robert Phillips of Mill Creek Hundred, New Castle County, and Ann Gregg, hundred and county afsd. 28-3-1770 at Hockessin meeting house.

James Wilson of Mill Creek Hundred, New Castle County, and Elizabeth Clark of same place. 13-11-1772 at Hockessin meeting house.

William Wilson, son of Thomas Wilson and Ann his wife, and Hannah Backhouse, daughter of John Backhouse and Mary his wife, both of Christiana Hundred, New Castle County. 30-12-1772 at Center.

Caleb Sharpless, Chester County, and Ruhene Jordan of Hockessin, New Castle County. 20-10-1773 at Hockessin meeting house.

Samuel Gregg, son of Samuel Gregg, dec'd., and Dinah Chandler, both of Christiana Hundred, New Castle County. 24-11-1773 at Center meeting house.

Adam Kirk, son of Adam Kirk of Christiana Hundred, New Castle County, and Esther Wilson, daughter of Joseph Wilson, county afsd. 30-3-1774 at Center meeting house.

David Greave, son of Jonathan Greave of Christiana Hundred, New Castle County, and Rachel Battin, daughter of Richard Battin of the same place. 18-15-1774 at Center meeting house.

John Gibson, son of Thomas Gibson of Pennsbury Twp., Chester County, and Mary Gregg, daughter of Samuel Gregg of Christiana Hundred, New Castle County. 26-10-1774 at Center.

Adam Williamson of Brandywine Hundred, New Castle County, son of John Williamson of Newtown in Chester County, and Mary Gilpin, daughter of Joseph Gilpin of Christiana Hundred, New Castle County. 19-10-1774 at Center.

Joseph Taylor, son of Jesse Taylor, of New Linton Twp., Chester County, and Jane Walter, daughter of James Walter of Wilmington, New Castle County. 19-10-1775.

Christopher Hollingsworth of Christiana Hundred, New Castle County, widower, and Sarah Webb of Kennett, Chester County, widow of William Webb. 28-12-1775 at Kennett meeting house.

James Wilson and Amy Dixson, both of Mill Creek Hundred, New Castle County. 23-4-1777 at Hockessin meeting house.

WILMINGTON MONTHLY MEETING

BIRTHS AND DEATHS

Benjamin Ferris son of David and Mary Ferris in Wilmington was born 8/5/1740; Sarah Ferriss b. 18/11/1741; Samuel Ferriss b. 5/9/1743; Mary Ferriss b. 17/2(12?)/1745; Deborah Ferriss b. 30/8/1746; Samuel Ferriss deceased 22/4/1748; Benjamin Ferriss d. 17/3/1771; Deborah Ferriss d. 1/3/1773; David Ferris d. 5/12/1779, in his 73rd year and 25th year of his ministry; Mary, wife of above David Ferriss d. "in the 7th year of her age" 10/12/1785.

Hannah Ferriss, daughter of Zechariah and, Elizabeth Ferriss b. 28/9/1743; John Ferriss b. 10/8/1746; Phebe Ferriss b. 30/8/1748; Elizabeth Ferriss b. 2/10/1750; Lydia Ferriss b. 6/8/1752. Phebe Ferriss daughter of Zechh. and Eliza. Ferriss d. 29/2/1753; Lydia Ferriss d. 8/5/1753; Elizabeth Ferriss mother of the aforesaid children, d. aged 75 years, 14/10/1784; Zachariah Ferriss their father, d. aged 85 years, 1 month, 24 days, 6/1/1803.

Deborah and Rachel Ferriss daughters of John and Abigail Ferriss b. 7/12/1738; Nathan Ferriss b. 7/6/1740; Rosannah Ferriss b. 7/11/1741; Ziba Ferriss b. 13/6/1743; Mathew Ferriss b. 14/1/1745; Elisabeth Ferriss their 7th child b. 7/12/1746.

Rebecca Minshall daughter of Griffith and Sarah Minshall of Wilmington b. at Wilmington, 4/2/1741 os; Robert Minshall b. at Wilmington 4/10/1742; Sarah Minshall b. at Wilmington 23/8/1744; Griffith Minshall b. at Wilmington 13/3/1754 ns; Sarah Minshall wife of Griffith Minshall and mother of the abovesaid children d. 11/6/1766; Rebecca Minshall afsd. d. 9/4/1796; Mercy Minshall, second wife of Griffith Minshall d. 24/12/1797; Griffith Minshall, the elder, d. 11/5/1801; Robert Minshall d. ca. 1818.

Moses Forman son of Alexr. Forman and Esther his wife b. 26/8/1742; Aaron Forman 2nd son b.

10/8/1744; Miriam Forman b. 18/11/1746; Mary Forman b. 21/5/1750; Elisabeth Forman b. 17/8/1753; Rachel Forman b. 4/10/1756; Leah Forman b. 25/5/1759; John Forman b. 26/9/1762; Susanna Forman b. 25/11/1765. Aron Forman son of Alexdr. and Esther his d. 16/5/1774.

John Perry b. at Sandwich in New England, 30/4/1713; Margret his wife b. at Marlborough in Chester Co., PA, 16/8/1720; Mary Perry their daughter b. at Marlborough, 2/7/1739; Eliphal Perry their son, b. at Marlboro, 15/1/1742; Nathan Perry their son b. at Wilmington, 19/7/1747; Rest Perry their daughter b. at Wilmington, 28/6/1751; John Perry b. at Wilmington, 11/1/1754; Ruth Perry b. at Wilmington, 15/8/1756; Sarah Perry b. at Wilmington, 26/11/1759. John Perry Father of the above children d. after being in the station of an elder, 30/8/1787. Mary Perry their daughter d. at Marlborough, 11/7/1741; Eliphal their son d. at Wilmington, 2/2/1748; Nathan their son d. at Wilmington, 19/6/1750; Ruth Perry their daughter d. 17/10/1763; Margarett Perry mother of the above children d. 12/12/1772. John Perry their son d. 2/9/1777.

Hannah Canby daughter of Oliver Canby and Elisabeth his wife b. 22/10/1746; William Canby b. 25/7/1748; Samuel Canby b. 26/5/1751; Mary Canby b. 10/8/1754. Hannah Canby daughter of Oliver and Elisabeth canby d. 26/1/1747. Oliver Canby father of the above children d. 30/11/1754.

Joseph Hewes son of William Hewes b. 1/3/1710. Ann Hewes his wife and dau of Joseph Worth b. 21/5/1708.
They m. 12/7/;1733. Their children: James Hewes b. 4/9/1734; Elizabeth b. 8/10/1736; Joseph Hewes b. 3/2/1739; Edward Hewes b. 9/7/1741; Sarah Hewes b. 3/11/1743/4; Moses Hewes b. 12/11/1745/6; Deborah Hewes b. 2/7/1748; Joseph Hewes d. 6 days old. Moses Hewes afsd. deceased in Little Brittain. Sarah afsd. went from Little brittain with her husband Eleazar Brown to Redstone Settlement and there deceased. ["All old stile."]

Jane Carsan dau of Richard and Ann his first wife b. 9/4/1739. Dinah Carsan dau of Richard and Martha Carsan his second wife b. 21/4/1744; Phebe Carsan their dau b. 22/1/1746; Hannah their dau b. 30/4/1748; Richard Carsan their son b. 3/7/1750; Miriam Carsan their dau b. 14/5/1753. Richard Carsan father of the above children d. 26/7/1782. Richard Carsan their above said son d. Martha Carsan mother of the above children d. 21/3/1790. Hannah Carsan afsd. d. 17/10/1801.

Thomas Clark b. 30/9/1707. Merebiah Clark b. 20/10/1710. Children of Thos. and Meribiah Clark: Sarah Clark b. 14/12/1732; Samuel Clark b. 16/8/1735; Elizabeth b. 4/9/1739; Lydia b. 17/2/1745; Thomas b. 23/12/1747; Mary b. 17/10/1750; William b. 16/10/1757. "New Stile."

Joshua Way son of Joshua Way and Elizabeth his wife b. 8/7/1750 half an hour past two o'clock in the morning.

Joshua and Deborah Littler's children: John b. 26/12/1739; Sarah b. 18/2/1742; Hannah b. 8/8/1744; Deborah b. 23/12/1746; Mary b. 22/8/1749; Joshua b. 3/2/1752; Rachel b. 5/10/1754; Deborah b. 30/12/1756. Deborah d. beginning of the 9th month 1747; Joshua d. 6/4/1757; Rachel d. 11/6/1757; Deborah d. 7/8/1757; Deborah Littler mother of the above d. 24/3/1773; Joshua Littler father of the above d. 26/11/1774.

Children of James and Elinor Robinson: Mary b. 8/8/1743; Francis b. 13/1/1746; Rachel b. 7/5/1754; James b. 27/1/1757; Thomas b. 16/12/1759. Elinor wife of James Robinson and mother of the above children d. aged 69 years and 8 days, 29/4/1790. James Robinson father of the afsd. children d. aged 71 years, 6 months and 3 days, 6/5/1790.

William Troth son of Henry Troth and Sarah his wife b. 2/1/1754; Samuel b. 3/9/1755; Henry b. 20/2/1758; Elisabeth b. 31/1/1761; John b. 30/8/1763.

Children of James and Margaret Lea: Sarah b. 25/2/1742; Frances b. 2/11/1743; Elizabeth b. 5/11/1744; Isaac b. 13/7/1746; Margaret b. 23/12/1748; Sarah b. 31/1/1753; Abraham Marshall b. 6/2/1755; Frances b. 21/2/1757; James b. 28/3/1759; John Lea their 10th child b. 11/3/1762. James Lea the father of the aforesaid children d. 2/10/1798. Margaret Lea the mother d. 31/1/1805, aged 81 years. Sarah d. 19/8/1751; Frances d. 17/8/1751; Isaac d. 12/1/1746/7; Abraham Marshall d. 29/3/1759; John d. [no date]; Sarah d. 29/8/1802.

Children of Nicholas and Mary Robinson: Rebekah b. 14/9/1752; Francis b. 24/6/1757; Elisabeth b. 28/3/1760; William b. 20/1/1764; Mary b. 30/8/1766; Francis son of Nicholas and Mary d. 3/7/1785; Mary mother of afsd. children d. 12/5/1792; Elisabeth Robinson d. 6/2/1807.

Paschall Sellers son of Joseph and Hannah Sellers b. 12/7/1753; Hannah Sellers b. 2/7/1758.

Children of Garret and Mary Blackford: William b. 30/9/1752; Samuel b. 16/9/1756; Garret b. 19/6/1758; John b. 9/1/1760; Thomas b. 28/9/1761; Elisabeth b. 10/9/1763; Joseph and Benjamin b. 10/8/1766.

Children of Nicholas and Sarah Wilson: Jane b. 20/2/1753; Thomas b. 11/9/1754; Robert b. 17/11/1756. Sarah Wilson d. 24/6/1802.

Elisabeth Richardson dau of Robert and Sarah Richardson b. 10/11/1751; John Richardson son of the above b. 31/10/1753; Mary Richardson b. 9/3/1758; Ann Richardson b. 3/8/1760; Robert Richardson parent of the above d. 18/6/1761; Sarah Richardson afsd. d. 29/6/1793; Mary Richardson afsd. d. 7/9/1795.

Thomas Wollaston b. 8/3/1728; Hannah Wollaston his wife b. 9/2/1738. Their children: Joshua b. 9/3/1759; Sarah b. 3/10/1761; James b. 10/10/1763; Jeremiah b. 29/6/1765; Catherine b. 15/10/1770; Ann b. 27/2/1777; Thomas afsd. d. 2/9/1796(?); Hannah aforesd. d. 12/9/1796.

Elizabeth Warner dau of William and Mary Warner b. 25/5/1732; Ann Warner b. 9/12/1733/4; Mary Warner b. 26/11/1735, d. 18/11/1736; Mary Warner b. 1/10/1737, d. 28/6/1746; William Warner b. 28/6/1739; John Warner b. 14/6/1741; Joseph Warner b. 29/9/1742; Benjamin Warner b. 15/7/1744; James Warner b. 31/1/1746; David and Jonathan b. and d. same day, 9/10/1748; Mary Warner wife of William Warner and mother of the above children d. 15/10/1748. Samuel Warner son of William and Sarah Warner b. 25/6/1755; Daniel Warner b. 1/12/1757.

Philip Bonsall son of Vincent Bonsall and Grace his wife b. 28/10/1747. Hannah Bonsall dau of Vincent and Sarah Bonsall b. 13/6/1758; Sarah Bonsall d. aged 70 years, 3 months, 3 days, 25/7/1788; Vincent Bonsall d. 10/1/1796.

Philip Jones son of William and Rebekah Jones b. 17/11/1740/1. William Jones b. 22/8/1744; Joseph Jones their 3rd son b. 11/5/1748; Rebekah Jones d. 25/4/1777; William Jones parent of the above d. 11/2/1767, aged 54 years wanting 2 days.

Sarah Stapler dau of John Stapler and Rachel his wife b. 23/5/1746, m. John Littler. Rachel Stapler d. 11/7/1783. John Stapler d. 30/8/1793. Jemima his second wife d. 31/7/1796.

Jacob Wolliston son of Joseph and Deborah Wolliston (deceased) b. 10/7/1743; William Wolliston b. 10/5/1745; Elisabeth Wolliston b. 23/11/1747; Catherine Wolliston b. 3/11/1753; Joseph Wolliston b. 18/10/1755.

William Woodcock son of Robert and Rachel Woodcock b. 3/11/1719; Anthony Woodcock b. 4/1/1724; Ruth Woodcock b. 21/10/1727; Robert Woodcock b. 28/4/1729; Bancroft Woodcock b. 18/7/1732.

Ezekiel Andrews son of William and Miriam Andrews b. 21/11/1729; Hannah Andrews b. 14/5/1732; Ruth Andrews b. 23/7/1734; John Andrews b. 2/6/1736.

William Milner son of Samuel and Mary Milner b. 23/4/1742; John Milner b. 4/9/1744; Sarah Milner dau of sd. Samuel Milner and Elisabeth his wife b. 29/2/1750; Elisabeth Milner b. 29/3/1752; Samuel Milner b. 20/3/1754.

Charles Robinson son of Volentine and Elisabeth Robinson b. 31/8/1741. Thomas Robinson b. 7/9/1743.

Nathan Wood d. in his 77th year, 28/10/1767. Hannah Wood his wife d. 6/9/1768.

Rebekah Poole dau of William and Martha Poole b. 3/8/1755; Rebekah d. 30/4/1772. Joseph Poole b. 3/7/1757. Hannah Poole b. 14/1/1759, d. 21/12/1759. Martha Poole d. 26/2/1760.

Pathenah Beeson dau of Thomas Beeson b. 12/2/1757; Lydia Beeson b. 14/11/1758, d. 25/11/1758; David Beeson b. 16/12/1759; Jonathan Beeson b. 18/7/1762; Aloe b. 3/2/1765; Thomas Beeson b. 10/7/1767; John Beeson b. 22/3/1770, d. 9/3/1775. Thomas Beeson father of the above d. 22/3/1790.

William Byrnes son of Daniel Byrnes and Dinah his wife b. 22/7/1759; Joshua Byrnes b. 3/7/1762; Lydia Byrnes 19/7/1767; Joseph Byrnes b. 16/12/1769; Caleb Byrnes b. 21/9/1771.

Rebekah Woodcock dau of William and Elisabeth Woodcock b. 6/10/1751; William Woodcock b. 1/10/1753; Elisabeth Woodcock died the ...[sic]; William Woodcock and Elisabeth his second wife had issue: Samuel b. 11/8/1764; Elisabeth b. 6/12/1761.

Benjamin Yarnall and Elisabeth his wife m. 30/4/1761. Their issue: Stephen b. 22/4/1762; Jonathan b. 4/11/1763 (1769?); Benjamin b. 1/10/1773, d. 18/9//1798.

Rachel Woodcock dau of Bancroft Woodcock and Ruth his wife b. 13/10/1760; Isaac Woodcock b. 6/8/1764. Ruth Woodcock wife of Bancroft Woodcock and mother of the aforementioned children d. aged 63 years, 3 months and ---

days, 30/12/1797 at Phila. Rachel James, formerly Woodcock, d. in Phila 28/10/1798.

Richard Reynolds son of Henry and Rebekah Reynolds b. 23/9/1758; Ann Reynolds b. 12/7/1760, d. 27/12/1763. Rebekah wife of Henry Reynolds d. 25nd and buried 27th of 10th month 1769. Joseph Reynolds son of Henry and Elisabeth Reynolds b. 21/5/1769. Elizabeth Reynolds aforesd. wife of Henry Reynolds d. 25/7/1788. Sarah Reynolds dau of Henry and Elisabeth Reynolds b. 6/12/1770; Benjamin b. 23/4/1772; Betty Reynolds b. 16/1/1775. Henry Reynolds aforesd. d. 25/7/1792.

Joseph Hobson son of John and Elisabeth Hobson b. 9/9/1758. Joseph Hobson d. 19/7/1764. Francis Hobson b. 18/6/1760, d. 19/4/1763. John Hobson b. 31/10/1763. Samuel Hobson b. 25/7/1770; Samuel d. 12/9/1778.

Mary Folwell dau of Gouldsmith and Sarah Folwell b. 3/7/1760, d. 21/6/1775; Edward Folwell b. 21/3/1762; Elisabeth Folwell b. 4/10/1763, d. 6/12/1797; Sarah Folwell b. 14/9/1766, d. 5/11/1774; Joseph Folwell b. 2/8/1768, d. --- [blank].

Mary Carter dau of Jeremiah Carter and Rachel his wife b. 25/7/1758; Lydia Carter b. 27/11/1760, d. 16/10/1763; Thomas Carter b. 9/4/1762, d. 28/11/1763; Rachel Carter above said d. 27/9/1763. Tacy Carter dau of Jeremiah Carter and Rebecca his wife b. 15/4/1766, d. 20/8/1769.

Joseph Newlin b. 29/9/1718 and Phebe his wife b. 26/2/1722. Joseph Newlin d. 28/11/1768(?). Phebe his wife d. 27/1/1775. Their issue: Elisabeth Newlin b. 7/3/1742; Edith Newlin b. 10/12/1745; Ellis Newlin b. 26/9/1749; Nathaniel Newlin b. 20/8/1760.

Joseph Tatnall b. ---? and Elisabeth his wife b. 5/11/1744; they m. 31/1/1765; their issue: Sarah b. 27/11/1765.

Ezekiel Andrews and Rebekah his wife m.
28/5/1761. Ezekiel d. 4/3/1772. Rebekah, late
wife of Thomas Shipley, d. 7/2/1797. Issue of
Ezekiah and Rebekah Andrews: Mary b. 3/3/1764,
James b. 17/7/1765(?), John Andrews b.
14/6/1769.

John Andrews (b. 2/6/1736) and Sarah his wife,
dau of David Ferris, b. 18/11/1741. They m.
25/8/1763. John Andrews d. 21/11/1778; Sarah
Andrews d. 22/12/1793. Their issue: Samuel b.
15/7/1764; Isaac b. 5/7/1767; David b.
25/9/1769, d. 23/8/1770; Hannah b. 2/6/1771, d.
19/5/1772; Deborah Andrews b. 5/10/1773;
Benjamin Andrews b. 20/12/1774; Mary Andrews b.
23/12/1777.

Benjamin Ferris son of David and Mary Ferris b.
in Wilmington 8/5/1740. Hannah his wife, dau of
James and Miriam Brown, b. at Nottingham
22/7/1737; had one son named David b. 20/7/1766;
he d. 22/8/1767. Hannah Ferris wife of Benjamin
Ferris d. 13/11/1767 just as the clock struck
four in the afternoon; buried on the 15th in
Friends burial ground in Wilmington. Benjamin
Ferriss d. 17/3/1771.

John White son of William White and Ann his wife
b. 12/2/1762; Esther their dau b. 11/8/1764;
Jane White 3rd child b. 9/1/1767; Joseph White
4th child b. 14/4/1769, d. 29/10/1798; Elisabeth
White b. 26/9/1771. William White d.
16/10/1791.

Amos Jones son of Philip Jones and Edith his
wife b. 1/6/1768; William Jones their son b.
10/2/1772; Joseph Jones their son b. 28/2/1774;
Edith Jones their dau b. 10/9/1776. Philip
Jones the father d. 17/5/1783. Edith Jones the
mother d. 25/5/1794. Joseph Jones d. 2/7/1775.

Isaac Kightley son of James Kightly and
Elisabeth his wife b. 9/8/1770. Deborah
Keightly b. 8/11/1772.

Mary Parvin dau of Benjamin and Sarah Parvin b.
18/3/1771.

Children of Benjamin Jacobs and Prudence his
wife: Joseph b. 1/3/1757; Mary b. 16/9/1758, d.
28/9/1764; Rachel b. 15/1/1761; Benjamin b.
24/4/1763; Mary b. 10/7/1765, d. 11/12/1768;
John b. 6/4/1768, d. 18/8/1769; Hannah b.
24/6/1770; Sarah b. 11/2/1773; Bettee b.
27/7/1777.

Children of William Ashburnham and Rosanna his
wife: Hannah b. 11/2/1769, d. 26/1/1805; John b.
16/9/1770, d. 2/8/1774. William Ashburnham
father of the above d. 18/1/1777. Hannah
Ashbournham 28/1/1805 [sic].

Children of William Marshall and Mary his wife:
James b. 29/4/1761; Edward b. 3/9/1765; Joseph
b. 7/12/1767; William b. 18/4/1770; Samuel b.
7/10/1772; Mary b. 4/5/1775.

Children of John and Hannah Way: Thomas b.
21/10/1758; Phebe b. 29/7/1760; Martha b.
28/5/1762; Ann b. 7/4/1764; Hannah b. 29/7/1766;
Mary b. 10/11/1770; Lydia b. 18/3/1773.

Children of Caleb and Lydia Seal: William b.
18/6/1756, d. 16/12/1774; Joshua b. 5/9/1759;
Sarah b. 2/3/1763; Hannah b. 21/1/1769; Lydia b.
3/6/1771, d. 28/10/1792; Rachel b. 6/4/1774, d.
16/12/1774; William b. 29/10/1776. Lydia the
mother d. 9/4/1780. Caleb and Alice Seal had
issue: Caleb b. 13/10/1792.

Children of Henry and Ann Paschal: Frances b.
24/2/1771; Margarett b. 13/9/1772; Mary b.
3/12/1775; Ann b. 7/12/1777; Elizabeth b.
11/1/1780; Hannah b. 25/3/1782; John b.
7/4/1783; Thomas b. 27/5/1785; Sarah b.
14/7/1787; Martha b. 27/10/1789.

Children of Ziba Ferris and Edith his wife: Mary
b. 16/3/1771, d. 9/9/1773; Deborah Ferriss b.
2/3/1773; John Ferris b. 10/12/1775, d.
1/11/1802; Edith Ferris b. 18/4/1778; Benjamin
Ferris b. 7/8/1780; Zeba Ferriss b. 25/1/1786.
Ziba Ferriss the father of the aforesd. children
d. aged 50 years, 10 months, 11 days, 24/4/1794.
Edith Ferriss the mother of the aforesaid
children d. 2/9/1815 in her 73d year.

William Poole son of William and Elisabeth Poole the second wife b. 4/8/1764. William Poole the father d. 6/4/1779. Elizabeth Poole the mother d. 16/11/1789.

Thomas Shipley b. 24/4/1718, d. 1/11/1789. Mary his wife b. 1/9/1719, d. 21/2/1771. They m. 15/9/1743. William their son b. 9/3/1746, d. 2/13/1816, aged about 70 years; Samuel b. 30/6/1747, d. 4/7/1747; Martha b. 2/8/1748, d. 6/12/1748; Mary b. 2/7/1750, d. ca. 1797; Thomas b. 9/7/1751, d. 30?/6/1752; Joseph b. 11/11/1752, d. 20/7/1832; Sarah b. 6/9/1755; Ann b. 29/1/1758; Anna b. 22/9/1760.

Martha Howard d. 3/12/1772.

Jeremiah Woolaston father of the forgoing Thomas Wooleston d. 2/11/1772.

James son of John and Elenor Owens b. about 26/8/1772. Elenor Owens the mother d. 4/9/1772. John Owens the father d. 22/12/1772. James Owens the above child d. 20/12/1774.

Mary Harvey d. 27/10/1774.

Thomas Milhouse son of John and Margaret Milhous d. 23/2/1777.

Elisabeth Robinson widow of Francis Robinson d. 10/9/1777.

Antient and esteemed Friend Elisabeth Shipley d. 16/10/1777 in her 87th year; buried at London Grove. Also our Antient and esteemed Friend Esther White d. 5/12/1777 in her 77th year. They were near and dear companions.

Hannah Morgan d. 31/8/1776.

Kathrine Lightfoott a minister, d. 27/5/1780.

Rachel Stapler wife of John Stapler and dau of Thomas and Mary West d. 11/7/1783 in her 63rd year; appointed elder of this meeting 10/4/1771 in which station she stood until her deceased, aged 62 years, 2 months and 20 days.

William Shipley d. 19/12/1768, husband of esteemed Friend Elisabeth Shipley. They were some of the first settlers of this town in the year 1736.

John Serrell d. 13/1/1788.

John Hains d. 1/1/1790.

Edward Tatnall father to Joseph d. 7/1/1790.

Joseph Reynolds son of Henry and Sarah Reynolds from Darby d. at the Island of St. Domingo, 31/10/1789.

Joseph West, son of Thomas and Mary West, d. 7/5/1790, aged near 62 years; appointed to station of elder 7th month 1779 in which station he stood until his decease.

Ann Gilpin d. age 86 years, 5 months, 15/2/1791.

Elizabeth Musgrave d. 2/4/1791.

Edith Sharples, dau of Benj. Sharpless, dec'd., d. 11/4/1789.

Elizabeth Yarnall d. 18/6/1792, aged 58 years, 4 months and 13 days.

Henry Reynolds d. 25/7/1792.

Jane Farson d. 7/12/1792, aged 88 years, 2 months and 22 days.

James Buckingham d. 23/1/1793, aged 69 years, 10 months, 23 days.

Margaret Weldon d. 14/3/1793.

Deborah Hollingsworth d. 9/4/1793.

Sarah Whitelock d. 21/5/1793.

Margaret Weldon widow (see above), d. 14/3/1793.

Waine Thomas d. in the meeting house yard sudden, 16/6/1793.

Ephraim Yarnall d. 25/9/1793.

Mary Gilpin d. aged 86 years, 31/10/1794.

Samuel Milner, son of James and Sarah Milner d. aged 46 years, 5/3/1758. Elizabeth Milner wife of aforesd. Samuel d. aged 75 years, 2/11/1790.

William Cloud d. 15/9/1795.

Jemima Stapler d. 31/7/1796.

Lydia Webb d. aged 53 years, 11 months, 22 days, 2/2/1797.

Benjamin Mendenhall, d. aged 67 years, 10 months, 17/2/1797.

Jane Thomas, wife of Evan Thomas, d. 25/11/1797.

Letice Welsh d. in Wilmington, 5/3/1798.

Evan Thomas, d. 4/7/1798.

Jane Smith d. 22/9/1798.

Joseph Brown son of James and Elisath. Brown b. 30/3/1770. James Brown d. 4/3/1772; Miriam Brown dau of the above d. 25/8/1769.

Children of John and Hannah Stewart: Elisabeth Stuart b. 27/9/1759; Martha b. 10/8/1762; George Stuart b. 6/3/1767; Ann b. 10/9/1769.

Children of Charles and Mary West: Caleb b. 15/11/1763; Abigail b. 28/11/1765; Sarah b. 9/9/1767; Mary b. 6/8/1769. All born in Phila. William West their son b. at Wilmington 26/9/1771, d. -/1/1858. John Steward d. 6th month 1772. Hannah Steward d. 20/9/1779.

Children of Job and Elizabeth Sinkler: John b. 20/9/1772; Mary b. 18/2/1774; Hannah b. 11/2/1776; Kezia b. 9/4/1779; Abraham b. 19/10/1782.

Children of John and Sarah Littler: Rachel b.
29/6/1765; Deborah b. 5/3/1768; Sarah b.
21/4/1769; Hannah b. 20/8/1771; John Stapler
Littler b. 26/1/1773; Sidney b. 3/5/1775.
Rachel Littler d. 14/8/1769; Deborah d.
23/4/1768; Hannah d. 17/10/1771; Sarah mother of
the foregoing children d. 6/11/1783.

William Starr son of Isaac Starr b. 27/3/1731.
Jane Hoops dau of Joshua Hoops b. 12/7/1732.
They m. at Goshen 3/11/1757. Their issue:
Hannah b. 9/12/1758; Isaac b. 30/9/1760;
Margarett b. 1/4/1763; William Lightfoot b.
7/11/1765; Joshua b. 16/9/1769; Caleb b.
13/8/1772. William Starr the father d.
16/6/1787. Jane Starr d. 16/5/1812. Hannah
Troth dau of Wm. and Jane d. 11/3/1828.

Nathan Wood son of Nathan Wood and Rebekah
Trimble m. and had issue: Hannah b. 11/8/1775;
Rachel b. 26/10/1777; William b. 25/6/1779;
Joseph b. 9/9/1781. Nathan Wood father of the
children here mentioned d. 11/10/1793. Hannah
Wood d. 23/6/1780. William Wood d.
13/4/1780(?).

William Canby son of Oliver Canby and Martha
Marriott and had issue: Oliver b. 15/3/1775;
Sarah b. 1/11/1776, d. 9/9/1777; Fanny b.
11/6/1778; Mary b. 14/2/1780; Anna b.
29/12/1784; Merrit b. 19/10/1787.

John Hill and Ann his wife had issue: James b.
18/3/1774; John b. 19/11/1775; George b.
29/3/1777, d. 14/1/1791; Isaac b. 26/9/1779;
Mary b. 23/4/1781; Joanna b. 26/3/1783; Howard
b. 13/12/1784; Ann b. 1/8/1787; Thomas b.
21/11/1789.

Joseph Marot and Elizabeth his wife had issue:
Ann b. 18/7/1785; William b. 5/6/1790; Joseph b.
31/3/1792; Samuel b. 29/6/1794; Devenport b.
19/1/1799. Joseph the father d. 30/8/1798.

Phebe Yarnall dau of John and Elisabeth Yarnall
b. 20/4/1776; Rachel their 2nd dau b. 18/8/1778;
Edith their 3d dau b. 7/8/1780; John b.

15/9/1782. John Yarnall the father d.
24/9/1799.

Jane Sheward dau of Caleb and Hannah Sheward b.
1/8/1772; Caleb son of the above b. 7/4/1777.
Caleb Sheward the father d. 17/8/1785; Benjamin
their son d. 18/9/1798; Hannah d. 8/3/1804.

Simon and Rebekah Johnson had issue: Ruth b.
28/4/1759; Robert b. 8/9/1761; Daniel b.
8/1/1766; Caleb b. 6/4/1768; Rebekah b.
18/5/1773; Simon b. 8/4/1776.

Edward Hewes son of Joseph Hewes and Mary his
wife, dau of Daniel Stubbs had issue: Joseph b.
5/9/1771; Vincent b. 21/5/1773; Ann b.
15/10/1775; Orpah b. 9/6/1778; John b.
10/5/1781; Mary b. 5/10/1783, d. 1/10/1785;
James b. 3/9/1785, d. 13/4/1788; Aron b.
11/3/1787; Deborah b. 12/7/1789; Hannah b.
14/9/1791, d. 25/7/1796.

Isaac Starr and Elisabeth his wife had issue:
Isaac b. 15/3/1764; Acquila b. 3/4/1767; Elisha
b. 20/1/1770; Phebe b. 5/2/1773; Isaac and
Rachel his wife dau of Robert Green and late
widow of John Prichett (?), deceased, had issue:
Elisabeth Starr b. 7/2/1780. Elisabeth Starr
the mother d. 21/11/1776; Isaac Starr the father
d. 1811 aged 83 years and ?; Isaac Starr their
son d. 12/9/1799.

Benjamin Canby son of Thomas Canby and Susanna
his wife dau of Joshua Littler had issue:
Deborah b. 19/10/1762; Thomas b. 9/6/1765;
Hannah b. 17/10/1768, d. 2/4/1769; Joshua b.
15/10/1771; Benjamin b. 30/10/1775; Susanna b.
1/1/1781.

Moses Bryan and Mary his wife had issue:
Elisabeth b. 8/3/1776; Thomas b. 28/1/1778;
James b. 2/3/1780; Joseph b. 1/9/1782.

Robert Johnson son of Joshua Johnson and Mary
his wife had issue: Elisabeth b. 24/2/1763;
Joshua b. 8/8/1765; Sarah b. 19/9/1768; Mary b.
28/4/1771.

Joseph England and Abigail his wife had issue: Elisabeth b. 30/1/1751; Margarett b. 10/11/1753; Joanna b. 5/7/1757; Sarah b. 7/4/1761; Joseph b. 2/1/1763; Abigail b. 5/2/1765. Joseph England d. aged 67 years, 2 months, 23 days, 5/2/1791; Abigail England d. aged 74 years, 11 months, 10 days, 13/5/1800. Margaret their dau d. aged 34-10-28, 7/10/1788. Joanna their dau d. aged 32-4-4, 9/11/1789. Abigail their dau d. aged 31-10-20, 25/12/1796.

Joseph and Catharine Rotherum had issue: Catharine b. 4/2/1756.

William Wolaston son of Joseph Wollaston and Elisabeth his wife dau of Joseph England had issue as follows: Jacob b. 27/10/1772; Joseph b. 2/3/1776; Mary b. 12/2/1778; Deborah b. 11/1/1780; George b. 17/4/1782; Joanna b. 12/2/1784; Elisabeth b. 2/11/1785; Levy b. 23/9/1787; Abigail b. 21/8/1789; Allice b. 12/7/1791; Lydia b. 10/10/1792. William Wolaston d. aged 49-4-12, 22/9/1794. Elizabeth Wollaston d. 9th month 1799.

Joseph and Amey Chambers had issue as follows: Sarah b. 24/7/1769; Elisabeth b. 20/11/1770; William b. 26/10/1772, d. 16/4/1775; James b. 16/3/1775, d. 1/11/1777; Mary b. 13/8/1777; William b. 12/8/1780; Joseph b. 21/12/1782; Emmy b. 4/5/1787.

Joel and Amey Lewis had issue: John b. 19/3/1774; Abigail b. 27/1/1775.

Samuel and Jane Reynolds had issue: Thomas b. 1/2/1757; Margarett b. 9/9/1760; Abraham b. 4/9/1762; Samuel b. 23/4/1769. Jane Reynolds wife of Samuel Reynolds d. 17/11/1779 and was the first person buried in Friends Burying Ground at White Clay Creek.

Samuel Kendal and Rebekah his wife had issue: Jesse b. 11/9/1741; Hannah b. 7/7/1746.

Jesse Kendal son of John Kendal and Mary his wife, dau of William Marshall had issue: Isaac b. 7/3/1764; John b. 20/6/1766; James b.

16/10/1768. Jesse Kendal parent of the foregoing children d. 4/11/1769. Mary the mother of the foregoing children d. 15/9/1802.

Richard Richardson son of John Richardson and Sarah his wife dau of Edward Tatnall has issue: Joseph b. 19/2/1767; Elisabeth b. 20/7/1771; Ashton b. 6/5/1776; Ann b. 20/10/1778; John b. 18/5/1783. Richard Richardson d. 10/9/1797. John Richardson d. 9/30/1859, 20 minutes of 10 A.M.

Caleb Byrnes (d. 11/1/1794) son of Daniel Byrnes and Mary his wife (d. 5/1/1794) had issue: Martha b. 18/4/1765; Jonathan b. 16/4/1768; Rachel b. 4/3/1771; Daniel b. 17/9/1773. Rachel Byrnes their dau d. 29/-/1804.

Joseph Tatnall son of Edward Tatnall and Elisabeth his wife dau of James Lea had issue: Sarah b. 27/11/1765; Margarett b. 23/8/1767; Elisabeth b. 28/7/1770, d. 1805; Edward b. 6/8/1772, d. ca. 10 days old; Ann b. 9/4/1775; Joseph b. 26/3/1777, d. 2/10/1798; Esther Tatnall b. 13/9/1779; Edward b. 20/6/1782; Thomas Tatnall b. 13/6/1785, d. 1/10/1798.

Samuel Canby son of Oliver Canby and Frances his wife dau of James Lea has issue: Elisabeth b. 2/9/1776; Margarett b. 16/8/1778; James b. 30/1/1781; Ann b. 5/6/1783; Esther b. 19/6/1785; Sarah b. 12/3/1788; Samuel b. 17/5/1790; Thomas b. 10/6/1792, d. ca. 1/8/1792; Frances b. 5/12/1793; Mary b. 17/2/1796, d. 23/7/1796; Mary 2nd b. 28/7/1798.

Job Harvey son of Benja. Harvey and Sarah (d. 10/4/1793) his wife dau of Edward Dawes had issue: Jonathan b. 30/11/1761; Benjamin b. 4/3/1764, d. 18/6/1803; Abner b. 16/6/1766; Mary b. 1/3/1769; Isaac b. 1/7/1771; Samuel b. 9/9/1773; Joseph b. 15/7/1776.

Philip Bonsall (d. 4/10/1803) son of Vincent Bonsall and Cathrine his wife dau of Caleb Harrison had issue: Vincent b. 30/4/1773; Caleb b. 26/7/1775; Isaac b. 16/7/1778; Grace b. 4/1/1781, d. 5/8/1783; Elenor b. 19/3/1783; Mary

b. 12/8//1785, d. 5/9/1793; Philip Bonsall b. 25/12/1787, d. 5/10/1783; Phillip Bonsall and Hannah his second wife (dau of Stephen Ogden b. 21/8/1752) has issue: Stephen Bonsal b. 29/9/1791; Hannah Bonsall b. 14/11/1793.

Vincent Gilpin son of Joseph Gilpin and Abigail his wife had issue: Edward b. 27/4/1760; Ann b. 13/8/1762; Hannah b. 27/12/1764; James b. 11/1/1769; William b. 18/8/1775; Gertrude b. 13/8/1778.

Jacob Bennett and Susanna his wife had issue: Alice b. 8/6/1752; Jacob b. 19/10/1754; Ann b. 9/5/1757; Sarah b. 3/2/1759; Susanna b. 4/10/1766.

George Spackman (d. 4/9/1798) son of Isaac Spackman old England and Thomsin his wife dau of Samuel Bond had issue: Mary b. 13/3/1776; Ann b. 28/12/1777; Samuel Spackman b. 4/2/1780; Hesther b. 16/4/1782.

Joseph Shipley son of Thomas Shipley and Mary his wife dau of Samll. Levis had issue: Samuel b. 12/2/1777; Mary b. 27/12/1778; Thomas b. 30/9/1780; John b. 25/12/1782; Rebekah b. 3/5/1785, d. 4/9/1786; Anna b. 26/7/1788; Elizabeth b. 10/6/1789; Sarah b. 3/3/1791; Margaret b. 18/12/1793.

Richard Dickenson and Phebe his wife (d. 13/1/1788) dau of Richard Carsan had issue: Carsan Dickenson b. 8/8/1767; Samuel Dickenson b. 14/2/1771, d. 14/2/1790.

Joseph Coleman and Sarah (d. 25/2/1778) his wife dau of Griffith Minshall had issue: Griffith Coleman b. 20/2/1778, d. 29/3/1778.

George Martin and Elisabeth his wife had issue: Sarah b. 7/9/1777.

William Brown and Dorcas his wife had issue: Elisabeth Brown b. at Nantuckett; Mary Macy Brown b. 11/7/1778.

Isaac Wilson (son of Jno. Wilson at Deer Creek) and Susanna his wife had issue: Alisanna Wilson b. 20/1/1790.

Jeremiah Woolston and Elisabeth his wife had issue: Martha b. 25/6/1755; Sarah b. 18/5/1757; Hannah b. 4/9/1759; Jeremiah b. 15/12/1761; Samuel b. 27/7/1764, d. 25/2/1765; Benjamin b. 7/6/1766; Elisabeth b. 8/10/1769.

John Milner son of Samuel Milner and Phebe his wife dau of John Larken had issue: Samuel b. 10/10/1768; William b. 28/12/1770 (1771?); Larkin b. 5/8/1774; Mary b. 16/9/1776; Esther b. 4/3/1779; Lydia b. 11/2/1781; Sidney b. 27/8/1783; Beulah b. 7/7/1785; Anna b. 17/12/1787; John b. 8/12/1789; Harriot b. 2/9/1794.

John Ferriss son of Ziba and Edith Ferriss and Sarah his wife had issue: John Ferriss b. 21/9/1801. John Ferriss d. aged 26 years, 10 months, 21 days, 1/11/1802.

Joseph Warner (d. aged 57 years) son of William Warner and Mary his wife dau of Philip Yarnall had issue: John b. 6/1/1773; William b. 16/11/1774; Susanna b. 22/11/1776; Joseph b. 20/4/1780; Mary b. 25/1/1783; Jesse b. 30/12/1785, d. 25/11/1793; Hesther b. 18/11/1787, d. 12/9/1802.

James Pierce (d. 1/4/1789) son of James Pierce of Goshen and Miriam his wife dau of Richard Carsan of this borough had issue: Mary b. 9/2/1781; Richard b. 13/5/1783; Martha b. at Chichester 10/1/1786; Hannah b. at Chichester 15/5/1788, d. 23/9/1791; Aaron Chandler (son of the above Miriam) b. 30/9/1794.

Joshua (d. 29/7/1777, aged 59 years, 3 months) and Ruth Byrnes had issue: Sarah b. 29/10/1750; Rachel b. 17/1/1754; Joshua b. 22/10/1756; Betsey b. 28/12/1759; Sarah the second b. 25/4/1760; Samuel b. 21/2/1762; James b. 1/2/1764; Thomas b. 1/2/1766.

Thomas (d. 7/8/1798) and Sarah Byrnes had issue:
Hannah Pancoast Byrnes b. 29/7/1796; Thomas
Byrnes b. 11/10/1798.

John and Rachel (d. 8/10/1780) Lewden had issue:
Esther b. 8/10/1764, d. 23/6/1769; Jeremiah b.
26/12/1767; Mary b. 9/2/1769, d. 15/9/1769;
Josiah b. at Christiana Bridge 28/9/1770; Esther
b. 9/4/1773; John b. 5/7/1775, d. 4/8/1775; John
b. 5/4/1777; Rachel b. 8/10/1780, d. 15/10/1780.

Joseph Townsend son of Joseph Townsend of East
Bradford Chester County and Hannah his wife dau
of Zechariah Ferriss of this borough had issue:
Joseph b. 1/3/1775; Lydia b. 19/8/1776;
Elizabeth b. 14/2/1779; Sarah b. 17/11/1780;
John Ferriss Townsend b. 29/11/1783; Isaac
Townsend b. 5/3/1786; Ann b. 11/12/1787.

Joseph Johnson and Sarah his wife had issue:
Martha b. 2/12/1796.

Thomas Brian son of William Brian of Waterford
in Ireland and Ann his wife dau of David Kells
of Armagh in Ireland had issue: Mary b.
3/8/1781; Rebecca b. 15/3/1783, d. 24/7/1785;
Thomas b. 3/9/1784, d. 1/7/1789; David b.
12/6/1786; Ann b. 17/8/1788, d. 7/9/1789.

John Martin (d. at Phila 28/12/1795) son of John
Martin late of Birmingham dec'd., and Rebecca
his wife dau of Henry Reynolds late of
Chichester dec/d, had issue: Hannah b.
18/2/1776; James b. 27/11/1777; John b.
1/2/1780; Elizabeth b. 16/4/1785; Joseph
Reynolds Martin b. 25/9/1791; Henry Martin b.
16/10/1794, d. 21/9/1795.

Joshua Stroud son of James and Elizabeth Stroud
late of Plimoth dec'd., and Martha his wife dau
of Caleb and Mary Byrnes had issue: Samuel b.
13/11/1785, d. 1793; Caleb b. 13/7/1787; Mary b.
25/8/1789; Elizabeth b. 27/7/1793.

Isaac and Lydia Stroud had issue born at
Wilmington, Lydia their dau b. 1/4/1783.

Samuel Marshall son of William Marshall and ---
his wife and Elisabeth his wife dau of Tobias
Vandever had issue: William b. 19/10/1776; James
b. 15/2/1779; Jane b. 26(20?)/1/1782.

Timothy Hanson (d. 20/10/1798) son of Samuel
Hanson of Little Creek and Mary (d. 24/2/1790)
his wife dau of Caleb Way: Susanna ["their
daughter, Zane" b. 6/10/1775, d. 26/4/1800;
Elizabeth b. 13/7/1778.

Gerard Blackford son of Gerard Blackford and
Sarah his wife dau of Jonathan Price had issue:
Joseph b. 18/8/1782; Jacob b. 23/4/1784; Lydia
b. 31/1/1788; George b. 5/3/1790; Mary b.
4/2/1793; Sally b. 24/2/1798.

Joshua Seal son of Caleb Seal and Lydia his wife
dau of Isaac Richards of Newgarden had issue:
Caleb b. 19/4/1784, d. 8/3/1789; Isaac b.
11/7/1786; Joshua b. 21/11/1788, d. 21/1/1790;
William b. 19/12/1790, d. 1794; Thomas b.
1/3/1793; Mary R. b. 5/9/1795; Lydia b.
29/5/1798.

John Mitchel and Tacy his wife had issue: Esther
b. 20/10/1781, d. 5/10/1782; Mary b. 2/9/1783.

James Harlan and Elisabeth his wife had issue:
Mary b. 5/4/1785.

Thomas Lea son of John Lea late of Chester and
Sarah his wife dau of Joseph Tatnall had issue:
Joseph b. 5/12/1785; Mary b. 18/3/1787; John b.
18/9/1788, d. 1/1/1789; Thomas b. 29/10/1789;
John b. 15/3/1794; Edward b. 19/2/1797, d.
18/3/1797; Edward b. 28/3/1798; Tatnall b.
16/4/1799; Sarah b. 16/10/1802; William b.
17/5/1805.

John Fairlam and Susanna his wife had issue:
Rebekah b. 10/4/1785.

Stephen Wilson (son of Isaac Wilson of Bucks
County) and Mersey his wife had issue: Benjamin
b. 19/6/1784; Oliver b. 20/9/1786; Sarah b.
14/12/1788, d. 16/2/1791; Isaac b. 18/8/1791;
Betty b. 30/12/1793; Joseph b. 11/5/1795.

Hugh Judge son of Hugh Judge and Susannah his
wife dau of Joseph Hatton of Ireland had issue:
Thomas Lightfoot Judge b. 27/9/1777; Hannah
Logan Judge b. 21/12/1778; Susanna Judge b.
4/9/1781; Margarett b. 4/3/1783; Phebe b.
27/8/1785; Esther b. ---; Rachel b. 7/1/1790.

Jacob Clayton (son of Joshua Clayton) and Hannah
his wife (dau of Isaac Miller) had issue: Lydia
b. 24/4/1785; Martha b. 4/7/1787, d. 13/1/1789;
Isaac b. 3/2/1789.

William Byrnes son of Daniel and Dinah Byrnes
and Anna (d. 14/9/1786 shortly after the birth
of the child) his wife dau of Thomas and Mary
Shipley had issue: Thomas Shipley Byrnes b.
14/9/1786.

Stephen Wilson son of Isaac Wilson of Bucks
County and Mercy his wife had issue: Benjamin b.
19/6/1784; Oliver b. 20/9/1786.

Henry Troth son of Henry and Sarah Troth and
Hannah his wife dau of William and Jane Starr
had issue: William b. 14/10/1784; Sarah b.
8/12/1787; John b. 20/2/1790; Jane b. 1/11/1791;
Margaret b. 14/1/1794.

James Reynolds (son of Henry Reynolds late of
Chichester and Sarah his wife) and Hannah his
wife (dau of John and Hannah Webster late of
Baltimore) had issue: Henry b. 2/3/1786; Sarah
Way Reynolds b. 18/12/1787.

Nathan Milner and Mary his wife dau of Daniel
Sharpley of Brandywine Hundred had issue:
Cathrine b. 2/9/1775; Esther b. 29/9/1777;
Joseph b. 23/11/1780; Cyrus b. 1/11/1782; Daniel
b. 14/11/1784; Rachel b. 24/9/1786; Isaac b.
14/3/1789; Jehu b. 21/7/1791; Mary b. 14/2/1794;
Elizabeth b. 4/7/1796.

John Kendall (d. 12/1/1845, aged 79-5-11) son of
Jesse and Mary Kendle and Mary his wife dau of
James and Deborah Gibbons had issue: Deborah b.
3/3/1788.

Isaac Jackson and Elisabeth his wife had issue:
Sarah b. 16/9/1786; Sidney b. 23/2/1788.

Nathaniel Richards son of Isaac Richards of
Newgarden and Lydia (d. 2/8/1822, age 60-10-21)
his wife dau of John Prichett of Brandywine
Hundred had issue: Mary b. 15/10/1786; John b.
26/4/1788, d. 5/12/1789; Rachel b. 24/6/1790, d.
9/10/1818; Isaac b. 24/2/1792; Betsey b.
20/6/1794, d. 28/10/1794; William b. 15/7/1795;
Ann b. 17/11/1797; Jesse b. 29/10/1799; Lydia P.
b. 25/9/1801. Ann Canby formerly Richards d.
2/10/1826.

Adam Williamson son of John Williamson and Mary
his wife dau of Joseph and Mary Gilpin had
issue: Lydia b. 6/8/1775; Nicholas Gilpin
Williamson b. 8/11/1777; Harry Buckley
Williamson b. 22/2/1781; Henrietta b. 22/5/1783,
d. 30/11/1795; Harriot b. 27/11/1785; Alvina b.
18/4/1788; Mary Ann b. 4/4/1791; George b.
14/10/1793.

Isaac Yearsley and Mary his wife had issue:
Isaac Yearsley b. 26/10/1788; James Yearsley
b. ---; Thomas Yearsley b. 23/8/1791.

Thomas Robinson son of James and Elenor Robinson
and Mary his wife dau of Jacob and Betty Wilson
had issue: Samuel b. 15/6/1788, d. 15/5/1790;
John b. 8/2/1790; William b. 4/4/1792; Elisabeth
b. 26/3/1794; Thomas Wilson Robinson b.
6/8/1799; Mary b. 20/3/1802; Ellinor b.
28/12/1805; James b. 8/2/1808.

James Robinson son of James and Elenor Robinson
and Betty (d. 15/11/1786) his wife dau of Jacob
and Betty Wilson had issue: Jacob Wilson
Robinson b. 8/7/1786.

Eli Mendinhall (son of Benjamin Mendinhall and
Hannah his wife) and Phebe (d. 30/9/1802 age 36-
3-11) his wife dau of John Pritchet late of
Brandywine Hundred had issue: Joseph b.
7/12/1789; Rachel b. 26/12/1792; Hannah b.
26/12/1794; Benjamin b. 18/8/1796, d.
13/10/1797; Jesse P. b. 22/5/1798; Lydia b.
11/3/1800. d. 17/11/1802; Phebe b. 8/1/1802, d.

4/11/1802. Eli Mendinhall and Mary his wife had issue: Lydia b. 6/9/1805; Saml. b. 26/4/1810(?), d. 10/15/1810; Mary b. 31/10/1807, d. 15/7/1824.

John White and Mary his wife had issue: Nicholas Robinson White b. 16/7/1791; William b. 20/10/1793; Mary Robinson White b. 16/11/1795, d. 21/1/1797; Rebecca b. 26/6/1797; Joseph b. 29/1/1800; John b. 22/1/1802; Ann b. 25/12/1804; Mary b. 12/1/1806; Elizabeth b. 16/3/1803.

William Poole son of William Poole and Elizabeth his wife and Sarah Poole dau of Benjamin and Martha Sharpless m. 5/5/1791 and had issue: Elizabeth b. 28/4/1792; Rebeckah b. 21/8/1793, d. 13/8/1794; Mary b. 21/2/1795; Samuel S. b. 13/11/1796; Hannah b. 10/10/1798; William Shipley Poole b. 4/1/1801; Sarah b. 28/1/1804.

Joshua Hallowell and Hannah his wife had issue: Margaret Hallowell b. 17/10/1775; Jesse b. 1/10/1777; Joshua b. 19/9/1779; Hannah b. 16/10/1781; William b. 30/1/1784; Joseph b. 13/10/1785; Rebecah b. 13/12/1787; James b. 14/4/1790; John b. 4/8/1792.

Joseph Shallcross and Orpah (d. 1806) his wife had issue: John Shallcross b. 12/10/1756; Hannah b. 9/8/1758; Joseph b. 12/12/1759; Thomas b. 14/8/1764; Mary b. 3/5/1766; William b. 14/9/1769; Isaac b. 21/11/1771; Betty b. 22/8/1775.

Jonas Canby and Sarah (d. 9th month 1799) his wife had issue: Mary b. 17/8/1791; Esther b. 6/12/1793; Sally b. 3/1/1799.

James Gilpin (d. 1/10/1798) and Sarah his wife had issue: Samuel Stapler Gilpin b. 11/8/1793; Sidney Ann Gilpin b. 28/2/1795; John Littler Gilpin b. 10/3/1797; Hannah James Gilpin (dau) b. 9/3/1799.

James Brian and Sarah (d. 23/10/1802) his wife had issue: Ann Brian b. 10/10/1789.

Isaac Dixson and Emmy his wife had issue [inserted here is "John Dixson their son came with his parents born 18/1/1777] Margaret Dixson came here with her parents by Certificate. Margaret d. 25/7/1783. Elizabeth their daughter b. 10/4/1784, d. 13/1/1788; Isaac their son b. 22/7/1786; Ann their dau b. 1/3/1789, d. 18/7/1796; Mary their dau b. 2/8/1791; Sarah their dau b. 19/1/1794, d. 13/10/1796; Emey their dau b. 21/4/1796, d. 25/7/1799.

Thomas Shallcross (son of Joseph and Orpah Shallcross) and Deborah Claypool Shallcross (d. 1797) (dau of Jonathan and Grace Potts) had issue: Jonathan Potts Shallcross b. 17/9/1790, d. 3/9/1794; Sarah Shallcross b. 18/3/1792, d. 5/4/1794; John Shallcross b. 23/1/1794, d. 31/5/1794.

Vincent Bonsal and Sarah his wife had issue: William b. 24/3/1797; Catherine b. 27/11/1798.

Abraham Bonsall and Mary his wife had issue: Anna b. 17/8/1793.

James Iddings and Mary his wife had issue: Ann b. 31/3/1781; Hannah b. 16/4/1783; Joseph b. 25/11/1785; Caleb Peirce Iddings b. 1/12/1788.

William Warner (son of Joseph Warner) and Esther his wife (dau of Joseph Tatnall) had issue: Joseph Tatnall Warner b. 30/4/1800; Ann Warner b. 3/1/1802.

John Elliott (d. at the Island 29/8/1799) and Sarah his wife had issue: James b. at Stanton 5/8/1792; William b. at Stanton 3/3/1794; Mary b. at Brandywine 2/12/1795.

Jesse Shenton Zane and Susanah (d. 26/4/1800) dau of Timothy Hanson his wife had issue: Mary Hanson Zane b. 19/12/1795; Nathan Shenton Zane b. 18/3/1797; Hester Zane b. 18/7/1798; Timothy Hanson Zane b. 19/4/1800.

Abraham Ford and Elizabeth (d. 13/7/1797, age 45 years) his wife were received into membership after which had issue: Joseph b. 9/5/1792. The following received into membership: Ann their dau b. 4/12/1779; Mary their dau b. 12/11/1782;

William their son b. 1/1/1785; Isaac their son b. 7/7/1789.

Robert Squibb and Mary his wife had issue: James Robinson Squibb b. 11/6/1796; Samuel b. 27/3/1799, d. 3/8/1801; Jacob Hewes Squibb b. 29/1/1801; Thomas Jefferson Squibb b. 7/2/1803; Robert b. 12/10/1805.

Parker Askew and Hannah his wife had issue: Rebecca b. 5/6/1781, d. 12/26/1826 at the ...?; William b. 14/4/1783, d. 12/7/1860; Peter b. 19/11/1785; Joseph b. 28/4/1788; Parker b. 29/12/1789; Sarah b. 28/1/1792; Elizabeth b. 15/11/1793; Molly b. 27/5/1796; Hannah [blank]

John Johnson son of Abraham Johnson and Hannah his wife dau of Caleb Sheward had issue: Martha b. 15/7/1791; Caleb b. 30/1/1794; Benjamin T.[?] b. 11/2/1800.

Joshua Seal and Ann his wife had issue: Talor b. 16/1/1793; William b. 27/8/1796.

Joseph Baily and Elizabeth had issue: Edward Tatnall Baily b. 6/2/1793; Samuel Baily b. 20/3/1794; Joseph Tatnall Baily b. 5/1/1799; Sarah Ann Baily b. 15/2/1801.

Thomas Wickersham and Sarah his wife had issue: James b. 2/12/1796; Elijah b. 29/11/1798; Samuel b. 15/3/1801, d. 17/6/1802.

Thomas Wilkinson and Alice his wife had issue: Joseph b. 7/10/1781; Alice b. 20/10/1783; Elizabeth b. 11/10/1785; Thomas b. in West Marlborough, Pennsylvania, 28/6/1787, d. in Wilmington 21/3/1790; James b. Wilmington, Delaware 5/8/1789; Thomas b. in Wilmington 19/9/1791, d. in Wilmington. [The first three children were born in the township of Londongrove in Pennsylvania.]

Nathan Sharples and Lydia his wife had issue: Edith b. 2/2/1797; Joseph P. b. 19/3/1799; Elizabeth b. 17/8/1801.

Mordecai Yarnall and Elizabeth his wife had
issue: Abner b. 17/12/1793; Esther b. 28/2/1797;
Rachel b. 15/7/1798; Joseph b. 3/2/1802.

Lydia Tilton d. 23/9/1798.
Sarah Reynolds from Chichester widow of Henry
Reynolds, d. 28/2/1798.

Joshua Johnson and Ann (d. 25/11/1804) his wife
had issue: Samuel Pennock Johnson b. 24/5/1794;
Sarah b. 7/1/1797; William b. 21/2/1799.

William Robinson and Elizabeth had issue: Hanson
b. 27/2/1799, d. 13/2/1800; Nicholas b.
7/12/1800, d. 28/6/1801; Francis (son) b.
7/8/1802, d. 18/3/1805; William b. 23/5/1804;
Samuel Hanson Robinson b. 7/1(?) 1806.

John Ferriss son of Zachariah Ferriss and Lydia
(d. 30/3/1782? aged 31-5-20) his wife dau of
Jonathan and Mary Zane of Phila m. 10/10/1771.
John Ferriss and Ann Gilpin dau of Vincent and
Abigail Gilpin m. 25/9/1783.

Joseph Bringhurst and Deborah had issue: William
b. 25/9/1800; Mary D. b. 4/7/1802(?); Joseph b.
26/9/1807.

Samuel and Ruth Nichols had issue: Lydia b.
17/9/1786; Hannah b. 8/3/1789; Joseph b.
21/6/1791, d. aged 10 months and some few days;
Margaret b. 17/1/1793; Ruth b. 15/10/1795, d.
age 11 months, 2 days; Elizabeth b. 29/9/1798.

John Richardson Latimer b. 10/12/1793. Mary
Richardson Latimer b. 29/7/1796. Henry Latimer
b. 21/5/1799. James Latimer b. 26/1/1802.

Thomas Spackman and Deborah his wife had issue:
Samuel C. b. 9/2/1796; Joseph b. 19/12/1799;
George b. 11/9/1801; Anna b. 18/9/1803.

Cyrus Newlin and Abigail (d. 25/11/1787) his
wife had issue: Robert b. 17/1/1778; Samuel b.
25/2/1781, d. 3/11/1782; Isaac b. 27/2/1783;
Cyrus b. 15/3/1785; Abigail b. 29/10/1787.
Cyrus Newlin and Sarah his second wife had

issue: Cyrus b. 26/2/1793, d. 4/9/1793; Mary b. 1/11/1795; Thomas Shipley Newlin b. 14/7/1799.

Thomas Stapler and Margaret his wife had issue: Mary b. 5/9/1780; Sarah b. 23/9/1782; Esther b. 14/1/1785; Stephen b. 22/5/1787; John b. 4/11/1789; William b. 21/12/1792.

Samuel Stroud and Elizabeth his wife had issue: Ann b. 16/12/1795; Mary b. 21/9/1797; Edward b. 19/1/1800; Samuel b. 20/1/1803; Sarah Richardson Stroud b. 21/6/1806.

Edward Gilpin and Lydia his wife had issue: Ann Ferris Gilpin b. 23/7/1791; Vincent b. 29/1/1795; John Ferris Gilpin b. 11/11/1796; Abigail b. 21/10/1798; Lydia Zane Gilpin b. 15/2/1802; Richard Baker Gilpin b. 12/4/1804.

Joshua Maule and Rebecca his wife had issue: Martha b. 30/9/1798; Hannah b. 3/2/1801, d. 13/8/1823; Mary b. 27/12/1802; Elizabeth b. 22/4/1805.

William Stapler and Mary his wife had issue: Rachel b. 25/8/1781, d. 9/1/1785; Joseph b. 17/9/1783; Hannah b. 11/8/1786; Esther b. 5/2/1789; Thomas and Stephen b. 2/8/1791.

John Saunders and Hannah his wife had issue: Israel b. 27/8/1794; Charles b. 30/8/1798; Mary Ann b. 29/7/1801; Elizabeth b. 22/8/1805.

Ellis Sanders and Hannah his wife had issue: Anne b. 4/1/1798.

John Webster and Lydia his wife had issue: Eliza b. 24/11/1794; Louissa b. 29/12/1800.

Jacob Alricks and Lydia (d. 7/11/1825) his wife had issue: William b. 7/4/1800, d. 17/10/1823; Mary Ann b. 18/4/1801, d. 2/3/1812; Sidney Ann b. 8/9/1803; Henry Sigpedus(?) b. 31/3/1806; Sarah b. 28/8/1802. [pencil annotation, "error."]

MARRIAGES

Robert Richardson of the borough of Wilmington son of John Richardson of Christiana Hundred & Sarah Shipley dau of William Shipley & Elisabeth his wife of the borough afsd., 6/10/1750.

Henry Troth of the borough of Wilmington and Sarah Paschall dau of William Paschall of Whiteland Township, Chester co., PA, 25/2/1751.
William Shipley, Junr. son of William Shipley of the borough of Wilmington and Sarah Rumford dau of Jonathan Rumford of the borough afsd., with consent of parents, 27/12/1753.

Daniel Jackson of the borough of Wilmington, cooper, and Ann Warner dau of William Warner of the borough afsd., having consent of parents, 23/5/1754.

William Poole of the borough of Wilmington and Martha Roberts of the borough afsd., 27/6/1754.

William Warner of the borough of Wilmington, turner, and Sarah Eldridge of the same place, 31/10/1754.

William Dean of the borough of Wilmington, Christiana Hundred, and Katherine King of the borough afsd., 16/1/1755.

John Stuart of Wilmington of Christiana Hundred son of Robert Stuart of Robinson Township in Berks Co., PA, and Hannah Lea dau of Isaac Lea of Wilmington, 10/6/1756.

William Marshall of the borough of Wilmington and Mary Tatnall dau of Edward Tatnall of the borough afsd., having consent of parents, 25/8/1757.

John Hobson of the township of Limerick in Phila Co., PA, yeoman, and Elisabeth Warner dau of William Warner of the borough of Wilmington, having consent of parents, 29/9/1757.
Joseph Hewes of the township of Penns Neck and county of Salem and province of West New Jersey and Rachel Bell of Wilmington, 16/4/1752.

William Evans son of William Evans of the
township of Lampeter and county of Lancaster,
PA, and Catherine Wollaston dau of Jeremiah
Wolaston and Catherine his wife in Mill Creek
Hundred, New castle Co., having consent of
parents, 19/9/1751.

William Morris Junr. of Trenton in Hunterdon
Co., West New Jersey and Rebekah Peters of
Wilmington, having consent of parents,
5/10/1752.

Thomas Canby Junr. of Wilmington and Elisabeth
Lewis dau of Robert Lewis and Mary his wife of
the town afsd., having consent of parents,
26/7/1753.

Gouldsmith Folwell of borough of Wilmington and
Sarah Cadwalder dau of John Cadwalader late of
Uwchland Township, Chester Co., dec'd., having
consent of parents, 31/5/1759.

Bancroft Woodcock of the borough of Wilmington,
goldsmith, and Ruth Andrews dau of William
Andrews late of county afsd., dec'd., having
consent of parents, 28/6/1759.

Samuel Wharton of the city of Phila, son of
Joseph Wharton of the township of Moyamensinsg
in the county of Phila, and Sarah Lewis of town
and county of New Castle, dau of Stephen Lewis,
late of the said place, dec'd., having consent
of parents, 15/2/1754.

Thomas Parry of the borough of Wilmington and
Catherine Dean of afsd. borough, 29/5/1760.

William Poole of the borough of Wilmington and
Elisabeth Canby of the borough afsd., having
consent of parents, 3/12/1761.

Thomas Underhill son of John Underhill of Cecil
County, Maryland, and Rachel Mendenhall dau of
Joseph Robinson late of Christiana Hundred, New
Castle Co., Del, dec'd., and widow of Joseph
Mendenhall of hundred afsd., dec'd., having
consent of parents, 25/7/1754.

William White of the borough of Wilmington, stay maker, son of John White of the city of Phila, and Ann McMullen, dau of David McMullen, late of Brandywine Hundred, dec'd., having consent of parents, 21/8/1760.

John Clempson of the township of Sadsbury, Lancaster Co., PA, and Elizabeth Way of the borough of Wilmington, 10/1/1755.

Job Harvey of the borough of Wilmington and Sarah Dawes of the borough afsd., having consent of parents, 30/10/1760.

Benjamin Canby of the borough of Wilmington son of Thomas Canby of Darby Township and Susannah Littler dau of Joshua Littler of the borough afsd., having consent of parents, 25/12/1760.

Henry Drinker of the city of Phila, merchant, son of Henry Drinker late of city afsd., dec'd. and Ann Swett dau of Benjamin Swett of the same place, having consent of parents, 4/5/1757.

Thomas Gilpin of Wilmington and Christiana Hundred and Ann Caudwell of the same place dau of Vincent Caudwell of Marlborough, Chester Co., PA, having consent of parents, 19/5/1757.

William Woodcock of the borough of Wilmington and Elizabeth Marshall of the same place, 22/1/1761.

Ezekiel Andrews of the borough of Wilmington and Rebekah Robinson of the borough of Wilmington, having consent of parents, 28/5/1761.

Benjamin Yarnall of borough of Wilmington and Elizabeth Folwell of the same place, having consent of parents, 30/4/1761.

Aaron Ashbridge of the township of Goshen in Chester Co., PA, and Mary Tomblinson of the borough of Wilmington, 4/6/1760.

Thomas Lamborn of township of London Grove, Chester co., PA, and Dinah Carsan of borough of Wilmington, having consent of parents, 1/4/1762.

Robert Johnson of Mill Creek Hundred, New Castle Co., son of Joshua Johnson of London Grove, Chester Co., PA, and Mary Wollaston of the Hundred afsd., having consent of parents, 3/6/1762.

William Troth of the borough of Wilmington and Lydia Osborne of the same place, having consent of parents, 4/8/1763.

John Andrews of the borough of Wilmington, son of William Andrews, late of the county afsd., dec'd., and Sarah Ferriss dau of David Ferriss of the borough afsd., having consent of parents, 25/8/1763.

John Littler of the borough of Wilmington, son of Joshua Little of the same place and Sarah Stapler, dau of John Stapler of the borough afsd., having consent of parents, 27/10/1763.

Philip Jones of the borough of Wilmington and Edith Newlin of the county afsd., having consent of parents, 31/5/1764.

William Jenkins son of Charles Jenkins of the city of Phila. and Hannah Littler dau of Joshua Littler of the borough of Wilmington, having consent of parents, 28/6/1764.

Jeremiah Carter of the borough of Wilmington and Rebekah Wiley of the borough afsd., 27/12/1764.

Joseph Tatnall of the borough of Wilmington son of Edward Tatnall of the same place and Elizabeth Lea dau of James Lea of the borough afsd., having consent of parents, 31/1/1765.

Richard Richardson (son of John Richardson, dec'd.) of Christian Hundred and Sarah Tatnall dau of Edward Tatnall of the borough of Wilmington, having consent of parents, 24/4/1766.

Hezekiah Niles (son of Tobias Niles, dec'd.) of the city of Phila and Mary Way dau of Francis Way of the borough of Wilmington, having consent of parents, 17/7/1766.

William Lightfoot son of Samuel Lightfoot of
Pikeland Township, Chester Co., PA, and Mary
Ferriss dau of David Ferriss of the borough of
Wilmington, having consent of parents,
14/8/1766.

Richard Dickinson son of Richard Dickinson of
Mount Holly in Burlington Co., West New Jersey,
and Phebe Carsan dau of Richard Carsan of the
borough of Wilmington, having consent of
parents, 16/10/1766.

Phineas Buckley of Bristol, Bucks Co., PA, son
of William Buckley of the same place, late
dec'd., and Mary Shipley, dau of Thomas Shipley
of the borough of Wilmington, having consent of
parents, 12/5/1768.

William Ashburnham of the borough of Wilmington
son of Thomas Ashburnham of the city of Phila,
and Rosanna Ferriss dau of John Ferriss late of
the borough afsd., dec'd., having consent of
parents, 19/5/1768.

Jonathan Woodnutt of the county of Salem and
province of West New Jersey and Betty Wilson
(relict of Jacob Wilson, dec'd.) of the county
of New Castle, 15/9/1768.

Edward Wells of the city of Phila, bricklayer,
and Sarah Littler dau of Joshua Littler of the
borough of Wilmington, having consent of
parents, 27/4/1769.

James Kightley of the borough of Wilmington,
school master and Elisabeth Wood of the same
place, 19/10/1769.

William Wollaston (son of Joseph Wollaston late
of the county of New Castle, dec'd.) and
Elisabeth England dau of Joseph England of
county afsd., having consent of parents,
4/10/1770.

Joseph Townsend of the borough of Wilmington,
sadler (son of Joseph Townsend of East Bradford
Township, Chester Co., PA) and Hannah Ferriss

dau of Zechariah Ferriss of the borough afsd., having consent of parents, 25/10/1770.

John Elliott of the city of Phila, son of John and Annabella Elliott of the said city, and Margaret Harvey, dau of Benjamin Harvey, late of Darby in Chester Co., dec'd. and Mary his wife now of the borough of Wilmington, having consent of parents, 4/4/1771.

Joseph Canby of Kent County, Maryland (son of Thomas Canby of said county, late dec'd.) and Hannah Lea dau of John Lea late of the borough of Chester in PA, dec'd., having consent of parents, 22/10/1772.

John Hill of the borough of Wilmington, house carpenter, and Ann Hunt of the said borough, having consent of parents, 17/6/1773.

James Marshall son of William Marshall, late of the borough of Wilmington, dec'd., and Margaret Lea dau of James Lea of the borough afsd., having consent of parents, 25/11/1773.

John Yarnall of the borough of Wilmington, son of Nathan Yarnall of Chester Co., PA, and Elisabeth Newlin, dau of Joseph Newlin, late of Christiana Hundred, New Castle Co., dec'd., having consent of parents, 3/2/1774.

Thomas Shipley of the borough of Wilmington and Rebekah Andrews of the borough afsd., having consent of parents, 27/4/1775.

Joseph Coleman of the borough of Wilmington son of Thomas Coleman, late of Prince Georges Co., Maryland and Sarah Minshall dau of Griffith Minshall of the borough of Wilmington afsd., having consent of parents, 14/9/1775.

Samuel Canby of the borough of Wilmington son of Oliver Canby, dec'd., and Frances Lea dau of James Lea of the borough of Wilmington, having consent of parents, 29/6/1775.

George Carsan son of George Carsan late of the township of Marlborough, Chester Co., PA,

dec'd., and Lydia James dau of Thomas James late
of the borough of Wilmington, dec'd.,
14/12/1775.

James Berry of Choptank in Maryland son of James
Berry, late of the same place, and Mary Bonsall
of Wilmington dau of Joseph Bonsal late of Darby
in PA, having consent of parents, 15/2/1776.

William Zane son of Jonathan and Mary Zane of
the city of Phila and Ann Bennett dau of Jacob
and Susanna Bennett of the borough of
Wilmington, having consent of parents,
16/5/1776.

George Martin of the borough of Wilmington son
of John Martin of the township of Birmingham,
Chester Co., PA, dec'd., and Elisabeth Reynolds
dau of Henry Reynolds late of the township of
Upper Chichester, Chester Co., PA., dec'd.,
having consent of parents, 28/11/1776.

Charles Wharton son of Joseph Wharton of the
city of Phila, dec'd., and Elisabeth Richardson
dau of Robert Richardson of the borough of
Wilmington, dec'd., having consent of parents,
22/10/1778.

Thomas Bryan son of William Bryan and Mary his
wife of the city of Waterford, Ireland, dec'd.,
and Ann Kells dau of David Kells of the parish
of Loughgoll, County Armaugh, Ireland, dec'd.,
and Mary his wife, 15/4/1779.

William Goodwin of the township of Elsenborough,
Salem Co. West New Jersey son of John Goodwin of
the town and county of Salem, province afsd.,
dec'd., and Elizabeth Brown, widow of James
Brown, late of the borough of Wilmington,
dec'd., 11/11/1779.

John Webster son of John Webster and Hannah his
wife of Chester Co., PA, and Lydia Mendinghall
dau of Benjamin Mendinghall and Hannah his wife
of the borough of Wilmington, 13/4/1780.

James Pierce son of James Pierce of Goshen in
Chester Co., PA, and Miriam Carsan dau of

Richard Carsan of the borough of Wilmington, 11/5/1780.

Thomas Newlin of Chester Co., PA, son of Nicholas Newlin late of the township afsd., dec'd., and Sarah Berry widow of Benjamin Berry late of Talbot Co., Maryland, dec'd., having consent of parents, 16/11/1780.

Gerard Blackford son of Garard Blackford of the borough of Wilmington and Sarah Price dau of Jonathan Price of London Grove Township, Chester Co., PA, having consent of parents, 12/7/1781.

Griffith Minshall of the borough of Wilmington and Mercy Dawes widow of Edward Dawes late of the borough of Wilmington, 13/12/1781.

Thomas Marriot of the city of Phila, tanner, son of Joseph Marriott of the said city and Mary his wife (dec'd.) and Mary Sheward dau of Caleb and Hannah Sheward of the borough of Wilmington, having consent of parents, 30/5/1782.

John Underhill son of Thomas Underhill of Cecil Co., Maryland and Elizabeth Johnson dau of Robert Johnson of Mill Creek Hundred, New castle Co., having consent of parents, 30/10/1782.

Joseph Price of Little Creek Hundred, Kent Co., Delaware and son of Isachar Price late of the city of Phila, dec'd., and Rosanna Ashburnham widow of William Ashburnham late of the borough of Wilmington, 12/6/1783.

Henry Troth of the borough of Wilmington, son of Henry and Sarah Troth of Talbot Co., Maryland, and Hannah Starr, dau of William and Jane Starr of Wilmington, having consent of parents, 18/9/1783.

John Ferriss son of Zechariah and Elizabeth Ferriss and Ann Gilpin dau of Vincent and Abigail Gilpin both of the borough of Wilmington, having consent of parents, 25/9/1783.

Eliakim Garretson son of Jedediah Garretson late of Hundred and County of New Castle Delaware and Esther his wife dec'd., and Lydia Windle dau of William Windle of East Marlborough Township, Chester Co., PA, and Mary his wife, having consent of parents, 27/11/1783.

James Reynolds of the borough of Wilmington, son of Henry Reynolds late of Upper Chichester, PA, dec'd., and Sarah his wife and Hannah Webster of the borough of Wilmington dau of John Webster late of the town of Baltimore, Maryland and Hannah his wife both dec'd., having consent of parent, 20/5/1784.

William Byrnes son of Daniel Byrnes of White Clay Creek Hundred, New Castle Co., Delaware, and Dinah his wife and Anna Shipley dau of Thomas Shipley of Christiana Hundred and county afsd., and Mary his wife dec'd., having consent of parents, 28/10/1784.

Joshua Stroud of Mill Creek Hundred, county of New castle, son of James Stroud of Plimouth Township PA and Elisabeth his wife dec'd., and Martha Byrnes dau of Caleb Byrnes of Mill Creek Hundred afsd., and Mary his wife, having consent of parents, 19/1/1785.

Thomas Lea son of John Lea late of the borough of Chester, Chester Co., dec'd., and Mary his wife and Sarah Tatnall dau of Joseph Tatnall of Brandywine Hundred and Elisabeth his wife, having consent of parents, 20/1/1785.

John Staples of the borough of Wilmington and Jemima Robinson of the same place, 16/6/1785.

James Robinson of the borough of Wilmington, son of James Robinson of the same place and Elenor his wife and Betty Wilson dau of Jacob Wilson late of White Clay Creek Hundred, New Castle Co., dec'd., and Betty his wife, having consent of parents, 21/7/1785.

Isaac Jackson son of Joseph Jackson late of Uwchland Township, Chester Co., PA, dec'd., and Esther his wife and Elisabeth Rea dau of John

Rea, late of Richland Township, Bucks Co., dec'd. and Sidney his wife, having consent of parents, 17/11/1785.

Samuel Nichols son of Joseph Nichols late of Christiana Hundred, New Castle Co., dec'd., and Margarett his wife and Ruth Mendinghall dau of Benjamin Mendinghall of the borough of Wilmington and Hannah Mendinghall, having consent of parents, 15/12/1785.

Nathaniel Richards of the borough of Wilmington, son of Isaac Richards of Newgarden Township, Chester Co., PA, and Lydia Prichett of the borough afsd., dau of John Prichett late of Brandywine Hundred, New castle Co., dec'd., 29/12/1785.

John Common of the township of Newgarden, Chester Co., PA, son of William Common of New London Township, county afsd., and Sarah his wife and Sarah Wollaston dau of Thomas Wollaston of Mill Creek Hundred, New Castle Co., and Hannah his wife, having consent of parents, 22/11/1786.

John James of the city of Phila son of John James and Ann his wife, late of the township of Goshen, Chester Co., PA, dec'd., and Rachel Woodcock dau of Bancroft and Ruth Woodcock of the borough of Wilmington, having consent of parents, 11/10/1787.

Thomas Wickersham of Talbott Co., Maryland son of Isaac Wickersham of Reading Township, Berks Co., PA and Mary his wife and Sarah Johnson dau of James Johnson of North Carolina and Margarett his wife, dec'd., having consent of parents, 11/10/1787.

Eli Mendinghall of the borough of Wilmington, son of Benjamin and Hannah Mendinghall of the borough afsd., and Phebe Pritchett of the same place dau of John Pritchett late of Brandywine Hundred, county afsd., dec'd., having consent of parents, 18/10/1787.

Thomas Robinson of Brandywine Hundred, New Castle Co., Delaware, son of James and Elenor Robinson of the borough of Wilmington, and Mary Wilson dau of Jacob Wilson late of White Clay Creek Hundred, county afsd., dec'd., and Betty his wife, having consent of parents, 25/10/1787.

Caleb Seal of the borough of Wilmington son of William Seal and Hannah his wife late of the township of Birmingham, Chester Co. and Alice Clark dau of Walter Clark, late of the township of East Bradford, Chester Co., dec'd., 22/11/1787.

John Kendall son of Jessee Kendall of Christiana Hundred, New Castle Co., and Mary Gibbons dau of James Gibbons of the same hundred, having consent of parents, 26/4/1787.

John Poles Seal of West Town, Chester Co., PA, and Mary Jackson of the borough of Wilmington, 17/9/1788.

Solomon Phillips son of James Phillips and Ruth his wife, dec'd., and Martha Nichols dau of Samuel Nichols, dec'd. and Elisabeth his wife in the borough of Wilmington, 22/10/1788.

Joseph Wilkinson of Queen Anne's Co., Maryland, son of Joseph Wilkinson late of Paxton Township, Lancaster Co., PA, dec'd., and Elizabeth his wife and Margarett Starr dau of William Starr late of the borough of Wilmington and Jane Starr, having consent of parents, 13/11/1788.

William Richards of Newgarden Township, Chester Co., PA, son of Isaac Richards and Mary his wife, the latter dec'd., and Cathrine Philips of Christianna Hundred in New Castle Co., Delaware, dau of Robert Phillips and Cathrine his wife, the latter dec'd., having consent of parents, 19/11/1788.

Ellis Sanders son of John and Ann Sanders of Mill Creek Hundred, New Castle Co., and Edith Yarnall dau of Ephraim and Sarah Yarnall of hundred and county afsd., having consent of parents, 1/4/1789.

Gerard Blackford of the borough of Wilmington and Elizabeth Serrell widow of John Serrell, late of the borough afsd., dec'd., 30/4/1789.

Richard Jacobs of the township of East Whiteland, Chester Co., PA, and Phebe Eaves widow of James Eaves, late of the borough of Wilmington, 30/7/1789.

Vincent Bonsall of the borough of Wilmington, and Mary Askew of the same place, widow of William Askew, late of Millcreek Hundred, county afsd., dec'd., 24/9/1789.

Thomas Shallcross son of Joseph and Orpah Shallcross of the borough of Wilmington, and Deborah Claypool Potts dau of Jonathan Potts late of Potts Grove in Montgomery Co., Pa, dec'd., and Grace his wife, having consent of parents, 22/10/1789.

Samuel Stroud of Mill Creek Hundred of New Castle Co., son of James and Ann Stroud late of Plimoth Township, Montgomery Co., PA, dec'.d, and Elizabeth Richardson dau of Richard and Sarah Richardson of Christiana Hundred, New castle Co., having consent of parents, 29/10/1789.

Abraham Gibbons of Leacock Township, Lancaster Co., PA, son of Joseph Gibbons, late of Chester Co., dec'd., and Mary Canby dau of Oliver Canby late of the borough of Wilmington, dec'd., 27/5/1790.

Cyrus Newlin of the borough of Wilmington, and Sarah Shipley dau of Thomas Shipley and Mary his wife of the borough afsd., having consent of parents, 24/6/1790.

John Johnson of the borough of Wilmington son of Abraham Johnson, dec'd., and Martha his wife of Darby Township, Chester Co., and Hannah Sheward dau of Caleb Sheward, dec'd., and Hannah his wife of the borough of Wilmington, 7/10/1790.

John White son of William and Ann White and Mary Robinson dau of Nicholas and Mary Robinson, both of the borough of Wilmington, having consent of parents, 21/10/1790.

Abraham Bonsall son of Jesse Bonsall, dec'd., and Ruth his wife of Darby Township, Delaware co., PA, and Mary Andrews dau of Ezekiel Andrews, dec'd., of the borough of Wilmington, having consent of parents, 28/10/1790.

Joseph Bailey of the borough of Wilmington son of Isaac Baily and Lydia his wife of the township of West Marlborough, Chester Co., PA, and Elizabeth Tatnall dau of Joseph Tatnall and Elizabeth his wife of Brandywine Hundred, New Castle Co., having consent of parents, 25/11/1790.

Henry Reynolds of the borough of Wilmington and Mary Kendal of the borough of Wilmington, 30/6/1791.

John Elliot son of John Elliot late of the borough of Wilmington, dec'd., and Rebecca his wife, and Sarah Johnson dau of Robert and Mary Johnson, of Mill Creek Hundred, county afsd., having consent of parents, 26/10/1791.

Joseph Thomas of Stanton in Mill Creek Hundred, New castle Co., son of Evan and Jane Thomas of Lower Doublin in Phila Co., and Elizabeth Chambers, dau of Joseph and Emmey Chambers of Mill Creek Hundred afsd., having consent of parents, 19/10/1791.

James Gilpin son of Vincent and Abigail Gilpin and Sarah Littler dau of John and Sarah Littler, both of the borough of Wilmington, having consent of parents, 26/4/1792.

Timothy Hanson of the borough of Wilmington son of Samuel Hanson of Kent Co., Delaware and Priscilla his wife, dec'd., and Mary Robinson dau of James Robinson of the borough of Wilmington and Elinor his wife, both dec'd., 17/5/1792.

John Jones of Little Brittain in Lancaster Co., son of John and Lydia Jones, the former dec'd., and Ann Shipley of the borough of Wilmington, dau of Thomas and Mary Shipley, dec'd., 20/9/1792.

Samuel Coope son of Samuel Coope and Deborah his wife, the latter dec'd., of the township of East Bradford Co., Chester Co., PA and Elizabeth Blackford dau of Gerard Blackford and Mary his wife, the latter dec['d., of the borough of Wilmington, having consent of parents, 25/10/1792.

Richard Barnard son of Richard Barnard and Lettice his wife of Newlin Township, Chester Co., PA, and Sarah Chambers dau of Joseph Chambers and Emmy his wife of Mill Creek Hundred, New Castle Co., having consent of parents, 24/10/1792.

Robert Leslie son of Thomas Leslie, late of Bohemia Manor, Cecil Co., Maryland, dec'd., and Rachel Rogers dau of Enos Rogers, late of Baltimore Town, Maryland, dec'd., having consent of parents, 20/3/1793.

Isaac Starr son of Isaac Starr and Elizabeth his wife, the latter dec'd., of the borough of Wilmington, and Margaret Tatnall dau of Joseph Tatnall and Elizabeth his wife of Brandywine Hundred, having consent of parents, 26/12/1793.

William Elliott of the borough of Wilmington son of John Elliott, dec'd., and Rebeckah his wife of county afsd., and Esther Griffith dau of Evan Griffith, dec'd., and Rebeckah his wife late of York County, PA, having consent of parents, 22/5/1794.

David Chandler son of Swithin Chandler late of Christiana Hundred, New Castle Co., dec'd., and Miriam Peirce, widow, dau of Richard Carson of the borough of Wilmington, 12/6/1794.

Jesse Shenton Zane son of Joel Zane and Esther his wife of the borough of Wilmington and Susannah Hanson dau of Timothy Hanson and Mary his wife, the latter dec'd., of the same place, having consent of parents, 18/9/1794.

Thomas Sipple son of Garret Sipple and Elizabeth
his wife, the latter dec'd., of Kent Co.,
Delaware, and Ann Tatnall dau of Joseph Tatnall
and Elizabeth his wife of Brandywine Hundred,
New Castle Co., having consent of parents,
25/9/1794.

Thomas Downing son of Richard Downing and
Elizabeth his wife of the township of East Caln,
Chester Co., and Mary Spackman dau of George
Spackman and Thomzin his wife of the borough of
Wilmington, having consent of parents,
25/12/1794.

Robert Squibb of the borough of Wilmington, son
of Nathaniel Squibb of Chester Township,
Delaware Co., PA, and Mary Hamilton dau of
Thomas Hamilton and Rachel his wife of the
borough of Wilmington, having consent of
parents, 21/5/1795.

John Biddle son of Owen and Sarah Biddle of the
city of Phila, the latter dec'd., and Elizabeth
Canby, dau of Samuel Canby and Frances Canby of
the borough of Wilmington, having consent of
parents, 15/9/1796.

William Dixon Phillips of Christianna Hundred,
New Castle Co., son of Robert and Ann Phillips
of Mill Creek Hundred Co., and Phebe Starr dau
of Isaac and Elizabeth Starr, the latter dec'd.,
of the borough of Wilmington, having consent of
parents, 20/10/1796.

Reuben Haines of West Nottingham in Cecil Co.
son of Job Haines of the same place and of
Esther his wife and Mary Johnson dau of Robert
Johnson of Mill Creek Hundred of New Castle Co.,
and Mary his wife, having consent of parents,
19/4/1797.

William Warner of the borough of Wilmington, son
of Joseph Warner and Mary his wife of said
borough, and Esther Tatnall of Brandywine
Hundred, New Castle Co., dau of Joseph Tatnall
and Elizabeth his wife of said hundred, having
consent of parents, 19/4/1798.

William Robinson of the borough of Wilmington, son of Nicholas Robinson and Mary his wife, the latter dec'd., of the afsd. place, and Elizabeth Hanson dau of Timothy Hanson and Mary his wife of the afsd. place, the latter dec'd., having consent of parents, 24/5/1798.

Charles Green of Kent Co. Delaware, son of Charles Green and Rosamon his wife, both dec'd., and Hannah Squibb of the borough of Wilmington, dau of Nathaniel Squibb and Margery his wife, the latter dec'd. of Chester Township, Delaware Co., PA, having consent of parents, 15/11/1798.

Thomas Squibb of the borough of Wilmington, son of Nathaniel Squibb and Margery his wife, the latter dec'd., of Chester Township, Delaware Co., PA, and Rachel Foster dau of Francis Foster and Elizabeth his wife, dec'd., of the township of West Marlborough, Chester Co., PA, 16/5/1799.

Joseph Bringhurst, junior, late of the city of Phila, but now of the borough of Wilmington, merchant, son of James Bringhurst of said city, and Anna his wife, the later dec'd., and Deborah Ferriss borough of Wilmington, dau of Ziba Ferriss late of the same borough, dec'd., and Edith his wife, having consent of surviving parents, 11/7/1799.

Isaac Baily widower of the township of East Marlborough, Chester Co., PA, and Sarah Yarnall, widow of Mill Creek Hundred, New Castle Co., 22/8/1799.

John Ferriss, Junior, of Christiana Hundred, New Castle co., son of Ziba Ferriss of the said hundred, and Edith his wife, the former dec'd., and Sarah Harlan of Mill Creek Hundred, county afsd., dau of Caleb Harlan and Ann his wife of the same place, having consent of surviving parents, 22/10/1800.

CERTIFICATES OF REMOVAL

Received by Wilmington Monthly Meeting from indicated monthly meetings

MMtg at the Oblong 17/6/1750 to MMtg at Center and Kennet in Pa. Sarah Ferris.
Chester MMtg at Providence 27/6/1750 to Wilmington MMtg. Hannah Lewes.
East Nottingham MMtg 16/12/1750/1. Catherine Rotheram.
MMtg at Phila 27/10/1751. Rachel Bell. who lived amongst us (which was but short).
MMtg at Buckingham 7/8(?) 1751. Elizabeth Kennerd wife of Anthony Kennard.
Meeting at Ballycane 12/7/1752. Elizabeth Robinson who removed with her husband Francis Robinson some years past with the compass of "our MMtg and now desiring our certificate. ... We also some years ago gave her a certificate to the same purpose which with her daughter was taken by the french and ...?"
MMtg of Newark held at Kennett 2/5/1752. Dinah Burns.
MMtg at Newgarden 31/3/1753. Mary Wolleston wife of James Woolleston.
MMtg of Newark at Center 1/6/1754. Cathren Sharpless.
MMtg of Concord 6/1/1755. Orpha Shallcross.
MMtg of Newark at Kennett 5/7/1755. Betty Caldwell.
MMtg of Newark held at Kennett 5/7/1755. Ann Caldwell
MMtg of Newark at Center 4/10/1755. Lydia wife of Caleb Sael
MMtg at Little Creek 22(?)/12/1755. Rachel Woodcock.
MMtg at Goshen 19/7/1756. Jane Carson, single.
From MMtg of Wilmington 14/10/1756, to MMtg of Phila Elisabeth Hough wife of Benja. Hough.
MMtg of Phila 25/3/1757. Ann Swett, single.
MMtg of Gwynedd 28/6/1757. Rebecca Shaw.
MMtg at Concord 3/10/1757. Susana England had behaved herself in some good degree orderly except for her outgoing in marriage for which offence she has made this meeting satisfaction.

Phila MMtg 28/1/1758. Susana. Hinton who soon after the decease of her husband removed to settle amongst you.
MMtg of Goshen in Chester co. 15/3/1758. Sarah Cadwalader, single.
MMtg at Goshen 17/7/1758. Elizabeth Fawkes wife of William Fawkes.
MMtg at Phila 28/7/1758. Susannah Lea, single.
MMtg of Newgarden 26/8/1758. Hannah Wolliston.
MMtg at Cape May or Egg Harbour, 2/10/1758. Susannah King.
MMtg at Warrington, 18/11/1758. To MMtg of Friends of Bradford in Chester Co. Mary James.
Chester MMtg 29/3/1759. Prudence wife of Jesse Woodward and their children, viz., Jesse, Sarah and Jane.
MMtg of Chester 27/8/1759. Mary widow of Othniel Tomblinson and her daughter Mary.
MMtg of Newgarden, 20/9/1759. Deborah Shaw, Junr. and Susanna Shaw.
Quarterly Meeting at Hampton in New England. 17/7/1760. Elizabeth Shipley.
Quarterly Meeting at Portsmouth in Rhode Island, 9/10/1760. Elizabeth Shipley, minister, [returning home].
MMtg of Phila 27/3/1761. Rebecca Robinson.
MMtg at Kennet at Center 16/4/1761. Bettey Wilson.
Chester MMtg 27/4/1761. Hannah Dawge(?).
Chester MMtg 29/6/1761. Rebecca widow of Thomas Wiley and her 3 children, Vincent, Martha and Mary. She and her husband came recommended from Exeter MMtg to us some years ago.
MMtg at East Nottingham 25/7/1761. Mary Chandler, single.
MMtg at East Nottingham in Chester Co., 30/1/1762. Hannah Folwell, single.
MMtg of Goshen 7/5/1762. Hannah Ellis, single.
Goshen MMtg, 9/7/1762. Susanna Hinton, single.
MMtg at East Nottingham, 2/10/1762. Prudence Jacob wife of ---? Jacob.
MMtg in Phila, 28/10/1763. Mary Kindall who is gone to reside with her husband Jesse Kendall ("a member of your meeting").

MMtg of Women Friends at Nine Partners in
    Dutchess Co., New York, 15/9/1763. Rosannah
    Ferris, single.
MMtg at Radnor 8/12/1763. Mary Davies, single.
MMtg at Kennett 17/5/1764. Susannah daughter of
    Richard Thatcher, dec'd.
MMtg at Concord, 4/7/1764. Rebekah Pilkinton,
    wife of Vincent Pilkinton.
MMtg of Concord 8/8/1764. Hannah Grubb, widow,
    single.

[MINUTES]
MMtg in Wilmington 16/11/1763. The preparative
    meeting enters a complaint against Jane
    McKinley formerly Richardson for
    accomplishing her marriage by a priest with
    a man not of our Society.
14/11/1764 Jane McKinley acknowledged her
    accomplishing her marriage by the assistance
    of Presbyterian parson with a man of that
    profession.

CERTIFICATES OF REMOVAL (RECEIVED)
MMtg at Phila 25/1/1765. Sarah Wood, she having
    lived sometime with Friends in New York
    City, single.
Chester MMtg, 27/5/1765. Abigal Gilpin, wife of
    Vincent Gilpin.
MMtg at Concord 7/3/1765. Rachel Seal, wife of
    William Seal.
MMtg at Kennett, 11/7/1765. Mary Hill. She
    hath lately made satisfaction for her
    misconduct in and about the time of her
    marriage.
MMtg of Uwchlan 5/12/1765. Hannah Ferriss,
    being removed with her husband.
MMtg at Concord, 9/4/1766. Elizth. wife of
    Henry Reynolds.
MMtg at Newgarden 7/6/1766. Ann Newberrey,
    single.
Exeter MMtg 25/6/1766. Mary Bonsall, single.
Duck Creek MMtg at Little Creek, 26/7/1766.
    Ruth Byrnes and her four children, Rachal,
    Samuel, James and Thomas Byrnes.
MMtg at Newgarden, 2/8/1766. Lidia Warner.
MMtg of Kennet, 10/16/1766. Hannah Harris,
    single.

MMtg of Nottingham 27/6/1767. Elizabeth Robinson.
MMtg of Phila, 1/29/1768. Martha Hayward, single.
MMtg at Phila, 29/4/1768. Sarah Way, wife of Joseph Way.
MMtg of Phila, 27/5/1768. Hannah Stewart, wife of John Stewart and her two daughters, Elizabeth and Martha.
MMtg at Concord, 8/6/1768. Martha wife of James Marshall.
MMtg at Goshen 8/7/1768. Lydia James, single.
Cissel MMtg at Kent Co., Maryland, 13/7/1768. Susannah Nuland, she being but 10 years old.
MMtg at Concord, 5/10/1768. Jane Stroud wife of Thomas Stroud.
MMtg of Cissil in Kent co., Maryland, 11/1/1769. Ann Jackson and her five children, viz., Joseph, William, Margaret, Elizabeth and Daniel.
Chester MMtg, 30/1/1769. Mary wife of Joseph Warner (she hath acknowledge her outgoing in marriage).
Chester MMtg, 27/2/1769. Edith wife of Ziba Ferris.
MMtg at Middletown, Bucks Co., 2/3/1769. Rebekah Poole.
MMtg at Uwchlan, 5/10/1769. Mary Jackson, single.
Gwinedd, 28/11/1769. Rachel Wilson lately joined in marriage with a friend of your meeting and has removed within the verge thereof. And for her cousin, Rebecca Woodcock who came recommended from Phila, single.
MMtg in Chesterfield, 7/12/1769. Martha Moor who remained a short time with us, single.
MMtg at Phila, 26/1/1770. Mercy Dawes, wife of Edward Dawes, with four children, Hannah Gray, George Gray, Sarah Gray and Samuel Gray.
MMtg of East Nottingham 31/?/1770. Susanna Folwel, single.
Chester MMtg, 29/10/1770. Elizabeth and Esther Yarnall, single.
Salem MMtg, 25/6/1770. Betty Woodnutt.
MMtg at Abington, 25/2/1771. Sarah Hurst, single.

MMtg at Phila, 26/4/1771. Hannah Humphreys, wife of Richard Humphreys.
Burlington MMtg, 3/6/1771. Phebe Dickison, wife of Richard Dickison.
MMtg at Thirdhaven, 276/1771. Sarah Parvin, wife of Benjamin Parvin.
MMtg at Phila 28/6/1771. Mary West, wife of Charles West, mariner.
MMtg of Newgarden, 7/9/1771. Sarah Corrington, single.
MMtg at Little Creek, 26/10/1771. Elizabeth Hanson and her three daughters, Lydia, Susannah and Anne Hanson. Lydia is single, the other two are young.
MMtg of Duck Creek, 26/10/1771. Ann Farson, living with a friend belonging to your meeting.
Newgarden MMtg, 2/11/1771. Jain Newland, wife of Ellis Newland.
MMtg at Phila, 29/11/1771. Amey Bonsall, single.
MMtg at Phila, 29/11/1771. Lydia Ferris, wife of John Ferris.
MMtg at Kennet, 14/5/1772. Betty Woodnut (clear of any marriage engagements) and children, Mary, Betty Wilson and Hannah Woodnut.
Nottingham MMtg, 30/5/1772. Hannah and Lydia, daughters of Isaac Williams and Lydia his wife.
MMtg of Kennett, 11/6/1772. Elizabeth Keightly.
MMtg of Duck Creek, 27/6/1772. Mary Preston and children, vizt., Mary Pennell, Hannah Lea, Ann Lea, Thomas Lea and Jonas Preston. They came well recommended from Chester MMtg. Clear of marriage engagements.
Chester MMtg, 27/7/1772. Catharine Bonsal, wife of Philip Bonsal.
Uwchlan MMtg, 6/8/1772. Hannah Morgan, daughter of William Morgan, single.
Uwchlan MMtg, 6/8/1772. Elizabeth Morgan, daughter of William Morgan, single.
MMtg of Kennet, 13/5/1773. Elizabeth and Hannah Battin, daughters of Richard Battin, single.
MMtg at Nantuckett, Mass, 31/5/1773. Dorcas Brown, about to remove with her husband.
MMtg at Salem, 29/6/1773. Rebecca Page, daughter of John(?) and Rebecca Page.

MMtg at Darby, 2/9/1773. Mary Chandly to dwell with her husband.

MMtg at Nantucket, New England, 29/11/1773. Hephsibah Coffin resident among you, with her uncle and aunt William and Darcus Brown, in her minority.

MMtg at Nantucket, 29/11/1773. William Brown's daughter, Elizabeth.

MMtg at NewGarden, 1/1/1774. Susanna Harlan, single.

MMtg at Falls in Bucks Co., PA, 3/8/1774. Martha Canby, wife of William Canby.

MMtg at Chesterfield in West New Jersey, 1/9/1774. Ann Robinson.

MMtg of Concord, 5/10/1774. Betty Gilpin, single.

MMtg at Haverford, 11/10/1774. Margaret Findly, wife of Robert Findly.

MMtg at Caecil, Kent Co., Maryland. Hannah Canby.

Nottingham MMtg, 31/12/1774. Mary Carter.

MMtg at Est Nottingham, 31/12/1774. Rebekah Wood, being lately married.

MMtg at Concord, 3/5/1775. Rebeccah Reynolds, single.

MMtg at Concord 3/5/1775. Elizabeth Reynolds, single.

MMtg at concord, 3/5/1775. Sarah Reynolds, widow.

MMtg at Kennett, 11/5/1775. Mary Williamson, wife of Adam Williamson.

MMtg at Uwchlan, 10/8/1775. Tamzin Speakman, wife of George Speakman.

MMtg at Sadsbury, 20/9/1775. Sarah Rason(?), daughter of Sarah Whitelock(?), single.

MMtg at Phila, 22/9/1775. Mary Bryan, wife of Moses Bryan.

MMtg for the Southern Dist. of Phila, 25/10/1775. Lydia Shirley.

MMtg of Newgarden, 8/18/1775. Mary Str...?, single.

MMtg at Concord, 6/12/1775. Sarah Clayton, daughter of David Clayton.

MMtg of Concord, 5/6/1776. Jane Gest.

Chester MMtg, ?/8/1776. Abigail, wife of Cyrus Newlin.

Chester MMtg 26/8/1776. Mary Shipley, wife of Joseph Shipley.

MMtg at Phila, 5/4/1777. Ann Kells who some
   years since came recommended from New
   Garden, single.
Concord, 7/5/1777. Elizabeth Brinton and her
   three children, Jacob, John and Hannah.
Kennett MMtg 12/6/1777. Elizabeth Stewart,
   single.
MMtg at Newgarden, 2/8?/1777. Ruth Pyle, single
Concord MMtg 8/9/1777. Sarah Reynolds, single.
MMtg of Phila, 31/10/1777. Sarah Dougherty,
   single.
MMtg of Kennet, 12/2/1778. Hannah Wilson,
   single.
MMtg of Duck Creek held at Little Creek,
   28/2/1778. Phebe Dickinson who removed some
   time ago from you to reside within the verge
   of this meeting and has since returned.
MMtg at Concord, 3/6/1778. Phebe Milner.
Chester MMtg, 26/10/1778. Lydia, daughter of
   David Yarnall.
MMtg for the southern Dist of Phila,
   6(?)/5/1779. Rebecca Elliot and son
   William, a minor. She is free from marriage
   engagement.
MMtg at Darby, 3/6/1779. Mary Iraharn, widow.
MMtg of Kennett, 17/6/1779. Margret Wilson.
MMtg at Concord, 7/7/1779. Jamima Robeson,
   disowned by our MMtg some years ago for her
   outgoing in marriage, hath lately made full
   satisfaction.
MMtg of Duck Creek, 28/8/1779. Catherine
   Lightfoot.
MMtg of Newgarden, 1/5/1779. Dinah Jackson,
   wife of Joshua Jackson.
MMtg of Concord, 8/9/1779. Rachel Star.
MMtg of Duck Creek at Little creek, 23/10/1779.
   Sarah Berry, widow of Benjn. Berry and her
   child, Mary Berry.
MMtg of Northern Dist. of Phila, 26/10/1779.
   Hannah Woolston, single.
MMtg at Third Haven 28/10/1779. Elizabeth
   Osborne and children, Hannah, Sarah, Lydia,
   Elizabeth, Ann and Susannah Osborn with
   Elizabeth Atkinson an apprentice.
Chester MMtg, 27/12/1779. Mary, daughter of
   John Colbourn.
MMtg Middletown, Bucks Co., 1/2/1780. Margaret
   Stapler.

Newgarden MMtg 4/3/1780. Grace Mason, single.
MMtg of Kennett, 6/3/1780. Mary Wolaston, wife of George Wolaston, and two children, vizt., Harmon and John Gregg.
Kennet MMtg, 13/4/1780. Ruth Gest, single.
Chester MMtg, 24/4/1780. Catherine, wife of Peter Hill.
Chester MMtg, 24/4/1780. Mary, daughter of John Fairlamb, dec'd., single.
Warrington MMtg, 10/6/1780. Deborah Hallinsworth, wife of John, who sometime past came recommended to us from Sadsbury MMtg.
Kennet MMtg, 15/6/1780. Sarah Hastings.
Thirdhaven MMtg, 28/9/1780. Ann Atkinson, single.
MMtg of Phila for Southern Dist., 22/11/1780. Mary Green and four children, John, Ellis, Ann and Sarah.
MMtg at Abington, 25/12/1780. Mary Stapler.
MMtg for Northern Dist. of Phila, 23/1/1781. Hester Lane, wife of Joel Lane and three children, Mary, Jesse Shenton and Rebecca, they being in their minority.
Nottingham MMtg, 31/3/1781. Mary Carter, single.
MMtg at Concord, 3/4/1781. Alce Clark, single.
MMtg at Caecil, Kent co., Maryland, 13?/6?/1781. Elisabeth Devenport.
Kennet MMtg, 12/7/1781. Elizabeth Lee, wife of James Lee, Junr.
MMtg at Concord, 5/6/1782. Lidia Prichard, single.
MMtg at Abington, 26/8/1782. Rachel Stroud, wife of James Stroud.
MMtg of Duck Creek at Little Creek, 28/9/1782. Rachel Byrne, single.
Newgarden MMtg, 5/10/1782. Lydia Windle, single.
MMtg of Concord, 4/12/1782. Mary Jackson, single.
MMtg of Bradford, 13/3/1783. Sarah Mendenhall, single.
MMtg of Phila 25/4/1783. Hannah Webster.
MMtg at Goshen, 6/6/1783. Phebe, wife of Sampson Barnett.
MMtg at Darby, 3/7/1783. Ann Pasehall and 7 children, Francis, Margaret, Mary,

Ann, Elizabeth, Hannah and John, they in
their minority.
Newgarden MMtg, 5/7/1783. Hannah Harlan,
single.
Newgarden MMtg, 2/8/1783. Lydia, wife of Joshua
Seal.
Kennet MMtg, 11/9/1783. Eleanor Buckingham,
single.
Newgarden MMtg, 1/11/1783. Sarah Johnston,
young woman.
Concord MMtg, 5/11/1783. Susanna Dougharty,
Junr., single.
MMtg of Fairfax, 22/11/1783. Sarah Hurst,
single.
MMtg at Concord, 3/12/1783. Susanna Dougharty,
single.
New Garden MMtg, 7/2/1784. Lydia, wife of John
Warner, and 5 children, Mary, Joseph,
Rachel, Levi and Nanny Warner.
MMtg of Newgarden, 6/3/1784. Sarah Leonard,
single.
Nottingham MMtg, 28/3/1784. Sarah Stubbs,
single.
MMtg of Uwchlan, 8/4/1784. Elizabeth Rea,
single.
MMtg of Newgarden, 1/5/1784. Joanna Davis, wife
of Isaac Davis.
Concord MMtg, 5/5/1784. Hannah Dutton, wife of
Francis Dutton.
Kennet MMtg, 13/5/1784. Patience Jordan,
daughter of Rachel Jordan, single.
MMtg of Kennet, 13/5/1784. Rachel Jordan,
single.
Horsham MMtg at Bybury, 2/6/1784. Mary Malne
who removed with her husband.
Kennet MMtg, 14/10/1784. Betty Nickols, single.
Kennet MMtg, 14/10/1784. Martha Nickols,
single.
MMtg of Duck Creek at Little Creek, 23/10/1784.
Mary Bostick, wife of John and children,
Lardner, Mary and John Bostick.
Goshen MMtg, 5/11/1784. Susanna, wife of John
Fairlamb.
MMtg of Kennett, 11/11/1784. Hannah, wife of
Jacob Cleaton.
MMtg at Thirdhaven on Choptank, 30/12/1784.
Sarah Pashil Troth daughter of Henry Troth,
single.

Kennett MMtg, 13/1/1785. Lidia, wife of Joshua Webb.
Nottingham MMtg at Little Britain, 4/4/1785. Betty Wilson, single.
MMtg of Kennett, 12/5/1785. Mary Jordan, single.
Newgarden MMtg, 4/6/1785. Susannah wife of John Jackson, Junr. and three of her children, Rachel, Joseph and Samuel Jackson.
MMtg of Kennett, 11/8/1785. Jane Dowdle, single.
Newgarden MMtg, 3/9/1785. Rachel Mash, single.
MMtg at Ceasil in Kent Co., Maryland, 14/9/1785. Sarah Wallis a child.
Exeter MMtg, 26/10/1725. Grace Potts, widow of Jonathan Potts.
Falls [? torn]. Hannah Lundy who removed with her husband, and her four children, Sarah, Richard, Elizabeth and Eleazer.
Nottingham MMtg at Little Brittain, 3/4/1786. Addah Stubs, single.
Bradford MMtg, 12/5/1786. Elizabeth Forman.
MMtg of Duck Creek at Little Creek, 27/?/1786. Mary Hanson, single.
Kennett MMtg, 15/6/1786. Martha Levis, single.
Kennett MMtg, 15/6/1786. Hannah Levis and Pheby Levis, single.
Newgarden MMtg, 1?/7/1786. Mary Commons, daughter of John Commons.
Nottingham MMtg, 29/7/1786. Mary Wilson who was recommended from Uwchlan MMtg while she lived with her mother - single.
Chester MMtg, 31/7/1786. Mary Preston, single.
Goshen MMtg, 10/11/1786. Jane Griffith, single.
Concord MMtg, 6/12/1786. Phebe Eves, single.
Newgarden MMtg, 5/5/1787. Phebe Harlen.
MMtg at Warrington, 9/6/1787. Hannah and Deborah Phillips, both minors, who placed with Jehu and Deborah Holingsworth, members of your meeting.
7/11/1787. Lydia Rotharam acknowledges being deficient for not caution her daughter against going out in her marriage.
Sadsbury MMtg, 23/1/1788. Hester Griffith.
Falls MMtg, Pennsylvania, 6/8/1788. Sarah Shipley who came to us recommended by certificate from you, having returned, single.

Horsham MMtg, 3/10/1788. Lydia Williams, formerly a member of your meeting, having initiated a concern to attempt to a reconciliation with friends.
Concord MMtg, 3/6/1789. Sarah Wilson, single.
Darby MMtg, 30/7/1787. Mary Andrews, single.
Concord MMtg, 5/8/1789. Mariam Peirce and two of her children, Martha and Hannah.
Gunpowder MMtg, 29/8/1789. Sarah Rogers, single.
Gunpowder MMtg, 29/8/1789. Margaret Rogers, widow, with her two daughters, Rachel and Mary.
15?/9/1790, Kennett MMtg. Rebecca Johnston, single.
Kennet MMtg, 13/5/1790. Ann Tate, single.
Northern Dist. of Phila, 23/11/1790. Sarah Littler, single.
MMtg of Phila, 26/11/1790. Esther Fussell, wife of Jacob Fussell and her children, Ann, Susanna, Jacob, Esther and Elizabeth who are in their minority except Ann.
Chester MMtg, 29/11/1790. Catharine Shalcross wife of Joseph.
Kennett MMtg, 12/3/1791. Ruth Logue, single.
Newgarden MMtg, 2/4/1791. Ann and Lydia Cloud, single.
Newgarden MMtg, 2/4/1791. Ann Cloud and her three minor children, Susannah, William and Caleb Cloud, she being removed with her husband.
MMtg of Bradford, 15/4/1791. Elisabeth Thomas wife of John Thomas.
Newgarden MMtg, 4/6/1791. Abigail Harlan, being settled with her husband.
Chester MMtg, 27/6/1791. Sarah wife of William Poole.
MMtg of Kennet, 16/6/1791. Margret Nichols.
MMtg of Duck creek, 7/23/1791. Rachel Byrnes.
To Friends at New Garden in Pennsylvania. From Shrewsbury MMtg at New Dale, County of Salop?, 17/8/1791. Beth Story having informed us of her intention to return to her father in America and that he resided within the compass of your meeting... She hat continued a member of our MMtg since she was recommended to it by certificate form

Kennet MMtg, Chester County in Pennsylvania, dated 13/10/1785, single.
MMtg of Phila, 26/8/1791. Martha Whitelock.
MMtg of Phila, 7/10/1791. Elizabeth Blackford, single.
Kennet MMtg, 17/11/1791. Jean Hollingsworth, Junr., single.
MMtg of Phila for the Northern Dist., 3/1/1792. Sarah Pusey, a minor.
Pipe Creek MMtg [Maryland], 17/3/1792. Ann Wright, daughter of Joseph and Mary Wright, single.
Kennett MMtg, 17/5/1792. Elisabeth Thomson, single.
Sadsbury MMtg, 20/6/1792. Esther Griffith, single.
Bradford MMtg, 16/11/1792. Ann Chalfant, single.
London Grove MMtg, 28/11/1792. Ann wife of Joshua Johnson.
MMtg at Goshen, 11/1/1793. Sarah wife of John Sanders, Junr..
Bradford MMtg, 14/12/1792. Rachel wife of John Burges.
MMtg at Salem, 25/2/1793. Hannah Byrnes.
Bradford MMtg, 12/4/1793. Lydia Harrison, Junr., single.
Nottingham MMtg, 30/3/1793. Sarah Jacobs.
Kennet MMtg, 13/6/1793. Mary Gilpin.
London Grove MMtg, 3/7/1793. Margaret Carrington, single.
Kennett MMtg, 11/7/1793. Jane Shipley, having lately given satisfaction to us for which she was disowned.
Bradford MMtg, 14/3/1794. Sarah Chalfant, single.
New Garden MMtg, 3/5/1794. Margaret Coward, single.
Kennett MMtg, 17/7/1794. Rachel Foster, single.
Kennet MMtg, 15/5/1794. Margaret wife of John Taylor.
MMtg of Phila, 26/9/1794. Anne Evans wife of Samuel Evans.
MMtg of Kennett, 11/12/1794. Hannah wife of Ellis Sanders.
MMtg at Duck Creek, 11/4/1795. Sarah Townsend, a minor, placed as an apprentice within the verge of your meeting.

Chester MMtg, 27/4/1795. Susannah, wife of William Cloud.
MMtg of Phila, Northern Dist., 5/20/1795. Parnel Gorham, single, and her four children, Jonathan, Mary, James and Deborah.
New Garden MMtg, 6/6/1795. Hannah Common.
Bradford MMtg, 12/6/1795. Deborah, wife of Thomas Spackman, Junr.
Ceacil MMtg, 15/8/1795. Margaret Wilkinson and her two children, Isaac and Hannah Wilkinson.
Redstone MMtg, 25/9/1795. Jane Smith, single.
MMtg of Phila, Southern Dist., 23/12/1795. Sarah Byrns being removed with her husband, Thomas Byrnes.
MMtg at Darby, 28/7/1796. Sarah Bonsall, having removed to reside with her husband, a member of your meeting.
Chester MMtg, 28/11/1796. Hannah Squib, single.
Horsham MMtg, 30/11/1796. Jane Thomas, having removed with her husband Evan Thomas.
MMtg at Middletown, Bucks County, 8/12/1796. Elizabeth Woolston, single.
MMtg at Darby, 3/8/1797. Mary Rudulph, single.
Kennett MMtg, 17/8/1797. Anne(?) Sanders having removed to live with her husband.
MMtg of Phila for Southern Dist., 23/8/1797. Lettice Welsh.
New Garden MMtg, 7/10/1797. Ann Lee.
Newgarden MMtg, 3/2/1798. Mary Sharp, single.
MMtg at Darby, 2/11/1797. Elizabeth Pedrick, single.
MMtg at Duck Creek, 7/4/1798. Ann Sipple and her daughter Eliza Tatnall Sipple, a child.
London Grove MMtg, 29/8/1798. Abigail Harlan, being removed with her husband.
Kennett MMtg, 12/7/1798. Alice, wife of Nathan Sanders, having removed to settle with her husband.
Kennett MMtg, 14/3/1799. Rachel wife of William Seal.
Ceacil MMtg, 17/11/1798. Rebecca Hoops and her two children, Hannah and Francis, minors.
MMtg of Phila, 31/5/1799. Ann Osborn, single.
MMtg of Phila, Southern dist., 25/12/1799. Margaret Starr and two minor children, Elizabeth Tatnall Starr and Isaac Starr.

Lydia Hussey acknowledges her accomplishing her marriage by the assistance of a magistrate with a man in membership with the same religious Society "for which misconduct I was justly disowned."

Sadsbury MMtg, 22/1/1800. Hannah Philips, single.
MMtg of Phila, 30/5/1800. Hannah Ashburnham, single.
Concord MMtg, 4/6/1800. Lydia Gilpin.
Concord MMtg, 8/10/1800. Hannah Hastings, single.
MMtg of Duck Creek, 6/9/1800. Sophiah Edmonson, a minor.
Sadsbury MMtg, 10/22/1800. Susanna Harvey, single.
MMtg of Phila, 28/11/1800. Grace Smith.
MMtg of Phila, 11/28/1800. Sarah Marriott, single.

RECORDS OF CERTIFICATES OF REMOVAL GRANTED BY WILMINGTON MONTHLY MEETING TO THE FOLLOWING MONTHLY MEETINGS

11/2/1751/MMtg at North Wales, Richard Richardson, wife and children.
13/4/1750 or 1751? to Salem MMtg, Jos. Hewes(?) who served an apprenticeship among us with a Friend.
10/11/1750, to MMtg at Duck Creek. Isaac Wood, clear of marriage engagements.
13/4/1751. To MMtg at Derby(?). Jno. Knowles and his wife.
12/7/1751. To Chester MMtg at Providence. Ben Hance, wife and three children.
8/6/1751. To MMtg at Salem. Francis Hinkley(?).
12/10/1751. To MMtg at Gwined. Elizth. Stalford(?)
12/10/1751. MMtg at Providence in Chester co. Lydia Minshall.
25/9/1752. Nottingham MMtg. Gidion Person.
12/4/1753. To MMtg at West River, Maryland. Richard Johns.
10/1/1754. MMtg at Goshen. John Griffith, wife and children.

10/3/1757. MMtg at the oblong in the Province of New York. Deborah Ferriss dau of John Ferriss, dec'd.
14/4/1757. MMtg at Phila. Hannah wife of John Webster having removed with her husband.
12/6/1755. MMtg at Phila. Sarah Way and children, dau Shusanna (clear of marriage engagements), Joseph, Saml., Sarah and Nicholas, who removed with her husband.
11/9/1755. To Goshen MMtg. Robert James.
12/6/1755. To MMtg at Phila. Rebecca and Mary Lea, clear of marriage engagements.
10/7/1755. To MMtg at Nottingham. Stephen Cock (Cook?). clear of marriage engagements.
19?/9/1755. To MMtg at Cecil in Maryland. Saml. Way, clear of marriage engagements.
11/9/1755. To MMtg at North Wales. John Forman(?) (clear of marriage engagements), and his children, Robert and Alexr.
12/11/1755. To Chesterfield MMtg in West Jersey. James Hewes, clear of marriage engagements.
14/10/1756. To MMtg of West River in Maryland. Cornelius Garrison.
To MMtg at Darby in Chester Co. Thos. Canby with his wife Sarah and children. 9/12/1756. Dau Martha is clear of marriage engagements and the small children are Nathan and Joseph.
8/9/1757. To MMtg at Nottingham. Joseph Hewes and his wife Ann and children: Elizath. and Sarah, clear of marriage engagements, Deborah Young.
13/10/1757. To MMtg at Hattonfield in West New Jersey. Saml. Clark, clear of marriage engagements.
9/3/1758. To MMtg Derby. James, Samuel, Rebecca and Mary Marshall, four of the children of William Marshall, late of the borough of Wilmington, dec'd.
14/9/1758. William West and dau Sarah, very young.
11/8/1757. To MMtg at Cecil in Maryland. Daniel Byrn and Dinah his wife.
8/12/1757. To MMtg of Nottingham. Thomas Littler, clear of marriage engagements.
11/5/1757. To Chester MMtg. For Wm. Jones for his son Philip Jones who is bound apprentice.

11/5/1758. To Chester MMtg. Joshua Littler for his son John Littler who is bound apprentice.

13/7/1758. To MMtg in Phila. Saml. Morton, clear of marriage engagements.

11/1/1759. To MMtg at Phila. John Andrew, clear of marriage engagements.

12/4/1759. To MMtg at Phila. Ann Lea, clear of marriage engagements.

10/5/1759. To MMtg at Cecil in Maryland. Daniel Jackson for self, wife and brother in law Joseph Warner.

13/9/1759. To MMtg in Phila. Benjamin Swett, clear of marriage engagements.

8/11/1759. To MMtg at Gwinedd. Ruth Evans (lately left a widow) and her children, Daniel, Lemuel, Elijah and Samuel.

13/12/1759. Rebekah Robinson, clear of marriage engagements.

To MMtg at Phila. Joseph Pemberton, clear of marriage engagements. 13/12/1759.

10/1/1759. To MMtg at New Garden. Jacob Wolliston, apprentice.

To MMtg at Salem. Susannah King. 10/1/1760.

----. To MMtg at Phila. Sarah Wilson, widow, and her son Robert.

14/5/1760. To MMtg in Wilmington. John Warner an apprentice.

16/4/1760. To Phila MMtg. Thomas Robinson son of Valentine Robinson an apprentice.

11/6/1760. To New Garden MMtg. John Pusey, clear of marriage engagements.

16/7/1760. To New Ark MMtg. Sarah Clark, clear of marriage engagements.

10/9/1760. To Goshen MMtg. Mary Ashbridge and her dau. M---.

15/10/1760. To Kennet MMtg. James Wilson, clear of marriage engagements.

16/4/1760. To Chester MMtg. William Milner son of Samuel Milner, dec'd., an apprentice.

12/11/1760. To MMtg at Duck Creek. Children of Daniel and Esther Fen: Daniel, Evan, Phebe and Rachel. Phebe and Rachel clear of marriage engagements; Daniel and Evan being young.

12/11/1760. To MMtg at Phila. Joshua Byrnes, and wife and dau Rachel.

To MMtg at Hopewell. 11/3/1760. Owen Williams, who went away in debt but has given satisfaction.
15/6/1761. To MMtg of Gun Powder in Maryland. William Moore, wife and children, Alice (clear of marriage engagements), William, Mary, David, Jonathan, Stephen and Margaret.
14/10/1761. To MMtg at Nottingham. Jeremiah Wolliston for three children of Joseph Wolliston, dec'd., viz., Elizabeth, Catherine and Joseph Wolliston.
14/10/1761. To MMtg in Phila. Jane wife of William Wilton.
11/11/1761. To MMtg at Phila. Sarah Wood, clear of marriage engagements.
11/11/1761. To MMtg at Goshen. Susanna Hinton, clear of marriage engagements.
16/12/1761. To MMtg at Phila. Philip Jones, having a short stay here (since he served his apprenticeship in the compass of another meeting).
13/1/1762. To Goshen MMtg. Martha Eldridge, clear of marriage engagements.
13/1/1762. To Goshen MMtg. Joseph and Rebekah Stran(?) and their children, Deborah and Mary.
10/2/1762. To MMtg at Duck Creek. Susannah Hanson, clear of marriage engagements.
10/2/1762. To MMtg at Cecil in Maryland. Mary Canby who is removed with her parents, clear of marriage engagements.
10/2/1762. To MMtg at Nottingham. John Smith and Dorothy his wife produced within certificate to our meeting 8th month last and in the 10th month following the removed to settle within the verge of your meeting.
14/4/1762. To MMtg at Phila. Philip Bonsall, apprentice.
14/4/1762. To Kennet MMtg. Mary Chandler, clear of marriage engagements.
12/5/1762. To MMtg at New Garden. Dinah wife of Thomas Lamborn.
12/5/1762. To MMtg on the Oblong in New York Government. Mathew Ferriss.
12/5/1762. To MMtg held on the Oblong New York Government. Rosannah Ferriss, clear of marriage engagements.

12/5/1762. To MMtg at Duck Creek. Thomas Parry and Catherine his wife.

16/6/1762. To Cecil MMtg in Maryland. William Warner, his wife Sarah and three of their children, Benjamin, Samuel and Daniel.

16/6/1762. To ??, William Warner, Junr., clear of marriage engagements.

14/7/1762. To MMtg at Phila. Thomas Canby, Junr. for himself and two children, Sarah and Eli.

15/9/1762. To Concord MMtg. Lydia Garretson (clear of marriage engagements) and her three children, Joseph, Garret and Elizabeth.

15/9/1762. To New Garden MMtg. James Garretson, son of Eliakim Garetson, dec/d. apprentice.

12/1/1763. To MMtg at Kennet. Mary West dau of William West, clear of marriage engagements.

12/1/1763. To MMtg at Shrewsbury. Lydia Clark, clear of marriage engagements.

16/2/1763. To MMtg in Phila. Elisabeth Clark, clear of marriage engagements.

16/3/1763. To Warrington MMtg. Robert Thornbury, and children, Thomas, Joseph, Sarah, Susanna and Mary. A few years past was recommended to us by a certificate from Sadsbury MMtg (we understand he was insolvent and had delivered up his effects to his creditors). He and two oldest daus are clear of marriage engagements. The rest are young.

11/5/1763. To Concord MMtg. Hannah Grubb, clear of marriage engagements.

13/4/1763. To Nottingham MMtg. John Lewden.

10/8/1763. To Phila MMtg. William Canby, apprentice.

14/9/1763. To Nottingham MMtg. Edward Hewes, clear of marriage engagements.

14/9/1763. To New Garden MMtg. Hannah Bennet, clear of marriage engagements.

14/9/1763. To Kennet MMtg. Deborah Bennet who lately came recommended with her parents from your meeting, clear of marriage engagements.

14/12/1763. To Chester MMtg. David Ogden, Zibiah his wife and two children, Ann and Sarah, both young.

11/1/1764. To MMtg in Phila. Thomas Redman, clear of marriage engagements.

14/3/1764. To Gunpowder MMtg. Sarah Wilson being removed with her husband with her two children, Ruth and Hannah, being young.
11/4/1764. To MMtg at Phila. Meribah Clark, widow of Thos. Clark and three children, Thomas, William and Mary who are young.
11/4/1764. To MMtg at Goshen. Thomas Ellis, being young, who came recommended to us in your certificate for Henry Reynolds, but has since returned.
13/6/1764. To MMtg at Kennet. Jesse Eldridge, an apprentice.
11/4/1764. To MMtg of Goshen. Hannah Ellis, clear of marriage engagements.
15/8/1764. To MMtg of Chester at Providence. Thomas James, Junr., clear of marriage engagements.
16/5/1764. To Fairfax MMtg in Virginia. Providence wife of Jesse Woodward, about to remove with her husband, and three children, Sarah, Jane and Prudence, being young.
13/6/1764. To Darby MMtg. Joseph Sellers, for wife Hannah and two children, Hannah and Sarah, being young.
12/9/1764. To MMtg at Nottingham. Ezekiel Andrews and Rebekah his wife and their daughter Mary.
10/10/1764. To MMtg at Phila. Hannah wife of William Jenkins.
14/11/1764. To MMtg at Third Haven in Maryland. Henry Troth and his wife and their children, William, Samuel, Henry, John and Elizabeth, being young.
14/11/1764. To Third Haven MMtg in Maryland. Solomon Edmondson, an apprentice, clear of marriage engagements.
13/3/1765. To Goshen MMtg. Lydia James who several years ago removed to live within the verge of your meeting.
12/12/1764. To MMtg in Phila. Mary Davis, clear of marriage engagements.
To MMtg at Phila. Hannah Stuart, about to remove with her husband and children, Elisabeth and Martha, young.
10/9/1765. To Richland MMtg. Martha Christy.
12/12/1765. To MMtg at Third Haven. William Troth, Lydia his wife and three of his children, Henry, William and Hannah.

15/5/1765. To MMtg at Gun Powder in Maryland. Robert Forman, clear of marriage engagements.
12/12/1765. To New Garden MMtg. William Hays, clear of marriage engagements.
10/7/1765. To MMtg in Phila. Joseph Elliot, son of Obediah Elliot who hath for several years past resided with his father within the verge of your meeting.
10/7/1765. To Concord MMtg. John Buckley's four children, Beulah, Mary, John(?) and Daniel.
14/8/1765. To Cecil MMtg in Maryland. Benjamin Canby, Susannah his wife and one child, Deborah.
14/8/1765. To MMtg at Nottingham. Gouldsmith Folwell and Sarah his wife and three children, Edward, Mary and Elisabeth, being young.
14/8/1765. To New Garden MMtg. Antient Friend, John Smith and Dorothy his wife.
11/9/1765. To Salem MMtg in New England. Abner Dawes, a young man, who plans to stay a while for his health.
Endorsement on John Baker's certificate to Can Creek MMtg in North Carolina, who produced the within certificate to us and being now about to return.
16/10/1765. To MMtg at Cane Creek, North Carolina. Minshall Littler, clear of marriage engagements.
11/12/1765. To Uwchlan MMtg. James Eldridge, clear of marriage engagements.
12/2/1766. To MMtg at Phila. Josiah Dawes, an apprentice in Phila.
16/4/1766. To MMtg at Nottingham. Hannah and Susanna Folwell, clear of marriage engagements.
16/4/1766. To MMtg at Haddonfield, West Jersey. Garret Blackford and wife and their six children, William, Samuel, Garret, John, Thomas and Elisabeth.
14/5/1766. To Kennett MMtg. Samuel and Jehu Hollingsworth children of Jehu Hollingsworth.
11/6/1766. To New Garden MMtg. William Swayne, Junr., clear of marriage engagements.
11/6/1766. To New Garden MMtg. Hannah Black, clear of marriage engagements.

16/7/1766. To Sadsbury MMtg. Joshua Way, son of Josua Way, dec'd., who several years, since was removed with his mother Elisabeth Clempson to live within the verge of your meeting.
13/8/1766. To MMtg at Cecil, Maryland. James Warner.
15/10/1766. To MMtg at Uwchlan. Mary wife of William Lightfoot.
12/11/1766. To MMtg at Sadsbury. Rumford Dawes, clear of marriage engagements.
[The following certificate was apparently returned without being used.] 12/11/1766. To Duck Creek MMtg. Rebekah Morris being removed with her husband.
12/11/1766. To Concord MMtg. William Seal, Rachel his wife and seven children, Hannah (clear of marriage engagements), Joseph, William, Caleb, Benjamin, Thomas and Rachel.
12/11/1766. To Duck Creek MMtg, certificate for Rebecah Morris who has removed with her husband.
10/12/1766. To MMtg at Burlington. Richard Dickinson and Phebe his wife.
10/12/1766. To Nottingham MMtg. Elisabeth Robinson, clear of marriage engagements.
10/12/1766 to Nottingham MMtg. Elizabeth Robinson, single.
11/2/1767. To MMtg at Gunpowder. Meriam Hopkins who is removed with her husband.
11/2/1767. To Sadsbury MMtg. Margaret Starr and dau Phebe. Her outward affairs are settled except for her husband's estate to which she is an executrix. She and dau are clear of marriage engagements.
11/2/1767. To Nottingham MMtg. Mary Carter, a child.
11/2/1767. To Chester MMtg. John James, clear of marriage engagements.
10/6/1767. To Exeter MMtg. Vincent Wiley, clear of marriage engagements.
15/4/1767. To MMtg at Naitsworth in Gloucestershire Great Britain. Susanna Hinton to return to reside in her native land. She is clear of marriage engagements.
/7/1767. To Concord MMtg. William Townsend (with his master Alexander Foreman), clear of marriage engagements.

15/7/1767. To Dear Creek MMtg. Hannah, wife of George Robinson.

15/7/1767. To Gunpowder MMtg. Elisabeth Smith wife of John Smith and their four children, Joshua, John, Mary and Pusey.

12/8/1767. To MMtg in Phila. Sarah Marshall who when young removed to live within the compass of your meeting.

16/9/1767. To MMtg at the Oblong in New York Government. Abigail Ferriss widow who several settled within the verge of your meeting.

16/9/1767. To Phila MMtg. Mary Richardson, clear of marriage engagements.

11/11/1767. To MMtg on Nantucket. Sarah Barney companion to our esteemed Friend Comfort Hoag in her religious visit.

11/11/1767. To MMtg at Hampton, New Hampshire. Esteemed Friend Comfort Hoag in her religious visit.

The following certificate is crossed through with an X. 13/1/1768. To Concord MMtg. Alexander Forman, wife Esther and five children, Mary, Elisabeth, Rachel, John and Susanna. Alexander for some years past has by mismanaging his outward affairs fell considerably short of paying his debts, for which with other misconduct her made an acknowledgment ...Mary is clear of marriage engagements. [Returned for an amendment]

16/3/1768. To MMtg at New Garden. Lydia wife of John Warner who lately came recommended from you to us being now returned - and dau Mary.

13/4/1768. To MMtg at Concord. Jonathan Yarnall, a child who lives with a Friend of your meeting.

15/6/1768. To MMtg of Duck Creek. L--- Janney who sometime ago came recommended from you as an apprentice who has served part of this time.

15/6/1768. To Newgarden MMtg. Mary Starr, clear of marriage engagements.

15/6/1768. To Darby MMtg. Henry Hayes and his five children, Magdalen, Elisabeth, Mary, Margaret and Henry. His oldest daus, Magdalen and Elisabeth are clear of marriage engagements.

13/7/1768. To New Garden MMtg. Ann Bryan.

15/6/1768. To MMtg at Phila. James Yarnall, clear of marriage engagements.
10/8/1768. To MMtg at Nottingham. Jeremiah Brown, clear of marriage engagements.
13/7/1768. To Falls MMtg. Mary Buckley wife of Phineas Buckley.
15/9/1768. To Darby MMtg. William Horne Junr., having served out his apprenticeship; clear of marriage engagements.
14/9/1768. To Gunpowder MMtg. John Brown; clear of marriage engagements.
14/9/1768. To Concord MMtg. Aaron Forman; clear of marriage engagements.
10/12/1768. To Duck Creek MMtg. Hannah Harris; clear of marriage engagements.
12/10/1768. To Fairfax MMtg in Virginia. Jesse Woodward Junr.; clear of marriage engagements.
14/12/1768. To Salem MMtg. Betty Woodnutt wife of Jonathan Woodnutt with her two young children, Mary and Betty Wilson.
14/12/1768. To MMtg at New Garden. Simon Gregg, clear of marriage engagements.
13/4/1768. Alexander Forman, wife Esther and five children, Mary, Elisabeth, Rachel, John and Susanna. Some years past Alexander by imprudently engaging in business he was not qualified for; became unable to pay his debts, although he gave up his effects to his creditors and made satisfaction in some degree for his missteps. Part of his debts remain unpaid. Mary is clear of marriage engagements.
11/1/1769. To MMtg at Concord. Miriam Forman, clear of marriage engagements.
15/2/1769. To Friends in Barbados. Isaac Harvey to reside on your Island for some time on account of Trade.
15/3/1769. To MMtg at Mamaraneck in New York Government. Elisabeth Ferriss, clear of marriage engagements.
12/4/1769. To Deer Creek MMtg, Maryland. David Scholifield, wife Rachel, and three children, Samuel, John and Enoch.
14/6/1769. To Phila MMtg. Sarah Wells, wife of Edward Wells.
14/6/1769. To MMtg in Grace Church Street or elsewhere in London. Goldsmith Folwell,

going to London concerning some temporal affairs.

12/7/1769. To MMtg in Phila. Jonathan and Miriam Cu...ad who are bound to different Friends within the compass of your meeting.

12/7/1769. To New Garden MMtg. Isaac Johnson being returned to settle within the compass of your meeting. Clear of marriage engagements.

11/10/1769. To New Garden MMtg. George Starr.

15/11/1769. To Cane Creek MMtg in Orange Co., North Carolina. Joseph Cloud.

13/12/1769. To MMtg in Phila. Enoch Welsh, bound an apprentice.

13/12/1769. To MMtg in Phila. Cephas Dawes son of Edward Dawes, an apprentice.

11/4/1770. To MMtg at Duck Creek. Timothy Hanson having served out his apprenticeship is returned to your meeting. Clear of marriage engagements.

11/4/1770. To Warrington MMtg. Vincent Pilkinton, wife Rebecca and two children, Thomas and Richard.

12/9/1770. To MMtg in Phila. James Brown for his son Israel who he hath placed as an apprentice to a Friend within the compass of your meeting.

13/2/1771. To Darby MMtg. Thomas Laycock, clear of marriage engagements.

To Duck Creek MMtg in Kent co., Delaware re Friend Jane Farson who sometime since removed herself from you and had your certificate to Friends of Savoy MMtg, London and remained there some time and then acquainted them with her intention of removing to within the compass of our MMtg and now she hath acquainted us of her intention to remove again to you and requests our certificate. Clear of engagements of marriage that we know of here. 21/2/1771

13/3/1771. To Kennett MMtg. James Kightly and Elisabeth his wife, son Isaac.

12/6/1771. To MMtg at Phila. Margarett Elliot about to remove with her husband.

14/8/1771. To Dear Creek MMtg in Maryland. Moses Forman, clear of marriage engagements.

10/7/1771. To MMtg at Phila. Caleb Bickham, wife Rachel and their children, Abel, Thomas, Abiah and Joseph, also an apprentice girl named Mary Penyard.

11/12/1771. To Phila MMtg. Jane Wilson who has for some years past resided with her mother Sarah Wilson, widow, within the compass of your meeting.

13/11/1771. To MMtg in Phila. Abraham Conrod who we are informed is placed under the care of a Friend within the compass of your meeting.

11/12/1771. To Cecil MMtg in Maryland. Thomas Wilson who is placed with a Friend of your meeting.

15/1/1772. To MMtg at Gunpowder, Maryland. Elisabeth Colegate being returned to reside within the compass of your meeting.

12/2/1772. To MMtg in Phila. Benjamin Chandler, Junr., clear of marriage engagements.

12/2/1772. To Duck Creek MMtg. Silvia Sipple who was recommended to us as an apprentice to a Friend of our Meeting and is returned to live within the compass of your meeting.

11/3/1772. To MMtg at Phila. George Gray who is placed an apprentice to a Friend within the compass of your meeting.

13/5/1772. To Kennett MMtg. Esther Wilson dau of Joseph Wilson, clear of marriage engagements.

10/6/1772. To Kennett MMtg. Thomas Welsh.

13/7/1772. To Kennett MMtg. David Chandler having served out his apprenticeship. Clear of marriage engagements.

14/10/1772. To MMtg in Phila. William Jackson, who is bound apprentice to a Friend within the compass of your meeting.

11/11/1772. To Phila MMtg. Sarah Carrington, clear of marriage engagements.

16/12/1772. To Cecil MMtg, Maryland. Hannah wife of Joseph Canby.

16/12/1772. To Kennett MMtg. Elisabeth Kightley and her two children, Isaac and Deborah.

15/12/1772. To Gwynedd MMtg. Elijah Evans who came here recommended with Caleb Byrnes.

13/1/1773. To Duck Creek MMtg. Ann Farson, clear of marriage engagements.

13/1/1773. To Third Haven, Maryland. Benjamin Parvin, wife Sarah and their dau Mary.

16/6/1773. To Kennett MMtg. Betty Woodnutt, clear of marriage engagements.

16/6/1773. To Phila MMtg. James Brown, bound an apprentice to a Friend within the compass of your meeting.

14/4/1773. To Darby MMtg. Henry Paschall, wife Ann and two children, Francis and Margret.

4/8/1773. To Phila MMtg. Richard Humphries. (owns Negroes).

13/9/1773. To Kennett MMtg. Elisabeth and Martha Stewart who are placed with different Friends within the compass of your meeting.

13/10/1773. To Cecil MMtg. Susanna Newlin who is returned to live with her father within the compass of your meeting.

12/1/1774. To Hopewell MMtg. James Wright being returned to live within the compass of your meeting.

13/4/1774. To Phila MMtg. Rumford Dawes and Mary his wife and dau Martha.

13/4/1774. To Phila MMtg. Jonathan Dawes, clear of marriage engagements.

13/4/1774. To Phila MMtg. Abijah Dawes, clear of marriage engagements.

13/4/1774. To New Garden MMtg. Susanna Thatcher, clear of marriage engagements.

11/5/1774. To Goshen MMtg. Alexander Dean.

11/8/1774. To Chesterfield MMtg in New Jersey. William Dean.

15/6/1774. To Concord MMtg. Nathan Sharpless, being returned to live within the compass of your meeting, clear of marriage engagements.

15/6/1774. To Duck Creek MMtg. Abel Janny, having returned to settle within the compass of your meeting, clear of marriage engagements.

10/8/1774. To Kennett MMtg. Jno. Way, wife Hannah and their seven children, Thomas, Phebe, Martha, Ann, Hannah, Mary and Lidya.

12/10/1774. To Phila MMtg. Joseph Webb who came recommended to us from your meeting about 8 years since, in about a year after as near as we can recollect he went to the West Indies, is lately returned. Clear of marriage engagements.

12/10/1774. To MMtg of Newgarden. George Carsan, clear of marriage engagements.

16/11/1774. To Newgarden MMtg. Susannah Harlan, a young woman who lately came recommended from you and residing a short time amongst us, clear of marriage engagements.

11/1/1775. To Phila MMtg. Sarah Hurst, clear of marriage engagements.

15/3/1775. To Duck Creek MMtg. Phebe Dickinson. Her husband about 4 years since went away and left considerable debts unpaid which yet remain; she is clear of debt of her own contracting since he left her as far as appears.

12/4/1775. To Phila MMtg. Benjamin Bryan, clear of marriage engagements.

10/5/1775. To Duck Creek MMtg. Mary wife of William Corbit. She was out going in marriage for which she has made satisfaction.

14/6/1775. To Phila MMtg. William Zane, having served out his apprenticeship is returned. Clear of marriage engagements.

12/7/1775. To Bradford MMtg. Benjamin Few, clear of marriage engagements.

16/8/1775. To Newgarden MMtg. Rebekah Chambers having accompanied a committee of this meeting in a visit to the families of Friends.

16/8/1775. To MMtg in Northern Dist. of Phila. Susanna Swett, widow.

13/9/1775. To Cecil MMtg, Maryland. Joseph Wilkinson.

15/11/1775. To MMtg for the Northern Dist. of Phila. Ann Jackson (clear of marriage engagements) and three children, Joseph, Elisabeth and Daniel Jackson.

13/8/1775. To Nottingham MMtg. Nathaniel ---, an apprentice.

10/1/1776. To Kennet MMtg. Hannah Wilson.

13/3/1776. To Phila MMtg. Benjamin Harvey, who is placed with Rumford Dawes a Friend within the compass of your meeting.

10/4/1776. To Newgarden MMtg. Lidia Carsan wife of George Carsan.

10/4/1776. To Nottingham MMtg. Jeremiah Carter for his dau Mary Carter.

15/5/1776. To Duck Creek MMtg. Jonathan Rowland, having served out his apprenticeship and being returned.

13/5/1776. To Third Haven MMtg, Maryland. Esteemed Friend Mary Berry who is removed to settle with her husband within the compass of your meeting.
12/6/1776. To Nottingham MMtg. John Hill and wife Ann and their two young children.
10/7/1776. To MMtg at Concord. Isaac Williams, Junior, clear of marriage engagements.
10/7/1776. To MMtg at Concord. Isaac Williams and Lydia his wife and their two children, Ennion and Mary.
10/7/1776. To Concord MMtg. Hannah Williams, clear of marriage engagements.
10/7/1776. To MMtg at Concord. Lydia Williams, clear of marriage engagements.
18/7/1776. To Newgarden MMtg in North Carolina. Stephen Hewet, clear of marriage engagements.
14/8/1776. To Newgarden MMtg. Hadly Johnson, clear of marriage engagements.
11/9/1776. To Newgarden MMtg. Mary Starr who is again removed to live within the verge of your meeting; after her short stay here, clear of marriage engagements.
11/9/1776. To MMtg of the Southern Dist. of Phila. Ann wife of William ...?
11/9/1776. To Goshen MMtg. Joseph Yarnall, clear of marriage engagements.
18/11/1776. To MMtg at Nottingham. Thomas Stubbs, clear of marriage engagements.
13/11/1776. To Newgarden MMtg. Samuel Denock, clear of marriage engagements.
11/12/1776. To Concord MMtg. Joseph Dingee, clear of marriage engagements.
12/2/1777. To MMtg in Phila. for the Northern Dist. Mary Littler, clear of marriage engagements.
20/3/1777. To Bradford MMtg. Richard Batten Junr. (after a short stay amongst us).
11/6/1777. To Duck Creek MMtg. Ann Corbitt being settled with her husband.
11/6/1777. To Kennett MMtg. Orpah Cloud being returned to live within the compass of your meeting, clear of marriage engagements.
11/6/1777. To Kennett MMtg. Betty Swain being returned, clear of marriage engagements.
11/6/1777. To Kennett MMtg. Ann Morgan, clear of marriage engagements.

16/7/1777. To Newgarden MMtg. Hannah Batten,
clear of marriage engagements.
16/7/1777. To Kennett MMtg. Elisabeth Batten,
clear of marriage engagements.
12/11/1777. To Concord MMtg. Michael Shipon,
clear of marriage engagements.
15/10/1777. To Haddonfield MMtg. Elgas Brown who
is placed an apprentice to a Friend of your
meeting.
15/10/1777. To MMtg at Third Haven in Maryland.
Samuel Troth, clear of marriage engagements.
11/3/1778. To Nottingham MMtg. Stephen Yarnall.
11/3/1778. To Nottingham MMtg. Edward Folwell.
4/3/1778. To Concord MMtg. Joseph Guest.
11/3/1778. To MMtg at Deer Creek. William
Morgan, clear of marriage engagements.
11/2/1778. To Concord MMtg. George Martin, wife
Elisabeth, and their child, Sarah.
13/5/1778. To Kennett MMtg. Vincent Stubbs,
clear of marriage engagements.
13/5/1778. To Newgarden MMtg. Martha Whitelock,
clear of marriage engagements.
13/5/1778. To Newgarden MMtg. Phebe Johnson,
clear of marriage engagements.
10/6/1778. To Nottingham MMtg. Thomas Waren(?),
clear of marriage engagements.
10/6/1778. To Gunpowder MMtg. Mary Hill, clear
of marriage engagements.
10/6/1778. To MMtg at Deer Creek. Jesse Morgan,
clear of marriage engagements.
15/5/1778. To Nottingham MMtg. Mary Chandlee
wife of Benja. Chandlee.
12/8/1778. To MMtg at Duck Creek. Mary Preston
(clear of marriage engagements) and son
Jonas.
12/8/1778. To Gunpowder MMtg, Maryland. John
Smith.
14/10/1778. To Phila MMtg for the Southern Dist.
Children of Aaron Musgraves Junr., viz.,
four children, Alice (clear of marriage
engagements), Mary, James and Israel
Musgrave.
14/10/1778. To Newgarden MMtg. John Milhouse,
wife Margarett and two daus, Ruth and Lidia,
clear of marriage engagements.
12/11/1778. To Duck Creek MMtg. Thomas Lea,
clear of marriage engagements.

11/11/1778. To Salem MMtg. Rebekah Lewden, clear of marriage engagements.
4/11/1778. To Duck Creek MMtg. Hannah Canby, clear of marriage engagements.
13/1/1779. To Concord MMtg. Rachel Stoops; has lately attended meetings at Chichester.
13/1/1779. To MMtg for Southern Dist. of Phila. Elisabeth Wharten wife of Charles Wharton.
10/3/1779. To MMtg in Phila for the Northern Dist. Hannah Wood---, clear of marriage engagements.
12/5/1779. To Phila MMtg. Amey Bonsall, clear of marriage engagements.
16/6/1779. To Nottingham MMtg. Benjamin Hough and son Benjamin, both clear of marriage engagements.
16/6/1779. To Hoosick and Saratoga MMtg. Hephzibah Coffin, clear of marriage engagements.
16/6/1779. To Chesterfield MMtg. Sarah Clayton, clear of marriage engagements.
To Bradford MMtg. Alexander Forman, wife Esther and their two children, John and Susanna.
13/10/1779. To Uwchland MMtg. Sarah Daugherty, clear of marriage engagements.
21/1/1780. To Duck Creek MMtg. William Brown, wife Dorcas and their two children, Elisabeth and Mary Macy Brown.
12/1/1780. To Salem MMtg. Elisa. wife of William Goodwin and three of her children, Hesther (clear of marriage engagements), Elisabeth (clear of marriage engagements) and Joseph Brown.
12/1/1780. To Haverford MMtg. Margaret wife of Robert Finley.
15/3/1780. To Nottingham MMtg. Benja. and Hannah Jacob, children of Benja. Jacobs, dec'd.
12/4/1780. To Kennet MMtg. Elizabeth Hugou.
10/5/1780. To MMtg at Concord. Mary Jackson, clear of marriage engagements.
12/7/1780. To Concord MMtg. Sarah Reynolds Junior, clear of marriage engagements.
16/8/1780. To Phila MMtg. Samuel Andrew, an apprentice with a friend of your meeting.
Endorsement on Shem Hills certificate 13/9/1780. To Dear Creek MMtg in Maryland. Shem Hill son of William Hill being returned.

13/9/1780. To Concord MMtg. William Starr Junr., apprentice with a friend of your meeting.
13/9/1780. To Kennet MMtg. Rebecca Morgan, clear of marriage engagements.
15/11/1780. To Third Haven. Jeremiah Cook, clear of marriage engagements.
13/12/1780. To Kennet MMtg. Richard Painter, clear of marriage engagements.
13/12/1780. To Cecil MMtg, Maryland. Mary Mifflin after a short stay.
10/1/1781. To Phila MMtg. Edward Dawes son of Jonathan Dawes who lives with his father.
11/4/1781. To Gunpowder MMtg in Maryland. Samuel Gray who has for some time resided with his brother in Baltimore Town who came recommended to us from Phila MMtg when young.
16/5/1781. To Middle Town MMtg in Bucks Co. Hannah Woolston, clear of marriage engagements.
16/5/1781. To Falls MMtg in Bucks Co. Sarah Shipley, clear of marriage engagements.
13/6/1781. To MMtg in Phila for the Southern Dist. Jeremiah Lewden, he being placed to school within the compass of your meeting.
10/10/1781. To Concord MMtg. Sarah, wife of Thomas Newlin and dau Mary Berry.
10/10/1781. To Phila MMtg. Mary Green (clear of marriage engagements) and four children, John, Ellis, Ann and Sarah Green.
14/11/1781. To Phila MMtg. Abigail West, a young woman.
12/12/1781. To Concord MMtg. William Waron, clear of marriage engagements.
12/12/1781. To Chesterfield MMtg, West New Jersey. James Robinson, Junr., clear of marriage engagements.
12/12/1781. To Cecil MMtg in Maryland. Elizabeth Devenport.
12/12/1781. To Duck Creek MMtg. Rachel Byrnes, clear of marriage engagements.
12/12/1781. To Kennet MMtg. Ann Wilson, clear of marriage engagements.
13/3/1782. To Goshen MMtg. Simon Johnson for his son Daniel Johnson, an apprentice.
12/6/1782. To Concord MMtg. Thomas Reynolds, clear of marriage engagements.

12/6/1782. To Newgarden MMtg. David Miller being returned, having served as an apprentice.
10/7/1782. To Gunpowder MMtg in Maryland. Robert Woodcock and wife Deborah. Some years ago they were disowned by this meeting for going out in marriage but they have lately made satisfaction.
14/8/1782. To Phila MMtg. Joseph Sharpless, clear of marriage engagements.
11/9/1782. To MMtg in Phila for the Northern Dist. Mary Marriot, wife of Thomas Marriot.
11/9/1782. To Kennett MMtg. Isaac Mendenhall Junr, who has lately made satisfaction for going out in his marriage for which he was some years past disowned by this meeting.
16/10/1782. To Concord MMtg. Harlon Cloud who some time ago returned to live within the compass of your meeting. Clear of marriage engagements.
13/11/1782. To Nottingham MMtg. Thomas Wearing, clear of marriage engagements.
13/11/1782. To Phila MMtg. Isaac Andrew, being placed an apprentice.
11/12/1782. To Nottingham MMtg. Elizabeth Underhill wife of John Underhill.
15/1/1783. To Phila MMtg. Samuel Dickinson.
12/2/1783. To MMtg at Third Haven in Maryland. David Hull, clear of marriage engagements.
12/3/1783. To MMtg in Phila. Isaac Harvey, being placed with his uncle within the compass of your meeting.
16/4/1783. To MMtg at Concord. Elizabeth Atkinson, clear of marriage engagements.
14/5/1783. To Duck Creek MMtg. David Farson.
6/11/1783. To Kennett MMtg. Joseph Quaintance, wife Susanah and their two children, Samuel and William Quaintance.
11/6/1783. To MMtg of the Northern Dist. in Phila. Elizabeth Osborn and daughters, Hannah, Sarah, Lydia, Elizabeth, Ann and Susanna Osborn. Her daus are adults and clear of marriage engagements.
13/8/1783. To Fairfax MMtg in Virginia. Andrew Scholfield, clear of marriage engagements.
13/8/1783. To Duck Creek MMtg. Roseannah Price, wife of Joseph Price and her dau Hannah Ashburnham.

12/11/1783. To Nottingham MMtg. Thomas Waring, clear of marriage engagements.
12/11/1783. To Phila MMtg. John Elliot, clear of marriage engagements.
14/1/1784. To MMtg for the Southern Dist. in Phila. Susanna Bennet, young woman, clear of marriage engagements.
14/4/1784. To Newgarden MMtg. Thomas Hutton, Junr., clear of marriage engagements.
14/4/1784. To MMtg in Phila for the Southern Dist. Sarah Bennet, clear of marriage engagements.
12//5/1784. To Concord MMtg. James Pierce, wife Miriam and their two children, Mary and Richard.
12/5/1784. To Cecil MMtg, Maryland. Jonathan Devonport, clear of marriage engagements.
12/5/1784. To Kennet MMtg. Aquilla Jones, clear of marriage engagements.
16/6/1784. Bradford MMtg. Moses Mershall, clear of marriage engagements.
14/7/1784. MMtg for the Northern Dist. in Phila. Sarah Litler.
14/7/1784. To Phila MMtg. Joshua Byrnes, clear of marriage engagements.
14/7/1784. To Chester MMtg. Isaac Wood after a short stay being the last of his apprenticeship, clear of marriage engagements.
14/7/1784. To Newgarden MMtg. Job Sinclair and son Abraham Sinclair, infant. Sickness of himself and family has reduced his circumstances; clear of marriage engagements.
11/8/1784. To Newgarden MMtg. Hannah Hadly.
15/9/1784. To MMtg of the Southern Dist. in Phila. Moses Bryen, wife Mary, and their four children, Elizabeth, Thomas, James and Joseph.
15/9/1784. To Chester MMtg. George Harris, clear of marriage engagements.
15/9/1784. To Darby MMtg. Keziah Sinklear, dau of Job Sinlear, being placed with her grandfather, Abraham Musgrove.
13/10/1784. To Fairfax MMtg. Abraham Randall, wife Jane, and their five children, Ann, Elizabeth, Mary, Rachel and Abraham.

13/10/1784. To MMtg for the Southern Dist. in Phila. Daniel Byrnes and Dinah his wife and their two young children, Joseph and Caleb.
13/10/1784. To MMtg for the Southern Dist. in Phila. Lydia Byrne dau of Daniel Byrnes, clear of marriage engagements.
13/10/1784. To Bradford MMtg. Daniel Warner, clear of marriage engagements.
10/11/1784. To MMtg in Phila for the Northern Dist. Jonathan Harvey, clear of marriage engagements.
10/11/1784. To Southern government. Hugh Judge on a religious visit.
15/12/1784. To Horsham MMtg. Sarah Hurst, clear of marriage engagements.
15/12/1784. To Gunpowder MMtg. Grace Mason, clear of marriage engagements.
12/1/1785. To Concord MMtg. Samuel Marshall with his three young children, William, James and Jane.
16/2/1785. To Nottingham MMtg. Ruth Pyle, clear of marriage engagements.
16/2/1785. To Concord MMtg. Samuel Townsend.
16/3/1785. To Phila MMtg. Caleb Lowns, clear of marriage engagements.
11/5/1785. To Kennett MMtg. Elizabeth Taylor.
11/5/1785. To Chester MMtg. Susannah Dougherty, clear of marriage engagements.
11/5/1785. To Chester MMtg. Susanna Dougherty Junr., clear of marriage engagements.
11/5/1785. To Mount Holley MMtg. Lydia Shirly, to removed with her husband.
11/5/1785. To Concord MMtg. Eli Few.
11/5/1785. To MMtg of Phila for the Northern Dist. Isaac Stroud, wife Lydia and their three children, Thomas, Mary and Elizabeth.
15/6/1785. To New Garden MMtg. William Chambers, clear of marriage engagements.
15/6/1785. To Chester MMtg. Mary Cobourn, clear of marriage engagements.
14/9/1785. To Darby MMtg. Nehemiah Davis and wife Ellinor, and six children, Mary, Sarah, Elizabeth, William, Dorrithy and Susanah Davis. Since the above application Nehemiah is deceased. After a short stay with us. The young women clear of marriage engagements.
14/9/1785. To New Garden MMtg. Hannah Hurford, clear of marriage engagements.

14/9/1785. To Sadsbury MMtg. Abraham Reynolds, clear of marriage engagements.
14/9/1785. To New Garden MMtg. Rachel Bernard, clear of marriage engagements.
12/10/1785. To Concord MMtg. Job Lancaster.
12/10/1785. To Gunpowder MMtg in Maryland. John and Tacy Mitchell and dau Mary, infant.
16/11/1785. To MMtg of Friends for Southern Dist. in Phila. Daniel Britt, clear of marriage engagements.
16/11/1785. To Crooked Run MMtg in Virginia. Jonathan Lukens, clear of marriage engagements.
14/12/1785. To Third Haven MMtg in Maryland. Betty wife of John Dickenson who has condemned her marriage by the assistance of a Priest and much deviating from plainness in dress for which she was disowned by this meeting several years past.
11/1/1786. To Abington MMtg. Benjamin Harper, clear of marriage engagements.
11/1/1786. To New Garden MMtg. James Harlan, wife Elizabeth and their children, Ellwood, Hannah and Mary.
15/2/1786. To Kennett MMtg. Ruth Nichols wife of Samuel Nichols.
15/2/1786. To Kennett MMtg. William Shipley son of William Shipley, clear of marriage engagements.
15/3/1786. To New Garden MMtg. Joseph Newlin son of Ellis Newlin, being placed with his uncle Benjamin Mason.
15/3/1786. To Nottingham MMtg. Sarah and Betty Jacob, daus of Benjamin Jacob, dec'd.
12/4/1786. To Horsham MMtg. Mary Melone wife of James Melone.
12/4/1786. To Goshen MMtg. John Fairlamb and wife Susanna and dau Rebeccah.
10/5/1786. To Concord MMtg. Abraham Jeffryes, clear of marriage engagements.
10/5/1786. To MMtg for the Southern Dist. in Phila. Sarah West, clear of marriage engagements.
10/5/1786. To Kennett MMtg. John Gibson and Mary his wife and their four children, Thomas, Joshua, Joseph and Betty.

10/5/1786. To Kennet MMtg. John Phillips and wife Lydia and their two children, Mahlon and William.

14/6/1786. To Darby MMtg. Abraham Bonsall, clear of marriage engagements.

14/6/1786. To Concord MMtg. Joseph Hatton, clear of marriage engagements.

14/6/1786. To New Garden MMtg. Phillip Yarnall, an apprentice to a Friend within the compass of your meeting.

14/6/1786. To Kennet MMtg. Eli Phillips, clear of marriage engagements.

12/7/1786. To Cecil MMtg in Maryland. Thomas Browning, a minor who some time past came recommended to us being place an apprentice with a man not a member of our Society.

16/8/1786. To MMtg of Phila for the Southern Dist. Timcon Warner, he being placed an apprentice within the compass of your meeting by his father who is not a member to a man of another Society.

16/8/1786. To MMtg in New York. Phebe Dickenson for her son Carson Dickenson who has removed to reside with his uncle within the compass of your meeting.

11/10/1786. To Third Haven MMtg. John Dickinson.

15/11/1786. To Uwchland MMtg. Susannah Hatton, a minor.

15/11/1786. To MMtg for the Southern Dist. in Phila. Elizabeth Hobson being removed with her husband.

15/11/1786. To Middletown MMtg, Bucks Co. Elizabeth Woolston junr.

13/12/1786. To Nottingham MMtg. Thomas Waring, clear of marriage engagements.

10/1/1787. To Concord MMtg. Samuel Morton Junr.

10/1/1787. To Kennet MMtg. Joshua Gibson and wife Lydia and their five small children, Hannah, John, Lydia, Deborah and Susanna.

14/3/1787. To MMtg at New Garden. Sarah Commons, wife of John Commons.

14/3/1787. To Concord MMtg. William Phillips, a minor, who is placed an apprentice to a Friend within the compass of your meeting.

14/3/1787. To Chester MMtg. Amos Bond, clear of marriage engagements.

11/4/1787. To MMtg at Guinedd. Levi Lukins, clear of marriage engagements.

11/4/1787. To Duck Creek MMtg. Thomas Foulke, clear of marriage engagements.
16/5/1787. To Exeter MMtg. Ephraim Parvin, clear of marriage engagements.
16/5/1787. To Chester MMtg. Benjamin Yarnall, minor.
16/5/1787. To Phila MMtg. Mary West, clear of marriage engagements.
11/4/1787. To Chester MMtg. Catherine Hill wife of Peter Hill.
13/6/1787. To MMtg for the Northern Dist of Phila. Sarah Price, being removed to live with a Friend within the compass of your meeting.
13/6/1787. To Gunpowder MMtg in Maryland. Thomas Byrnes, clear of marriage engagements.
13/6/1787. To MMtg for the Southern Dist. of Phila. Ann Evans, clear of marriage engagements.
13/6/1787. To Concord MMtg. James Marshall and wife Margret.
13/6/1787. To Goshen MMtg. John Saunders for his son Amos, he being placed an apprentice.
13/6/1787. To MMtg for the Southern Dist Phila. Rachel Jacobs, clear of marriage engagements.
13/6/1787. To Duck Creek MMtg. Thomas Stroud, clear of marriage engagements.
13/6/1787. To Cecil MMtg. Sarah Troth, clear of marriage engagements.
11/7/1787. To Darby MMtg. James Andrews, clear of marriage engagements.
11/7/1787. To MMtg in New York. Isaac Sharpless, clear of marriage engagements.
11/7/1787. To MMtg in New York. Carson Dickenson, hath removed with the consent of his mother.
11/7/1787. To Kennet MMtg. Jehu Dixon, clear of marriage engagements.
11/7/1787. To Chester MMtg. Phebe Iddons, minor.
15/8/1787. To Salem MMtg. Joseph P---, minor.
15/8/1787. To Phila MMtg. Elizabeth Forman, clear of marriage engagements.
12/9/1787. To Westland MMtg. John Dixon and wife Mary, and their three young children, Rebecca, Elizabeth and Susanna.

12/9/1787. To Phila MMtg for the Southern Dist. William Byrnes (clear of marriage engagements) and son Thomas.

10/10/1787. To Concord MMtg. Nicholas Newlin who some years ago came recommended by you.

10/10/1787. To Kennet MMtg. William Tate, minor, to reside with a Friend within the compass of your meeting.

10/10/1787. To Haverford MMtg. Humphrey Ellis, clear of marriage engagements.

14/11/1787. To Phila for Northern Dist. Aaron Roberts, clear of marriage engagements.

14/11/1787. To Concord MMtg. Susanna Martin wife of Joseph Martin and her two children, Mordecai and Lazarus.

14/11/1787. To Third Haven MMtg. Sarah Wickersham being removed with her husband.

12/12/1787. To New Garden MMtg. Sarah Stubbs, clear of marriage engagements.

12/12/1787. To Exeter MMtg. Hannah Eddings being removed with her husband, and her five children, Jane, Hannah, Samuel, Thomas and Rachel.

12/12/1787. To Abington MMtg. Susanna Canby, a child who is placed with a relation within the compass of your meeting.

3/2/1788. To MMtg in Phila for the Northern Dist. Caleb Starr who is put apprentice to Joseph James within the compass of your meeting.

13/2/1788. To Kennet MMtg. Rebecca, Simon and David Johnson, children of Simon Johnson, dec'd., who are placed with their relations within the compass of your meeting.

12/3/1778. To Kennet MMtg. Hermon and John Gregg.

16/4/1778. To Horsham MMtg. Benjamin Longstreth, clear of marriage engagements.

14/5/1788. To Cecil MMtg in Maryland. Phebe Harlan wife of Henry Harlan (who left her some years since).

14/5/1788. To Cecil MMtg. Gerard Blackford, wife Sarah and three children, Joseph, Jacob and Lydia Blackford.

11/6/1788. To MMtg in Phila for the Southern Dist. Alexander Wilson, clear of marriage engagements.

11/6/1788. To MMtg in Phila for the Northern
Dist. Benjamin Canby son of Benjamin Canby,
placed an apprentice to Samuel Taylor within
the compass of your meeting.
11/6/1788. To Newgarden MMtg. Jacob Wood, wife
Isable and their seven children, Joseph,
John, Elizabeth, Jacob, Joshua, Enos and
Lewis.
16/7/1788. To MMtg in Phila for the Northern
Dist. John Knowles, minor, placed an
apprentice to John Gibbons, member of your
meeting.
16/7/1788. To MMtg of Darby. Alice Serrel, clear
of marriage engagements.
13/8/1778. To Phila MMtg. Rachel James wife of
John James being removed with her husband.
13/8/1788. To Mount Holly MMtg. Sarah Hughes who
has removed with her husband.
10/9/1788. To Westland MMtg. David Townsend,
clear of marriage engagements.
15/10/1788. To Kennett MMtg. James Lea Junr. and
wife Elizabeth and their four children,
John, James, Thomas and Margaret Lea.
15/10/1788. To Kennett MMtg. Joannah Davis who
has removed to reside with her husband.
15/10/1788. To Kennet MMtg. Esther Griffith.
15/10/1788. To Darby MMtg. Mary Andrews, clear
of marriage engagements.
15/10/1788. To Chester MMtg. Susanna Dutton,
minor.
15/10/1788. To Westland MMtg. James Reynolds and
wife Hannah and their two children, Henry
and Sarah Way Reynolds.
12/11/1788. To Kennet MMtg. Evan Bailey and wife
Hannah.
12/11/1788. To Westland MMtg. Solomon Phillips
and wife Martha.
12/11/1788. To Westland MMtg. Mary Bostick about
to remove with her husband and her four
young children, Lardner, Mary, John and
Kezia Bostick.
12/11/1788. To Concord MMtg. Mary Seal wife of
John Polas Seal, removed with her husband.
10/12/1788. To Kennet MMtg. Thomas and Jane
Temple and son Edward and dau Jane.
11/12/1788. To MMtg of Cape May. Hannah Townsend
being removed to live with her husband and

her 5 children, Elizabeth, Sarah, John, Isaac and Ann Townsend.

10/12/1788. To MMtg in Dublin or elsewhere in Ireland. James Robinson, junior, on account of trade.

14/1/1789. To Middleton MMtg. Lydia Williams, residing with her husband.

11/2/1789. To Bradford MMtg. Isaac Mendenhall, clear of marriage engagements.

11/2/1789. To Cecil MMtg. Margret, wife of Joseph Wilkinson.

11/2/1789. To Duck Creek MMtg. Hannah Ashburnham.

11/2/1789. To Bradford MMtg. John Kendall and wife Mary, and dau Deborah.

11/3/1789. To Duck Creek MMtg. James Cox, clear of marriage engagements.

15/4/1789. To Friend in New York and New England governments. Antient and esteemed Friend Zachariah Ferriss.

15/4;/1789. To Newgarden MMtg. Catharine wife of William Richards to live with her husband.

15/4/1790. To Guinedd MMtg. Edward Stroud, son of Edward Stroud, dec'd., minor.

13/5/1789. To Friends in New York and New England Governments. Robert Johnson to accompany ancient Friend Zachariah Ferriss.

13/5/1789. To Concord MMtg. Thomas Wilson, wife Hannah and son George Wilson, minor.

13/5/1789. To Kennet MMtg. Martha Levis, clear of marriage engagements.

13/5/1789. To Kennet MMtg. Hannah Levis, clear of marriage engagements.

13/5/1789. To Kennet MMtg. Phebe Levis, clear of marriage engagements.

10/6/1789. To Salem MMtg. Ann Lightfoot, clear of marriage engagements.

10/6/1789. To Chester MMtg. Ann Griffith, clear of marriage engagements.

15/7/1789. To Haverford MMtg. Nathan Jones.

15/7/1789. To Murderkill MMtg. Samuel Foulke, clear of marriage engagements.

15/7/1789. To Phila. MMtg. Martha Chapman, clear of marriage engagements.

12/8/1789. To Phila. MMtg Elizabeth Blackford, junior, clear of marriage engagements.

12/8/1789. To Northern Dist. in Phila. Susana Wilson, clear of marriage engagements.

12/8/1789. To Westland MMtg. Isaac Gregg, having for a considerable time resided at Pittsburgh, clear of marriage engagements.
16/9/1789. To Phila. MMtg. Benjamin Stackhous, minor, placed an apprentice within the compass of your meeting.
16/9/1789. To Motherkiln MMtg. Mary Hanson, being returned to her former habitation, clear of marriage engagements.
14/10/1789. To Uwchlan MMtg. Phebe Jacobs, wife of Richard Jacobs, being removed to live with her husband.
14/10/1789. To Saratoga MMtg, New York Government. Abraham Reynolds, clear of marriage engagements.
11/11/1789. To Uwchlan MMtg. Isaac and Elizabeth Jackson and their two children, Sarah and Sidney Jackson.
11/11/1789. To Sadsbury MMtg. Samuel gibbons.
11/11/1789. To Middletown MMtg, Bucks Co. Richard and Eliezar Lundys, being young.
13/1/1790. To Friends of New York and New England Governments. Hugh Judge, religious visit.
14/4/1790. To Exeter MMtg. Samuel Wallace.
14/4/1790. To Friends of the Southern Governments. Ancient and esteemed Friend Zacharia Ferris, on a religious visit.
12/5/1790. To Friends of the Southern Governments, esteemed friend Gerard Blackford, to accompany Zachariah Ferris in his religious visit.
12/5/1790. To Chester MMtg. Ambrose Taylor and Mary his wife and their six children, Jacob, Mordecai, Stephen, Abijah, Peter and Mary Taylor.
16/6/1790. To Sadsbury MMtg. James Gibbons and Deborah his wife and their three children, Daniel, Rebecca and Rachel.
16/6/1790. To Saratoga MMtg. Samuel Reynolds, clear of marriage engagements.
16/6/1790. To Phila. MMtg. James and John Hill, minors.
16/6/1790. To New Garden MMtg. Joshua Stroud and Martha his wife and their three small children, Samuel, Caleb and Mary.
16/6/1790. To Bradford MMtg. James Kendall, clear of marriage engagements.

16/6/1790. To Chester MMtg. Mary Preston, clear of marriage engagements.

11/8/1790. To Sadsbury MMtg. Esteemed Friend Mary Gibbons, wife of Abraham Gibbons, to live with her husband.

15/9/1790. To MMtg at Darby. Ann Paschall, about to remove with her husband and her eight minor children, Mary, Ann, Elizabeth, Hannah, John, Thomas, Sarah, and Martha Paschall.

15/9/1790. To MMtg at Darby. Frances Paschall (female), clear of marriage engagements.

15/9/1790. To MMtg at Darby. Margaret Paschall, clear of marriage engagements.

15/9/1790. To Motherkill MMtg. Thomas Pennell (endorsement), who produced a certificate and in a few weeks after returned to reside within the compass of your meeting.

15/9/1790. To Cornwall MMtg in New York Government. Joshua Byrnes, clear of marriage engagements.

15/9/1790. To Cornwall MMtg in New York Government. Celeb Byrnes, Junr., clear of marriage engagements.

13/10/1790. To Uwchland MMtg. Alice Woodward, clear of marriage engagements.

13/10/1790. To MMtg at Warrington. Stephen Hayes, clear of marriage engagements.

10/11/1790. To MMtg at Kennett. John Sinkler, minor, with his master.

10/11/1790. To MMtg at Phila. Ann Hill for her son George Hill, being placed apprentice to a friend of your meeting.

15/12/1790. To Kennett MMtg. Lydia Seal, to reside a while within the compass of your meeting, clear of marriage engagements.

15/12/1790. To Darby MMtg. Mary Bonsall, wife of Abrm. Bonsall.

15/12/1790. To MMtg for the Northern Dist. of Phila. John Lewden for his son Josiah Lewden.

15/12/1790. To Duck Creek MMtg. Rachel Byrnes, clear of marriage engagements.

15/12/1790. To Horsham MMtg. Caleb Pierce, Junr., clear of marriage engagements.

16/2/1790. To MMtg of New Garden. Levi Lamburn, having served out his apprenticeship and

returned to reside within the compass of your meeting.
16/2/1791. To MMtg at Phila. Indorsement. William Stackhouse.
13/4/1791. To MMtg in Phila for the southern Dist. Jonathan Harvey, clear of marriage engagements.
13/4/1791. To Uwchlan MMtg. Solomon Fussell, clear of marriage engagements.
13/4/1791. to Third Haven MMtg, Maryland. Baynard Wilson, having served out his apprenticeship.
11/5/1791. To Phila. MMtg. Sarah Lundy, clear of marriage engagements.
11/5/1791. To Concord MMtg. Isaac Yearsley and Mary his wife and their three children, James, Isaac and Thomas.
11/5/1791. To Friends in Pennsylvania and New Jersey. Antient and esteemed Friend Zachariah Ferriss, religious visit.
15/6/1791. To MMtg at Concord. Ezekiel Wilson and wife Rachel, and their two children, Samuel and Peter Wilson.
13/7/1791. To MMtg in the Southern Dist. of Phila. Ann Brian and two children, Mary and David Bryan.
7/13/1791. To Concord MMtg. Oliver Canby who is placed an apprentice to a Friend of your meeting.
13/7/1791. To Concord MMtg. Elisha Starr, clear of marriage engagements.
10/8/1791. To Cornwall MMtg in the state of New York. John Andrews, clear of marriage engagements.
14/9/1791. To MMtg at Gunpowder. Edward Marshall, clear of marriage engagements.
14/9/1791. To Goshen MMtg. Jane Clayton, clear of marriage engagements.
12/10/1791. To Phila. MMtg for the Southern Dist. Ann Hill for her son Isaac Hill, minor.
12/10/1791. To Phila. MMtg for the Northern Dist. Mary Hill, minor.
12/10/1791. To MMtg at Deer Creek. Isaac Wilson, wife Susanna and young child Alisanna.
16/11/1791. To Concord MMtg. Thomas Wilson, Junior, clear of marriage engagements.

15/2/1792. To MMtg at Concord. Ephraim Yarnall for his son who hath put his son Holton Yarnall an apprentice within the compass of your meeting.
15/2/1792. To MMtg at Newgarden. Samuel Jackson, minor, who is placed with William Jackson, a Friend of your meeting.
15/2/1792. To MMtg at Gunpowder. Joseph and Thomas Jackson, minor children of John Jackson who have gone to reside with their father within the compass of your meeting.
15/2/1792. To MMtg at Third Haven. Mary Atkinson.
14/3/1792. To MMtg of Gunpowder. Rachel Jackson who is gone to reside with her father in Baltimore, clear of marriage engagements.
14/3/1792. To MMtg at Concord. Isaac Townsend, minor.
11/4/1792. To MMtg at Westland. Betty Johnson, having removed with her husband, Caleb Johnson.
16/5/1792. To Kennet MMtg. Ruth Logu, clear of marriage engagements.
16/5/1792. To Kennet MMtg. Jean Hollingsworth, clear of marriage engagements.
16/5/1792. To MMtg in Phila. Ann Hill, wife of John Hill, and four minor children, Joanna, Howard, Ann and Thomas.
16/5/1792. To Exeter MMtg. Martha Chapman, clear of marriage engagements.
11/7/1792. To MMtg at Cane Creek, North Carolina. Joshua Buckingham, clear of marriage engagements.
12/9/1792. To New Garden MMtg. William Seal, who is placed an apprentice to a Friend within the compass of your meeting.
12/9/1792. To Chester MMtg. John Kendal, wife Mary and their two young children, Jesse and Deborah.
12/9/1792. To MMtg at Pipe Creek [Maryland]. Ann Wright, being returned to reside within the compass of your meeting, clear of marriage engagements.
12/9/1792. To Bradford MMtg. Elizabeth Thomas, wife of John Thomas.
10/10/1792. To Bradford MMtg. John Sinkler, who is placed an apprentice within the compass of your meeting.

10/10/1792. To Bradford MMtg. Deborah Coope, having returned to live within the compass of your meeting.
10/10/1792. To MMtg in New York. Thomas Buckley, clear of marriage engagements.
10/10/1792. To Purchase MMtg, New York. Esteemed Friends Hugh and Susannah Judge and their children, Thomas, Hannah, Susannah, Margaret, Pheby, Esther and Rachel.
14/11/1792. To Nottingham MMtg. Ann Jones, wife of John Jones.
14/11/1792. To Purchase MMtg, State of New York. Margaret Reynolds, clear of marriage engagements.
14/11/1792. To MMtg at Duck Creek. 14/11/1792. Israel Corbit, son of Israel.
12/12/1792. To Kennet MMtg. Ann Peirce, clear of marriage engagements.
12/12/1792. To MMtg at Bradford. Sarah Bernard, being removed to reside with her husband within the compass of your meeting.
12/12/1792. To Sadsbury MMtg. Alice Evans, being returned to live within the compass of your meeting.
16/1/1793. To Kennet MMtg. Phebe Peirce.
16/1/1793. To Bradford MMtg. Elizabeth Coope wife of Samuel Cooper, Junr.
16/1/1793. To MMtg in Phila for the Northern Dist. Caleb Sheward, who is placed an apprentice to a Friend within the compass of your meeting.
13/2/1793. To MMtg for Northern Dist., Phila. John Lewden who is placed apprentice to a Friend of your Meeting, minor.
22/5/1793. To Kennet MMtg. John Sanders, junr. and wife Sarah.
22/5/1793. To MMtg for Northern Dist. Phila. Alice Temple being removed with her husband and her three children, Thomas, Mary and William Temple.
22/5/1793. To MMtg for the Northern Dist. Phila. Sarah Wilson about to remove with her husband.
12/6/1793. To MMtg for Northern Dist. Phila. Hannah Lundy.
12/6/1793. To MMtg of Middletown, Bucks Co. Elizabeth Lundy, dau of Hannah Lundy.

12/6/1793. To MMtg of Upper Springfield, New Jersey. Rachel Lundy, dau of Hannah Lundy.
12/6/1793. To MMtg at Sadsbury. James Jackson, Junr., clear of marriage engagements.
12/6/1793. To MMtg of Little York, PA. Hannah Phillips, clear of marriage engagements.
12/6/1793. To MMtg of Little York. Deborah Phillips, minor.
12/6/1793. To MMtg of Cecil [Maryland]. Jesse Hoops, clear of marriage engagements.
12/6/1793. To Goshen MMtg. John Saunders for his son Nathan Saunders, minor, who is placed an apprentice with a Friend of your meeting.
10/7/1793. To MMtg for the Northern Dist. Phila. Benjamin Woolston, clear of marriage engagements.
10/7/1793. To Concord MMtg. Hannah Hallowell, being removed with her husband, and her nine children, Margaret, Jesse, Joshua, Hannah, William, Joseph, Rebecah, James and John.
10/7/1793. To Cecil MMtg, Kent Co., Maryland. Sarah Wallace, clear of marriage engagements.
14/8/1793. To Rahway MMtg. Elizabeth Porter, clear of marriage engagements.
16/10/1793. To Kennett MMtg. David Chandler, clear of marriage engagements.
12/2/1794. To MMtg for the Southern Dist. Phila. William Harlan, clear of marriage engagements.
12/3/1794. To MMtg at Exeter. Esteemed Friends Jesse and Rachel Hains and their four minor children, Mary, Jacob, Reuben and Jesse Hains.
12/3/1793. To MMtg at Exeter. Jacob and Hannah Clayton and their four minor children, Lydia, Isaac, Joshua and Hannah.
16/4/1793. To Nottingham MMtg. William Wollaston, being placed apprentice within the compass of your meeting.
16/4/1794. To MMtg at London Grove. Margaret Carrington, clear of marriage engagements.
14/5/1794. To MMtg at Exeter. Grace Potts, clear of marriage engagements.
11/6/1794. To MMtg at Bradford. Rachel Burgess, wife of John Burgess.
16/7/1794. To MMtg of London Grove. James Wollaston.

13/8/1794. To Phila MMtg. John Lewis.
3/8/1794. To MMtg of Phila. Hezekiah Niles, minor, who is put apprentice to Benjamin Johnson within the compass of your meeting.
13/8/1794. Rachel Bond, being settled with her husband.
13/8/1794. To MMtg of Nottingham. Indorsement. Elizabeth Jacobs, being returned to live within the compass of your meeting.
10/9/1794. To MMtg of Phila. Sarah Bennet, clear of marriage engagements.
15/10/1794. To MMtg of Bradford. Richard Baker, Junr.
12/11/1794. To MMtg for the southern Dist., Phila. Edith Jones, clear of marriage engagements.
12/11/1794. To MMtg of Concord. Isaac G. Gilpin, no obstruction to his present engagement in marriage with a member of your meeting.
10/12/1794. To MMtg at Duck Creek. Ann Sipple, wife of Thomas Sipple.
10/12/1794. To MMtg at Nottingham. Charles Johnson, wife Mary and their three children, Lydia, William and Jethrew Johnson.
10/12/1794. To MMtg in Phila for the Northern Dist. Sarah Reynolds, clear of marriage engagements.
10/12/1794. To MMtg for the Northern Dist., Phila. Joseph Hewes, clear of marriage engagements.
11/2/1795. To MMtg at London Grove. Abigail Harlan, wife of William Harlan.
11/2/1795. Uwchland MMtg. Mary wife of Thomas Downing.
11/2/1795. To MMtg for the Southern Dist. of Phila. Phebo Jones, a young woman, clear of marriage engagements.
11/2/1795. to MMtg at Newgarden. Margaret Conrad, clear of marriage engagements.
15/4/1795. To Nottingham MMtg. Robert Lefley, wife Rachel and their dau Margaret.
15/4/1795. To MMtg of Phila. William Dawson, clear of marriage engagements.
15/4/1795. To MMtg in Phila for the Southern Dist. Isaac Starr, Junr. and wife Mary.
15/4/1795. To Phila MMtg. Thomas Worrell, clear of marriage engagements.

15/4/1795. To MMtg in Phila for the southern Dist. Jesse Pritchet, clear of marriage engagements.

13/5/1795. To MMtg at Nottingham. Sarah Jacobs, clear of marriage engagements.

13/5/1795. To MMtg of Bradford. Abraham Bonsall, wife Mary and their two children, Rebecah and Anna Bonsall.

13/5/1795. To Redstone MMtg. Henry Troth and Hannah his wife and their five small children, William, Sarah, John, Jane and Margaret.

10/6/1795. To Londongrove MMtg. Sarah Rogers, clear of marriage engagements.

15/7/1795. To MMtg at Duck Creek. Samuel Marshall, clear of marriage engagements.

15/7/1795. To Bradford MMtg. Samuel Fisher, clear of marriage engagements, after a short abode with us.

15/7/1795. To Darby MMtg. John Foreman, clear of marriage engagements.

12/8/1795. To Londongrove MMtg. Margaret Rodgers, widow, and dau Mary, minor.

12/8/1795. To MMtg at Bradford. Matilda Clempson, clear of marriage engagements.

12/8/1795. To MMtg at New Cornwall, New York. James Byrnes, clear of marriage engagements.

16/9/1795. To MMtg of Redstone, PA. Jonathan Sharpless, wife Eddith and their two children, Samuel and Elizabeth, minors.

16/9/1795. To Bradford MMtg. James Clampson and wife Hannah, having returned with their family to settle within the compass of your meeting with their six minor children, John, Rachel, Mary, Ann, Elizabeth and James.

16/9/1795. To Phila MMtg. William Elliott and wife Esther.

14/10/1795. To MMtg at Darby. Catherine Shallcross, being removed with her husband within the compass of your meeting.

16/12/1795. To MMtg at Westland. Hannah Townsend, wife of Joseph Townsend and her three minor children, Elizabeth, Sarah and John Ferriss Townsend.

16/12/1795. To Chester MMtg. Susanna Cloud, having returned to reside within the compass of your meeting.

13/1/1796. To MMtg of Phila. Benjn. Andrews, clear of marriage engagements.
13/1/1796. To MMtg of Piles Grove. Ephraim Barnes, clear of marriage engagements.
13/4/1796. To MMtg at Nottingham. Isaac Shortledge, being young when he left us.
7/?/1796. To MMtg of Phila. Benjamin Ferriss, being put an apprentice with a Friend of your meeting.
10/8/1796. To MMtg at Kennet. Catherine Milner, having removed with her parents, clear of marriage engagements.
10/8/1796. To MMtg at Goshen. Hannah Sinclair, a young woman.
14/9/1796. To Phila MMtg. Samuel Spackman, a young man who is placed with a friend within the compass of your meeting.
12/10/1796. To MMtg of Rahway. Joshua Mott who for a number of years past has resided within the compass of your meeting.
16/11/1796. To Phila MMtg. Elizabeth, wife of John Biddle.
16/11/1796. To MMtg of Phila. James Canby, minor, being placed an apprentice with a Friend of your meeting.
16/11/1796. To Phila MMtg. Ruth, wife of Bancroft Woodcock.
16/11/1796. To Phila MMtg. Sidney Litler, clear of marriage engagements.
16/11/1796. To MMtg in Baltimore. Samuel and Hannah Byrnes and dau Ruth and Sarah Townsend an apprentice girl, both minors.
14/12/1796. To Concord MMtg. Catharine Perkins, clear of marriage engagements.
14/12/1796. To MMtg in Baltimore. Daniel Byrnes, young man, clear of marriage engagements.
11/1/1797. To MMtg of Phila for the Southern Dist. Thomas Shipley, an apprentice to William Buckley, minor, within the compass of your meeting.
15/3/1797. To Phila MMtg. Ann Robinson, clear of marriage engagements.
15/3/1797. To MMtg of Kennett. John Wilson, clear of marriage engagements.
12/4/1797. Indorsement. Elijah Pearson, having returned after a short residence here, having satisfied his late master for that part of his time which remained unexpired.

12/4/1797. To MMtg of Phila. Samuel Smith and Lidia his wife and son Albin Gilpin Smith.

10/5/1797. To MMtg of Whiteoak Swamp, Virginia. Joseph Johnson and wife Sarah and infant dau, Martha.

14/6/1797. To Phila MMtg. Jane Dowdle, clear of marriage engagements.

14/6/1797. To MMtg in Phila for the Northern Dist. William Coale, minor, who is placed as an apprentice with Budd and Bartram within the compass of your meeting.

14/6/1797. To MMtg of Phila. for the Southern Dist. Phebe, wife of Sampson Barnet, considering the difficulties of her situation.

12/7/1797. To MMtg at Nottingham. Mary Haines, wife of Reuben Haines.

12/7/1797. To MMtg of Baltimore. Stephen Wilson and Mercy his wife and their five children, minors, Benjamin, Oliver, Isaac, Betty and Joseph Wilson.

12/7/1797. To MMtg of Kennett. Nathan Milner and Mary his wife, and their eight minor children, Joseph, Cyrus, Daniel, Rachel, Isaac, Jehu, Mary and Elizabeth Milner.

12/7/1797. To Concord MMtg. George Luff, young, who is placed an apprentice with a member of your meeting.

13/9/1797. To MMtg of Bradford. Benjamin Blackford.

15/11/1797. To MMtg in Phila for the Northern Dist. Larkin Milner, clear of marriage engagements.

10/1/1798. To MMtg on the Island of Nantucket for the Northern Dist. Parnel Gorham, for herself, clear of marriage engagements, and her four children, Jonathan, Mary, James and Deborah Gorham.

14/3/1798. To Duck Creek MMtg. James Iddings, wife Mary and their four minor children, Ann, Hannah, Joseph and Caleb Pierce Iddings.

14/3/1798. To MMtg in Phila for the Southern Dist. James Martin, who is placed apprentice with Samuel Richards, Junior, within the compass of your meeting.

4/11/1798. To MMtg of Phila for the Southern Dist. Joshua Seal, wife Ann and their two children, Taylor and William Seal.
11/4/1798. To Duck Creek MMtg. Margaret, wife of John Taylor.
11/4/1798. To MMtg of Baltimore. Thomas Meeteer for his son Thomas, he being placed an apprentice to a Friend of your meeting.
16/5/1798. To MMtg of Darby. Abraham Johnson, clear of marriage engagements.
13/6/1798. To MMtg at Goshen. William Jones, clear of marriage engagements.
13/6/1798. To MMtg at Concord. Elisha Starr, clear of marriage engagements.
11/7/1798. To Newgarden MMtg. Thomas and Alice Wilkinson and their five children, Joseph, Alice, Elizabeth, James and Thomas.
15/8/1798. To Motherkiln MMtg. Nathaniel Luff, being returned to reside within the compass of your meeting with his son Thomas, a minor.
15/8/1798. To MMtg at Redstone. Samuel Gibson, clear of marriage engagements.
15/8/1798. To MMtg at Redstone. Thomas Gibson, minor.
15/8/1798. To MMtg of Phila. John Wickersham, minor, placed with his uncle, Amos Wickersham within the compass of your meeting.
10/10/1798. To MMtg at Bradford. Jesse Merridith, clear of marriage engagements.
10/10/1798. to MMtg at Concord. Nathaniel Luff for his dau Susannah Luff, minor.
14/11/1798. To Baltimore MMtg. Ruth Byrnes, clear of marriage engagements.
12/12/1798. To Southern Dist in Phila. Sarah Byrnes and her two children, Hannah and Thomas Byrnes.
12/12/1798. To MMtg at London Grove. Caleb Bonsall, clear of marriage engagements.
16/1/1799. To Duck Creek MMtg. Hannah Green, wife of Charles Green.
13/2/1799. To Redstone MMtg. Joseph Townsend, junr., clear of marriage engagements.
13/2/1799. To Redstone MMtg. Isaac Townsend, he being about to go to his parents within the compass of your meeting.

13/3/1799. To MMtg at Nottingham. Rachel Jordan, clear of marriage engagements.
13/3/1799. To MMtg at Nottingham. Patience Jordan, clear of marriage engagements.
10/4/1799. To Third Haven MMtg. Ann Edmondson, having returned.
10/4/1799. To MMtg of Baltimore. Vincent Bonsall and wife Sarah and their minor children, William and Catharine Bonsall.
10/7/1799. To Nottingham MMtg. Lydia Harrison, junr., clear of marriage engagements.
10/7/1799. To Nottingham MMtg. George and Lydia Harrison.
10/7/1799. To Chester MMtg. Abraham Hoopes, being returned to live within the compass of your meeting, clear of marriage engagements.
10/7/1799. To MMtg of Bradford. Sarah Yarnall for her son Ephraim Yarnall who is place an apprentice with a Friend of your meeting.
10/7/1799. To Chester MMtg. Robert Newlin (Newtin?).
14/8/1799. To Kennett MMtg. William Hollingsworth, clear of marriage engagements.
11/9/1799. To Kennett MMtg. Glovier Buckingham, clear of marriage engagements.
11/9/1799. To Kennett MMtg. Mary Buckingham, clear of marriage engagements.
11/9/1799. To MMtg at London Grove. Sarah Chalfont, clear of marriage engagements.
16/10/1799. To Kennet MMtg. Sarah Baily, who hath removed with her husband within the compass of your meeting.
16/10/1799. To Spring MMtg of North Carolina. Ann Lee, wife of Samuel Lee.
11/9/1799. To Kennett MMtg. Richard Buckingham.
11/12/1799. To Kennett MMtg. Thomas Jackson, clear of marriage engagements.
12/2/1800. To Baltimore MMtg. Joseph Hewes, clear of marriage engagements.
11/6/1800. To MMtg of Phila for the Southern Dist. Joseph Blackford, bound an apprentice to Samuel Shin, member of your meeting.
13/8/1800. To MMtg at Bradford. Mary Canby, minor, who is placed with a friend of your meeting.
13/8/1800. To Kennett MMtg. Samuel Hollingsworth, minor.

10/9/1800. To MMtg of the Southern Dist. of
   Phila. Betty Shallcross, clear of marriage
   engagements.
10/9/1800. To Uwchland MMtg. Joanna Wollaston,
   clear of marriage engagements.
10/9/1800. To Phila MMtg for Southern Dist.
   Joshua Stroud, wife Martha and their minor
   children, Mary and Elizabeth.
15/10/1800. To Kennet MMtg. Marib Yarnall, clear
   of marriage engagements.
12/11/1800. To Pipe Creek MMtg. Lydia Hussey,
   being removed with her husband.

PENCADER PRESBYTERIAN CHURCH
Glasgow, Delaware

Marriages
(Performed by Rev. William Chealy)

Nov 8, 1796	Benjamin Stuart Taylor and Mary Biddle.
Dec 22, 1796	David Higgins and Rachel Wallace.
Dec 29, 1796	Wm. Johnson and Alice Martin.
Feb 2, 1797	Wm. Faris and Elana Huckel.
Feb 2, 1797	Samuel Bradley and Elenor Warnock.
Mar 13, 1797	John Price and Ann Bouldin, of Back Creek, Cecil Co.
Mar 13, 1797	Philip Bensance and Mary Andras, of St. Georges Hd.
Mar 29, 1797	Thomas Murphy and Eliz. Christfield, of Kent Co.
Apr 20, 1797	Bejm. C. McHannan and Hetty Skeggs, of Warwick, Kent Co.
Apr 20, 1797	Robert Maxwell, Esq., and Francina Bayard Shields, both of Middletown.
May 2, 1797	Thos. McMoling and Ann Williams, of Pencader Hd.
Apr 27, 1797	Wm. More, of Cecil Co., and Margaret Wiley, at Elk.
May 16, 1797	Richard Hamley, of Christain, and Henerata Carson, Pencader.
May 30, 1797	Thos. Sharp and Christana Haughay, both of St. Georges Hd.
June 21, 1797	John Rogers and Ann Cohoon of Pencader. "P.S. payd for ye licence only Dol. 2 1/2."
Aug 11, 1797	Samuel Shakespear and Susanna Edinbarough.
Sep 14, 1797	Ehud Sharp and Margaret Allin, of Christiana Hd.
Oct 10, 1797	John Wright and Ann Staats, of St. Georges Hd.
Oct 24, 1797	Jacob Allin and Elizabeth Wilson, of Pencader.
Oct 28, 1797	Wm. E. Sewall and Fanny Russell, of Cecil Co., Md.
Nov 9, 1797	William See and Rachel Bryan, both of Pencader Hd.

Nov 16, 1797	Reuben Sugar and Mary McDade, both of St. Georges.
Dec 7, 1797	Matheas Hanson and Mary Ann Watson, both of Cecil Co.
Dec 18, 1797	Wm. Milligin and Susanna Van Sant, of Pencader.
Dec 26, 1797	Robert King and Elizabeth Scot, of St. Georges.
Jan 4, 1798	Richard Bamberry and Ketrine Besten, of Town Point.
Jan 4, 1798	Alexander Perry and Rebekah Rice, my housekeeper, both of Pencader.
Jan 9, 1798	William Barr and Araminta Turner, both of Cecil Co.
Jan 25, 1798	John Holms and Elizabeth Williams, of Pencader.
Jan 30, 1798	John Boldin and Sarah Richardson, both of Cecil Co.
Feb 1, 1798	Joshua David and Sidney Elles, of Pencader.
Feb 26, 1798	John Jones and Sarah Burchal, of N.C. Co.
May 1, 1798	Benj. Taylor and Keity Armstrong, of St. Georges.
May 17, 1798	Lewis Curlett and Elizabeth Porter, of Pencader.
May 19, 1798	George Smith and Anne Bartley, of St. Georges.
May 27, 1798	Richard Bouldin and Mary Harding, both of Cecil Co.
May 31, 1798	James Watson and Senna Vanlear, both of N.C. Co.
June 12, 1798	Wm. B. Hackett and Mary Cox, of Queen Anns Co.
July 1, 1798	Genkin Evans and Elizabeth Bell, of Pencader.
July 24, 1798	Zebulon Beaston and Asaneth Thomas, of Cecil Co.
Aug 2, 1798	Samuel Betts and Ann Finley, both of Queen Ann Co.
Sep 20, 1798	Jesse Gilbert and Jain Shakisper, of Pencader.
Oct 27, 1798	Laurance Miles and Jain Thomas, of Pencader.
Nov 13, 1798	Samuel Sharp and Isablea Laurance, of Pencader.
Dec 8, 1798	Bolding Biddle and Rachel Bolding.

Dec 27, 1798	William Crow and Rebecca Cosden, of Cecil Co.
Jan 1, 1799	William Mansfield and Sarah Ervin of St. Georges.
Jan 17, 1799	Edward Cosden and Elizabeth Henderson, of Cecil Co.
Jan 23, 1799	David Howell and Hetty Lyons, of St. Georges.
Jan 24, 1799	Spencer Price and Mary Hyett, St. Georges.
Feb 14, 1799	Philip Dealry and Hester Everson, of St. Georges.
Feb 19, 1799	Wm. Joans and Mary Herman, of Pencader Hd.
Feb 27, 1799	Christopher Jones and Ann Van Winkle, Pencader Hd.
Mar 3, 1799	John A. Penintong and Elizabeth Mansfield, St. Georges.
Mar 5, 1799	Robert Can and Mary Price, both of St. Georges.
Mar 7, 1799	Wm. Jester and Hetty La Farge, both of St. Georges.
Mar 21, 1799	Jeremiah Hukinn and Rebecca Everson, both of St. Georges.
Apr 23, 1799	Wm. Dunlap and Sarah McClay, Pencader.
May 9, 1799	John Culbertson and Sarah Foster, Pencader.
May 12, 1799	John Higney and Ann Johns, Pencader.
May 30, 1799	Jeremiah Hukin and Mary Can, of St. Georges.
May 30, 1799	William Eakin and Rachel Griffith, St. Georges.
June 13, 1799	Andrew Anderson and Margaret Pennington, both of Elkton.
June 27, 1799	Thos. W. Clark and Louisa McWilliams, New Castle town.
July 4, 1799	Samuel Allin and Rebecca Armstrong, both of Newark.
July 7, 1799	Daniel Richardson and Elizabeth Hart, both of Elkton.
Aug 7, 1799	James Stewart and Agnes Porter, both of Pencader.
Aug 15, 1799	Henry Hukin and Sarah Griffith, Pencader.
Aug 27, 1799	Levey Biddle and Sarah Boulton, of Cecil Co.

Aug 27, 1799	Thomas Armstrong and Lydia Smith, both of St. Georges.
Sep 5, 1799	Jesse Holton and Elizabeth Boys, both of St. Georges.
Sep 30, 1799	Joseph Ireland and Ann Cru, St. Georges Hd.
Oct 19, 1799	James Allcorn and Ann Dodd, both of Pencader Hd.
Nov 21, 1799	Sath Stewart and Elizabeth Tweedy, both of Pencader Hd.
Nov 26, 1799	Thomas Ninbey(?) and Ann Pritchard, of Mill Creek Hd.
Dec 3, 1799	Wm. Chant and Sarah Prayer, of Pencader Hd.
Dec 3, 1799	John Simonton and Abigail Bolding, St. Georges Hd.
Dec 4, 1799	James Merrie and Margaret Durraham, St. Georges.
Dec 5, 1799	Oliver Howell and Eleanor Thomas, Pencader Hd.
Dec 19, 1799	James Wallace and Jinny Bolding, Elkton.
Dec 24, 1799	James Miles and Mary Thomas, St. Georges Hd.
Dec 28, 1799	William Ellis and Rebecca Sproat, of Cecil Co.
Dec 31, 1799	Joseph Cochran and Sarah Gordin, Pencader.
Jan 2, 1800	Joseph Hall and Elizabeth Alexander, Elkton.
Jan 8, 1800	Robert Hardcastle and Elizabeth Bayard, St. Georges.
Jan 9, 1800	Gerrit Chasnut and Mary Miller, Iron Hill.
Jan 16, 1800	Duglis Morrison and Elizabeth Wilson, White Clay Creek Hd.
Jan 21, 1800	Thomas Jones and Mary Whittim, both of Cecil Co.
Jan 25, 1800	Black Isiak and Durcus, servants of Ellis James.
Jan 30, 1800	Alexander M. Harris and Ann Lindsey, Pencader.
Jan 30, 1800	James Stewart, Jr. and Ann Whann, Pencader.
Feb 5, 1800	Benjamin Bantam and Elizabeth Evertson, both of St. Georges.
Feb 27, 1800	Joseph Higons and Johana Berry, St. Georges.

EARLY CHURCH RECORDS OF NEW CASTLE COUNTY

Mar 13, 1800	Joshua Elison and Christanna Huckin.
Mar 13, 1800	Mathew Cantwill and Mary Pugh, of Pencader.
Mar 20, 1800	Jesse Bolden and Hannah Griffith, Pencader.
Mar 25, 1800	Samuel McLaughtling and Hetty Shannon, St. Georges.
Mar 25, 1800	John Carnber(?) and Jan Vail, both of St. Georges.
Apr 3, 1800	John Robinson and Jane Stewart, Christiana Hundred.
Apr 9, 1800	James Price and Elizabeth Below, St. Georges.
Apr 29, 1800	John Christfield and Rachel Hull, Head of Sarcifix.
June 2, 1800	Benjamion Ravis and Sarah Cochran, St. Georges.
June 5, 1800	John Hair and Mary Boldin, Nigh Elk.
July 2, 1800	John Patterson and Nancy Faris, both of St. Georges.
July 24, 1800	James Whitelock and Amelia Thatcher, both of Pencader.
July 24, 1800	Samuel McGregor and Nancy Douglas, both of St. Georges.
Oct 24, 1800	Joseph Lee(?) and Sarah Baker, Pencader.
Nov 27, 1800	Owen Lloyd and Ann Smith, of St. Georges.
Dec 18, 1800	Thomas Bowen and Ann Roberts, Pencader.

BAPTISMS
Administered by Rev. William Chealy

July 29, 1796	John of Jacob and Charity Cazier.
Sep 21, 1796	Richard Thomson of Francis and Sarah Haughey, born Mar 15.
Apr 2, 1797	Isaac of Isaac and Johanna Thing (or King?), born Mar 14.
May 4, 1797	Agnes of Robert and Mary Allen, born Jan 9.
May 6, 1797	Rebecca, adult, of William and Elizabeth Woodland.
May 6, 1797	Sarah, adult, of William and Elizabeth Woodland.

May 21, 1797	John Harmon of Jaocb and --- Strats (Streets?).
May 31, 1797	William of James and Ann Dunlap, age 21 years.
June 4, 1797	Charles Glen of Charles and Mary Stuart.
June 8, 1797	Rachel of John and Ann Cruson.
June 10, 1797	James of Francis and Mary More, age 1 year, 8 months.
June 14, 1797	Ann of Jacob and Temperance King, age 1 year, 8 months.
June 25, 1797	Robert of Robert and Mathew Bartlet.
July 25, 1797	Wm. Elixander of Elixander Perry and Ann, age 2 years, 6 months.
July 25, 1797	Isick Lee of Elixander Perry and Ann.
Aug 13, 1797	Eliza of John and Mary Porter, age 7 weeks.
Aug 19, 1797	John of Elisha and Sarah James.
Sep 6, 1797	Robert of John and Mary Cochran.
Nov 9, 1797	Susana of David and Susana Lebo.
Dec 24, 1797	William Black, adult.
Feb 2, 1798	Sarah Hamly of Jos. and Sarah Thomas.
Feb 18, 1798	Susanna Elixander, adult.
Feb 18, 1798	Margaret Penninten, adult.
Mar 25, 1798	Hannah Elizabeth Hamblin, Richard Chichester Jonson and Sally Glasock.
May 2, 1798	Sarah of Nimrod and Dealy Pennington.
May 6, 1798	Jesse Forester of Wm. and Ann Bunker.
May 17, 1798	Margaret of Mart and Susanna Carr.
May 12, 1798	Sarah of Francis and Sarah Haughey.
May 17, 1798	Elixander Smith of James and Margaret Bolding.
May 19, 1798	Ann of Jacob and Temperance King.
May 21, 1798	Sarah Thompson of Samuel and Mary Crow.
May 31, 1798	William of James and Lydia Stewart.
July 1, 1798	Jain Fearis of Wm. and Margaret James, born Nov 8, 1797.

EARLY CHURCH RECORDS OF NEW CASTLE COUNTY

July 15, 1797	John of Thos. and Elizabeth Murphy.
Sep 2, 1798	Thomas Carson of Richard and Henerata Hamby - of Christian bondage.
Sep 5, 1798	William of Andrew and Lidia Elison, born Oct 7, 1780.
Sep 5, 1798	Rachel of Andrew and Lidia Elison, born Feb 16, 1786.
Sep 5, 1798	Andrew of Andrew and Lidia Elison, born Feb 21, 1788.
Sep 5, 1798	Hester of Andrew and Lidia Elison, born Sep 12, 1794.
Sep 30, 1798	Charles of Thomas and Mary Murrow, born Feb 3, 1798.
Feb 1, 1799	John of John and Peggy Gamble.
Feb 5, 1799	Elsha of Elia Cole and Sarah.
Feb 5, 1799	Sarah of Wm. and Elinor Price.
June 18, 1799	Henry of Jacob and Charity Cazier.
July 9, 1799	Ebner of John and Ann Crawford.
July 9, 1799	Mary of John and Ann Crawford.
July 9, 1799	Jane of John and Ann Crawford.
Aug 8, 1799	David Montgomery of John and May Porter.
Aug 8, 1799	Margaret Stewart and Susana of John and Margaret Derragh, of New Castle.
Aug 11, 1799	Hannah of Archable and Rebecca Armstrong.
Sep 3, 1799	Margaret Bach of Robert and Francine Maxwill.
Oct 1799	Mary Ann of James Backen, born Sep 11, 1796.
Oct 1799	Robert of James Backen, born Nov 22, 1798.
Oct 1799	James Thomson, born Feb 13, 1799.
Oct 19, 1799	Samuel Dunlap, aged 18.
Oct 19, 1799	Mary Dunlap, aged 16.
Oct 19, 1799	Sarah Pryor, aged 23.
Nov 10, 1799	Joel of Wm. and Rachel Evans.
Nov 10, 1799	Elizabeth of Francis and Elizabeth Smith, aged 10.
Jan 1, 1800	William Chealy of Levi and Jane Bolden, born Oct 29, 1799.
Jan 1, 1800	Margaret Black (named for grandm.), of Levi and Jane Bolden, born 29, 1799.

Mar 11, 1800	Elinor of Elixander and Elizabeth Vail.
Apr 1800	Jane Elsbury, adult.
June 7, 1800	Debora of Robert and Debora Smith.
June 15, 1800	Ann Shearon, adult.
June 15, 1800	Mary Dowson, adult.
June 22, 1800	Thomas Kean, of Francis and Sarah Haughey.

ASBURY METHODIST EPISCOPAL CHURCH

BAPTISMS

April 14, 1799	Phoebe Rodney, adult. D. Fiddler, minister.
March 25, 1798	Rebecca Sharpless, young woman. E. Cooper, minister.
April 8, 1798	Rebecca Sturgis, born March 24, 1786. Parents: Jonathan and Mary. E. Cooper, minister.
April 2, 1793	Lemuel Green Sturgis, born July 2, 1792. Parents Jonathan and Mary. L. Green, minister.
November 25, 1798	William Smith. E. Cooper, minister.
May 1, 1800	Maria Sturgis, born March 1, 1800 of Jonathan and Mary. D. Fiddler, minister
May 14, 1800	Mary Saunders, adult. D. Fiddler, minister.
December 13, 1797	Ann Thompson, born September 30, 1785. William Thompson, born April 17, 1788. Rebecca Thompson, born August 3, 1791. Martha Thompson, born November 25, 1797. Rachel Thompson, born December 19, 1794. [Children of John and Ann Thompson. E. Cooper, minister.]
March 13, 1798	George Washington Worrell, born March 8, 1798. Parents: Edward and Rebecca. E. Cooper, minister.
November 30, 1800	William Worrell, born October 5, 1800 of Edward and Rebecca. Jos. Everett, minister.
April 8, 1798	William Witsell, born January 1, 1798. Parents: Henry and Rachel. E. Cooper, minister.
February 1795	John Dickinson Wood, born September 1, 1794 of Samuel and Patience. N. Cook, minister.

April 8, 1798	Maria Ervin Wood, born March 3, 1797. E. Wood, minister.
June 26, 1799	Michael Wolf, born September 30, 1798 of Jacob and Rebecca. D. Fiddler, minister.
July 28, 1799	Charles Williams, born June 13, 1798 of Charles and Christianna. D. Fiddler, minister.
October 7, 1799	James Witsell, born July 11, 1799 of Henry and Rachel. E. Cooper, minister.
January 10, 1813	Samuel Walker, born December 15, 1791 of William and Ruth. J. Bateman, minister.
March 5, 1799	Elizabeth Foudray Bray, born May 18, 1798 of Elkanah and Susanah. Danl. Fiddler, minister.
April 17, 1795	John Colesbury, born April 2, 1795 of Henry and Allice. E. Pelham, minister.
April 8, 1798	Elizabeth Campbell, adult. E. Cooper, minister.
April 9, 1798	Henry Williams Colesbury, born September 12, 1797 of Henry and Allice. E. Cooper, minister.
January 23, 1800	John Collins, born July 30, 1798 of James and Lidia. Dan'l. Fiddler, minister.
January 23, 1800	James Collins, born January 11, 1800 of James and Lidia. Dan'l. Fiddler, minister.
October 4, 1805	Mary Criston, born October 1800 of Philip and Mary. J. Moore, minister.
June 30, 1800	Cornelia Devany, aged 11 months of William and Sarah. C. Kendall, minister.
June 30, 1800	Ann Kitty Devany, aged 3 years of William and Sarah. C. Kendall, minister.

MARRIAGES

1788 - John Miller and Eleanor Latimer
    Samuel Foudray and Ann Wood
1791 - Robert Rumsey and Elizabeth Colesbury
    Jonathan Sturgis and Mary Mehollen

1793 – Samuel Wood and Patience Irwin
1796 – James Krampton and Elizabeth Derrick
1797 – Thomas McCorkle and Ann Osborne
       John Food and Sarah Bostick
       Olden Griffin and Rebecca Griffin
       Thomas Hyatt and Sarah Whitsill
       James Hudson and Letitia Kelley
       James Lynch and Elizabeth Windemire
       Henry Witsill and Rachel Smith
1798 – Alexander Abbott and Mary Sulivan
       John Francis and Jane Hersche
       James Mitten and Elizabeth Trampton
       William Norris and Margaretta McGuire
       Samuel Arren and Elizbeth McGill
1799 – Joseph Bates and Ann West
       James Bevard and Maria Anderson
       William North and Elinor Robison
       John Paynter and Rebecca Fredd
       George Reed and Elinor Reed
       William Smith and Rachel Jennett

ST. PETERS' CATHOLIC CHURCH
Wilmington, Delaware

Transcribed by Rev. Edward B. Carley, 1985. All the following entries have been translated from the French.

Riviere, Pierre Victor, 26 Jan 1796, Claude Riviere; Jeanne Louise Francoise Elizabeth Riviere; sponors: Pierre Bauduy, Victoire Basili; priest: Etienne Faure

Bauduy, Felicite Alexandre Marie, Nov 1796, Pierre Marie Joseph Bauguy, Therese Jeanne Julienne Bretton des Chappelles; sponsors: Alexandre Francois, Bretton des Chappellas brother of mother of child, Felicite Marguerite Clementine Joseph Hamon (nee Bauduy) sister of the father

St. Martin, Bernard, 78 yrs of age, buried Mar 26 1797

DuPont - De Gault, Marie Francoise Angelique Jeanne Louise Dupont, Wilmington, 25 Aug 1795, Pierre Henry Dupont de Gault; Marie Catherine Elizabeth Vienot(?) de Vanclaire (Vanblanc?); sponsors: Francois Breuil, Jeanne Coustier de Ste marie

Vidal, Jean Francois Marie Felix Stanislas, Wilmington, Nov 1796; Jean Vidal, Marie Anne Elizabetjh de Lingender; sponsors: Francois Breuil, Marguerite Felicite Bosse

Marie Michel (negro), 20 yrs old, bapt Oct 15 17907; sponsors: Michael Lally de la Neuveville, Elizabeth Garesche, slave off Lally de la Neuveville; manumission also granted eodem die.

Fournier, De'sire' Francoise Virginie, Port au Prince, 17 Oct 1793, Francois Fournier, Marie Francoise Clemintine Solle'el; sponsors: Louis Malingre, Marguerite Desire' Sollee' (Follee'?)

Dupont de Gault, Pierre Marie Jean Eli Auguste, Wilm, 21 Aug 1797; Pierre Henry Dupont de Gault;

Marie Catherine Eliz. Vienot Vaublanc(?);
sponsors: Jean Garrasche' du Rocher, Mme.
Elizabeth Brossay

d'Orbigny, Louise Jeanne Elizabeth Victoire,
Wilm, 27 Nov 1797; Martin B---(?) de
Moine(?)D'Orbigny; Cecile Victoire Bazile;
sponsors: Louis Florent Bazile, Dame Victoire
Dulet(?) Bazile

Bretton-Deshapelles, Alexandre Joseph Pierre
Jean ---(?), Wilm, 13 Nov 1797; Alexandre
Francois Bretton Des Chapelles, Louise Marie
Adelaide Bouduy; sponsors: Joseph de Saque'
Destoourer (paternal uncle), Helene Cruon(?)
Veuve Bauduy

Priest: Cibot, vice-prefect, Cure'

de Sassenay, Claire Ettienne Eugenie, 10 Aug
1799, Claude Henry Etienne Bernard de Sassenay,
Fortunee' Prudence Julienne Claudius Bretton-de
Chapelles; sponsors: Gaspard Ettienne Bernard de
Sassenay, Louise --- Claudine
Bretton-Deschapelles

Keating, Gaudefroi Jean Jules, 16 Sep 1798; Jean
Keating, Eulalie Victorie Mathusine Cldine
Bretton-Des-Chapelles; sponsors: Gaudefroi
Keating, Jeane Juliene --- Bretton Descapelles

Keating, Hippolyte Louis Guillaume, 11 Aug 1799,
Jean Keating, Eulalie Victorie Claudine Mat.
Bretton des Chapelles; sponsors: Guillaume
Keating (uncle of child), Louise Jacque Claudine
Bretton-des Chapelles

Daughter of Andr' Noel (?) Mario Zoe' Marieanne,
5 Apr 1800, dau of Andre' a free negro and
Laurette, his wife, mulatress; sponsors: Mr.
Dumont Lagrange, Marie Louise. (Note: I believe
Andre's surname to be Noel. - E.B.Carley)

Hurli, Eugenie, bapt Aug 11 1800, Michael Hurli,
Marguerite Kuque)?), sponsors: A. Jean, Marie

de Vaujoyeux, Guillaume, 28 Feb 1799, Guillaume Francois Marguerite Hamon De Vaujoyeux, Felicite' Marguerite Clementine Josephine Bauduy; sponsors: Etienne Darnanud, Helenna, widow Bauduy, grandmother

Bauduy, Etienne, 21 Mar 1800, Louis-Alexandre Amelie Bauguy, Victoire Agathe Mathurina Darnaud; sponsors: Louis Etienne Damand, his grandfather; Helenne, widow, Bauguy, his grandmother

Esteol, Jean Baptiste, native of Montpellier, 78 yrs old, buried Jan 9 1801

Dupont-de Gault, Pierre Marie Jean Elie Auguste 21 Apr 1797, buried Jan 19 1801

MARRIAGE BONDS OF NEWCASTLE COUNTY
Transcribed by Gilbert Cope

3 Nov 1744 Adam Cooper of Chester County, Margaret Maxwell of same, surety, Jno. Finney, wit: Richd. McWilliam.

5 Nov 1744 John Firth of Salem County, carpenter, Judith Vickery of same; surety, George Monrow of New Castle (did not sign), wit: Richd. McWilliam.

21 Nov 1744 James Gradey of Chester County, yeoman, (mark), Anne Turtle of same, surety, Francis Johnston of N.C. Co., cooper, wit: Richd. McWilliam.

12 Feb 1744 Samuel Platt of Philadelphia County, yeoman, Anne Reynolds of New Castle County, surety, George Reynolds of New Castle Hd, wit: Patrick Flynn, Richd. McWilliam.

14 Feb 1744 William Clark of New Castle Hd, yeoman, Alice Armor of New Castle County, surety, John VanGezell, wit: Richard McWilliam.

20 Feb 1744 Jacob Martin of New Castle County, yeoman, Elizabeth Alexander of same, surety, William Flucker of same county, wit: Richard McWilliam.

24 Apr 1747 Jacob Alexander of Caecil County, yeoman, Rebecca Booth of same county, surety, Francis Alexander of New Castle County, wit: Richard McWilliam.

9 Dec 1749 David M'Canliss of Pencader Hd, weaver, (mark), Agnes Parson, widow, surety, Joseph Moore, wit: Richd. McWilliam.

14 Apr 1750 John Rogers Junr. of New Castle County, sadler, Isabella Miller of same county, spinster, surety, Caleb Pusey of same county, wit: Richard McWilliam.

16 Apr 1750 Joseph Jaquett of New Castle County, carpenter, Susannah Jaquett of same county, surety, Samuel Silsbee, wit: Richard McWilliam.

19 Apr 1750 John Elder of Pencader Hd, yeoman, Mary Tweedy of New Castle County, spinster, surety, Alexander Elder, wit: Richard McWilliam.

3 May 1750 Andrew M'Knight of New Castle County, yeoman, Abigail M'Donald, surety,

Walter Shetford (Thretford?), wit: Richd. McWilliam.

3 May 1750 William Neal or Neill of Chester County, yeoman, Mary Clinton of same, spinster, surety, Ezekiel Boggs, wit: Richd. McWilliam.

9 May 1750 Philip Vn. Luvenigh of town of New Castle, sadler, Mary Stallcop of New Castle County, surety, John Gilbert of New Castle, saddler, wit: Richd. McWilliam.

12 May 1750 Richard Buffington of Chester County, Ann Woodward of Chester Co., spinster, surety, Andrew Frazer of Christiana Hd (his mark), wit: Richard McWilliam.

19 May 1750 John Evans of Pencader Hd, yeoman, Ann Rees of Pencader Hd, spinster, surety, Joseph Thomas of Pencader, wit: Richd. McWilliam.

22 May 1750 Thomas Groom of Bucks County, yeoman, Lydia Goforth of New Castle Co., spinster, surety, William Goforth of New Castle Co., yeoman, wit: Richd. McWilliam.

23 May 1750 Robert Bryan of New Castle Hd, yeomnan, Hester Garritson of New Castle Co., widow, surety, John Scott of New Castle Co., Inholder, wit: Caleb Pusey, Charles McCarthy.

29 May 1750 Patrick Culford (or Colford) of Philadelphia Co. joiner, Cathrine Rice of New Castle Co., widow, Sur, John Kelly of New Castle town, Wits: Geo. Ross, Gertrude Ross.

31 May 1750 Joseph England of Mill Creek Hd, miller, Abigail Rotheram of New Castle Co., single woman, surety, Charles Black of Mill Creek, blacksmith, wit: David Finney, Charles McCarthy.

2 Jun 1750 Thomas Ogle Junior of Christiana Hd, yeoman, Katherine Springer of New Castle Co., spinster, surety, George James of Christiana Hd, yeoman, wit: Richd. McWilliam.

8 Jun 1750 Thomas Eaken of Pencader Hd, yeoman, Elizabeth Fraiser of Cecil Co., spinster, surety, William Clark of New Castle Co., yeoman, wit: Richd. McWilliam.

5 Nov 1750 Thomas Bennett of Appoquinimink Hd, yeoman, Alice Conoway of Salem Co.,

spinster, surety, Thomas Basset of
Appoquinimink Hd, wit: Richd. McWilliam.
26 Nov 1750 William Anderson of St Georges Hd,
blacksmith, Mary Ashburry of New Castle Co.,
spinster, surety, James Pander of St.
Georges, yeoman, wit: Richd. McWilliam.
9 Feb 1750 James Harris of White Clay Creek Hd,
yeoman, Elizabeth Lewis of New Castle Co.,
widow, surety, Thomas Rice of Mill Creek Hd,
yeoman, wit: Richd. McWilliam.
18 Mar 1750 Ambrose Granthum of New Castle town
(his mark), Christiana Corneluson of same
place, spinster, Sureties, George Monro of
same place, wit: Richd. McWilliam.
9 Sep 1751 Thomas Kelly of Mill Creek Hd,
yeoman, Mary Patterson of Mill Creek, widow,
surety, James Kelly of Mill Creek, yeoman,
wit: Richd. McWilliam.
3 Oct 1751 James Pringle of New Castle Hd,
farmer, Catharine Scott of New Castle
County, widow, surety, John Bryan of New
Castle Hd, yeoman, wit: Richd. McWilliam.
14 Jan 1752 Robert Richardson of New Castle Hd,
yeoman, Hannah Lewden of the same place,
surety, Thomas Moore of same place, wit:
Richard McWilliam.
17 Feb 1752 Daniel McDavett of New Castle Co.,
yeoman, Elizabeth Moran of New Castle Hd,
spinster, surety, John Bryan of same co.,
wit: Richd. McWilliam.
18 Mar 1752 Samuel Kirkpatrick of Red Lyon Hd,
weaver, Jane Davis of Pencader Hd, widow,
surety, John Rankin of New Castle Hd,
Innholder, wit: Richd. McWilliam.
24 Jul 1752 John Sturgis of Chester Co., weaver,
Agnes Allen of same co., widow, surety,
Ezekiel Boggs of New Castle Co., Innholder,
wit: Richd. McWilliam.
24 Aug 1752 William Whealand of Cecil County
(Factor for Bayard & Bouchell), Jeany Young
of same place, (Not signed by any one but
granted at request of P. Bayard and H(?)
Bouchell by letter).
19 Dec 1753 Joseph Inloe of Penns Neck, Salem
Co., yeoman (Signed Ealeu?), Margaret Janes
of Salem Co., spinster, surety, Robert
Morrisson of New Castle, blacksmith, wit:
Richd. McWilliam.

9 Nov 1754 William Robinson of New Castle Co., yeoman, Mary Dushane of same co., surety, John Thompson of same co., yeoman, wit: Charles McCarthy.
21 Nov 1754 Thomas Thomas of Pencader Hd, yeoman, Elizabeth Thomas of same place, widow, surety, Hugh Haughey of same hd, weaver, wit: Richd. McWilliam.
22 Jan 1755 Titus Van Hecklin (Vancecklan) of St Georges Hd, blacksmith, Mary Van Degrift of the same place, spinster, surety, John See of same place, yeoman, wit: William Spencer.
14 Nov 1755 Robert Patterson of Chester Co., chapman, Sarah Harvey of Chester Co., spinster, surety, Robert Harvey of same co., yeoman, wit: Richd. McWilliam.
5 Dec 1755 Evan Thomas of Red Lyon Hd, Mary Clemens of New Castle Co., spinster, surety, John Hance of Red Lyon Hd, wit: Richd. Spencer.
17 Apr 1756 John Post of New Castle co., cordwainer, Mary Gravenseat of New Castle Hd, spinster, surety, John Bryan of same co., yeoman, wit: Richd. McWilliam.
7 May 1756 John Crombie (signed Crummey) of New Castle co., carpenter, Margaret Pearce of New Castle Co., spinster, surety, Thomas Glenn of same co., taylor, wit: Richd. McWilliam.
5 Jul 1756 David Miles of White Clay Creek Hd, miller, Sarah Cantral of the same hd, spinster, surety, William Eynon of same hd, tanner, wit: Richd. McWilliam.
4 Sep 1756 Alexander Cummins of New Castle Hd, labourer (his mark) Mary Barber of New Castle town, widow, surety, Matthew Cannon (his mark) of New Castle Hd, wit: William Spenser Junr., Francis O'Cain.
19 Mar 1757 David Porter of New Castle Hd, yeoman, Margaret Houston, spinster, surety, Robert Bryan of same place, yeoman, wit: William Spencer Junr.
14 May 1757 Alexander Neill of Chester Co., yeoman, Elizabeth Faires of Chester Co., spinster, surety, John Henderson of New Castle Co., wit: William Spencer Junr.
14 May 1759 Charles Graham of London Britain, labourer, Grissel Cooper, surety, William

Ramsey of New Castle Co., yeoman, wit: Wm. Spencer Junr.

10 Mar 1760 Samuel Addair (Adear) of Pencader Hd, yeoman, Ann Eakin of New Castle Co., single woman, surety, William Ferris (Faries) of Pencader, carpenter, wit: Wm. Spencer Junr.

22 Apr 1760 John Buller of Chester Co., yeoman, Hannah Hayes of Chester Co., widow, surety, Robert McLoren of New Castle Town, wit: Wm. Spencer Junr.

14 May 1760 John Piles (his mark, Hester Patterson of said Hd, single woman, surety, James David (his mark), wit: Wm. Spencer Junr.

13 Nov 1760 Robert Barr of Mill Creek Hd, yeoman, Sarah Bullock, single woman, surety, Hector Graham of Mill Creek Hd, wit: Wm. Spencer Junr.

11 Mar 1761 William Gillespie of Cecil Co., Cooper, Elizabeth Ferguison of Cecil Co., widow, surety, William Spencer of New Castle, Innholder, wit: Wm. Spencer Junr.

12 May 1761 Thomas Sutton of St. Georges hd, Taylor, Catherine Kittle of same place, single woman, surety, Michael Dushane of same hd, wit: Rd. McWilliam.

27 May 1761 Joseph Parks of Chester Co., tanner, Anne Sinkler of Chester Co., widow, surety, Daniel McLonen of New Castle town, Innholder, wit: Rd. McWilliam.

11 Jun 1761 Alexander McMechen of White Clay Creek Hd, Mary Steel, single woman, surety, William Spencer of town of New Castle, wit: Wm. Spencer Junr.

4 Jul 1761 John Golden of St. Georges Hd, yeoman, Jane Williams of same place, widow, surety, Joseph Pierce of same hd, wit: Rd. McWilliam.

6 Jul 1761 Paul Jaquet of White Clay Creek, yeoman, Sarah Steel, single woman, surety, John Lindsey of same place, Taylor & Wm Spencer of New Castle, wit: Wm. Spencer, Junr.

6 Jul 1761 John Lindsey of White Clay Creek Hd, Taylor, Jane Solomon, widow, surety, Wm. Spencer of said Co., wit: Wm. Spencer Junr.

17 Jul 1761 Thomas Bravard, Cecil Co., Hannah Cruizer, single woman, surety, Isaac Alexander of New Castle Co., wit: Wm. Spencer Jr.

18 Jul 1761 James Fossett (his mark) of Red Lyon Hd, laborer, Margaret Cann of Red Lyon Hd, widow, surety, Dad. [David] Williams of same place, yeoman, wit: Rd. McWillaam.

25 Aug Jacob Morton of New Castle Hd, yeoman, Mary Whitely of same hd, single woman, surety, Peter Morton of same place, yeoman, wit: Rd. McWilliam.

23 Oct 1761 John Jurik (his mark), White Clay Creek, yeoman, Catherine Burns of same hd, single woman, surety, William Spencer of New Castle, Innholder, wit: Sam Dougall, George Hutchison (his mark).

12 Nov 1761 Thos. Sproul, New Castle, carpenter, Sarah Rea of same place, widow, surety, John Thompson, wit: Daniel Thane, Mary Thane.

4 Jan 1762 Joseph Williams, farmer, of Pencader Hd, Ann Harden, surety, David Howell Junr. farmer, of Pencader, wit: Saml. Dougal.

12 Mar 1762 Richard Tobin of Red Lyon Hd, Mary Truax, surety, James Huston of Red Lyon Hd.

3 May 1762 Thomas Smith of St. Georges Hd, Mary Bryant of same place, surety, John King, wit: Sam Dougle.

2 Jun 1762 William Penland of St. Georges Hd, Annis Donnal of Newlondon township Chester Co., single woman, surety, John Rankin of New Castle Hd, wit: Sam. Dougall.

5 Aug 1762 Wm. McCrea of White Clay Creek Hd, merchant, Eddath Chambers of Philadelphia, widow, surety, Jas. McMechen Esq., White Clay Creek, wit: David Wilkins, Robert Wallaoe.

25 Dec 1762 Andrew Wilson (his mark) of White Clay Creek, yeoman, Jane Jaquet of same hd, spinster, surety, William Spencer of said co., Innholder, wit: Rd. William.

15 Jan 1763 James Ross of White Clay Creek Hd, Rebecca McMechen of Mill Creek Hd, single woman, surety, Daniel McLonen of town of New Castle, wit: Samuel Janvier, Sam Dougall.

11 Mar 1763 Daniel Moody (his mark) of New Castle Hd, Jannet Eakin of same hd, single woman, surety, William Spencer of same place, wit: Sm. Dougall.

14 May 1764 Thomas Flannagan of White Clay Creek Hd, Catherine Crulin of same hd, surety, Andrew Allen of same place, wit: Alexr. Montgomery.

22 Apr 1765 Samuel Vail of St. Georges Hd Christiana Chuck, surety, Wm. Penland of same hd, wit: Will Spencer, Stephen Spencer.

30 Jul 1765 John Jones of New Castle Co., yeoman, Mary Bolton, surety, Abel Evans of same co., wit: Robert Jones, Jacob Moore.

5 Aug 1765 Thomas Thomas (his mark) of East Nottingham Township, Esther Jones of New Castle Co., surety, Zachariah Jones of New Castle Co., wit: Alexr. Montgomery, Jacob Moore.

8 Aug 1765 Robert McIlheran of the town of New Castle, yeoman, Mary Donald of New Castle, single woman, surety, Not signed by any one).

14 Aug 1765 Robert Jones of Pencader Hd, Jane Bolton, surety, John Jones of Pencader, wit: Andrew Ross, Jacob Moore.

16 Aug 1765 Alexander Purse of New Castle Co., joiner, Esther Thompson of same co., spinster, surety, Hugh Wiley of same co., wit: Geo. Shaw, Jacob Moore.

23 Aug 1765 David Finney of the town & county of New Castle, Esqr., Ann Thompson of same co., surety, Tho. McKean of the town of New Castle, Esqr., wit: Alexr. Montgomery, Jacob Moore.

31 Oct 1765 Gustavus Grimes of New Castle, Labourer, Jane Conn of same town, single woman, surety, Stephn. Spencer of same place, wit: Richd. McWilliam.

22 Nov 1765 John White of Pencader Hd, Hannah John of same hd, surety, John Evans of same co., wit: Alexr. Montgomery.

9 Dec 1765 David Lewis of Pendcader Hd, Elizabeth Lewis of same hd, surety, Thomas Wattson of same place, wit: Stephen Spencer, Alexr. Montgomery.

26 Dec 1765 Henry Hiland of Christiana Hd, carpenter, Mary Robinson of same place, single woman, surety, Morton Morton of New Castle Hd, wit: Rd. Mcwilliam.

28 Dec 1765 Robert Bryan of New Castle Hd, Rebecca Webster, of same hd, widow, surety,

Wm. Clark of same place, yeoman, wit: Rd. McWilliam.
31 Dec 1765 James Peery of St. Georges Hd, Elizabeth Donald of Red Lyon Hd, surety, James Houston of same place, yeoman, wit: Alexr. Montgomery.
25 Feb 1766 Hugh Martin of New Castle Hd, Jane Thompson of same hd, surety, Saml. Ruth of same place, wit: Alexr. Montgomery.
25 Mar 1766 Jonathan Payne of New Castle Hd, Elizabeth Harriss of same co., widow, surety, George Ogle of Christiana Hd, wit: Alexr. Montgomery.
7 Apr 1766 David Howel Junr. of Pencader Hd, Anne Williams of same place, surety, Joshua Williams of same hd, wit: James Van Dike, Alexr. Montgomery.
9 Apr 1766 Samuel Bradford of White Clay Creek Hd, Catherine Lewis of same place, surety, Wm. Pettigrew of same co., wit: Jeremiah McCrackin (mark), Alexr. Montgomery.
9 Jun 1766 Daniel Murphy of Redlyon Hd, Mary Ann Fairis of Pencader Hd, surety, Alexander Eakin of same co., wit: Ax. Montgomery, Davd. Thompson.
9 Jun 1766 John Glascow of Chester Co., (signed Glasgow), Mary McDowell of same co., surety, Michael Randel, wit: James Brydin, John Glasgow, shoumekr.
16 Jun 1766 Jeremiah Cloud of Kennet Township, Chester Co., farmer, Hester Harry of Marlborough, single woman, surety, Silas Harry of same place, yeoman, wit: Rd. McWilliam.
26 Jun 1766 Matthew Robinson (his mark) of New Castle Hd, Alice Gray of same hd, surety, Robt. McLonen of same co., wit: Nathl. Silsbee Jr., Ax. Montgomery.
3 Jul 1766 James Gibson of New Castle Hd, Mary Fuller of same co., widow, surety, John Stewart of same co., wit: Alexr. Montgomery.
8 Jul 1766 James Townsley (his mark) of Lancaster Co., Margaret McDill of same co., surety, John Steuart of the town of New Castle, wit: Andrew Ross, Alexr. Montgomery.
7 Aug 1766 James Kelley of Pencader Hd, Sarah Reaber of same hd, surety, William McMechen of same co., wit: Alexr. Montgomery.

11 Aug 1766 John Clark of Red Lyon Hd, Mary Adams of White Clay Creek Hd, surety, Thomas Tobin Junr of same hd, wit: Andrew Ross, Alexr. Montgomery.

4 Sep 1766 Jacob Fairis of Pencader (signed Fearis or Ferris), Caziah Sharp of same place, surety, Wm. Eakins of same co., wit: Jno. Reece Junr., Alexr. Montgomery.

9 Sep 1766 David Lewis of Mill Creek Hd, Agnes Abrams of same co., surety, John Ball of New Castle Hd, wit: Alexander Montgomery, Richard McWilliam.

6 Nov 1766 Thomas Tobin Junr of Redlyon Hd, Rachel Smith of White Clay Creek Hd, surety, Danl. McLonen of New Castle town, wit: Stephn. Spencer, Alexr. Montgomery.

13 Nov 1766 Charles Hughes (his mark) of the county of Chester, Margaret Gobby of the same co., surety, Peter Gobby (his mark) of the same province, wit: Edward Wall, Alexr. Montgomery.

18 Nov 1766 Nathan Oldham of Cecil Co., planter, Elizabeth Giles of same place, single woman, surety, Zachariah V [Van] Leuvenigh of New Castle town, tanner, wit: Rd. McWilliam.

20 Nov 1766 Abraham Venneman of Penns Neck, Salem Co., shop joiner, Rebecca Dougherty of same place, single woman, surety, Treviss Jenkins of same place, marriner, wit: Rd. McWilliam.

27 Nov 1766 James Boyd of the town of New Castle, Sarah Janvier, surety, Richd. Janvier of New Castle town, wit: Willm. McKinney, Alexr. Montgomery.

10 Dec 1766 Ephraim Yarnall of Mill Creek Hd, Sarah Holton of the same co., surety, James Armstrong of Redlyon Hd, wit: Robt. McMun, Alexander Mongtomery.

20 Jan 1767 William Mullican of White Clay Creek Hd, Elizabeth Wood, surety, John Garritson of New Castle Hd, wit: Jno. Yeates, Alexr. Mongtomery.

10 Feb 1767 David Hunter of New London township, Chester Co., Jean Finney of the same township, surety, Archd. Finney of New London, wit: Robert Hunter, John Finney, Walter Finney.

24 Feb 1767 Robart Bonting of Chester Co.,
Margaret Heas of same co., surety, Jno.
Cooper of Chester Co., wit: Jno. Singleton,
Wm. McDowell.
10 Feb 1767 William Rutherford of Chester Co.,
yeoman, Sarah Tarner of the same co., single
woman, surety, Robt. McLonen, of New Castle,
Innholder, wit: Rd. McWilliam.
17 Feb 1767 Mark Elliot of Brandywine Hd,
yeoman, Jane Mclalee of New Castle Hd,
single woman, surety, Jno. Elliot of New
Castle Hd, farmer, wit: Rd. McWilliam.
17 Feb 1767 Hugh Miller of Phags Mannor in the
county of Chester, Mary Fairis of the same
co., surety, Robt. Finney of the county of
New Castle, wit: Robert Smith, Alexander
Montgomery.
3 Mar 1767 Robt. McMullen of Pencader Hd, Ann
Williams of the same hd, surety, Veazey Rice
of Pencader Hd, wit: Alexander Montgomery.
24 Mar 1767 Benjamin Whitting of Chester Co.,
Sarah Hughes, surety, Thomas Whitting of
Chester Co., wit: Samuel Wilson, A.
Montgomery.
2 Apr 1767 Thomas January of the town of New
Castle, Jane Clark, surety, Stephn. Spencer
of New Castle, wit: A. Montgomery.
2 Apr 1767 Edward Swainey (his mark) of the
town of New Castle, labourer, Judith Bestida
of same place, single woman, surety, John
Steuart of same place, taylor, wit: Rd.
McWilliam.
20 Apr 1767 Thomas Sutherland of New Castle Hd,
Jane Beaty of same co., surety, Jno.
Armstrong Junr. of Christiana Hd, wit: A.
Montgomery.
23 Apr 1767 John Elliot of New Castle Hd, Mary
Shaw of the same co., surety, Evan Thomas of
Redlyon Hd, wit: A. Montgomery.
30 May 1767 John Long of West New Jersey,
farmer, Rebecca Wright of Penn's Neck in
West New Jersey, single woman, surety, John
Passmore of New Castle, Innholder, wit: Rd.
McWilliam.
31 Mar 1768 John Clark of New Castle Co.,
farmer, Mary Welsh of same co., spinster,
surety, Thomas Moore of same co., wit: Rd.
McWilliam.

15 Sep 1774 John Lyon of New Castle Hd, Sarah Williams of the same hd, spinster, surety, George Anderson of White Clay Creek, blacksmith, wit: Jas. Booth.

3 Dec 1774 Charles Stewart of White Clay Creek Hd, Mary Barr of the same hd, spinster, surety, Isaac Hershey of same place, wit: Jas. Booth.

2 Nov 1775 Erick Fillpot (signed Philpot) of Penn's Neck, New Jersey, Catherine Mains of Pennsneck, surety, Richd. January, wit: Rd. McWilliam Jr., Wm. McWilliam.

17 Jan 1776 John Keith of Appoquinimink Hd, Isabella Anderson of the same hd, widow, surety, Abraham Staats (his mark) of same place, wit: Jas. Booth.

12 Mar 1776 Francis Alexander of Pencader Hd, farmer, Eleanor Simonton of White Clay Creek Hd, single woman, surety, John Simonton of White Clay Creek, miller, wit: Rd. McWilliam (Endorsed, "a license to be made out for Mr. Edwards this date).

17 Mar 1777 Stephen Foreman of the city of Philadelphia, mariner, Rachel Thomas of the county of New Castle, spinster, surety, Anthony Morris (signed Anthony Thomas of Phil., silversmith, wit: Jas. Booth.

24 Mar 1777 John Henderson of Appoquinimink Hd, husbandman, Ann Clark of same hd, surety, Robert Meers of same place, wit: Wm. McWilliam.

26 Mar 1777 Robert Rodgers of White Clay Creek Hd, Mary Downing of New Castle Hd, surety, William Graham of White Clay Creek Hd, wit: Jas. Booth.

28 Mar 1777 James Kinnear of New Castle Hd, Ann Riddles of same place, spinster, surety, Adam Dayet of same hd, wit: Jas. Booth.

29 Mar 1777 James Wynkoop of St. Georges Hd, practitioner of physick, Hester Peterson of same place, surety, Abram Wynkoop of Appoquinimink Hd, wit: Rd. McWilliam, Jr.

16 Apr 1777 James Gamble of Christiana Hd, Lydia Springer of same place, surety, Robert Oram of Mill Creek Hd, wit: Rd. McWilliam, Jr.

16 Apr 1777 Joseph Leman of the town of New Castle, Mary Scantling of same place,

surety, Thomas Nodes(?) of same place, wit:
Rd. McWilliam Jr.
23 Apr 1777 Andrew Morton of New Castle Hd,
Rachel Walraven of same place, surety, David
Morton of same place, wit: Jas. Booth.
15 May 1777 Jesse Bowen of Pencader Hd, Susanna
Whan of same place, surety, David Howel of
Pencader, wit: Jas. Booth.
19 May 1777 Benjamin Pierce of Cecil County
(signed Benja. Pearce), Lydia Moody of
Appoquinimink Hd, Spinster, surety, Isaac
Allman of Appoquinimink, wit: Jas. Booth.
19 May 1777 Thomas Hackett, weaver, of New
Castle Hd, Frances McElroy of same place,
widow, surety, William Milligan of same
(Signed Jas. Milligen), wit: Rd. McWilliam
Jr., Patk. Mooney.
7 Jun 1777 John McCord of St. Georges Hd,
cordwainer, Ann McCord of same hd, surety,
Charles Divin (his mark) of Pencader,
taylor, wit: Rd. McWilliam, Jr., Patk.
Mooney.
16 Jun 1777 Benjamin John of Appoquinimink Hd,
Eliz. Scott of Cecil Co., surety, Jehu John
of Appoquinimink, wit: Rd. McWilliam Jr.,
Richd. Spencer.
23 Jun 1777 Donaldson Yeates of Kent Co.,
merchant, Mary Syng of the county of
Philadelphia, surety, Isaac Grantham, Esq.
of New Castle Co., wit: Jas. Booth (see
Penna. Mag. V. 22 No., 2).
24 Jun 1777 John Barclay of White Clay Creek Hd,
Mercht., Eleanor Porter of New Castle Hd,
surety, David Finney Esq. of Mill Creek Hd,
wit: Jas Booth.
3 Jul 1777 Thomas Matthews of New Castle Co.,
Ann Kirk of same co., surety, William
Matthews of same co., wit: Jas. Booth.
21 Jul 1777 William McGinnis (McGinnies) of New
Castle Hd, farmer, Susanna Bell of same hd,
surety, James Garretson Jr. of same place,
carpenter, wit: Steph. McWilliam.
21 Jul 1777 Samuel Cameron of Redlion Hd (made
his mark), Martha McCowan of Pencader Hd,
surety, Daniel Smith (his mark) of New
Castle Hd, wit: Jas. Booth.
5 Aug 1777 James Boggs, cordwainer, of New
Castle Hd, Hannah Sankey of same hd, surety,

James Read, Tavern Keeper, of same hd, wit: Step: McWilliam.

14 Apr 1782 James Wilson of New Castle Co., Mary Poulson, surety, William Anderson of same co., wit: Archd. Alexander, Geo: W. Janvier.

1 Aug 1780 Stephen Massy of Kent Co., Maryland, Ann Reynolds of New Castle Co., surety, George Reynolds of New Castle Co., wit: Jo: Burn, John Platt.

8 Aug 1786 George Kerker of New Castle Co., yeoman, Martha Hennon of the same co., surety, George Hennon of same co., wit: Rebekah McCrery, James Gallahar.

29 Dec 1786 Thomas Taylor of New Castle Co., Letitia Ford of the same co., surety, Matthew Thompson of same co., wit: Hannah Bryan, Rebekah McCrery.

2 Jan 1787 William Morgan of New Castle Co., Martha Williams of same co., surety, John Morgan of the county aforesaid, wit: Peter Jaton or Gatow?, Samuel Allen.

25 Jan 1787 John Baily of New Castle Co., yeoman (John Bayly Junr.), Jean Simpson of same co., surety, John Platt of same co., wit: Jno. Graham, Jas. Simpson.

15 Mar 1787 James Lutten of Cecil Co., yeoman, Ealenor Taylor of same co., surety, John Taylor of same county (signed in German?) Wit: Robert Litton, John Miller.

15 Mar 1787 David Gormley of New Castle co., Mary Post of the same co., surety, William Scott of same co., wit: Laurence Doullir(?), Christopher Willet.

5 Apr 1787 Alexander Smith of New Castle Co., yeoman, Nancy Kirkwood of same co., surety, Alexander McBeath of same co., storekeeper, wit: Wm. Steel, Robt. McBeath.

24 Apr 1787 William McCaskey of Cecil Co., yeoman, Elizabeth McCown of same co., surety, James Kilgore of Cecil Co., wit: James Johnston, Jos. Wallace (On back, -9 Marriage Bonds returned by Mr. McCrery this 12th Sept, 1787).

8 Nov 1787 David Millen of ye Burrow of Wilmington, Margaret Kennedy of same town, spinster, surety, John Moore of Wilmington, wit: James Gilliland, Robert Miller, William Newell.

13 Dec 1787 John Marshall of New Castle Co.,
Elizabeth Turner of same co., surety, Thomas
Turner of New Castle Co., wit: Robert Bryan,
Andrew Morton.
27 Dec 1787 Charles Springer of New Castle Co.,
Elizabeth Rice, of same co., surety, John
Graham of same co., wit: Margret Ogle, Polly
Rice.
1 Feb 1788 Henry Brattan of St. Georges Hd,
Rachel Stetts of same hd, spinner, surety,
Benjamin Brattan of same hd, wit: James
Brattan, John McCabe, Alexander Flynn.
23 Apr 1788 Hugh Montgomery of New Castle Co.,
Rebecca Ball of same co., surety, Valentine
Best of same co., wit: Pas. Springer, Thomas
Springer.
15 May 1788 Isaac Scothorn of New Castle Co.,
Jean Ferguson of same co., surety, Nathan
Boys of same co., wit: John Ball (On back,
Marriage Bonds taken in President Collin's
administration: retd. by Rev. Wm.
McKennan.).
3 Sep 1788 Jonathan Groves of White Clay Creek
Hd, Johanna Sauce(?) of same hd, widow,
surety, William Dawson of same hd, wit:
Richard Goss (his mark), Joseph Walker.
23 Dec 1788 Zebdiel Carmean of Caroline Co.,
Md., Elizabeth Moloston of Kent Co., Del.,
surety, Jacob Carmean of Kent Co., Del.,
wit: Lewis Deweese, Thomas Deweese.
23 Dec 1788 John Ervin of New Castle Co., Sarah
Ball, surety, Wm. Bracken of same co., wit:
Hugh Long, James Ball, Hugh Martin.
24 Dec 1788 David Jester of Kent Co., Del,
Catherine Sipple of the same Co., surety,
Nathan Bowman of Kent Co., wit: William
Walker, Thomas Jester.
1 Feb 1789 John Tanner of Little Creek Hd, Kent
Co., Catherin Crippen of same place (she
signs Cathrin Tanner.) surety, Joseph Harper
of Little Creek, wit: William Jesop, Wm.
Howett.
12 Feb 1789 Edward Oldham Junr. of Cecil Co.,
Judith Oglevee of same co., surety, Edward
Oldham Senr. of same co., wit: Edward
Oglevee, Elisha Oldham.
3 Mar 1789 Jacob Merydith of Kent Co., Del,
Martha Merydith of same place, surety,

Joshua Deweese of same co., wit: Joshua
Meredith, Danniel Meredith.

12 Mar 1789 Samuel Merydith (his mark) of Kent
Co., Del, Mary Breadley of same co., surety,
Lemuel Wheeler of same co., wit: Armwell
Lockwood, Thomas Jackson.

15 Mar 1789 John Smyth of Cedar Creek Hd, Sussex
Co., Rhoda Young of same place, sureties,
John T. Campbell Esq and Nephtali Carpenter
of same co., wit: Nathl. Young, Robert P.
Campbell.

26 Mar 1789 William Murphy of Mispillion Hd,
Kent Co., Jennie Cary of Cedar Creek Hd,
Sussex Co., surety, George Cowan, John
Snowden, wit: William Wilents(?), David
Vankirk.

2 Apr 1789 Jeroboam Beauchamp of Murderkiln Hd,
Kent Co., Mary Downam of same place, surety,
Costen Beauchamp, Joshua Beauchamp of same,
wit: John Thomas, John Gooding.

30 Apr 1789 Jesse Peterson of Appoquinimink Hd,
New Castle Co., Sarah Hackett of same place,
surety, Joseph Hacket of same place (All
three sign), wit: William Jessop, John
Person(?).

7 May 1789 William Wade late of New Castle Co.,
Elizabeth Edgin of Kent Co., Del., surety,
William Frasar of Kent Co., wit: Cary
Fimlinson, John Gibbs.

16 Jul 1789 John Arters of Kent Co., Del., Sarah
Williams of same, surety, William Johnson of
same co., wit: John Tomlin, Patrick
Brendergast.

13 Aug 1789 Stephen Jones of Mispillion Hd, Kent
Co., Eleanor Scott of same place, surety,
Nathan Scott & Curtis Jones of same hd, wit:
Jacob Callaway, Nathan Harrington (his
mark).

3 Sep 1789 John Hollensworth (mark) of Kent
Co., on Del., Elizabeth Harper of same co.,
surety, Isaiah Latchem of same co., wit:
Alexander White, Thomas Smith.

"Marriage Bonds retd. by the Revd. Joshua
Deweese, Nov 89". This was written on a bond
shown on page 222.

15 Sep 1789 Elias Poynter of Cedar Creek Hd,
Sussex Co., Leah Broton of same place,
surety, Rattlife Poynter, William Poynter of

Cedar Cr., wit: Jacob Ludwick, Daniel Webb Dickinson.
19 Sep 1789 Tyrell Tribit of Murderkiln Hd, Kent Co., Esther Stradley of Mispillion Hd, Kent Co., surety, Thomas Stradley, John Tribet of Murderkiln, wit: John Greer Junr.
24 Sep 1789 Jonathan Badger of Murderkiln Hd, Agnes Broadaway of same place, surety, Daniel Reynolds, Abraham Knotts of same hd, wit: Wm. Gaskines.
12 Nov 1789 James Bell of Kent Co., in Del., Nancy Moleston of the same co., surety, Thomas Sipple of same co., wit: William Bell Junr, Thos. Johnson.
31 Dec 1789 Ezekiel Reid of Mispillion Hd, Kent Co., Nancy Brinkley, of same place, surety, Zadock Sipple, William Jacobs of same (marks), wit: George Saxon.
31 Dec 1789 Joseph Hazlett of Mispillion Hd, Kent Co., Mary Draper of Cedar Creek Hd, surety, Nathaniel Young, Nephtali Carpenter of Cedar Cr., wit: Wm. Adams.
31 Dec 1789 Matthew Morris of Kent co., (Mor sen), Sarah Redden of same co., surety, Jabes Fisher of same place, wit: William Green Ser., William Thompson, Jr.
31 Dec 1789 John Muncey of Kent Co., Del, Elizabeth Hudson of same place, surety, Bedwell Maxwell of Kent Co., wit: Thos. Houldson, Rachel Stewart (her mark).
3 Jan 1790 Frederick Pratt, Jemima Virdin, surety, William Virdin, Thomas Lockwood, wit: John Virdin, George Pratt.
7 Jan 1790 David Thompson of New Castle Co., Fanny Aitkin, surety, William McKinnan Jur. of same co., wit: Samuel Veazey, John Thompson.
7 Jan 1790 William Thomas Jur., Rebecca Soward, surety, Thomas Soward, James Jones, wit: George Soward, Sint [Saint] Legor Neal.
21 Jan 1790 William Thompson of Kent Co., Del, Margaret Kelley of same co., surety, David Young of Kent Co., wit: Lamuel Whitehead, William Beauchamp.
28 Jan 1790 Thomas Bedwill, Mary Lovitt, surety, Moses Kinsey(?) and James Jones, wit: William Virdin, Solomon Dill.

4 Feb 1790 William Wilson of New Castle Co., Elioner Scothorn of same Co., spinster, surety, Nathan Scothorn of same co., wit: David Magee, Robert Creighton.

8 Feb 1790 John Verdin of Murderkiln Hd, Kent Co., Katherine Wright of same place, surety, Zadok Sipple (his mark), Waitman Booth, wit: Andrew Saxton.

18 Feb 1790 John Peg of Murderkiln Hd, Kent Co., Sarah Meredith of Queen Ann's Co., Md., surety, Charles Townsend (mark), Joseph Barker of Mispillion Hd, wit: Saml. Foulke.

21 Feb 1790 James Lucas of Kent Co., Del., (his mark), Mary Hudson, surety, Andrew Rash, William Wilson (his mark), wit: Solomon Truitt, David Wells.

23 Feb 1790 John Barton of Mill Creek Hd, yeoman, Rebecca Kenney of same place, surety, Samuel Kelly of New Castle Co., wit: Valentine Best.

25 Feb 1790 Alexander Donnel of Miln Creek Hd, Jean Huston of same hd, surety, Jacob Moore of Miln Creek, wit: Edwd. Armstrong, James Ocheltree.

4 Mar 1790 John McNamee of New Castle Co., Mary Gold of same co., spinster, surety, Peter Springer of same co., wit: Valentine Best, Thos. Canby.

6 Mar 1790 William Burton of Sussex Co., Del., Ann Bagwell of same co., surety, Benjamin Burton of Sussex Co., wit: Robt. Prettyman, Peter Burton.

6 Mar 1790 William Walker of Mispillion Hd, Kent Co., Susannah Canby of Mispillion Hd, surety, John Pettigrew, James Douglass of Mispillion, wit: Daniel Webb Dickinson, James Rosmier(?) (mark).

14 Mar 1790 Andrew Williams of Kent Co., Elizabeth Powell, surety, Solomon Wilson (mark) William Wallace of same, wit: Mark Powell, Joseph Nickerson.

18 Mar 1790 Thomas Deweese of Mispillion Hd, Kent co., Katherine Spencer of same hd, surety, Joshua Deweese, David Dewees of Mispillion, wit: Bidwell Maxwell.

18 Mar 1790 Joseph Furbe(?), Martha Morgan, both of Murderkiln Hd.

MARRIAGE BONDS OF NEWCASTLE COUNTY 247

23 Mar 1790 John Collins, Ann Smith, both of Brandywine Hd.
1 Apr 1790 John Doughty of Kent Co., Mary Tanner.
1 Apr 1790 James Teat, Naomi Shaw(?) both of Murderkiln Hd.
7 Apr 1790 Benjamin Jones, Elizabeth Doney.
8 Apr 1790 Robert Smith of Brandywine Hd, Elizabeth Boggs of New Castle Hd.
8 Apr 1790 Caleb Luffe of Kent Co., Margaret Williamson of same co.
8 Apr 1790 Isaac Menough of Md., Margaret Jones of New Castle Co.
11 Apr 1790 Thos. Dickson, Kent Co., Mary Rees.
11 Apr 1790 John Davis of Kent Co., Betsy Pennell of same co.
14 Apr 1790 James Jones, Tanner, of Kent Co., Mary Thomas.
20 Apr 1790 Wm. May of Christiana Hd, Susanna Gallacher.
4 May 1790 Beriah Foster, Mary Welden, both of Brandywine Hd.
16 May 1790 John Walker, Mary Darling (Married by Thos. Jackson same date).
20 May 1790 Thomas Bowman of Kent Co., Mary Smith of same.
27 May 1790 John Fouracors of Kent Co., Rachel Davis.
2 Jun 1790 Daniel Newman of Kent Co., Sarah Howell.
5 Jun 1790 John Appleton, Elizabeth Mitchell.
7 Jun 1791 Ashel Philo Philps of Sussex Co., Agness Houston of same.
10 Jun 1790 Wm. Underlin, Elizabeth McCoomb (Married same date by Thos. Jackson).
17 Jun 1790 Archable Jackson, Rachel Slawter.
24 Jun 1790 John Hegens, Ruhamy Buckley.
24 Jun 1790 John Ailes, Elizabeth Houston, both of Mispillion Hd.
11 Jul 1790 Joshua Hart of Kent Co., Sarah Rich.
14 Jul 1790 Day Willin of Kent Co., Namy Berrey.
17 Jul 1790 Robert Lathem of Duck Creek Hd, Mary Conwell of same.
27 Jul 1790 Samuel Jones, Susannah Doney.
29 Jul 1790 John Hill of Kent Co., Mary Woodley.
1 Aug 1790 John Smallwood, Elizabeth Pigeon.
1 Aug 1790 Sidney Burrus, Hannah Shepperd.
5 Aug 1790 Francis Erwin, Nancy Peters.

5 Aug 1790 James Howard, Fornney Chadwick.
5 Aug 1790 Robert McMullen of Pencader, Sarah Underwood of same.
10 Aug 1790 Jonathan Murphy of Murderkiln, Rachel Williams of same.
11 Aug 1790 John McNath of Mispillion Hd, Mary Arnett of same.
15 Aug 1790 Sorden Lister of Mispillion Hd, Agnes Gibbs of same.
22 Aug 1790 John Loftus of Murderkiln Hd, Barbara Bostwick of same.
27 Aug 1790 John Lee, Elizabeth Budd.
27 Aug 1790 Hezzekiah Beck (mark), Ann Reed.
8 Sep 1790 John Brown of Sussex Co., Eleanor Wright of same.
8 Sep 1790 Vincent Bessex of Mispillion Hd, Mary Minas of same.
9 Sep 1790 David Aaron of Kent Co., Grace Hardin.
11 Sep 1790 Jacob Bostwick of Murderkiln Hd, Mary Coppage of Mispillion Hd.
16 Sep 1790 Robert Appleton, Sine Reed.
21 Sep 1790 Matthew Travers of Mispillion, Margaret Dogherty of same.
23 Sep 1790 Israel Graham of Mispillion Hd, Sarah Lewis of same.
26 Sep 1790 James Sutton, Elizabeth Dulany.
28 Sep 1790 Timothy Sweany, Elizabeth Newcomb.
29 Sep 1790 Thos. Soward, Sarah Burch.
2 Oct 1790 Wm. Mifflin of Mispillion Hd, Mary Rowland of same.
7 Oct 1790 Lowdman Warring, Mary Carter.
13 Oct 1790 Thomas Harper of Sussex Co., Catherine Tredwell of same.
14 Oct 1790 John Colter of Sussex Co., Elizabeth Hall of same.
14 Oct 1790 Sml. Barr of New Castle Co., Ann Gitchell.
14 Oct 1790 Ebenezer Farrow (mark), Elizabeth M'Daniel.
19 Oct 1790 John Lister of Caroline Co., Md., Nancy Hartshorn of Kent Co., Del.
26 Oct 1790 Clayton Coldwell, Rachel Watkins.
27 Oct 1790 Benj. McMullen of Pencader Hd, Mary Flin of same.
31 Oct 1790 Garret Jones, Sarah Soward.
9 Nov 1790 Michael Nagel of Christiana Hd, Elenor McLean.

11 Nov 1790 Thomas Culbreath of New Castle Co., Mary Hamilton
1 Jan 1791 Philip Lewis of Kent County Del., Dorcas Armitage of New Castle Co., surety-James Snow of Kent Co.
15 Jan 1791 Sml. Jaquet of the borough of Wilmington, Sarah Jefferies of same.
20 Jan 1791 Sml. Bready of Pencader Hd, Margaret Post of same.
3 Feb 1791 Philip Mathews of Sussex Co., -- Lourana -- of same.
17 Mar 1791 John Robinson of Sussex Co., Bridget Conway of same.
30 Mar 1791 Peter Gordy of Sussex Co., Mary Sandress of same.
31 Mar 1791 John Griffith of New Castle Co., Reachel Harssey of same, surety, Benj. Hearsey.
5 Apr 1791 Benj. Davis of Pencader Hd, Jane Bowen of same.
16 Apr 1791 Sml. Underwood of Christiana Hd, Elizabeth Backhouse of Brandywine Hd.
21 Apr 1791 John Collins of Sussex Co., Bridget Ingram of same.
24 Apr 1791 Woodman Stockly of Sussex Co., Sarah Burton of same.
18 May 1791 Jenkin Evans of Pencader Hd, Mary Jones of Cecil Co., Md.
25 May 1791 Benj. Collins of Sussex Co., Mary Collins of same.
14 Jun 1791 Archibald Armstrong of Cecil Co., Md, Rebecah Morton of New Castle Co.
26 Jun 1791 Thomas Brereton(?) of Sussex Co., Mary White of same.
7 Jul 1791 Joseph Copes of Sussex Co., Jane White of same, surety, Wm. Vaughan, wit: Joshua Hall, Wm. Hall.
28 Jul 1791 Abraham Harris of Sussex Co., Lovey Melson of same.
4 Aug 1791 Wm Ogle, Mary Jones.
11 Aug 1791 Jesse Scot of Sussex Co., Mary Taylour of same.
25 Aug 1791 Thomas Paramore of Sussex Co., Anna Jones of same.
16 Aug 1791 Robert Crosley of Delaware Co., Anne Harvey of same, surety, Rd. Meredith of Chester Co., wit: Thomas Ainger, Amor Porter.

21 Aug 1791 John Henderson, Sarah Dean.
25 Aug 1791 Thomas Jones of Wilmington, Catherine McClure of same.
 1 Sep 1791 Edward Penney, Catharine Peterman.
 3 Sep 1791 Charles Brown of Sussex Co., Sidney Turner of same.
 6 Sep 1791 James Hickey of Chester Co., Mary Windle of Christiana Hd.
13 Sep 1791 Moses Clayton of Bethel Township, Susannah Earl of same.
29 Sep 1791 Alexander Smith of Sussex Co., Lucilla Polk of same.
12 Oct 1791 Wm Kennerly of Sussex Co., Martha Kennerly.
13 Oct John Morris, Sary Hutson.
13 Oct Benj. Smith of Kent Co., Ann Passons.
 6 Nov 1791 Thomas Reynolds, Ann Reynolds.
10 Nov 1791 John Cowgill of Kent Co., Martha Stout.
 8 Dec 1791 John Burroughs of Queen Anns Co., Rachel Manson.
15 Dec 1791 John Lynch of Kent Co., Nancy Brown.
17 Dec 1791 James Wells, Kent Co., Catharine Truax.
21 Dec 1791 Robert Faries, Pencader Hd, Mary Clark.
19 Jan 1792 Peter King of St. George's Hd, Hannah Todd of Wilmington.
28 Feb 1792 James Jefferis of Brandywine Hd, Mary Perkins of same, surety, Thomas Jefferis of Christiana Hd, wit: Saml. Jaquet, Thos. Ainger.
 1 Mar 1792 Ebenezer Jones of Christiana Hd, Rebeckah Tryon of same.
14 Mar 1792 James Todd of Christiana Hd, Edith Hickman of same.
22 Mar 1792 Malachi Peten of Pencader Hd, Mary Preston of same.
10 Apr 1792 James Smith of Christiana Hd, Rebecah Morton of same.
10 Apr 1792 John Stewart, Md., Mary Elwood, of same.
 3 May 1792 James Gaskill of Christiana Hd, Ann Jones of same.
20 Jul 1793 Wm Baldwin of Christiana Hd, Susannah Crozer of same.
10 Aug 1792 Thos. Kirk of Christiana Hd, Hannah Kellam of Brandywine Hd.

16 Aug 1792 Jas. Smith, Chester Co., Hannah
   Talley, Brandywine Hd, surety, Jos. Talley,
   Brandywine Hd, wit: Curtis Talley, John
   Smith.
30 Aug 1792 Wm. Townsend of Wilmington, Mary
   Hedges of same.
 2 Sep 1792 Elisha Evens of Sussex Co., Nancy
   Smith.
20 Sep 1792 Isaac Eaton of New Castle Co.,
   Keziah Lewis.
 4 Oct 1792 Thos. Warrington of Christiana Hd,
   Elizabeth Hedges of same.
13 Oct 1792 James Shelley of Brandywine Hd, Mary
   Adear of Christiana Hd.
18 Oct 1792 Jesse Harry of Christiana Hd (or
   Bradford Township), Catharine Meers(?) of
   Bradford Township, surety, Joseph Lawson.
18 Oct 1792 John Kyle of Christiana Hd, Mary
   Smith of same.
23 Oct 1792 Joseph Underwood of Pencader Hd,
   Else Ginn.
25 Oct 1792 Parker Otwell of Sussex Co.,
   Elizabeth Short of same.
 1 Nov 1792 Wm. Berry of Kent Co., Sarah
   Montgomery of same.
15 Nov 1792 Reuben Anderson of Kent Co., Nancy
   Adams of same.
15 Dec 1792 John Jones of Somerset Co., Md.,
   Elizabeth Warren of Kent Co., Del.
27 Dec 1792 Boaz Hilford of Mispillion Hd, Sarah
   Morgan(?) of Kent Co.
31 Dec 1792 John Hyatt Esquire, of New Castle
   Co., Sarah Wattson of same.
 2 Jan 1792 John Dawson of Christiana Hd,
   Sebinah Genkins of Christiana Hd.
 3 Jan 1793 Edward Hemphill of Christiana Hd,
   Susanah Dunlap of same.
10 Jan 1793 John Dodds of Kent Co., Lydia Cooper
   of same.
17 Jan 1793 Jacob Rynhold (mark) of New Castle
   Co., Mary Evans of same.
24 Jan 1793 Thomas Miner(?) of Sussex Co., Ruth
   Shaffer (Shaver?) of same.
 4 Feb 1793 William Stewart of New Castle Co.,
   Lydia Sharp of same.
 7 Feb 1793 Peter Lowber of Murderkiln Hd, Agnes
   Warrington of same.
 9 Feb 1793 Benj. Berry of Kent Co., Sarah
   Turchess of same.

20 Feb 1793 Bethnel of Sussex Co., Mary Robinson of same.
21 Feb 1793 William Robinson of Kent Co., Minte Taylor of same.
25 Feb 1793 John Hart of Kent Co., Hannah Buckmaster.
25 Feb 1793 James White of Kent Co., Susanna Ryans of same.
28 Feb 1793 John Harper Jr. of Kent Co., Priscilla Bracher of same.
14 Mar 1793 Joseph Lewis of Christiana Hd, Mary Hamilton of same.
17 Mar 1793 Sml. Hyatt of St. George's Hd, Mary Stroud (?) of Brandywine Hd.
21 Mar 1793 Bedwell Maxwell of Murderkiln Hd, Sarah Grier of same.
11 Apr 1793 Wm Faussett(?) Jr. of Worcester, Md., Martha Campbel of Sussex Co., Del.
25 Apr 1793 Isaac Middleton of Christiana Hd, Martha Calvert of same.
29 Apr 1793 Jonathan Treviller of Marlborough Township, Ann Nulin of same, surety, Sml. Carlton of Cennet Township.
30 Apr 1793 Frederick Craig of Christiana Hd, Elizabeth French of same, surety, Peter Brynberg, wit: Evan Thomas, Caleb Eyre.
18 May 1793 William Mott of Murderkiln Hd, Mary Sullivan of same.
23 May 1793 Thomas Hooper of Sussex Co., Elizabeth Dallinar of Kent Co.
25 May 1793 John Provost (mark) of Wilmington, Sarah Petterson of same.
13 Jun 1793 Elisha Robinson of Duck Creek Hd (mark), Margaret Cooper of same.
6 Jul 1793 Thomas Lewis of Kent Co., Rebecca Bateman of same.
11 Jul 1793 Thomas Brown of Kent Co., Nancy Smith of same.
1 Aug 1793 Robert Kernahan of Duck Creek Hd, Margaret Cook of same.
7 Aug 1793 Brickers Townsend of Kent Co., Susanna Brown of same.
15 Aug 1793 Jesse Watson of Appoquinimick Hd, Frances Blainny of same.
22 Aug 1793 Geo. Smith of Duck Creek Hd, Elizabeth Wells of same.
4 Sep 1793 David Pleasanton of Jones Hd, Kent Co., Sarah Gordon of same.

5 Sep 1793 Daniel Lanman (mark) of Kent Co.,
    Margaret Brown of same.
 6 Sep 1793 John Mitchell, Jane Stewart.
18 Sep 1793 Thomas Rawlings of Christiana Hd,
    Jennet Clark of same.
25 Sep 1793 Cornelius Ryan of Sussex Co., Betsy
    Rayfield of same.
 3 Oct 1793 John Allen, Isobel Robison.
 4 Oct 1793 Benjamin Newpher of Christiana Hd,
    Catharine Bennet of same.
17 Oct 1793 Rd. Knowles, Esther McDowel.
31 Oct 1793 Reuben West of Sussex Co., Nancy
    Cottingham of same.
 3 Nov 1793 Minus Messic of Sussex Co., Hannah
    Philips of same.
 4 Nov 1793 Colin McNitt of Phila., Elizabeth
    McCalla, surety, John Foster of Wilmington.
 4 Nov 1793 James De La Cour of Montgomery
    County, Pa, Ann Ford of same, surety, Sml.
    Ford of Christiana Hd.
16 Nov 1793 Geo. Spain of Phila., sailmaker,
    Elizabeth Reynold, surety, Wm. Bassett of
    Wilmington.
19 Nov 1793 Charles Anderson of Christiana Hd,
    Racheil Paulson.
21 Nov 1793 Nathaniell Grubb of Delaware Co.,
    Margarett Babb, surety, Nath'l. Newlin of
    Delaware Co.
21 Nov 1793 Philip Ford of Brandywine Hd,
    Kathrine Perkins.
26 Nov 1793 Barkley McLean of Phila. city, Ann
    Jane Townley, surety, Donald Stewart.
28 Nov 1793 David Rees of Duck Creek Hd, Jemima
    Griffin of same.
16 Dec 1793 James Legg of Little Creek Hd, Sarah
    Clarke of same.
18 Dec 1793 Jonathan Beeson of Brandywine Hd,
    Elizabeth Shipley.
19 Dec 1793 Londay Howard of Sussex Co., Betsey
    Philips of same.
21 Dec 1793 John Currey (mark) of Christiana Hd,
    Hannah Dunn of same, surety, Neal Curry of
    Christiana Hd.
28 Dec 1793 Charles Collins of Brandywine Hd,
    Giles McNulty, surety, James McNulty of
    Brandywine Hd.
 2 Jan 1794 John Rodney of Sussex Co., Peggy
    Piper of same.

2 Jan 1794 John Spear (mark) of Duck Creek Hd, Elizabeth Ozburn of same.
6 Jan 1794 John Walraven of Christiana Hd, Mary Colesbery.
9 Jan 1794 Moses Ward of Sussex Co., Polly Callaway of same.
9 Jan 1794 John Burns of Lower Chichester, Sarah Truman. Surety, John Moore of Brandywine Hd.
13 Jan 1794 David Howell of Pencader Hd, Elizbeth Hukill.
18 Jan 1794 William Reynolds of Wilmington, Leah Barnett. Surety, William Jones Jur. of Wilmington.
21 Jan 1794 William Lenderman of Brandywine Hd, Elizabeth Stidham. Surety, David Killam of Brandywine Hd, farmer.
11 Feb 1794 Nickolas Haney of Wilmington (mark), Margrett Backster.
17 Feb 1794 George Grimes of Red Lyon Hd, Mary Henderson.
18 Feb 1794 Benjamin Rumsey of Wilmington, Mary Clark.
26 Feb 1794 William Polk of Sussex Co., Sarah Robinson of same.
20 Feb 1794 Robert Gilmour of Christiana Hd, Hannah Given.
27 Feb 1794 Coventer Ellingsworth(?) of Sussex Co., Polly Workman of same.
24 Feb 1794 Jonas Stidham of Christiana Hd, yeoman, Elizabeth Nebeker of same place.
27 Feb 1794 Joseph Holston of Brandywine Hd, Mary Steanes.
4 March 1794 Robert Clark of Pencader Hd, Elizabeth Law of Red Lyon Hd.
19 March 1794 John Grant of Chester Co., Susanna Ames. Surety, William Creery of Wilmington.
24 March 1794 Benjamin Hampton of Willistown Township, Mary M'Coy. Surety, Thomas Clarke of Wilmington.
7 April 1794 John Street of Wilmington, Mary Gilbert. Surety, Thomas LeTelier of Wilmington.
10 April 1794 Robert Allen of Red Lyon Hd, Mary Adair.
10 April 1794 Isaac Adams, Unyey Cordrey.

MARRIAGE BONDS OF NEWCASTLE COUNTY 255

23 April 1794 John Stapler Littler of
Wilmington, Nancy Broom. Surety, James M.
Broom of Wilmington.
1 May 1794 Gillis Smith of Sussex Co., Elloner
Ward of same. Sureties: Marshall Smith,
Isaac Benson.
17 May 1794 Samuel Day of Delaware Co., Hannah
Howell. Surety, Alexander Hopkins of
Delaware Co.
24 May 1794 William Miller of Wilmington, Rhoda
Heaton.
27 May 1794 John Simmons of Chester Co., Lydia
Taylor.
5 June 1794 James Martin of Sussex Co., Peggy
Anderson of same.
6 June 1794 Nathaniel Marshal of Wilmington,
Rebekah Vineman. Surety, James Tagart of
Wilmington.
24 June 1794 Charles Wilson of Chester Co., Ruth
Taylor. Surety, Thomas Wilson of Chester Co.
30 June 1794 John Crampton of Wilmington, Sarah
Harden.
11 July 1794 Isaac Wiltbank of Sussex Co., Mary
Stewart of same place, single woman. Surety,
Joseph Mason. Wit: Peter Clowes, Wm. Stuard.
12 July 1794 John Franklin of Sussex Co., Elin
Brerton, single woman of same co. Wit:
Nathan Jefferis, Stephen Wood.
17 July 1794 Thomas Dougherty of Wilmington,
Mary Ford.
19 July 1794 Jacob Colesbery of Wilmington,
Margaret Robinett.
19 July 1794 John Powell of Chester Co.,
Prudence M'Leer. Surety, Bezaleel Bentley.
21 July 1794 Drake Hodskin, Eunice Willing.
6 Aug 1794 Zadock Barker of Sussex Co., Sally
Prettyman, single woman of same co.
5 Aug 1794 John Walker of Sussex Co., Mary
Stevenson of same.
7 Aug 1794 Benjamin Salmon junr. of Sussex Co.,
Catharine Waples of same.
16 Aug 1794 Abraham M'Collom of Christiana Hd,
Rebekah Elliott.
21 Aug 1794 Samuel Hall of Sussex Co., Eunice
Serman of same co.
21 Aug 1794 William Wilkins of Chester Co.,
Rachel M'Coy. Surety, Mathew M'Cay.

27 Aug 1794 Cleland Boyd of Christiana Hd, Elliner Muckovoy.
31 Aug 1794 George Crawford of Sussex Co., Lovey Short of same.
4 Sep 1794 Thomas Napier of Brandywine Hd, Mary Carpenter.
15 Sep 1794 Michael Mullen of Wilmington (mark), Mary Culbertson of same place.
16 Sep 1794 William Rice of Mill Creek Hd, Sarah Bracken.
2 Oct 1794 Joshua Clows (mark) of Kent Co., Sarah Walker of same.
14 Oct 1794 John Devan of Brandywine Hd, Mary Kennedy.
30 Oct 1794 John Wilson of Chester Co., Elizabeth Craig. Surety, Nathan Simmons of Chester Co.
6 Nov 1794 Abram Gest of New Castle Co., Mary Robins.
6 Nov 1794 Samuel Carleton of New Castle Co., Rebekah Harlan. Surety, Joshua Bingham of New Castle Co.
12 Nov 1794 Esau Sharpley of Brandywine Hd, Rebekah Sharpley. Surety, Wm. Sharpley of Brandywine Hd.
13 Nov 1794 Benjamin Ready of Sussex Co., Anna Polk of same. Sureties, John Bacon, John Williams.
13 Nov 1794 Richard Radley of Sussex Co., Peggy M'Gee of same.
13 Nov 1794 John Hineman of Brandywine Hd, Sarah Righter.
19 Nov 1794 Jacob Backhouse of Brandywine Hd, Elizabeth Bratten.
19 Nov 1794 Jacob Lewis, Elizabeth Betts of Sussex Co. Sureties: Jonathan and Joseph Betts. Wit: John Betts.
20 Nov 1794 David Downing of Chester Co., Ann Evans. Surety, Joseph Commons of New Castle Co.
20 Nov 1794 Joseph Willcox of Cecil Co., Maryland (signed Wilcox), Hannah Morgan.
1794 John M'Dowel of Sussex Co., ---.
1 Dec 1794 Ebenezer Collins of Sussex Co., Sally Atkinson of same.
18 Dec 1794 Isaac Waples of Sussex Co., Sally Burton of same.

MARRIAGE BONDS OF NEWCASTLE COUNTY

20 Dec 1794 Thomas West of Sussex Co., Sally Stephenson of same. Surety, George West of Sussex Co.
Dec 1794 Joseph Waples of Sussex Co., Leah Prettyman, of same, single woman.
23 Dec 1794 Richard Green of Sussex Co., Mary Harmonson of same co., single woman. Wit: Mary Harmonson, Elizabeth Harmonson.
23 Dec 1794 Isaac Jones of Sussex Co., Lurena Wingate of same, single woman. Surety, Zachariah Jones. Wit: Wingate Jones, Josiah Martin.
24 Dec 1794 Roderick Lewis of Sussex Co., Mary Cirwithen of same, single woman.
24 Dec 1794 James Bratten of Brandywine Hd, Martha M'Bride. Surety, James Nixon.
30 Dec 1794 Isaac Hopkins of Sussex Co., Polly Short of same.
31 Dec 1794 Samuel Lee of the borough of Wilmington, Ann Sharp. Surety, Harlin Cloud of Wilmington.
14 Jan 1795 James Burton of Sussex Co., Polly Craig of same. Surety, William Craige.
17 Jan 1795 John Eastwick of Brandywine Hd, Rebeckah Cherrey.
20 Jan 1795 William Hobbs of Sussex Co., Jenny Bound of same.
26 Jan 1795 John Babtist Chassaing of Wilmington, Emelia Lagurd. Surety, Isaac H. Starr.
28 Jan 1795 William Fitcher of Sussex Co., Martha Little of same.
28 Jan 1795 Joshua Jones of Worcester Co., Maryland, Polly Morris of Sussex Co.
29 Jan 1795 Thomas Pierce of Mill Creek Hd, Rachiel Forgison.
2 Feb 1795 William Craige of Sussex Co., Nancy White of same.
5 Feb 1795 James Penington of Wilmington, Rebekah Charley. Surety, David Talley.
? Feb 1795 William Jones of Sussex Co., Elen Rodes Burton, single woman, of same.
17 Feb 1795 James Dyson of Christiana Hd, Sarah Stidham.
19 Feb 1795 Henry Logan of New Castle Co., Mary M'Calla.

24 Feb 1795 Jacob Resir (or Rasir) of Wilmington, Elizabeth Newel. Surety, Jeremiah Carter.
25 Feb 1795 Joseph Gibson of Christiana Hd, Ann Douglass. Surety, Clotworthy Barber.
26 Feb 1795 John Price of Chester Co., Elizabeth Smith. Surety, William Pennell.
27 Feb 1795 John Jefferis of Wilmington (mark), Rachel Bale. Surety, Niel Gallaher (mark).
28 Feb 1795 Samuel M'Collom (M'Chollam) of Wilmington, Martha M'Coy.
12 March 1795 Henry Crawford of New Castle Co., Hesther Beson.
17 March 1795 Ralph Lutton of New Castle Co., Mary Hannah.
18 March 1795 Benjamin Gest of New Castle Co., Kathrine Davis. Surety, Caleb Martin.
21 March 1795 George Weaver of New Castle Co., Mary M'Worter. Surety, John M'Whorter.
28 March 1795 William Hemingway of Wilmington, Sarah Hayes.
1 April 1795 Daniel Roach of Sussex Co., Martha Tull of same.
4 April 1795 Robert Shields of Wilmington, mariner, Elizabeth Jorden.
20 April 1795 Cornelius M'Dade (mark) of Wilmington, Mary Carr.
25 April 1795 James Starr of Sussex Co., Mary Stratton of same.
29 April 1795 Robert Hunter of Sussex Co., Prudence Hopkins of same.
5 May 1795 Fransis Fountain (mark) of Wilmington, Mary Ann Richardson.
6 May 1795 Joseph Booth of Wilmington, Mary Pennington.
7 May 1795 Thomas Hemmons of Sussex Co., Patience Stockly of same.
8 May 1795 Theodore Wilson of Sussex Co., Mary N. Kollick, single woman of same.
16 May 1795 Lewis Tousard of Wilmington, Anna Maria Geddess. Surety, Peter Bandery (Baudy?).
2 June 1795 Andrew Lindsey (mark) of New Castle Co., Isabella M'Calla.
4 June 1795 Jacob Morton of Christiana Hd, Rachaiel Harp.
18 June 1795 Anderson Hudson of Sussex Co., Ruth Mustard of same.

18 June 1795 Isaac Culin of Delaware Co., Hannah Carter. Surety, Thomas Enochs.
20 June 1795 Jacob Broomell of Delaware Co., Phebe Baker.
26 June 1795 George Bell of Wilmington, Ann Bell.
29 July 1795 James Stewart of Kent Co., Jane Barnitt of same.
4 July 1795 John Earl of Mill Creek Hd, Elizabeth Wilson.
6 July 1795 Robert Jones of Sussex Co., Anna Stewart of same.
8 July 1795 William Hart of New Castle Co., Margaret Mikeljohn.
9 July 1795 Jacob Richards of Brandywine Hd, Elizabeth James.
13 July 1795 Benjamin Draper of Sussex Co., Ruth Fisher of same.
15 July 1795 Adam Talley of Brandywine Hd, Rebekah Day.
18 July 1795 William Hemphill of Wilmington, Jane M'Intire.
23 July 1795 William White of Sussex Co., Polly Fisher of same. Surety, David Craige.
29 July 1795 Ebenezer Myers (mark) of Kent Co., Priscilla(?) Layton of same.
29 July 1795 Jacob Starr of New Castle Co., [no name].
25 Aug 1795 William John (mark) of Maryland, Ann Grimes of same.
6 Sep 1795 Sylvester Young of Wilmington, Ann M'Questen.
8 Sep 1795 William Bracken of Mill Creek Hd, Elioner Herdman.
6 Oct 1795 John Thelwell of Wilmington, Esther Jones.
8 Oct 1795 John Rumford of Wilmington, Priscilla Jefferis. Surety, Benjamin Marden.
15 Oct 1795 James Hogg of Wilmington, Elizabeth Robinson.
16 Oct 1795 James M'Mullan (mark) of Wilmington, Katharine Bryam.
29 Oct 1795 James D. Boss of Wilmington, Eliza M. Bancroft. Surety, David Bush.
1 Nov 1795 John Hart of Brandywine Hd, Deborah Conrod.
20 Nov 1795 George Ward of Kent Co., Anna White of same.

22 Nov 1795 Jonathan Savill of Wilmington, Harriott Farmer(?).
27 Nov 1795 Ashbery Sutton of St. Georges Hd, Mariah Beedle. Wit: Polly Hickman, Peter Hyatt.
10(or 6) Dec 1795 Benjamin Denny of Kent co., Polly Williams of same.
23 Dec 1795 Lazarus Pierce of Brandywine Hd, Sarah Lenderman.
31 Dec 1795 Patrick M'Niel (M'Neal?) of Wilmington, Elizbeth Jefferis.
1 Jan 1796 William Smith of Wilmington, Elizabeth Fletcher. Surety, Dutton Richards.
1 Jan 1796 Moses Lowther of Brandywine Hd, Mary Long.
2 Jan 1796 Richard Hancock of Wilmington, Rebekah Matson. Surety, William Foot.
2 Jan 1796 William Foot of Wilmington, Kittey Matson. Surety, Richard Hancock.
4 Jan 1796 Francis O'Daniel of Wilmington, Isabella French.
11(?) Jan 1796 Robert Scoolley (mark) of Kent Co., Polly Greenwood of same.
8 Jan 1796 Henry Hewitt of Christiana Hd, Susanna Grubb. Surety, Isaac Crawford of Christiana Hd.
8 Jan 1796 James Robinson of Christiana Hd, Rebekah M'Kennon.
8 Jan 1796 Robert M'Call of Wilmington, Elizabeth Calahen.
16 Jan 1796 John Byrnes of Wilmington, Mary Cox.
17 Jan 1796 Francis Dunlap of Wilmington, Honour Stidham.
19 Jan 1796 Enoch Wood of Kent Co., Rebekah Numbers of same.
27 Jan 1796 George Robinson of Sussex Co., Patty Blossom(?) of same.
28 Jan 1796 William Kinny of Sussex Co., Frances Flowers of same.
2 Feb 1796 John Horsey of Sussex Co., Gooding Goddard of same.
11 Feb 1796 Thomas Ward of Sussex Co., Betsy Callaway of same.
14 Feb 1796 Elisha Evans of Sussex Co., Elizabeth Russel.
18 Feb 1796 Bruffet Jones of Sussex Co., Elizabeth Johnson.

21 Feb 1796 William Houston of Indian River Hd, Sarah Barker.
25 Feb 1796 Gerherdus Dorman of Broadkiln Hd, Nancy Clark.
27 Feb 1796 Jacob White of Rehoboth Hd, Sussex Co., Katharine Jordan.
16 March 1796 Samuel Paynter of Sussex Co., Elizabeth Rowland.
23 March 1796 Joseph Cartwright of New Castle Co., Mary Francis of same.
27 March 1796 Jacob Starots (mark) of New Castle Co., Cathren Allfred(?).
24 March 1796 William Emerson of Sussex Co., Sally Hearn of same.
31 March 1796 Elijah Cohran(?) of Kent Co., Susannah Stark.
3 April 1796 Jacob Claten (mark) of New Castle Co., Angelica Mecay.
12 April 1796 Levin Winder of Sussex Co., Martha Willen of same.
15 April 1796 Cornelius Patten (mark) of New Castle Co., Mary Torten.
28 April 1796 Joseph Deakyne of New Castle Co., Ann Mann.
31 April 1796 John Thompson of Dagsborough Hd, Rachel Johnson.
7 May 1796 Nathan Davis of Kent Co., Alcy Mather of same.
10 May 1796 David Stauts (mark) of New Castle Co., Letesha Codereck of Kent Co.
10 May 1796 Richard Palmer of New Castle Co., Elizabeth Nutt.
14 May 1796 Benjamin West of Kent Co., Elizabeth Bassett.
14 May 1796 Robert Crumcalton (mark) of New Castle Co., Milcay Wharum of same.
22 May 1796 William S. Corbet of New Castle Co., Elizabeth Pell of same.
7 June 1796 Joseph Langford of Sussex Co., Sally Griffith of same.
9 June 1796 James Relph of Sussex Co., Mary Prichard of same.
12 June 1796 David Hall of New Jersey, Ann Wesley, surety, Mills M'Ilvain of Sussex Co.
15 June 1796 Robert Burton of Indian River Hd, Polley Stockley.
18 June 1796 Peery Pool of Indian River Hd, Helen M'Dowal of same.

6 July 1796 Isaac Callaway of Sussex Co., Nelly Adams Alexander of same.
7 July 1796 John R. Fassitt of Sussex Co., Ann Russell.
11 July 1796 Daniel Clifton of Lewis, Sussex Co., Kitty Hargis of same.
13(?) July 1796 Joseph Fisher (his mark) of Indian River Hd, Katharine Lingo of same.
19 July 1796 Nathaniel Russam(?), Leah Laws.
21 July 1796 Elijah Wright of Sussex Co., Mary Kenny of same.
28 July 1796 Jehu Ryland of Pencader Hd, Henrietta Harrison.
3 Aug 1796 Daniel Burton of Rehoboth, Sussex Co., Arcada Milby.
4 Aug Aaron Owens of Sussex Co., Ann Culver, of same.
25 Aug Matthew Walker of Sussex Co., Nelly Smith of same.
1 Sep William Calhoon of Sussex Co., Nancy Bevins of same.
20 Sep Andrew Smith of Sussex Co., Rhoda Hill Bryan of same.
5 Oct John Mustard of Sussex Co., Hetty Marsh.
6 Oct James Badly of Sussex Co., Mary Baily of same.
12 Oct Robert Willis of Sussex Co., Elizabeth King of same.
1 Nov Thomas Freeny of Sussex Co., Ellenor Benson of same.
8 Nov Manon Bull of Sussex Co., Polly Jane Pollock of same.
25 Nov James Maull of Sussex Co., Elizabeth Johnson of same.
30 Nov Caleb Rodney of Sussex Co., Elizabeth West of same.
8 Dec 1796 Job Messick of Dagsborough Hd, Sussex Co., Priscilla Townsend.
1 Feb 1797 Samuel Bready of Pencader Hd, Eleanor Warnock of same.
14 May 1800 (1801?) Jonath Kelly, Ann Ryan.
15 May George Ruth of New Castle Town, Sarah James.
25 July James Baker of New Castle Co., Mary Ann ---.
2 Sep William Davis (mark) of New Castle Co., Elizabeth Powell
30 Sep William Bruce, Margaret Griffith.

30 Sep James Couper Jr. of New Castle Co., Hanna
   M'Intire.
 7 Oct David Morton, Rebecca Cozier.
 9 Oct James Caldwell, Sarah Booth.
20 Oct Robert White, Mary Ternall.
23 Oct John Smith, Gertrude Gilpin.
-- Oct Wm. Slater of N.C. town, Martha Smith.
11 Dec Samuel Thomas, Elenor Philips.
24 Dec John Kinsey, Rebecca Porter.

INDEX

-A-

AARON, David, 248
ABBOTT, Alexander, 226
ABRAHAMS, Agnes, 50
ABRAMS, Agnes, 238
ACLAWERY, Bridget, 21
  Mary, 21
  Philip, 21
ACTEN, Mary, 46
ADAIR, Mary, 254
ADAMS, Ann, 63
  George, 53
  Isaac, 7, 254
  Margaret, 7
  Mary, 238
  Nancy, 251
  Nicolas, 5
  Packer, 5
  Thomas, 7
  William, 245
ADDAIR(ADEAR), Samuel, 234
ADEAR, Mary, 251
AICKEN, Elizabeth, 28
  John, 29, 66
  Mary, 28
  Mrs., 66
  Thomas, 28
AIKEN, Ann, 60
  David, 59
  Hannah, 25
  Joseph, 25
  Mary, 25
  Robert, 59
  Thomas, 1, 25
  William, 52
  William Derby, 25
AILES, John, 247
AINGER, Thomas, 249, 250
AITHREN, Thomas, 22
AITKIN, Fanny, 245
ALEXANDER, Archd., 242
  Elizabeth, 219, 230
  Francis, 230, 240
  Isaac, 235
  Jacob, 230
  John, 27, 58
  Jonathan, 51
  Margaret, 27
  Mary, 27, 50
  Nelly Adams, 262
ALICE, John, 25
  Susannah, 25
ALISON, Oliver, 86, 99
  Rachel, 88, 99
ALL, Joseph, 28
ALLCORN, George, 49
  James, 219
  Susannah, 64

ALLEN, Agnes, 220, 232
  Charles, 62
  Doherty, 11
  Dougherty, 43
  Eliza, 54
  John, 11, 115, 253
  Margaret, 11
  Mary, 9, 11, 220
  Rachel, 48
  Rebecca, 11
  Robert, 220, 254
  Samuel, 242
  William, 9, 11, 115
ALLFRED, Cathren, 261
ALLIN, Jacob, 216
  Margaret, 216
  Samuel, 218
ALLISON, Elizabeth, 51
  Samuel, 54
ALLMAN, Isaac, 241
ALRICKS, Ann, 5
  Henry Sigpedus, 146
  Jacob, 146
  James, 5
  Lydia, 146
  Mary Ann, 146
  Peter, 5
  Sarah, 146
  Sidney Ann, 146
  William, 146
AMBLER, David, 55
AMES, Susanna, 254
ANDERSON, Andrew, 218
  Ann, 44
  Charles, 253
  David, 6, 14, 16, 17
  Elizabeth, 53
  George, 240
  Isabella, 240
  James, 6
  Jane, 6, 14, 16, 17
  Joseph, 14
  Josiah, 14
  Maria, 226
  Peggy, 255
  Reuben, 251
  Richard, 59
  Ruth, 16
  Sarah, 14, 17
  Susannah, 35
  William, 14, 232, 242
ANDRAS, Mary, 216
ANDREW, Hannah, 112
  Isaac, 194
  John, 178
  Samuel, 192
ANDREWS, Benjamin, 127, 211
  David, 127

Deborah, 127
Elizabeth, 29
Ezekiel, 124, 127, 149, 159, 181
Hannah, 124, 127
Isaac, 127
James, 127, 199
John, 124, 127, 150, 205
Mary, 127, 159, 173, 181, 201
Miriam, 124
Rebekah, 127, 152, 181
Ruth, 124, 148
Samuel, 127
Sarah, 127
William, 29, 124, 148, 150
APPLETON, John, 247
Robert, 248
ARMITAGE, Dorcas, 92, 249
ARMOR, Alice, 230
Jane, 6, 13
John, 6
Samuel, 13
William, 6, 13
ARMSTRONG, Ann, 74
Archable, 222
Archibald, 249
Christopher, 56
Edwd., 246
Elizabeth, 6
Hannah, 222
Isabell, 6, 8
James, 56, 238
Jane, 62
John, 6, 8, 239
Keity, 217
Margaret, 54
Mrs., 66
Rebecca, 218, 222
Samuel, 57
Sarah, 8
Thomas, 219
William, 74
ARNETT, Mary, 248
ARREN, Samuel, 226
ARTERS, John, 244
ASBY, Richard, 55
ASHBRIDGE, Aaron, 149
Mary, 178
ASHBURNHAM, Hannah, 128, 176, 202
John, 128
Rosanna, 128, 154
Thomas, 151
William, 128, 151, 154
ASHBURRY, Mary, 232
ASHTON, Ann, 106
Robert, 106
ASKEW, Elizabeth, 144

Hannah, 144
Joseph, 144
Martha, 42
Mary, 158
Molly, 144
Parker, 144
Peter, 144
Rebecca, 144
Sarah, 144
William, 144, 158
ATKINSON, Ann, 170
Elizabeth, 169, 194
Lydia, 103
Mary, 206
Sally, 256
AUGUSTE, Pierre Marie Jean Eli, 227
AULL, Elizabeth, 34, 36
James, 34
John, 34, 36
Robert, 36
William, 34, 66, 74
AVERITE, Anne, 93
AYSEN, Sarah, 63

-B-

BABB, Elizabeth, 112
Lydia, 106
Margarett, 253
BABCOCK, Mary Ann, 67
BACKEN, James, 222
Mary Ann, 222
Robert, 222
BACKHOUSE, Elizabeth, 249
Hannah, 118
Jacob, 256
John, 118
Mary, 118
BACKSTER, Margrett, 254
BACON, John, 256
BADGER, Jonathan, 245
BADLY, James, 262
BAGWELL, Ann, 246
BAILEY, Evan, 201
Hannah, 201
Isaac, 159
Joseph, 159
Lydia, 159
BAILY, Edward Tatnall, 144
Elizabeth, 144
Isaac, 162
John, 242
Joseph, 144
Joseph Tatnall, 144
Mary, 262
Samuel, 144
Sarah, 214
Sarah Ann, 144
BAKER, James, 262
John, 182

Joshua, 116, 117
Lydia, 116
Margery, 116, 117
Phebe, 259
Richard, 209
Sarah, 117, 220
BALDWIN, Elizabeth, 60, 114
  John, 114
  Mary, 114
  William, 250
BALE, Rachel, 258
BALL, Ann, 41
  Hannah, 37
  Isabella, 37, 38
  James, 37, 38, 243
  James Washington, 38
  Jeremiah, 41
  John, 53, 238, 243
  Joseph, 67
  Mary, 37, 61
  Rebecca, 243
  Sarah, 243
  Susannah, 37
BALLEY, Joseph, 55
BAMBERRY, Richard, 217
BANCROFT, Eliza M., 259
BANDERY (BAUDUY), Peter, 258
BANTAM, Benjamin, 219
BARBER, Clotworthy, 258
  Mary, 233
  Thomas, 42
BARCLAY, John, 241
BARKER, Joseph, 246
  Mary, 53
  Samuel, 46
  Sarah, 64, 261
  Zadock, 255
BARNARD, Lettice, 160
  Richard, 160
BARNES, Ephraim, 211
  John, 9
  Margaret, 9
  Mary, 9
BARNET, Phebe, 212
  Sampson, 212
BARNETT, Leah, 254
  Phebe, 170
  Sampson, 170
BARNEY, Sarah, 184
BARNINGHAME, Charles Gookin, 65
BARNITT, Jane, 259
BAROW, Richart, 80
BARR, Mary, 55, 240
  Robert, 234
  Samuel, 63, 248
  William, 217
BARRAT, Benjamin, 111
BARROW, Richard, 98

  Sara, 82
  Sarah, 87, 98
BARTLET, Mathew, 221
  Robert, 221
BARTLEY, Anne, 217
BARTON, John, 246
BASILI, Victorie, 227
BASSET, Thomas, 232
BASSETT, Elizabeth, 261
  William, 253
BATEMAN, J., 225
  Rebecca, 252
BATES, Joseph, 226
BATTELL, Mary, 5
  William, 5
BATTEN, Elisabeth, 191
  Hannah, 191
  Richard, 190
BATTIN, Elizabeth, 167
  Hannah, 167
  Rachel, 119
  Richard, 119, 167
BATTLE, William, 41
BAUDUY, Etienne, 229
  Felicite Alexandre M., 227
  Helenna, 229
  Marguerite Clementine Jos, 229
  Pierre, 227
  Veuve, 228
BAUGUY, Helenne, 229
  Louis-Alexandre Amelie, 229
  Pierre Marie Joseph, 227
BAYARD, Elizabeth, 219
  P., 232
BAYLY, John, 242
BAZILE, Cecile Victoire, 228
  Louis Florent, 228
  Victoire Dulet, 228
BEACH, Susannah, 57
BEARD, David, 47
BEASON, Esther, 105
  Hannah, 107
BEASTON, Zebulon, 48, 217
BEATY, Jane, 239
BEAUCHAMP, Costen, 244
  Jeroboam, 244
  Joshua, 244
  William, 245
BECK, Hezzekiah, 248
BEDFORD, Gunning, 4, 5, 58, 73
  Mary, 4, 5
BEDOME, Joseph, 86
BEDWILL, Thomas, 245
BEEBY, Jane, 111
  Robert, 109

BEECH, Cathrine, 49
BEEDLE, Mariah, 260
BEESON, Aloe, 125
  David, 125
  John, 125
  Jonathan, 125, 253
  Lydia, 125
  Pathenah, 125
  Thomas, 125
BELL, Ann, 259
  Elizabeth, 217
  George, 259
  James, 245
  Rachel, 147, 163
  Robert, 47
  Susanna, 241
  William, 245
BELLEW, Frances, 53
BELLIEU, Elizabeth, 53
BELOW, Elizabeth, 220
BELVEAL, Frances, 53
BEMISH, Rachel, 87, 96
BENERS, Anna Eliza, 58
BENNET, Catharine, 253
  Deborah, 180
  Eliza, 63
  Hannah, 180
  Sarah, 195, 209
  Susanna, 195
BENNETT, Alice, 136
  Ann, 136, 153
  Jacob, 136
  Sarah, 136
  Susanna, 136, 153
  Thomas, 231
BENSANCE, Philip, 216
BENSO, Ellenor, 262
BENTLEY, Bezaleel, 255
  John, 79
  Mary, 77
BENTLY, Cheffrs (Jefferies), 84
BERNARD, Rachel, 197
  Sarah, 207
BERREY, Namy, 247
BERRY, Benjamin, 154, 169, 251
  James, 153
  Johana, 219
  John, 45
  Mary, 169, 190
  Sarah, 154, 169
  William, 55, 251
BESON, Hesther, 258
BESSEX, Vincent, 248
BEST, Valentine, 246
BESTEN, Ketrine, 217
BESTIDA, Judith, 239
BETHNEL, ---, 252
BETTS, Elizabeth, 256
  John, 256
  Jonathan, 256
  Joseph, 256
  Samuel, 217
BEVARD, Elizabeth, 60
  James, 226
BEVINS, Nancy, 262
BICKHAM, Abel, 187
  Abiah, 187
  Caleb, 187
  Joseph, 187
  Rachel, 187
  Thomas, 187
BIDDLE, Bolding, 217
  Elizabeth, 211
  John, 161, 211
  Levey, 218
  Mary, 216
  Owen, 161
  Sarah, 161
BIGUM, Catherine, 97
BILDERBACK, William, 50
BINGHAM, Joshua, 256
BIRD, Benoni, 58
  Elizabeth, 63
  John, 75
  John D., 1
  Mrs., 65
BIRK, Bridget, 45
BIRMINGHAM, Richard, 4
BISHOP, Henry, 4
  Nicholas, 4
BLACK, Elizabeth, 93
  Hannah, 182
  James R., 76
  William, 48, 221
BLACKBURN, Ingeber, 52
BLACKFORD, Benjamin, 123, 212
  Elisabeth, 123, 182
  Elizabeth, 160, 174, 202
  Garret, 123, 182
  George, 139
  Gerard, 139, 154, 158, 160, 200
  Jacob, 139, 200
  John, 123, 182
  Joseph, 123, 139, 200, 214
  Lydia, 139, 200
  Mary, 123, 139, 160
  Sally, 139
  Samuel, 123, 182
  Sarah, 139, 200
  Thomas, 123, 182
  William, 123, 182
BLAINNY, Frances, 252
BLANFORD, John, 66
BLANKFORD, Ann, 57
BLOSSOM, Patty, 260

BOEN, Richard, 77
BOGGS, Elizabeth, 247
　Ezekiel, 231, 232
　Hannah, 91, 96
　James, 241
　John, 85, 91, 93
　Joseph, 92
BOLDEN, Jane, 222
　Jesse, 220
　Levi, 222
　Margaret Black, 222
　Noble, 92, 100
　William Chealy, 222
BOLDIN, John, 217
　Mary, 220
BOLDING, Abigail, 219
　Elixander Smith, 221
　James, 221
　Jinny, 219
　Margaret, 221
　Rachel, 217
BOLDON, Mary, 93
BOLTON, Jane, 236
　John, 99
　Mary, 49, 236
BOMISH, Rachel, 82
BOND, Amos, 198
　John, 66, 72
　Rachel, 209
　Samuel, 136
　Thomas, 1
BONHAM, Hannah, 90, 95
　Rev., 86
BONNER, Ann, 57
BONSAL, Abraham, 143
　Anna, 143
　Catharine, 167
　Catherine, 143
　Mary, 143
　Philip, 167
　Sarah, 143
　Vincent, 143
　William, 143
BONSALL, Abraham, 159, 198, 210
　Abram., 204
　Amey, 167, 192
　Anna, 210
　Caleb, 135, 213
　Catharine, 214
　Cathrine, 135
　Elenor, 135
　Grace, 124, 135
　Hannah, 124, 136
　Isaac, 135
　Jesse, 159
　Joseph, 153
　Mary, 135, 153, 165, 204, 210

　Philip, 124, 135, 136, 179
　Rebecah, 210
　Sarah, 124, 175, 214
　Stephen, 136
　Vincent, 124, 135, 158, 214
　William, 214
BONTING, Robart, 239
BONTLER, Mary, 81
BONTLEY, Choffry, 80
BOORAM, Edward, 53
BOOTH, Ann, 24, 25, 26, 27, 28, 29, 76
　Elizabeth, 28
　George, 27
　George Clay, 24
　Hannah W., 76
　James, 1, 24, 25, 26, 27, 28, 29, 36, 55, 59, 64, 76, 240, 241
　Joseph, 36, 258
　Mary, 24, 62
　Rebecca, 230
　Sarah, 263
　Waitman, 246
　William, 29
BOSS, James D., 259
BOSSE, Marguerite Felicite, 227
BOSTICK, John, 171, 201
　Kezia, 201
　Lardner, 171, 201
　Mary, 171, 201
　Sarah, 226
BOSTWICK, Barbara, 248
　Jacob, 248
BOUCHELL, H., 232
BOUCHER, Elizabeth, 40
BOUDUY, Louise Marie Adelaide, 228
BOULDIN, Ann, 216
　Richard, 217
BOULTEN, Francis, 98
BOULTER, Shioni, 80
BOULTON, Francis, 81
　John, 78, 83
　Mary, 98
　Sarah, 218
BOUND, Jenny, 257
BOUNDS, John, 100
BOWAN, Thomas, 80
BOWEN, Ann, 91
　Jane, 90, 93, 96, 249
　Jesse, 241
　John, 81, 87, 90, 96, 99
　Leffis, 83
　Mary, 40, 78, 83
　Priscilla, 53
　Sarah, 32

Thomas, 91, 220
BOWMAN, Ann, 30
　Ann Booth, 37
　Hester, 64
　Ingeber Lefevre, 37
　James, 30
　James Lefevre, 32
　Jeremiah, 32, 33, 36, 37, 61
　John, 33, 60
　John Janvier, 33
　Mary, 30, 33
　Mary Eliza, 36
　Nathan, 243
　Susannah, 32, 33, 36, 37
　Thomas, 247
BOWON, Lottie, 82
BOYD, Cleland, 256
　Eliza, 64
　James, 50, 238
BOYS, Elizabeth, 219
　Nathan, 243
BRACHER, Priscilla, 252
BRACKEN, Sarah, 256
　William, 243, 259
BRACKIN, Henry, 49
BRADFORD, Catharine, 65, 72
　Cathrine, 16
　Elizabeth, 16
　Samuel, 9, 16, 237
BRADLEY, Henry, 41
　Hugh, 53
　Margaret, 53
　Samuel, 216
BRADY, John, 61
　Margarat, 61
BRANAN, Mary, 91
BRANEN, Mary, 95
BRANNAN, John, 55
BRANNEL, Eleanor, 20
　Hannah, 20
　Michael, 20
BRANNON, Catharine, 33
　John, 33
　Margaret, 33
BRANSON, Frances, 55
BRATCHEY, Elizabeth, 45
BRATTAN, Benjamin, 243
　Henry, 243
　James, 243
BRATTEN, Elizabeth, 256
　James, 257
BRAVARD, Thomas, 235
BRAY, Elizabeth Foudray, 225
　Elkanah, 225
　Susanah, 225
BREADLEY, Mary, 244
BREADY, Samuel, 249, 262
BRENDERGAST, Patrick, 244

BRERETON, Thomas, 249
BRERTON, Elin, 255
BRETTON DESCAPELLES, Jeane Juliene, 228
BRETTON DES CHAPELLAS,
　Eulalie Victorie Claudine, 228
　Fortunee' Prudence Julien, 228
　Louis Jacque Claudine, 228
BRETTON-DES CHAPELLES,
　Alexandre Francois, 228
　Claudine, 228
　Eulalie Victorie Mathusin, 228
BRETTON-DESHAPELLES,
　Alexandre Joseph Pierre J, 228
BREUIL, Francois, 227
BREWSTER, Elizabeth, 40, 42
BRIAN, Ann, 138, 142, 205
　David, 138, 205
　James, 142
　Mary, 138, 205
　Rebecca, 138
　Sarah, 142
　Thomas, 138
　William, 138
BRINGHURST, Anna, 162
　Deborah, 145
　James, 162
　Joseph, 145, 162
　Mary, 145
　William, 145
BRINKLEY, Nancy, 245
BRINTON, Elizabeth, 169
　Hannah, 169
　Jacob, 169
　John, 169
BRITCHARD, David, 54
BRITT, Daniel, 197
BROADAWAY, Agnes, 245
BROADFOOT, ---, 63
BROOKS, Timothy, 79
BROOM, James M., 255
　Nancy, 255
BROOMELL, Jacob, 259
BROSSAY, Elizabeth, 228
BROTON, Leah, 244
BROWN, Charles, 250
　Darcus, 168
　Dorcas, 136, 167, 192
　Eleazar, 121
　Elgas, 191
　Elisabeth, 131, 136, 192
　Elizabeth, 153, 168
　Israel, 186
　James, 131, 153, 186, 188
　Jeremiah, 185

John, 32, 185, 248
Joseph, 86, 131
Margaret, 63, 253
Mary, 32
Mary Macy, 136, 192
Miriam, 127, 131
Nancy, 250
Penelope, 40
Sarah, 44
Susanna, 252
Thomas, 252
William, 46, 136, 168, 192
BROWNE, Joseph, 94
BROWNING, Thomas, 198
BRUCE, William, 262
BRUOR, Phebeh, 81
BRYAM, Katherine, 259
BRYAN, Ann, 184
  Benjamin, 189
  Elisabeth, 133
  Hannah, 242
  Jacob, 93
  James, 133
  John, 232, 233
  Joseph, 133
  Mary, 53, 133, 153, 168
  Michael, 93
  Moses, 133, 168
  Rachel, 216
  Rhoda Hill, 262
  Robert, 49, 231, 233, 236, 243
  Thomas, 133, 153
  William, 153
BRYANT, Mary, 235
BRYDIN, James, 237
BRYEN, Elizabeth, 195
  James, 195
  Joseph, 195
  Mary, 195
  Moses, 195
  Thomas, 195
DRYNBERG, Peter, 252
BUCHEN, Zachria, 89
BUCHUN, Elizabeth, 89
BUCKINGHAM, ---, 99
  Eleanor, 171
  Glovier, 214
  Hannah, 89
  James, 130
  Jane, 89
  John, 87, 99, 112
  Joseph, 112
  Joshua, 206
  Margaret, 89
  Mary, 214
  Richard, 214
  Ruth, 90
  William, 87, 89, 99

BUCKINHAM, Jane, 91
  William, 91
BUCKLEY, Beulah, 182
  Daniel, 182
  John, 182
  Mary, 182, 185
  Phineas, 151, 185
  Ruhamy, 247
  Thomas, 207
  William, 151, 211
BUCKMASTER, Hannnah, 252
BUDD, Elizabeth, 248
BUFFINGTON, Richard, 231
BUKINGHAM, William, 86
BULL, Manon, 262
BULLES, John, 60
BULLOCK, George, 14
  Isabell, 14
  Sarah, 234
  Thomas, 14
BUNKER, Ann, 221
  Jesse Forester, 221
  William, 221
BURCH, Mary, 54
  Sarah, 248
BURCHAL, Sarah, 217
BURCHARD, Adam, 25
  David, 25
  George, 25
  Mary, 25
BURGES, John, 174
  Rachel, 174
BURGESS, John, 208
  Rachel, 208
BURK, Charles, 12
  Elizabeth, 12
  Sarah, 12
BURN, Jo., 242
BURNS, Catherine, 235
  Dinah, 163
  James, 6
  Jane, 55
  John, 254
BURROUGH, William, 47
BURROUGHS, Elizabeth, 106
  John, 250
BURROWS, Esther, 55
  Joshua, 63
BURRUS, Sidney, 247
BURTON, Benjamin, 246
  Daniel, 262
  Elen Rodes, 257
  James, 257
  Peter, 246
  Robert, 261
  Sally, 256
  Sarah, 249
  William, 246
BUSH, Ann, 10
  David, 10, 75

Eliza M., 259
Elizabeth, 10, 66
Sarah, 10
BUSHONG, Anthony, 43
BUTLER, Ann, 84
　Catharine, 7
　Mary, 7
　Michael, 44
　Shon, 80
　Simon, 78, 80, 84
BUTTLER, Ann, 81
BYRN, Daniel, 177
　Dinah, 177
BYRNE, Daniel, 112
　Joshua, 112
　Lydia, 196
　Rachel, 170
　Rebeccah, 112
BYRNES, Anna, 140
　Betsey, 137
　Caleb, 125, 135, 138, 155, 187, 196, 204
　Daniel, 113, 125, 135, 140, 155, 196, 211
　Dinah, 125, 140, 155, 196
　Hannah, 174, 211, 213
　Hannah Pancoast, 138
　James, 137, 165, 210
　John, 260
　Jonathan, 135
　Joseph, 125, 196
　Joshua, 125, 137, 178, 195, 204
　Lydia, 125
　Martha, 135, 155
　Mary, 135, 138, 155
　Rachal, 165
　Rachel, 135, 137, 173, 178, 193, 204
　Rebeccah, 113
　Ruth, 137, 165, 211, 213
　Samuel, 137, 165, 211
　Sarah, 137, 138, 175, 213
　Thomas, 137, 138, 165, 175, 199, 200, 213
　Thomas Shipley, 140
　William, 125, 140, 155, 200

-C-

CADER, David, 21
　Jane, 21
　Mary, 21
CADWALDER, John, 148
　Sarah, 148, 164
CAIL, Elizabeth, 56
CAIN, Robert, 104
CALAHEN, Elizabeth, 260
CALDWELL, Ann, 54, 163
　Betty, 163

　David, 48
　James, 263
CALENDER, Elizabeth, 4
　John, 4
　Nicolas, 4
CALHOON, William, 262
CALLAWAY, Betsy, 260
　Isaac, 262
　Jacob, 244
　Polly, 254
CALVERT, Anne, 102
　Martha, 252
CAMBLE, Mary, 100
CAMERON, Samuel, 241
CAMPBEL, Martha, 252
CAMPBELL, Ann, 15
　Catharine, 31
　Elizabeth, 225
　Isabella, 31
　James, 15, 16, 51
　John, 31
　John T. 244
　Mary, 15, 16
　Robert P., 244
　Samuel, 52
　Sarah, 16
　Thomas, 60
CAN, Mary, 218
　Robert, 218
CANADY, Margaret, 46
CANBY, Ann, 136, 141
　Anna, 132
　Benjamin, 133, 149, 182, 201
　Deborah, 133, 182
　Eli, 180
　Elisabeth, 121, 136, 148
　Elizabeth, 161
　Esther, 136, 142
　Fanny, 132
　Frances, 136, 161
　Hannah, 121, 133, 168, 187, 192
　James, 136, 211
　Jonas, 142
　Joseph, 152, 177, 187
　Joshua, 133
　Margarett, 136
　Martha, 132, 168, 177
　Mary, 121, 132, 142, 158, 179, 214
　Merrit, 132
　Oliver, 110, 121, 132, 136, 152, 158, 205
　Sally, 142
　Samuel, 121, 136, 152, 161
　Sarah, 132, 136, 142, 177, 180
　Susanna, 133, 200

Susannah, 182, 246
Thomas, 133, 136, 148, 149, 152, 177, 180, 246
William, 121, 132, 168, 180
CANE, William, 40
CANGLETON, David, 50
CANN, Ann, 23
  Catharine, 20
  Cathrine, 16, 19
  Elizabeth, 23
  Isaac, 23
  James, 23
  Jane, 23
  John, 3, 16, 19, 20, 23
  Margaret, 235
  Mary, 96
  Phoebe, 19, 20
  Rachel, 23
  William, 23
CANNON, Isaac, 52, 53
  Lydia, 52
  Matthew, 233
  Rachel, 52
CANSTON, Henrietta, 65
CANTRAL, Sarah, 233
CANTREL, Mary (Thomas), 88
CANTWELL, Sarah, 56
  Stephen, 86
CANTWILL, Mathew, 220
CARLETON, Samuel, 256
CARLEY, Edward B., 227
CARLILE, Kezia, 91
CARLISLE, Kezia, 96
CARLIT, Eliza, 49
CARLTON, Samuel, 252
CARMAN, Joseph, 93, 100
CARMEAN, Jacob, 243
  Zebdiel, 243
CARNBER, John, 220
CARNE, Elizabeth, 7, 8
  Grace, 7
  John, 7, 8
  William, 8
CARNEY, Thomas, 52
CARPENTER, George, 29
  James, 28
  Mary, 256
  Nephtali, 244, 245
  Sarah, 28
  William, 28
CARR, Margaret, 22, 221
  Mart, 221
  Mary, 258
  Susanna, 221
  William, 42
CARRINGTON, Margaret, 174, 208
  Sarah, 187
CARSAN, Ann, 122

Dinah, 122, 149
George, 152, 188, 189
Hannah, 122
Jane, 122
Lidia, 189
Martha, 122
Miriam, 122, 153
Phebe, 122, 151
Richard, 122, 136, 137, 151, 154
CARSON, Henerata, 216
  Jane, 163
  Richard, 107, 109, 160
  Thomas, 45
CARTER, Hannah, 259
  Jacob, 24
  James, 24, 65
  Jeremiah, 126, 150, 189, 258
  Lydia, 126
  Mary, 45, 126, 168, 170, 183, 189, 248
  Rachel, 126
  Rebecca, 24, 126
  Tacy, 126
  Thomas, 126
CARTMAN, Hannah, 43
CARTWRIGHT, Joseph, 261
CARY, Jennie, 244
CASHETY, Agnes, 27
  Ann, 27
  Elizabeth, 27
  Nicholas, 27
CASPERSON, Tobias, 46
CASTALOW, Mary, 62
CASTELLO, Joshua, 53
CAUDWELL, Ann, 149
  Vincent, 149
CAULK, John, 28
  Mary, 28
  William, 28
CAVENDER, Catherine, 56
CAZIER, Charity, 220, 222
  Christiana, 52
  Henry, 222
  Jacob, 220, 222
  John, 220
CH..AD, Jonathan, 186
  Miriam, 186
CHADWICK, Fornney, 248
CHALFANT, Ann, 174
  Sarah, 174
CHALFONT, Sarah, 214
CHALLENGER, Thomas, 64
CHAMBERLAIN, Mary, 77
  Peter, 77
CHAMBERLIN, Mary, 84
  Peter, 84
CHAMBERS, Amey, 134
  Eddath, 235

Elisabeth, 134
Elizabeth, 159
Emmey, 159
Emmy, 134, 160
James, 134
Joseph, 134, 159, 160
Mary, 134
Rebekah, 189
Sarah, 134, 160
William, 134, 196
CHAMPION, Flora, 93
  James, 93
  Mary, 41
CHANDLEE, Benja., 191
  Benjamin, 113
  Mary, 191
CHANDLER, Ann, 103, 104, 118
  Benjamin, 187
  Charity, 104
  Christopher, 118
  David, 160, 187, 208
  Dinah, 119
  Elizabeth, 117
  Jacob, 104, 114, 117
  Jane, 105
  Mary, 117, 164, 179
  Miriam, 113
  Phebe, 117
  Rachel, 105
  Sarah, 107, 114
  Swithin, 103, 104, 107, 117, 118, 160
  Thomas, 108, 111, 112, 117
CHANDLY, Mary, 168
CHANT, William, 219
CHAPMAN, Martha, 202, 206
CHARLES, Benjamin, 93
CHARLESON, John, 34
  Mary, 34
CHARLEY, Rebekah, 257
CHASNUT, Gerrit, 219
CHASSAING, John Babtist, 257
CHEALY, William, 220
CHEECK, Christian, 48
CHERREY, Rebeckah, 257
CHERRY, William, 118
CHESTERMAN, Ann, 34
  Elizabeth, 34
  Thomas, 34
CHETHAM, Edward, 42
  Hannah, 42
CHILDS, Abigel, 88
CHRISTFIELD, Eliz., 216
  John, 220
CHRISTY, Martha, 181
CHUCK, Christiana, 236
CINOLL, James, 13

John, 13
Susannah, 13
William, 13
CIRWITHEN, Mary, 257
CLAMPSON, Ann, 210
  Elizabeth, 210
  Hannah, 210
  James, 210
  John, 210
  Mary, 210
  Rachel, 210
CLARK, Alce, 170
  Alice, 157
  Ann, 240
  Cathrine, 17
  Elisabeth, 180
  Elizabeth, 118, 122
  George, 17
  Henry, 54
  James, 45, 57
  Jane, 50, 239
  Jennet, 253
  John, 47, 60, 109, 238, 239
  Joseph, 17
  Louisa, 62
  Lydia, 122, 180
  Margaret, 64
  Mary, 95, 122, 181, 250
  Matthew, 51
  Merebiah, 122
  Meribah, 181
  Nancy, 261
  Robert, 254
  Samuel, 115, 177, 122
  Sarah, 122, 178
  Thomas, 122, 181, 254
  Thomas W., 218
  Walter, 157
  Widow, 91
  William, 60, 122, 181, 230, 231
CLARKE, Ann, 49
  Catharine, 2
  Louisa, 31
  Mary, 254
  Richard, 2
  Sarah, 253
  Sarah Ann, 31
  Thomas, 31
  William, 60
CLARKSON, Harriet Rumsey, 29
  Hester Cox, 28
  Joseph, 28, 29, 31
  Mary, 28, 29, 31
  Robert Blackwell, 31
CLATEN, Jacob, 261
CLAWSON, Peter, 39
CLAY, Ann, 7, 55, 65, 71

Ann Booth, 35
Anna, 9
Catharine, 37
Curtis, 35, 37, 38, 61
Elizabeth, 9, 35, 37
Elizabeth Clay, 38
Ellen Lohra, 38
Emma Wood, 38
Jehu, 71
Mary, 57
Sarah, 61
Slater, 9, 71
Slator, 7
Thomas, 72
William, 1, 9, 29, 59, 72
CLAYTON, David, 168
Hannah, 140, 208
Isaac, 140, 208
Jacob, 140, 208
Jane, 205
Joshua, 140, 208
Lydia, 140, 208
Martha, 140
Moses, 250
Sarah, 168, 192
CLEANY, William, 40
CLEATON, Hannah, 171
Jacob, 171
CLEM, Catharine, 20
John, 20
Philip, 20
CLEMENT, Ann, 94
CLEMENTS, Hannah, 46
CLEMPSON, John, 149
Matilda, 210
CLIFTON, Daniel, 262
CLINTON, Mary, 231
CLOSE, Adam, 56
CLOUD, Ann, 173
Caleb, 173
Harlin, 257
Harlon, 194
Jeremiah, 49, 237
Joseph, 186
Orpah, 190
Lydia, 173
Susanna, 210
Susannah, 173, 175
William, 131, 173, 175
CLOWES, Peter, 255
CLOWS, Joshua, 256
CLUNGEON, Eleanor, 36, 37
Sarah Ann, 37
William, 36, 37
COALE, Bartram, 212
Budd, 212
William, 212
COBINE, Eleanor, 58
COBOURN, Mary, 196
COBURN, Agnus, 48

COCHRAN, Elijah, 261
John, 221
Joseph, 219
Mary, 221
Robert, 221
Sarah, 220
COCK (COOK), Stephen, 177
COCKEREL, John, 85
CODERECK, Letesha, 261
COFFIN, Hephsibah, 168
Hephzibah, 192
COHOON, Ann, 216
COLBOURN, John, 169
Mary, 169
COLDWELL, Clayton, 248
COLE, Ann, 2
Edward, 2
Elia, 222
Elizabeth, 2
Elsha, 222
Esther, 41
Sarah, 222
COLEGATE, Elisabeth, 187
COLEMAN, Griffith, 136
Joseph, 136, 152
Nicholas, 64
Sarah, 136
Thomas, 152
COLESBERRY, Ann, 9, 12
Ann Cathrine, 17
Catharine, 12
Cathrine, 17
Henry, 1, 9, 64
Isaac, 17
Jacob, 12, 17, 44, 66, 255
Levy, 12
Mary, 17, 254
Sarah, 12, 66
Swen, 9, 12
COLESBERY, Catharine, 14
Henry, 14
Jacob, 14
COLESBURY, Allice, 225
Elizabeth, 225
Henry, 225
Henry Williams, 225
John, 225
COLGAN, Charles, 37
James, 38
John, 37, 38, 62
Mary, 37, 38
COLINDER, Margret, 105
Nicholas, 105
COLLEY, Agnus, 45
COLLINS, Benj., 249
Charles, 253
Ebenezer, 256
James, 225
John, 16, 225, 247, 249

Lidia, 225
Mary, 57, 249
Reuben, 16
Susannah, 16
COLTER, John, 248
COMMON, Hannah, 175
John, 156, 172
William, 156
COMMONS, John, 198
Joseph, 256
Mary, 172
Sarah, 198
CONELL, Hannah M., 90
CONEY, Robert, 54
CONLY, Cathrine, 14
CONN, Jane, 49, 236
CONNEL, Robert, 60
CONNOLLY, Hannah, 96
CONNOR, Mary, 52
CONNOWAY, Hugh, 19
Jane, 93
Margaret, 19
William, 19
CONOWAY, Alice, 231
Margaret, 93
CONRAD, Margaret, 209
CONROD, Abraham, 187
Deborah, 259
CONWAY, Bridget, 249
James, 52
Thomas, 103
CONWELL, Mary, 247
COOCH, Hannah, 100
Sarah, 93
COOK, Isaac, 106
Jeremiah, 193
Margaret, 252
N., 224
COOLEY, Elizabeth, 93
COOPE, Deborah, 160, 207
Elizabeth, 207
Samuel, 160, 207
COOPER, Adam, 230
E., 224, 225
Grissel, 233
John, 239
Margaret, 252
COPE, Catharine, 7
John, 7
Mary, 7
William, 7
COPELAND, Ann, 17
William, 17
COPES, Joseph, 249
COPPAGE, Mary, 248
CORBET, William S., 261
CORBIT, Elizabeth, 39
Israel, 207
Mary, 189
William, 189

CORBITT, Ann, 190
CORDREY, Unyey, 254
CORK, Mr, 66
CORKE, Glevs, 29
Sarah, 29
CORKE(CAULK), Elizabeth, 29
Jacob, 29
James, 29
Lydia, 29
Oliver, 29
CORNELUSON, Christiana, 232
CORNISH, John, 92, 100
CORRINGTON, James R., 64
Sarah, 167
CORSON, Jane, 46
COSDEN, Edward, 218
Rebecca, 218
COTTINGHAM, Nancy, 253
COTTMAN, Mrs., 89
COUPER, James, 263
COUTTS, Hercules, 67
COWAN, George, 244
COWARD, Margaret, 174
COWEN, Elizabeth, 5, 12
Isabell, 12
Isabella, 5
Mark, 5, 12
COWGILL, John, 250
COWING, Mary, 50
COX, Alias, 89
James, 202
Margery, 108
Martha, 109
Mary, 217, 260
Paul, 52
Rebecah, 108
COZIER, Rebecca, 263
CRAHSUER, John, 54
CRAIG, Elizabeth, 256
Frederick, 252
Joseph, 22
Polly, 257
William, 22
CRAIGE, David, 259
William, 257
CRAMPTON, John, 255
CRAWFORD, Ann, 222
Anne, 93
Ebner, 222
Elizabeth, 48
George, 256
Henry, 258
Isaac, 260
Jane, 222
John, 222
Lydia, 51
Mary, 222
CREED, James, 51, 59
CREELIN, Catharine, 47
CREERY, William, 254

CREIGHTON, Robert, 246
CRESHEN, Anthony, 61
CRIPPEN, Catherin, 243
CROCKET, Benjamin, 44
  Jane, 55
CROFT, Edward, 64
CROMBIE (CRUMMEY), John, 233
CROOKS, Ann, 35
  Samuel, 35
  William, 35
CROSLEY, Robert, 249
CROW, John, 58
  Mary, 221
  Samuel, 221
  Sarah Thompson, 221
  William, 218
CROWLEY, Joanna, 104
CROXON, Archibald, 55
CROZER, Susannah, 250
CRU, Ann, 219
CRUGHTON, Margaret, 48
CRUIZER, Hannah, 235
CRULIN, Catherine, 236
CRUMCALTON, Robert, 261
CRUON, Helene, 228
CRUSON, Ann, 221
  John, 221
  Rachel, 221
CULBERTSON, John, 218
  Mary, 256
  Patrick, 48
CULBREATH, Thomas, 249
CULFORD(COLFORD), Patrick, 231
CULIN, Isaac, 259
CULP, George, 13, 16
  John, 16
  Phyllis, 13, 16
CULVER, Ann, 262
CUMBERLAND, Martha, 22
  Sarah, 20
  Thomas, 20, 22
  William, 22
CUMMINGS, Alex, 12
  Alexander, 11
  John Ramsey, 12
  Mary, 11, 12
CUMMINS, Alexander, 233
CUNNINGHAM, John, 43, 52
CURD, Sara, 81
CURETON, Susannah, 107
CURFY, Deborah, 45
CURLE, Richard, 110
  Samuel, 110
CURLET, James, 62
CURLETT, Lewis, 217
CURLEY, Hannah, 44
CURREY, John, 253
CURRIE, Samuel, 46
  William, 45
CURRY, Neal, 253
CURTIS, Jehu, 1, 69
  Mary, 42

-D-

DAFIS, Emlon, 81
  Martha, 81
DAFYDD (DAVID), Elizabeth, 81
  James, 84
  Jan'th, 82
  Margaret, 84
  Rhichart, 80
  Rhys, 80
  Richard, 82, 83
  Susana, 81
  Suusana, 81
  Thomas, 80
DALLINAR, Elizabeth, 252
DALTON, Mary, 8
  Miles, 8
  Susanna, 8
DAMAND, Louis Etienne, 229
DANIELS, Rose, 61
DANILLA, John, 40
DANNALAH, Mary, 50
DARBY, Elizabeth, 47
  Mary, 59
DARBYSHIRE, Elizabeth, 17
  Thomas, 17
DARLING, Mary, 247
DARNAUD, Etienne, 229
  Victoire Agathe Mathurina, 229
DATER, Osboorns, 82
DAUGHERTY, Sarah, 192
DAVERS, Hannah, 7
  James, 11
  Mary, 7, 11
  William, 7, 11
DAVID [See also Dafydd]
  Daniel, 86
  Eleanor, 79
  Elizabeth, 59, 77, 81
  Evan, 41
  Henry, 77
  Hugh, 78, 84, 99
  James, 77, 234
  Jane, 99
  Joannah, 201
  John, 94
  Jonathan, 86
  Joshua, 217
  Margaret, 58, 78
  Martha, 83
  Mary, 99
  Philip, 80, 84
  Rees, 78, 94, 99
  Righart (Richard), 77

Sarah, 51
Shonnet (Jennet), 77
Stephan, 95
Stephen, 81, 98
Susanna, 78, 83
Thomas, 78, 80, 95
DAVIES, Mary, 165
DAVINE, Abel, 99
DAVIS, Abagail, 51
  Abel, 87, 92, 96
  Benjamin, 249
  Daniel, 90
  David, 51, 79, 80, 81, 87, 90, 94, 95, 96
  Deborah, 90
  Dorrithy, 196
  Elenor, 90
  Elizabeth, 37, 83, 92, 196
  Ellinor, 196
  Emling, 83
  Emly, 79
  Enoch, 86
  Hannah, 90, 96
  Hester, 90
  Isaac, 171
  Isabell, 45
  James, 64
  Jane, 49, 232
  Janott, 82
  Joanna, 171
  John, 87, 99, 247
  Jonathan, 87, 97
  Kathrine, 258
  Martha, 36, 37
  Mary, 37, 46, 94, 181, 196
  Nathan, 261
  Nehemiah, 196
  Rachel, 89, 95, 247
  Rachel Saunders, 37
  Richard, 40
  Sally Ann, 37
  Samuel, 36, 37, 92
  Samuel Devear, 36
  Sarah, 92, 100, 196
  Susanah, 196
  Susannah, 37
  Thomas, 46, 87
  William, 57, 196, 262
DAVY, Nancy, 93
DAWES, Abijah, 188
  Abner, 182
  Cephas, 186
  Edward, 135, 154, 166, 193
  John, 111
  Jonathan, 188, 193
  Josiah, 182
  Martha, 188
  Mary, 111, 188
  Mercy, 154, 166
  Rumford, 183, 188, 189
  Sarah, 149
DAWGE, Hannah, 164
DAWSON, John, 251
  Rachel, 47
  William, 209, 243
DAY, John, 104
  Rebekah, 259
  Samuel, 255
DAYET, Adam, 240
DAYSON, Elizabeth, 25
  John, 25
DE GAULT, DuPont, 227
  Dupont, 227
  Marie Francoise Angelique, 227
  Pierre Henry Dupont, 227
DE LA COUR, James, 253
DE LA NEUVEVILLE, Lally, 227
  Michael Lally, 227
DE LINGENDER, Marie Anne Elizabetjh, 227
DE SASSENAY, Claire Ettienne Eugenie, 228
  Claude Henry Etienne Ber., 228
  Gaspard Ettienne Bernard, 228
DE STE MARIE, Jeanne Coustier, 227
DE VANCLAIRE, Marie Catherine Elizabeth, 227
DE VAUJOYEUX, Guillaume Francois Marger, 229
  Marie, 229
DEAKYNE, Joseph, 261
DEALRY, Philip, 218
DEAN, Alexander, 188
  Catherine, 148
  Sarah, 250
  William, 147, 188
DEATH, Hanna, 93
DELANY, Eleanor, 93
DELAPLAIN, Nehemiah, 63
DENN, William, 80
DENNIS, John, 108
  William, 51
DENNY, Benjamin, 260
DENOCK, Samuel, 190
DEPUTY, Joshua, 63
DERBY, Maria, 63
DERRAGH, John, 222
  Margaret, 222
  Margaret Stewart, 222
  Susana, 222
DERRICK, Anna, 59
  Elizabeth, 226

DES CHAPPELLES, Bretton, 227
  Therese Jeanne Julienne B, 227
DESIRE' SOLLEE', Marguerite, 227
DESTOOURER, Joseph de Saque', 228
DEVAN, Benjamin, 48
  John, 256
  Susannah, 53
DEVANY, Ann Kitty, 225
  Cornelia, 225
  Sarah, 225
  William, 225
DEVENALD, Mary, 87
  Rachel, 87
  Sarah, 87
DEVENPORT, Elisabeth, 170
  Elizabeth, 193
DEVENSHIRE, Elizabeth, 61
DEVERS, John, 35
  Susannah, 35
  Thomas, 35
DEVONALD, Daniel, 98
  Hannah, 87
  John, 99
  Judith, 88
  Mary, 87
DEVONALLT, John, 77
  Mary, 78
DEVONPORT, Jonathan, 195
DEWEESE, David, 246
  John, 244
  Joshua, 244, 246
  Lewis, 243
  Thomas, 243, 246
D'HAPPART, Joseph Leger, 60
DICKENSON, Betty, 197
  Carsan, 136
  Carson, 198, 199
  John, 197
  Phebe, 136, 198
  Richard, 136
  Samuel, 136
DICKEY, Elizabeth, 45
DICKINSON, Daniel Webb, 245, 246
  John, 198
  Phebe, 169, 183, 189
  Richard, 151, 183
  Samuel, 194
DICKISON, Phebe, 167
  Richard, 167
DICKSON, John, 103
  Ruth, 108
  Thomas, 105, 247
DILL, Solomon, 245
DIMPSEY, Edward, 15
  Peter, 15

Rosanna, 15
DINGEE, Joseph, 190
DISS, John, 56
DIVIN, Charles, 241
DIXON, Ann, 114
  Elizabeth, 115, 199
  George, 103
  Grace, 114
  Henry, 113, 115
  Jehu, 199
  John, 56, 114, 115, 199
  Katharine, 117
  Martha, 113
  Mary, 113, 199
  Rebecca, 199
  Ruth, 115
  Sarah, 114, 115
  Solomon, 115
  Susanna, 199
  William, 103, 115
DIXSON, Amy, 119
  Ann, 104, 108, 116, 143
  Deborah, 112
  Elizabeth, 143
  Emey, 143
  Emmy, 142
  Hannah, 107
  Isaac, 111, 142, 143
  John, 108, 111, 142
  Joseph, 108
  Margaret, 143
  Mary, 143
  Rebecah, 110
  Sarah, 108, 143
  Thomas, 112
  William, 102
DODD, Ann, 219
DODDS, John, 251
  Valentine, 54
DOFNALLT, Mary, 81
DOGHERTY, Margaret, 248
DOLBY, Joseph, 47
DONALD, Elizabeth, 49, 237
  Mary, 49, 236
DONEY, Elizabeth, 247
  Susannah, 247
DONNAL, Annis, 235
DONNALD, Elizabeth, 45
DONNEL, Alexander, 246
DONNELL, John, 56
DOORSH, Catharine, 60
DOPE, Catharine, 89
DORAN, Mary, 44
D'ORBIGNY, Louise Jeanne Elizabeth V, 228
  Martin B.. de Moine, 228
DORMAN, Gerherdus, 261
DORREL, Henry, 47
DORSEY, Ann, 63
  Louisa, 62

DOUFNALLT, Shon, 80
DOUGAL, Samuel, 235
DOUGALL, Sam, 235
DOUGHARTY, Susanna, 171
DOUGHERTY, Ann, 19
  Edward, 53
  Eleanor, 51
  Fanny, 14
  George, 57
  Margaret, 53
  Michael, 22
  Patrick, 14, 19
  Rebecca, 50, 238
  Sarah, 19, 169
  Susanna, 196
  Susannah, 196
  Thomas, 255
DOUGHTY, John, 247
DOUGLAS, John, 42
  Lettis, 99
  Nancy, 220
DOUGLASS, Ann, 258
  James, 246
  Lettice, 88
  Phillip, 99
DOULLIR, Laurence, 242
DOVENAL, John, 93
DOVENALD, Mary, 99
DOWDLE, Ann, 30
  Elizabeth, 30, 36
  Jane, 172, 212
  Martha, 29
  Robert, 30, 31
  Rosy, 36
DOWN, Walter, 99
DOWNAM, Mary, 244
DOWNE, Walter, 86
DOWNING, David, 256
  Elizabeth, 161
  Margery, 43
  Mary, 240
  Rebecca, 62
  Richard, 161
  Thomas, 161, 209
DOWNS, John, 23
  Martha, 23
  Rachel, 99
DOWSON, Mary, 223
DRAPER, Benjamin, 259
  Mary, 245
DRINKER, Henry, 149
DRUMMOND, Ann, 10
  Donald, 10
  Margaret, 10
DU ROCHER, Jean Garrasche, 228
DUCK, Elizabeth, 103
DUFF, Henry, 56
DUGLAS, Joshua, 83
DUGLASS, Philipp, 80
DUGLESS, Joshuia, 80
DULANY, Elizabeth, 248
DUNGAN, Levy, 85, 91
DUNLAP, Ann, 221
  Francis, 260
  James, 221
  Mary, 43, 222
  Samuel, 222
  Susanah, 251
  William, 218, 221
DUNLOP, Francis, 51
DUNN, Hannah, 253
  Jane, 53
  John, 63
DUNNING, Ann, 54
DUNSMORE, Gwentlian, 91
DUNWOODY, Mary, 58
DUPONT, Jeanne Louise, 227
DUPONT-DE GAULT, Pierre
Marie Jean Elie, 229
DURRAHAM, Margaret, 219
DUSHANE, Hester, 48
  Mary, 233
  Michael, 234
  Susanna, 93
DUTTON, Francis, 171
  Hannah, 171
  Susanna, 201
DYEL, Adam, 13
  Margaret, 13
  Mary, 13
DYER, Jane, 40
DYET, Sidney, 58
DYSON, James, 257

-E-

EAKEN, Thomas, 231
EAKIN, Alexander, 237
  Ann, 234
  Jannet, 235
  Jennet, 46
  William, 218
EAKINS, William, 238
EARL, John, 1, 259
  Susannah 250
EASTWICK, John, 257
EATON, George, 79
  Gwenllian, 79
  Isaac, 92, 251
  John, 79
  Joseph, 79
  Juan, 79
  Mary, 79
  Sarah, 47
EATTON, George, 84
  Gwen, 84
  Joseph, 84
  Juan, 83
  Mary, 84
EAVES, James, 158

Phebe, 158
ECKLES, John, 44
EDDINGS, Hannah, 200
 Jane, 200
 Rachel, 200
 Samuel, 200
 Thomas, 200
EDGAR, Ann, 63
EDGE, Andrew, 92, 96
 Sarah, 92, 96
EDGIN, Elizabeth, 244
EDINBAROUGH, Susanna, 216
EDMOND, Dyws, 83
 Evan, 77, 99
 Lewis, 77
 Luce, 99
 Lyns, 81
 Mary, 94
 Thomas, 78, 80, 95, 99
EDMONDSON, Ann, 214
 Solomon, 181
EDMONSON, Sophiah, 176
EDMUND, Mary, 81, 89, 99
 Thomas, 86, 99
EDMUNDS, Catherine, 84
 Evan, 84
EDWARD, Arthur, 78
 Arthyr, 80, 83
 Caterine, 99
 Catharine, 78
 Elizabeth, 82, 91
 Elizabeth (James), 87
 Jann, 81
 John, 77, 82, 99
 Joshua, 80
 Margaret, 82
 Rebecka, 82
 Rebeka, 99
 Richard, 78
 Sarah, 81, 82, 87
EDWARDS, Edward, 77, 80, 83, 99
 Elizabeth, 96
 Famer, 90
 Jaen, 77
 James, 90
 Jane, 83
 Mary, 82
 Richard, 42, 84
 Shan, 81
EFAN, Ann, 81
 Dafydd, 80
 Hugh, 80
 Shion, 80
 Thomas, 80, 82
EFANS, Lidia, 81
 Samuel, 80
 Shon, 80
ELDER, Alexander, 230
 John, 230

Mary, 47
ELDRDIGE, Martha, 179
ELDRIDGE, James, 182
 Jesse, 181
 Sarah, 147
ELISON, Andrew, 222
 Hester, 222
 Joshua, 220
 Lidia, 222
 Rachel, 222
 William, 222
ELIXANDER, Susanna, 221
ELLES, Sidniy, 217
ELLINGSWORTH, Coventer, 254
ELLIOT, James, 31
 John, 159, 195, 239
 Joseph, 182
 Margarett, 186
 Mark, 239
 Martha, 31
 Mary, 31, 61
 Obediah, 182
 Rebecca, 159, 169
 William, 169
ELLIOTT, Annabella, 152
 Chloe, 12, 14
 Cloe, 17
 Doctor, 65
 Esther, 210
 James, 143, 210
 John, 12, 14, 17, 50, 143, 152, 160, 239
 Joseph, 52
 Margaret, 14
 Mary, 48, 52, 143
 Rebeckah, 160
 Rebekah, 255
 Sarah, 143
 Susannah, 17
 William, 12, 143, 160
ELLIS, Evan, 110
 Hannah, 164, 181
 Humphrey, 200
 James, 51
 Lydia, 110
 Sarah, 111
 Thomas, 181
 William, 219
ELSBURY, Jane, 223
ELWALL, Jean, 109
ELWOOD, Mary, 250
EMERSON, William, 261
EMLY, Hanna, 41
EMPSON, Ebenezer, 3, 5
 Jonathan, 5
 William, 3
EMSON, Sarah, 78
ENGLAND, Abigail, 134
 Elisabeth, 134, 151
 Elizabeth, 113

Joanna, 134
John, 113
Joseph, 134, 151
Margarett, 134
Sarah, 134
Susana, 163
ENOCHS, Thomas, 259
ENOS, Ann, 23, 26
  Elizabeth, 21
  George, 23
  James, 6, 16
  Jane, 6, 11
  John, 26, 54
  Joseph, 1, 6, 11, 23, 26
  Mary, 16, 21, 26
  Rebecca, 6
  Samuel, 21
  Stephen, 6, 11
  Susannah, 6, 16
ERLE, John, 3
ERVIN, John, 243
  Sarah, 218
ERWIN, Francis, 247
ESHAM, Eliza, 24
  Sarah, 24
ESTEOL, Jean Baptiste, 229
ETON, Joseph, 80
ETTON, Guoullian, 81
  John, 82
  Mary, 81
  Shons, 80
  Shusan, 81
EVAN [See also Efan]
  Annie, 98
  Elizabeth, 82, 87
  Hugh, 78
  John, 96
  Margaret, 78
  Mary, 78
  Mary Ann, 98
  Nathaniel, 85
  Nathyaniel, 98
  Samuel, 78, 98
  Sarah, 97
  Thomas, 78, 98
  William, 81
EVANS [See also Efans]
  Abel, 236
  Alice, 207
  Ann, 174, 199, 256
  Caterine, 94
  Daniel, 178
  David, 99
  Deborah, 89
  Elijah, 178, 187
  Elisha, 260
  Genkin, 217
  Hughe, 94
  Jane, 44, 82, 87
  Jenkin, 249

Joel, 222
John, 78, 80, 83, 85, 94, 231, 236
Lemuel, 178
Lydia, 78, 93
Mary, 83, 88, 92, 251
Rachel, 222
Ruth, 178
Samuel, 45, 174, 178
Sara, 88
Thomas, 79, 99
Weize, 90
William, 148, 222
EVENS, Elisha, 251
EVERETT, Joseph, 224
EVERSON, Hester, 218
  Rebecca, 218
EVERTSON, Elizabeth, 219
EVES, Abraham, 30, 33, 36, 58
  Eliza, 6
  Elizabeth, 8, 11, 30, 33, 36
  Hannah, 6
  James, 8, 11
  Jane, 6
  John, 6, 8, 11
  John D., 67
  Margaretta Jane, 33
  Mary, 8, 11, 65, 70
  Mrs., 66
  Phebe, 172
  Samuel, 36
  Sarah, 8, 30
  Spencer, 33
EWEN, John, 23
  Phoebe, 23
  Sarah, 23
EWING, Alexander, 22
  John, 65
EYNON, Deborah, 92
  Hannah, 88
  Mary, 97
  William, 95, 99, 233
EYNOW, Hannah, 95
  Mary, 91
EYRE, Caleb, 252

-F-
FAIRES, Elizabeth, 233
FAIRIS, Mary, 239
  Mary Ann, 237
FAIRLAM, John, 139
  Rebekah, 139
  Susanna, 139
FAIRLAMB, John, 170, 171, 197
  Mary, 170
  Rebeccah, 197
  Susanna, 171, 197

FALCONER, Thomas, 39
FARA, Jane, 40
  Mary Catharina, 39
FARIES, Robert, 250
FARIS, Jacob, 238
  Nancy, 220
  William, 216
FARMER, Harriott, 260
FARR, Thomas, 86
FARRELL, Jane, 56
FARREN, John, 22
FARRIES, Zachariah, 107
FARROW, Ebenezer, 248
FARSON, Ann, 167, 187
  David, 194
  Jane, 130, 186
  Wilmington, 111
FASSITT, John R., 262
FAURE, Etienne, 227
FAUSSETT, William, 252
FAWKES, Elizabeth, 164
  William, 164
FEARIS, Jacob 238
FEN, Daniel, 178
  Esther, 178
  Evan, 178
  Phebe, 178
  Rachel, 178
FENISTER, Elrich, 22
  Rachel, 22
  William, 22
FERGUISON, Elizabeth, 234
FERGUSON, Agnes, 53
  Hugh, 62
  Jean, 243
FERIE, Rachel, 47
FERRAL, Gideon, 101
  Mary, 101
FERREL, Margaret, 42
FERRELL, William, 109
FERRIE, Eleanor, 27
  James, 27
  Rafello James, 27
FERRIS, Alexander, 49
  Benjamin, 120, 127, 128
  David, 120, 127
  Deborah, 128
  Edith, 128, 166
  Hannah, 127
  John, 128, 167
  Lydia, 167
  Mary, 120, 127, 128
  Rosannah, 165
  Sarah, 163
  William, 234
  Zacharia, 203
  Zachariah, 203
  Zeba, 128
  Ziba, 128, 166
FERRISS, Abigail, 120, 184
  Benjamin, 211
  David, 150, 151
  Deborah, 120, 162, 177
  Edith, 137, 162
  Elisabeth, 120, 185
  Elizabeth, 154
  Hannah, 120, 151, 165
  John, 120, 137, 145, 151, 154, 162, 177
  Lydia, 120, 145
  Mary, 120, 151
  Mathew, 179
  Matthew, 120
  Nathan, 120
  Phebe, 120
  Rachel, 120
  Rosanna, 151
  Rosannah, 120, 179
  Samuel, 120
  Sarah, 120, 137, 150
  Zachariah, 145, 202, 205
  Zechariah, 120, 138, 152, 154
  Ziba, 120, 137, 162
FEW, Benjamin, 189
  Eli, 196
  Elizabeth, 42
FIDDLER, D., 224, 225
FIERE, Abraham, 3
  Philip, 3
FILLPOT (PHILPOT), Erick, 240
FIMLINSON, Cary, 244
FINDLY, Margaret, 168
FINLEY, Ann, 217
  Margaret, 192
  Robert, 192
FINNEY, Archd., 238
  David, 236, 241
  Jean, 238
  John, 238
  Robert, 239
  Walter, 238
FIRTH, John, 230
FISHER, James, 245
  Joseph, 262
  Polly, 259
  Ruth, 259
  Samuel, 210
FISHERS, Mr., 100
FITCHER, William, 257
FITZGERALD, Annie, 57
  Nicholas, 13
  Sarah, 13
FIVER, Henry, 54
FLANNAGAN, Thomas, 47, 236
FLEMIN, Jane, 18
  Martha, 18
  William, 18
FLEMING, Thomas, 41

EARLY CHURCH RECORDS OF NEW CASTLE COUNTY

FLETCHER, Elizabeth, 260
FLIN, Mary, 248
FLINN, Mary, 93
FLOOD, Hannah, 93
　Joseph, 93
FLOUGH, Christian, 47
FLOWERS, Frances, 260
FLOYD, Ann, 54
　Cornelius, 21
　Rachel, 21
FLUCKER, William, 230
FLYNN, Alexander, 243
　Patrick, 230
FOGG, Charles, 53
FOLWEL, Samuel, 166
FOLWELL, Edward, 126, 182, 191
　Elisabeth, 126, 182
　Elizabeth, 149
　Goldsmith, 185
　Gouldsmith, 126, 148, 182
　Hannah, 164, 182
　Joseph, 126
　Mary, 113, 126, 182
　Sarah, 126, 182
　Susanna, 182
FOMSAND, Cornolius, 80
FOOD, John, 226
FOOT, William, 260
FOOTE, Benjamin, 36
　David, 35
　Elizabeth, 35
　James Ross, 31
　John, 32, 35, 36, 64
　Margaret, 32
　William Reynolds, 32
FORD, Abraham, 143
　Ann, 143, 253
　Elizabeth, 143
　Isaac, 144
　Joseph, 48, 143
　Letitia, 242
　Mary, 143, 255
　Philip, 253
　Samuel, 253
　William, 43, 144
FOREMAN, Alexander, 183
　John, 210
　Stephen, 240
FORGESTON, Fanney Ruffee, 92
FORGISON, Rachiel, 257
FORMAN, Aaron, 120, 185
　Alexander, 184, 185, 192
　Alexr., 120, 177
　Aron, 121
　Elisabeth, 121, 184, 185
　Elizabeth, 172, 199
　Esther, 120, 184, 185, 192
　John, 121, 177, 184, 185, 192
　Leah, 121
　Margaret, 82, 87
　Mary, 121, 184, 185
　Miriam, 121, 185
　Moses, 120, 186
　Rachel, 121, 184, 185
　Robert, 177, 182
　Susanna, 121, 184, 185, 192
　Widow, 81
FORREST, Margaret, 56
FOSSEN, Hannah, 54
FOSSETT, James, 235
FOSTER, Beriah, 247
　Elizabeth, 162
　Francis, 162
　John, 253
　Martha, 63
　Mary, 63
　Rachel, 162, 174
　Sarah, 218
FOUDRAY, Samuel, 225
FOULKE, Samuel, 202, 246
　Thomas, 199
FOUNTAIN, Fransis, 258
FOURACORS, John, 247
FOURNIER, De'sire'
　Francoise Virgin, 227
　Francois, 227
FOX, Joseph, 5
FRAISER, Elizabeth, 231
FRANCIS, John, 22, 226
　Maria, 22
　Mary, 261
　Phillip, 22
FRANCOIS, Alexandre, 227
FRANKLAND, Jane, 45
FRANKLIN, Benjamin, 69
　John, 255
FRASAR, William, 244
FRASER, Alexander, 3
FRAZER, Alice, 64
　Andrew, 231
FREDD, Rebecca, 226
FREEL, Sarah, 60
FREENY, Thomas, 262
FRENANTZ, Anthony, 8
　Frances, 8
　Ibred, 8
FRENCH, Ann, 41
　Avice, 5
　Elizabeth, 252
　Isabella, 260
　John, 3, 5, 37
　Mary, 39
　Parnel, 41
　Penelope, 37
　Sibylla, 3

Thomas, 39
FROGG, John, 65
FULLER, Mary, 50, 237
FULTON, Jane, 31
  John, 31
  Margaret, 31
  Matthew, 41
FURBE, Joseph, 246
FURGUSON, Ann, 43
FURNANES, Mary, 24
FURNISS, Robert, 47
FUSSELL, Ann, 173
  Elizabeth, 173
  Esther, 173
  Jacob, 173
  Solomon, 205
  Susanna, 173

-G-
GALAHA, Margaret, 60
GALLACHER, Susanna, 247
GALLAHAR, James, 242
GALLAHER, Niel, 258
GAMBLE, James, 240
  John, 222
  Peggy, 222
GANEAU, James, 41
GARDNER, James, 32
  John, 32
  Mary, 32, 43
  Rachel Ann, 32
  Rebecca, 32
GARESCHE, Elizabeth, 227
GARETS, John, 89
GARETSON, Eliakim, 180
GARISON, Powel, 3
  Sarah, 3
GARLAND, George, 72
  Mary, 40
  Ruth, 72
  William, 72
GARNER, Joseph, 87
GARRETSON, Ann, 106
  Cullender, 49
  Eliakim, 155
  Elikim, 109
  Elizabeth, 18, 180
  Esther, 155
  Garret, 180
  Hannah, 60
  James, 55, 61, 180, 241
  Jedediah, 155
  John, 106
  Joseph, 18, 180
  Lydia, 180
  Sarah, 18
GARRETTSON, Abraham, 19
  Cornelius, 8
  Hannah, 19
  John, 47
  Mary, 19
GARRISON, Ann, 48
  Cornelius, 177
  Joseph, 24
  Sarah, 24
GARRITSON, Ann, 103
  Garret, 105
  Hester, 231
  John, 105, 238
GASKILL, James, 250
GASKINES, William, 245
GASTON, Elizabeth, 30
  James, 30
  Mary, 30
GASTOW, Peter, 242
GAY, Richard, 45
GEDDESS, Anna Maria, 258
GENKINS, Sebinah, 251
GERILIUS, Lawrence, 22
  Peter Abraham, 22
GEST, Abram, 256
  Benjamin, 258
  Daniel, 113
  Jane, 168
  Ruth, 170
GIBBONS, Abraham, 158, 204
  Daniel, 203
  Deborah, 203
  James, 140, 157, 203
  John, 201
  Joseph, 158
  Mary, 157, 204
  Rachel, 203
  Rebecca, 203
  Samuel, 203
GIBBS, Agnes, 248
  John, 244
  Sarah, 45
GIBSON, Betty, 197
  Deborah, 198
  Edward, 14
  Elizabeth, 108
  Hannah, 198
  Henry, 49
  James, 50, 237
  John, 119, 197, 198
  Joseph, 197, 258
  Joshua, 197, 198
  Lydia, 198
  Mary, 197
  Samuel, 53, 213
  Susanna, 198
  Thomas, 119, 197, 213
GILBERT, Catherine, 23
  Cathrine, 16
  Eliza, 6
  Elizabeth, 23
  Jesse, 217
  John, 6, 16, 22, 27, 231
  Knight, 18

Mary, 22, 24, 28, 29, 254
Rachel Miller, 28
Rebecca, 26
Rhenere, 6
Rudy, 18
Sarah, 23, 24, 26, 27, 34
Stephen, 22, 23, 24, 26, 27, 28, 29, 34, 66
Susannah, 16
William, 18
GILBORN, Elizabeth, 17
Knight, 17
Rhoda, 17
GILES, Elizabeth, 50, 238
George, 61
GILL, Ann, 88
GILLALAN, John, 11
Margaret, 11
GILLAN, Rebecca, 43
GILLESPIE, Neal, 51
Thomas, 53
William, 234
GILLESPY, Eleanor, 19
Elizabeth, 21
Nathaniel, 21
Neil, 19
Sarah, 21
GILLILAND, James, 242
GILLMAN, Elizabeth, 31
John, 31
Robert, 31
GILLMORE, Elizabeth, 37
John, 37
Margaret, 37
GILLYARD, Elizabeth, 44
GILMAN, Catharine, 38
Elizabeth, 38
GILMOUR, Robert, 254
GILPIN, Abigail, 136, 145, 146, 154, 159
Abigal, 165
Ann, 130, 136, 145, 154
Ann Ferris, 146
Betty, 168
Edward, 136, 146
Gertrude, 136, 263
Gideon, 116
Hannah, 118, 136
Isaac G., 209
James, 136, 159
John, 32
John Ferris, 146
Joseph, 47, 116, 118, 119, 136, 141
Judith, 32
Lydia, 146, 176
Lydia Zane, 146
Mary, 116, 119, 131, 141, 174
Richard Baker, 146

Thomas, 149
Vincent, 136, 145, 146, 154, 159
William, 136
GINN, Else, 251
GIPLIN, Hannah James, 142
James, 142
John Littler, 142
Samuel Stapler, 142
Sarah, 142
Sidney Ann, 142
GITCHELL, Ann, 248
GIVEN, Hannah, 254
GLASCOW, Ann, 49
GLASFORD, Ann, 91
Hugh, 87, 97, 99
GLASGOW, John, 237
GLASOCK, Sally, 221
GLENN, Thomas, 233
GOARY, Richart, 80
GOBBY, Margaret, 238
Peter, 238
GODDARD, Gooding, 260
GOFORTH, John, 86
Lydia, 88, 231
Mary, 53
William, 43, 231
GOFTON, Charles, 66
GOLD, Mary, 246
GOLDEN, Hannah, 45
John, 234
GONNE, Henry, 1
GOODFELLOW, Ann, 58
GOODING, John, 244
GOODWIN, Elisa., 192
Hesther, 192
John, 153
Joseph Brown, 192
William, 153, 192
GOOKIN, Charles, 4
GORDIN, Sarah, 219
GORDON, James, 41
Jane, 7
John, 7
Robert, 39
Sarah, 252
GORDY, Peter, 249
GORHAM, Deborah, 175, 212
James, 175, 212
Jonathan, 175, 212
Mary, 175, 212
Parnel, 175, 212
GORMLEY, David, 242
GOSBORO, Margaret, 93
GOSS, Charles, 114
Richard, 243
GOTEER, Margaret, 92
GOTEERS, Francis, 100
GOTTIER, Francis, 101
GRADEY, James, 230

GRAFTON, Elizabeth, 68
  Hannah, 5, 65
  Mary, 5
  Richard, 1, 5, 42, 65,
  67, 68
GRAHAM, Charles, 233
  Hector, 234
  Israel, 248
  John, 242, 243
  William, 240
GRANGER, Lucy, 46
GRANT, Catherine, 55
  John, 254
  Mary, 27
  Patrick, 27, 58
  Thomas, 27
GRANTAM, Eliz'th, 93
  Phillis, 93
  Sharp, 93
GRANTHAM, Elizabeth, 101
  Isaac, 67, 241
  Jacob, 1
GRANTHUM, Ambrose, 232
GRAVE, Sarah, 115
GRAVENROOT, Ann Cathrine, 44
  Lucretia, 46
GRAVENSEAT, Mary, 233
GRAY, Alice, 50, 237
  George, 166, 187
  Hannah, 166
  Margaret, 55
  Samuel, 166, 193
  Sarah, 166
  William, 44
GREARES, Jane, 56
GREAVE, Ann, 116
  David, 119
  Hannah, 114
  Jane, 116, 118
  John, 105, 115, 116
  Jonathan, 107, 119
  Martha, 104
  Samuel, 104
  Sarah, 104
GREEMWATOR, John, 83
GREEN, Ann, 170, 193
  Charles, 162, 213
  Edward, 4, 40
  Ellis, 170, 193
  Hannah, 41, 213
  Henery, 106
  Humphries, 52
  James, 106
  John, 170, 193
  Joshua, 118
  Mary, 170, 193
  Richard, 257
  Robert, 133
  Rosamon, 162
  Sarah, 170, 193
  William, 245
GREENFIELD, Margaret, 46
GREENOUGH, Ebenoner, 63
GREENWOOD, Polly, 260
GREER, John, 245
GREGG, Abraham, 118
  Ann, 116, 118
  Betty, 116
  Dinah, 116
  Elizabeth, 112
  Emey, 103
  Emy, 116
  Herman, 113
  Hermon, 200
  Isaac, 203
  John, 103, 105, 200
  Joseph, 107
  Mary, 119
  Samuel, 107, 116, 119
  Sarah, 116
  Simon, 185
  Thomas, 105
  William, 103, 114, 118
GREGORY, Benjamin, 55
GRIER, Sarah, 252
GRIFFIN, Jemima, 253
  Margaret, 52
  Olden, 226
  Rebecca, 226
GRIFFITH, Ann, 202
  Benjamin, 79
  Daniel, 86, 95, 99
  Elinor, 97
  Elisha, 99
  Elizabeth, 77, 83
  Esther, 160, 174, 201
  Evan, 160
  Hannah, 220
  Hester, 172
  James, 92
  Jane, 172
  John, 78, 86, 93, 99, 176, 249
  Joseph, 85, 87, 91, 95, 97
  Judith, 77
  Katharine, 93
  Margaret, 262
  Martha, 85
  Mary, 90, 91
  Rachel, 78, 88, 96, 218
  Rebecca, 100
  Rebeckah, 160
  Sally, 261
  Samuel, 83, 91, 99
  Sara, 81
  Sarah, 93, 96, 218
  Seney, 93
  Susanna, 93

Thomas, 77, 83, 94, 99
William, 81
GRIFFITHS, Samuel, 77
GRIFFYTH, Elonor, 81
GRIMES, Ann, 259
  Cathrine, 17
  Elizabeth, 43
  George, 254
  Gustavus, 20, 49, 236
  Jane, 20
  John, 17, 55
  Joseph, 63
  Mary, 17, 20
GRINER, Catharine, 8
  John, 8
  Mary, 8
GRINWATER, John, 77
GRINWATOR, Shon, 80
GROOM, Thomas, 231
GROVES, Jonathan, 243
GRUBB, Hannah, 165, 180
  John, 118
  Nathanill, 253
  Prudence, 118
  Samuel, 116, 118
  Susanna, 260
  Susannah, 52
GRYFFYD(GRIFFITH), Benjamin, 84
GRYFFYTH, Benjamin, 80
  Elizabeth, 81
  Rachel, 81
  Samuel, 80
  Shon, 80
  Thomas, 80
GUEST, Joseph, 191
  William, 40
GUEY, Thomas, 2
  William, 2
GUMBLEE, John, 4
  Susanna, 4
GUMBLY, John, 2
  Ruth, 2
GUMBY, Susanna, 41
GUNN, Elizabeth, 57
GUTHRIE, William, 64
GUTTIER, Francis, 93

-H-
HACKETT, Joseph, 244
  Sarah, 244
  Thomas, 241
  Walter, 68
  William B., 217
HADLEY, Hannah, 110
  Joseph, 103, 110
  Simon, 103
HADLY, Hannah, 105, 195
  Simon, 105
HAFFRY, Joseph, 48

HAINES, Esther, 161
  Job, 161
  Mary, 212
  Reuben, 161, 212
HAINIS, Rebecca, 44
HAINS, Jacob, 208
  Jesse, 208
  John, 130
  Mary, 208
  Rachel, 208
  Reuben, 208
HAIR, Charles, 60
  John, 220
HALL, Aaron, 35
  Ann, 9, 24
  Archibald, 46
  Charity, 44
  David, 261
  Dorcas, 30, 35, 37, 66
  Dorothy, 72
  Elizabeth, 248
  James, 44
  Jane, 37
  John, 30, 35, 56, 67, 72, 87
  Joseph, 219
  Joshua, 249
  Lydia, 30
  Margaret Charlotte, 37
  Mrs., 65, 66
  R., 24
  Samuel, 255
  Sarah, 9, 46
  William, 9, 249
  William Thomas, 35
HALLINSWORTH, Deborah, 170
  John, 170
HALLIWELL, Richard, 1, 67
HALLOWELL, Hannah, 142, 208
  James, 142, 208
  Jesse, 142, 208
  John, 142, 208
  Joseph, 142, 208
  Joshua, 142, 208
  Margaret, 142, 208
  Rebecah, 142, 208
  William, 142, 208
HALY, Elizabeth, 40
HAMBLIN, Hannah Elizabeth, 221
HAMBY, Henerata, 222
  Richard, 222
  Thomas Carson, 222
HAMELL, Jennet, 51
HAMESON, John, 49
HAMILTON, Ann, 19
  Anne, 92
  Bridget, 34
  Catharine, 32
  James, 63

John, 8, 19, 34
Margaret, 19
Mary, 161, 249, 252
Rachel, 161
Rose, 8
Samuel, 51
Thomas, 8, 51, 161
William, 19
William Hamilton, 34
HAMLEY, Richard, 216
HAMMER, John, 109
HAMON, Felicite Marguerite Cleme, 227
HAMPTON, Benjamin, 254
HANCE, Ben, 176
 Benjamin, 108
 Eleanor, 48
 Elizabeth, 52
 Hance Miller, 10
 John, 233
 Nathaniel, 10
 Peter, 45
 Rachel, 45
HANCOCK, John, 57
 Richard, 260
HANDY, Abigail, 38
 Caesar, 38
 Henry, 38
HANEY, Nickolas, 254
HANNA, Margaret, 24
HANNAH, Agnes, 62
 Mary, 258
HANSON, Anne, 167
 Elizabeth, 139, 162, 167
 John, 4
 Lydia, 167
 Mary, 139, 160, 162, 172, 203
 Matheas, 217
 Peter, 4
 Priscilla, 159
 Samuel, 114, 139, 159
 Susanna (Zane), 139
 Susannah, 160, 167, 179
 Thomas, 115
 Timothy, 114, 115, 139, 143, 159, 160, 162, 186
HARBERT, Richart, 80
HARBORT, Sara, 81
HARDCASTLE, Robert, 219
HARDEN, Ann, 235
 Sarah, 255
HARDIN, Grace, 248
 Martha, 48
HARDING, Mary, 102, 217
HARE, Frederick, 92
HARGIS, Kitty, 262
HARLAN, Abigail, 111, 173, 175, 209
 Ann, 162

Caleb, 162
Dinah, 105
Elisabeth, 139
Elizabeth, 197
Ellwood, 197
George, 116
Hannah, 171, 197
James, 139, 197
Mary, 114, 139, 197
Michael, 105
Phebe, 200
Rebekah, 256
Sarah, 162
Susanna, 168
Susannah, 189
Thomas, 114
William, 208
HARLAND, George, 103
 Stephen, 45
HARLEN, Phebe, 172
HARMONSON, Elizabeth, 257
 Mary, 257
HARP, Ann Jane, 38
 David, 22, 24
 Fanny, 20
 John, 20, 22, 38
 Mary, 22, 38
 Rachaiel, 258
 Rachel, 24
 Rebecca, 24
 Rebecca Eleanor, 38
 Sarah, 20
HARPER, Benjamin, 197
 Elizabeth, 244
 John, 252
 Joseph, 243
 Thomas, 248
HARRINGTON, Nathan, 244
HARRIS, Abraham, 249
 Alexander M., 219
 Elizabeth, 7, 49, 104
 George, 195
 Hannah, 165, 185
 James, 7, 232
 John, 40, 41
 Mary, 52
 Rachel, 7
 Samuel, 49, 50
HARRISON, Caleb, 135
 George, 214
 Henrietta, 262
 Lydia, 174, 214
 Richard, 73
HARRISS, Elizabeth, 237
HARRY, Catherine, 98
 Cathoring Evan, 81
 David, 81, 98
 Elizabeth, 78, 81, 98
 Esther, 49
 Hester, 237

Jesse, 251
John, 78, 85, 98
Mary, 82, 106
Sarah, 98
Shion, 80
Silas, 237
Thomas, 80, 98
HARSSEY, Reachel, 249
HART, Catharine, 55
  Elizabeth, 218
  John, 252, 259
  Joshua, 247
  William, 259
HARTLEY, James, 31
  Lucinda, 31
  Washington, 31
HARTSHORN, Nancy, 248
HARTUNG, Elizabeth, 62
HARVEY, Abner, 135
  Alex, 15
  Alexander, 1, 8, 10, 12
  Andrew, 93, 101
  Ann, 8
  Anne, 249
  Benjamin, 135, 152, 189
  Elizabeth, 8, 10, 12, 15
  George, 12
  Isaac, 185, 194
  Job, 135, 149
  Jonathan, 135, 196, 205
  Joseph, 135
  Margaret, 152
  Mary, 129, 135, 152
  Robert, 233
  Samuel, 135
  Sarah, 135, 233
  Susanna, 176
HARWOOD, Katharine, 93, 96
HARY, Sarah, 88
HASTINGS, Hannah, 176
  Sarah, 170
HATTON, Joseph, 140, 198
  Susannah, 198
HAUGHAY, Christana, 216
HAUGHEY, Francis, 58, 220, 221, 223
  Hugh, 233
  Richard Thomas, 220
  Sarah, 220, 221, 223
  Thomas Kean, 223
HAUGHTON, Martha, 104
HAYES, Elisabeth, 184
  Henry, 184
  Magdalen, 184
  Margaret, 184
  Mary, 184
  Mordecai, 116
  Sarah, 258
  Stephen, 204
HAYS, Hannah, 39

Thomas, 106
William, 182
HAYWARD, Martha, 166
HAZLETT, Araminta, 11
  Frances, 15
  Jane, 11, 13, 15
  Joseph, 245
  Mary, 13
  William, 11, 13, 15, 52, 66
HAZLEY, James, 54
HEALD, Jacob, 118
  Mary, 118
HEARN, Sally, 261
HEARSEY, Benj., 249
HEAS, Margaret, 239
HEATH, Elizabeth, 88
HEATON, Rhoda, 255
HEDGES, Elizabeth, 251
  Mary, 251
HEGENS, John, 247
HEMINGWAY, William, 258
HEMMONS, Thomas, 258
HEMPHILL, Edward, 251
  William, 51, 259
HENDERSON, David, 93, 100
  Elizabeth, 218
  James, 43
  John, 233, 240, 250
  Margaret, 61
  Mary, 254
HENDRICKHAME, John, 40
HENDRICKSON, John, 59
  Judith, 91, 92, 97
HENDRY, John, 45
HENNON, George, 242
  Martha, 242
HENRY, Alexander, 64
  Andrew, 100
HERBERT, Richard, 79, 98
  Sarah, 79, 98
HERDMAN, Elinor, 259
HERMAN, Ephraim Aug., 2
  Mary, 2, 218
HERRING, Maria, 64
HERSCHE, Jane, 226
HERSHEY, Isaac, 240
HEWES, Ann, 121, 133, 177
  Aron, 133
  Deborah, 121, 133
  Edward, 121, 133, 180
  Elizabeth, 121
  Elizath., 177
  Hannah, 133
  James, 121, 133, 177
  John, 48, 133
  Joseph, 121, 133, 147, 176, 177, 209, 214
  Mary, 133
  Moses, 121

Orpah, 133
Sarah, 121, 177
Vincent, 133
William, 121
HEWET, Stephen, 190
HEWLITT, Henry, 260
HEYET, Godmah, 89
HEZLET, William, 54
HIATT, James, 81
HICKEY, James, 250
HICKLEN, William, 118
HICKLIN, Ann, 111
  Betty, 116
  Dinah, 113
  Mary, 113
  William, 113, 116
HICKMAN, Edith, 250
  Polly, 260
HICKS, Ann, 41
HIGGINS, David, 216
HIGNEY, John, 218
HIGONS, Joseph, 219
HILAND, Henry, 236
HILFORD, Boaz, 251
HILL, Ann, 132, 190, 204, 205, 206
  Catherine, 170, 199
  Frederick, 52
  George, 132, 204
  Howard, 132, 206
  Isaac, 92, 132, 205
  James, 132, 203
  Joanna, 132, 206
  John, 132, 152, 190, 203, 206, 247
  Joseph, 112
  Mary, 53, 132, 165, 191, 205
  Peter, 170, 199
  Shem, 192
  Susanna, 110
  Thomas, 132, 206
  William, 192
HILTON, Eliza, 38
  James, 38
  John, 38
  Sarah, 38
  Thomas, 38
  Washington, 38
HINEMAN, John, 256
HINKLEY, Francis, 176
HINSAY, Cornelius, 14
  Elizabeth, 14
  John, 14
HINSEY, Margaret, 96
HINTON, Ann, 18
  Dorcas, 54
  Rebecca, 18
  Susana, 164
  Susanna, 164, 179, 183

Thomas, 18
HIRE, Frederic, 100
HITHERINGTON, Jane, 54
HOAG, Comfort, 184
HOBBS, William, 257
HOBSON, Elisabeth, 126
  Elizabeth, 198
  Francis, 126
  Fransis, 102
  John, 126, 147
  Joseph, 126
  Samuel, 126
HODCHOSON, Thomas, 80
HODGES, Mary, 40
HODSKIN, Drake, 255
HOEY, Mary, 18
  Samuel, 18
HOGG, Elizabeth, 111
  George, 111
  James, 259
HOGMORE, Susannah, 62
HOLINSWORTH, Cathoring, 81
  Katherine, 84
  Stephen, 81
HOLINSWOTH, John, 80
HOLLAN, Rosanna, 44
HOLLAND, Joanna, 56
  John, 13, 51
  Margarett, 112
  Mary, 64
  Patrick, 13
  Susannah, 13
  Thomas, 55, 112
HOLLENSWORTH, John, 244
HOLLIDAY, William, 56
HOLLINGSWORTH, Amor, 117
  Ann, 39
  Anne Sword, 39
  Betty, 106
  Christopher, 117, 119
  Deborah, 130
  Jean, 174, 206
  Jehu, 182
  Judith, 117
  Levi, 39, 63
  Mary Evans, 39
  Samuel, 106, 182, 214
  Sarah 103
  Stephen, 4, 41
  Thomas, 103, 114, 117
  Volentine, 105
  William, 214
HOLLINS, Christopher, 40
HOLLINSWORTH, Catherine, 79
  Deborah, 172
  Enoch, 104
  Henry, 103
  Jacob, 105
  Jehu, 172
  Joseph, 104

Mary, 103
Samuel, 104
Stephen, 84
Valentine, 102
HOLMS, John, 217
HOLSEN, Ann, 17
  John, 17
  Thomas, 17
HOLSTON, Joseph, 254
HOLTON, Jesse, 219
  Sarah, 238
HOMAN, Mary, 16
  Matthias, 16
  Sarah, 16
HOOPER, Thomas, 252
HOOPES, Abraham, 214
  John, 102
HOOPS, Francis, 175
  Hannah, 175
  James, 208
  Jane, 132
  Joshua, 132
  Rebecca, 175
HOPKINS, Alexander, 255
  Isaac, 257
  Meriam, 183
  Prudence, 258
HORE, John, 3
  Mary, 3
HORNE, William, 185
HORSEY, John, 260
HOUGH, Benjamin, 163, 192
  Elisabeth, 163
HOULDSON, Thomas, 245
HOUSMAN, Joseph, 24
HOUSTON, Agness, 247
  Elizabeth, 247
  James, 237
  Margaret, 233
  Mary, 106
  Wiliam, 261
HOWARD, James, 248
  Londay, 253
  Martha, 129
HOWE, Jane, 47
HOWEL, David, 237, 241
  Ebenezer, 87
  Margaret, 88
  Moris, 81
  Rynal, 88
HOWELL, Benjamin, 31, 45
  David, 218, 235, 254
  Hannah, 255
  Hary, 82
  James, 81
  Joseph, 48
  Margaret, 31
  Mary, 46, 87
  Moris, 86
  Oliver, 219

Philippa Miller, 31
Rachel, 31
Reinald, 95
Rinall, 80
Sarah, 247
Thomas, 86
HOWETT, William, 243
HOWK, Margaret, 59
HOWLANDS, Daniel, 83
HOWLEY, Martha, 67
HOWOL, Jane, 82
  Mary, 82
HOWTS, Edward, 70
HUCKEL, Elana, 216
HUCKIN, Christana, 220
HUDSON, Anderson, 258
  Elizabeth, 245
  James, 226
  Mary, 246
HUGG, Enoch, 63
HUGH, David, 87
  Gownllian, 82
  Hall, 90
  Hanah, 90
  Isaac, 87
  Marey, 82
  Mary, 88, 98
  Phebe, 89
  Rachel, 89
  Sarah, 89
  William, 81, 89, 96
HUGHES, Charles, 238
  David, 91
  John, 86
  Mrs., 93
  Sarah, 50, 201, 239
HUGHS, Ann, 48
  Mary, 15
  Patrick, 15
  Prudence, 15
HUGOU, Elizabeth, 192
HUKILL, Elizabeth, 254
  Margaret, 64
HUKIN, Henry, 218
  Jeremiah, 218
HUKINN, Jeremiah, 218
HULL, David, 194
  Rachel, 220
HUME, Elizabeth, 52
HUMPHREYS, Elizabeth, 55
  Hannah, 167
  Richard, 167
HUMPHRIES, Richard, 188
HUNT, Ann, 152
HUNTER, Charles, 44
  David, 238
  Esther, 105
  Peter, 105
  Robert, 238, 258
HURFORD, Hannah, 196

John, 105
HURLI, Eugenie, 228
  Michael, 228
HURST, Sarah, 166, 171, 189, 196
HUSBANDS, Lydia, 49
HUSSEY, Ann, 104
  Christopher, 106
  Content, 106
  Elikim, 106
  Jedediah, 103
  John, 104
  Lydia, 176, 215
  Nathan, 103
  Rabucah, 103
HUSTON, Isabella, 46
  James, 235
  Jean, 246
HUTCHINSON, Thomas, 94
HUTCHISON, George, 235
HUTSON, Sary, 250
HUTTON, Andrew, 16, 48
  Elizabeth, 16
  John, 16
  Susannah, 51
  Thomas, 195
HYATT, Jane, 88
  John, 251
  Peter, 260
  Samuel, 252
  Thomas, 226
HYERS, Cathrine, 42
HYETT, Mary, 218
HYKIE, Margaret, 40

-I-
IDDINGS, Ann, 143, 212
  Caleb Peirce, 143
  Caleb Pierce, 212
  Hannah, 143, 212
  James, 143, 212
  Joseph, 143, 212
  Mary, 143, 212
IDDONS, Phebe, 199
IMLAY, Benjamin, 44
INGRAM, Bridget, 249
INLOE, Joseph, 232
INSTONS, John, 58
IRAHARN, Mary, 169
IRELAND, Joseph, 219
IRWIN, Patience, 226
ISAREL, Joseph, 23
  Mary, 23
  Rebecca, 23
  Susannah, 23
  William Pusey, 23
ISIAK, Black, 219
ISRAEL [See also Isarel.]
  Abigail, 26, 57, 63
  Deborah, 29

Elizabeth, 23
Esther, 31
George, 35
George Latimer, 27
Hannah, 26, 33
Isaac Grantham, 30
Jeremiah, 35
Joseph, 24, 26, 27, 29, 30, 31, 33, 35, 66, 75
Latitia, 26
Margaret, 29
Mary, 29, 33
Samuel, 29
Sarah, 29
Susanna, 75
Susannah, 24, 26, 27, 30, 31, 35

-J-
JACK, Edward, 60
JACKSON, Ann, 166, 189
  Archable, 247
  Daniel, 147, 166, 178, 189
  Dinah, 169
  Eleanor, 25, 28
  Elisabeth, 141, 189
  Elizabeth, 25, 74, 166, 203
  Erasmus, 60, 74
  Esther, 155
  Isaac, 141, 155, 203
  James, 208
  John, 172, 206
  Joseph, 155, 166, 172, 189, 206
  Joshua, 169
  Margaret, 166
  Mary, 157, 166, 170, 192
  Rachel, 172, 206
  Samuel, 25, 28, 57, 172, 206
  Sarah, 141, 203
  Sidney, 141, 203
  Susannah, 172
  Thomas, 206, 214, 244, 247
  William, 166, 187, 206
JACOB, Benjamin, 192, 197
  Betty, 197
  Hannah, 192
  Prudence, 164
  Sarah, 197
  Thomas, 105
JACOBS, Benjamin, 128
  Bettee, 128
  Elizabeth, 209
  Hannah, 128
  John, 128
  Joseph, 128

Mary, 128
Phebe, 203
Prudence, 128
Rachel, 128, 199
Richard, 158, 203
Sarah, 128, 174, 210
William, 245
JACQUET, Dorcas, 52
John, 53
JAMES, Abol, 98
Aboll, 81
Alice, 7, 44
Ann, 7, 107, 156
Daniel, 98
Danioll, 80
David, 85, 98
Elenor, 88
Elinor, 85, 87, 98
Elisha, 221
Elizabeth, 7, 64, 88, 259
Ellis, 219
George, 7, 231
Howel, 89
Jain Fearis, 221
James, 77, 78, 79, 80, 86, 94, 97, 98, 99
Jane, 99
Jennet, 49
John, 77, 81, 86, 91, 156, 183, 201, 221
Joseph, 78, 84, 200
Lydia, 153, 166, 181
Margaret, 81, 84, 221
Mary, 81, 89, 98, 164
Mr., 91
Phillip, 80, 98
Rachel, 126, 201
Robert, 177
Sara, 81
Sarah, 60, 77, 81, 82, 83, 89, 95, 98, 221, 262
Shon, 80
Susanna, 92
Thomas, 80, 87, 96, 98, 99, 153, 181
William, 87, 89, 95, 96, 221
JAMISON, John, 64
Joshua, 54
JANES, Margaret, 232
JANEY, Blakeston, 118
JANNEY, L, 184
JANNY, Abel, 188
JANUARY, Richard, 240
Thomas, 239
JANVIER, George W., 242
Jacob, 9, 43
Joseph, 55
Mary, 60
Mrs., 65

Rachel, 9
Rebecca, 9
Richard, 238
Samuel, 43, 235
Sarah, 50, 238
Thomas, 50
JAQUET, Christiana, 24, 65
Elizabeth, 24, 65
Elleanor, 3
Isaac, 24
Jane, 235
John, 24, 65
Paul, 234
Peter, 3, 4
Samuel, 249, 250
JAQUETT, Catharine, 70
Elizabeth, 70
John, 66, 70
Joseph, 230
Nicholas, 1
Peter, 70
Susannah, 230
JATON (GATOV), Peter, 242
JEAN, A., 228
JEFFERIES, Priscilla, 259
Sarah, 249
JEFFERIS, Elizabeth, 260
James, 250
John, 258
Nathan, 255
Thomas, 250
JEFFREYS, George, 42
JEFFRYES, Abraham, 197
JENKIN, Elanor, 82
Eleanor, 87, 98
Evan, 85, 96
John, 78, 79
Jones, 79
Rebeka, 82
Sarah, 82
Thomas, 81
William, 41
JENKINS, Charles, 150
David, 54
Hannah, 181
John, 78
Sarah, 57
Thomas, 83
Treviss, 238
William, 150, 181
JENNETT, Rachel, 226
JENNINGS, Edward, 1, 2
Sarah, 2
JESOP, William, 243
JESSOP, William, 244
JESTER, David, 243
Thomas, 243
William, 218
JOANS, William, 218
JOB, Andrew, 104

Mary, 104
JOHN, Ann, 93
  Benjamin, 241
  Daniel, 86, 97
  David, 87
  Easther, 78
  Elinor, 99
  Elizabeth, 78, 79, 96, 99
  Hannah, 49, 84, 236
  Hary, 82
  Jacob, 85, 96
  James, 96
  Jehu, 241
  Jenkin, 84
  John, 96
  Margaret, 88, 94
  Mary, 77, 82
  Morgan, 80
  Rebecca, 77
  Rebeka, 99
  Samuel, 77, 78, 79
  Susanna, 96
  Thomas, 39, 41, 77, 83, 85, 95, 98, 99
  William, 259
  Zacharies, 85
JOHNS, Ann, 22, 26, 28, 29, 218
  Elinor, 82
  Fidelia, 22
  Jacob, 97
  John, 28
  Kensey, 1, 22, 26, 28, 29, 38, 57, 76
  Morgan, 87
  Nancy, 76
  Richard, 176
  Sarah, 38
  Van Dyke, 29, 75
JOHNSON, Abraham, 144, 158, 213
  Ann, 145, 174
  Baldwin, 40
  Benjamin, 209
  Benjamin T., 144
  Betty, 206
  Breta, 58
  Caleb, 133, 144, 206
  Charles, 209
  Daniel, 133, 193
  David, 200
  Eleanor, 43
  Elisabeth, 133
  Elizabeth, 154, 260, 262
  George, 53
  Hadly, 190
  Hannah, 93, 144
  Isaac, 186
  James, 156
  Jethrew, 209
  John, 144, 158
  Joseph, 138, 212
  Joshua, 113, 133, 145, 150, 174
  Lydia, 209
  Margarett, 156
  Martha, 138, 144, 158, 212
  Mary, 133, 159, 161, 209
  Peter, 4
  Phebe, 191
  Rachel, 261
  Rebecca, 4, 200
  Rebekah, 133
  Robert, 133, 150, 154, 161, 202
  Ruth, 133
  Samuel Pennock, 145
  Sarah, 133, 138, 145, 156, 159, 212
  Simon, 133, 193, 200
  Thomas, 245
  William, 145, 209, 216
  William Gil, 52
JOHNSTON, Agnes, 22
  Anne, 3
  Barbara, 21
  Catharine, 13
  Charles, 22
  Eliza, 21
  Francis, 230
  Henry, 56
  James, 13, 61, 242
  John, 13
  Margaret, 21
  Peter, 3
  Rebecca, 56, 173
  Robert, 21
  Sarah, 171
  Susanna, 22
  Thomas, 21
  William, 21, 41
JOLEY, Mary, 89
JOLY, Jonathan, 87
JONES, Amos, 127
  Ann, 88, 99, 207, 250
  Anna, 249
  Annie, 88
  Aquilla, 195
  Benjamin, 86, 97, 247
  Bruffet, 260
  Christopher, 218
  Curtis, 244
  Dr., 94
  Ebenezer, 250
  Edith, 127, 209
  Elenor, 94
  Elinor, 81, 85
  Elizabeth, 52, 88, 98, 99
  Elrhys, 80

Epril Elizabeth, 82
Esther, 42, 236, 259
Garret, 248
Griffith, 86, 87, 94, 95
Hanah, 90
Hester, 91, 94
Hugh, 82
Isaac, 257
Jacob, 86
James, 41, 86, 91, 99, 245, 247
Jamos, 82
Jenet, 95
Jenkin, 99
Joanna, 92, 97
Johanna, 90
John, 41, 49, 79, 82, 86, 87, 91, 95, 97, 99, 159, 207, 217, 236, 251
Jordan, 94
Joseph, 124, 127
Joshua, 257
Lettice, 50
Lewis, 80, 83
Lydia, 159
Margaret, 247
Mary, 81, 82, 87, 88, 91, 93, 94, 95, 249
Morgan, 78, 86
Mrs., 66
Nathan, 202
Phebe, 209
Philip, 124, 127, 150, 177, 179
Rebekah, 124
Rees, 78, 86, 94, 99
Rev., 89
Robert, 236, 259
Samuel, 92, 247
Sarah, 50, 56, 88, 91
Shonn, 80
Stephen, 244
Susannah, 88
Thomas, 80, 82, 85, 219, 250
William, 124, 127, 177, 213, 254, 257
Wingate, 257
Zachariah, 95, 236, 257
Zachria, 87
JONSON, Mary, 89
  Richard Chicester, 221
JORDAN, Katharine, 261
  Mary, 172
  Patience, 171, 214
  Rachel, 171, 214
  Rosannah, 43
  Ruhene, 119
  Samuel, 53
  Susana, 118

JORDEN, Elizabeth, 258
JORMAN, Lewis, 81
JUBART, Mary, 47
JUDGE, Esther, 140, 207
  Hannah, 207
  Hannah Logan, 140
  Hugh, 140, 196, 203, 207
  Margaret, 207
  Margarett, 140
  Phebe, 140
  Pheby, 207
  Rachel, 140, 207
  Susanna, 140
  Susannah, 140, 207
  Thomas, 207
  Thomas Lightfoot, 140
JUNEY, Mary, 89
JURIK, John, 235
JUSTIS, Ann, 17
  David, 53, 64
  Elizabeth, 17
  Isaac, 17
  Thomas, 60

-K-

KARLAN, Cicily, 51
KARLIN, Edward, 47
KEAN, John, 56, 101
KEANE, Ann, 44
KEARNES, John, 26
  Mary, 26
KEARNS, John, 25
  Mary, 25
  William, 25
KEATING, Gaudefroi, 228
  Gaudefroi Jean Jules, 228
  Guillaume, 228
  Hippolyte Louis Guillaume, 228
  Jean, 228
KEELER, Sarah, 111
KEHOON, Elizabeth, 96
KEIGHTLY, Deborah, 127
  Elizabeth, 167
KEITH, John, 240
KELCH, Mary, 55
KELLAM, Hannah, 250
KELLEY, James, 237
  John, 231
  Letitia, 226
  Margaret, 245
KELLS, Ann, 153, 169
  David, 138, 153
  Mary, 153
KELLY, James, 232
  John, 43
  Jonath, 262
  Samuel, 246
  Thomas, 232
KENDAL, Deborah, 206

Hannah, 134
Isaac, 134
James, 134
Jesse, 134, 135, 206
John, 134, 206
Mary, 134, 135, 159, 206
Rebekah, 134
Samuel, 134
KENDALL, C., 225
Deborah, 140, 202
James, 203
Jesse, 140
Jessee, 157
John, 140, 157, 202
Mary, 140, 202
KENEDY, John, 51
KENIE, John, 22
KENNEDY, Ann, 59
Jane, 45
Margaret, 242
Mary, 256
KENNERD, Anthony, 163
Elizabeth, 163
KENNERLY, Martha, 250
William, 250
KENNEY, Rebecca, 246
KENNY, Mary, 262
KENT, Elizabeth, 47
Erasmus, 51
KENTON, Ann, 11
Thomas, 11
KEPPELE, Elizabeth, 54
KERKER, George, 242
KERNAHAN, Robert, 252
KETTLE, Cornelius, 3, 40
John, 53
Margaret, 3
KIDD, Agnes Emmeline, 37
Eliza Ann, 63
John, 36
Margaret, 36, 37
Thomas, 36
KIGHTLEY, Deborah, 187
Elisabeth, 127, 187
Isaac, 127, 187
James, 127, 151
KIGHTLY, Elisabeth, 186
Isaac, 186
James, 186
KILCRISS, Mary, 51
KILGORE, James, 242
KILLAM, David, 254
KILTY, William, 55
KIMBLE, Elisabeth, 92
John, 92
Sarah, 93
KINDALL, Jesse, 164
Mary, 164
KING, Ann, 27, 28, 31, 35, 221

Catherine, 23
David, 23, 28
Eleanor, 47
Elizabeth, 26, 262
George, 26
Jacob, 221
John, 29, 65, 235
Katherine, 147
Mary, 35, 67
Michael, 1, 27, 28, 29, 31, 35
Mrs., 66
Peter, 250
Robert, 217
Sarah, 27, 67
Susannah, 164, 178
Temperance, 221
Thomas, 27, 67
William, 22
KINKEAD, James, 44
Rebecca, 44
Sarah, 51
KINKEY, Fransiney, 100
Margery, 103
KINNEAR, James, 240
KINNY, William, 260
KINSEY, John, 263
Moses, 245
KIRK, Abigail, 105
Adam, 110, 119
Alphonsus, 105
Ann, 241
Elizabeth, 52
George, 20
Henry, 18
Isaac, 16
Jacob, 109
John, 16, 18, 20, 23, 109
Mary, 106
Patience, 20
Susannah, 16, 18
Thomas, 250
Timothy, 102
William, 109
KIRKLAND, Elizabeth, 46
KIRKPATRICK, Samuel, 232
KIRKWOOD, Nancy, 242
KITLEY, Francis, 57
KITTLE, Catherine, 234
KNARSBOROUGH, Margaret, 92
KNOTTS, Abraham, 245
KNOWLES, John, 176, 201
Richard, 253
KOLLICK, Mary N., 258
KRAMPTON, James, 226
KUGUE, Marguerite, 228
KUHN, Peter, 54
KYLE, John, 251

-L-
LA FARGE, Hetty, 218
LACKEY, Mrs., 65
LADLEY, Moses, 50
LADLY, Mary, 54
LAFFERTY, Cornelius, 48
LAGRANGE, Dumont, 228
LAGURD, Emelia, 257
LAMBORN, Dinah, 179
 Thomas, 149, 179
LAMBSON, Giles, 47
 Sarah, 55
 Thomas, 43
LAMBURN, Levi, 204
LAMPLEY, Judith, 103
LAMSON, Ann, 51
LANCASTER, Job, 197
LAND, Charity, 7, 15
 John, 1, 2, 3, 15
 Joseph, 3, 15
 Rebecca, 2
 Samuel, 7
 William, 7, 15
LANDERS, John, 60
LANE, Hester, 170
 Jesse Shenton, 170
 Joel, 170
 Mary, 170
 Rebecca, 170
LANGFORD, Joseph, 261
LANMAN, Daniel, 253
LANSLEY, James, 9
 Mary, 9
LAPSLEY, James, 44
LARAGAN, Rosanna, 51
LAREW, Shadrack, 50
LARKEN, John, 137
LARKINS, Jeremiah, 40
LATCHEM, Isaiah, 244
LATHAM, Elizabeth, 57
 Mrs., 26
LATHEM, Robert, 247
LATHIM, James, 45
LATIMER, Eleanor, 225
 Henry, 145
 James, 145
 John Richardson, 145
 Mary Richardson, 145
LATIMOR, Martha, 48
LAUGHERTY, John, 25
 Margaret, 25
LAUGHLIN, Isabella, 51
LAURANCE, Isablea, 217
LAVERDY, Francis, 56
LAW, Elizabeth, 12, 254
 Henry, 12
 Thomas, 12
 Unity, 12
LAWLER, John, 63
LAWS, Leah, 262

LAWSON, Joseph, 251
LAYCOCK, Thomas, 186
LAYTON, Priscilla, 259
LEA, Abraham, 123
 Ann, 167, 178
 Edward, 139
 Elizabeth, 123, 150, 201
 Frances, 123
 Francis, 152
 Hannah, 147, 152, 167
 Isaac, 123, 147
 James, 123, 135, 150, 152, 201
 John, 123, 139, 152, 155, 201
 Joseph, 139
 Margaret, 123, 152, 201
 Mary, 139, 155, 177
 Rebecca, 177
 Sarah, 123, 139
 Susannah, 164
 Tatnall, 139
 Thomas, 139, 155, 167, 191, 201
 William, 139
LEADAN, Elizabeth, 9
 James, 9
 Patrick, 9
LEBO, David, 221
 Susana, 221
LEDENER, Elizabeth, 48
LEE, Ann, 175, 214
 Elisabeth, 170
 James, 170
 John, 248
 Joseph, 220
 Samuel, 214, 257
LEES, Elizabeth, 25, 26
 Sarah, 25
 William, 1, 25, 26
 William Bond, 26
LEFEVER, James, 52
LEFEVRE, James, 74
 Susannah, 61
LEFLEY, Margaret, 209
 Rachel, 209
 Robert, 209
LEGARR, Elizabeth, 41
LEGG, James, 253
LEIPER, Alexander, 26
 Sarah, 26
LEMAN, Joseph, 240
LEMMON, Jacob, 99
LEMON, Elizabeth, 95
 Jacob, 95
LENDERMAN, Sarah, 260
 William, 254
LEONARD, James, 36
 Martha, 36
 Sarah, 171

LESLIE, Robert, 160
  Thomas, 160
LETELIER, Thomas, 254
LEUDEN, Elizabeth, 41
LEUVENIGH, Zachariah V., 238
LEVENSTEIN, Michael, 56
LEVIS, Hannah, 172, 202
  Martha, 172, 202
  Mary, 115
  Phebe, 202
  Pheby, 172
  Samuel, 112, 136
  Sarah, 114
  William, 114, 115
LEWDEN, Esther, 138
  Hannah, 232
  Jeremiah, 138, 193
  John, 48, 54, 138, 180, 204, 207
  Josiah, 138, 204
  Mary, 138
  Rachel, 138
  Rebekah, 192
LEWES, Hannah, 163
LEWIS, Agnes, 19, 20
  Amey, 134
  Ann, 15, 81, 84
  Catherine, 94, 237
  Cathrin, 81
  Dafydd, 80
  David, 19, 20, 50, 78, 236, 238
  Elizabeth, 83, 92, 148, 232, 236
  F.D., 84
  Garrett, 64
  George, 58
  Griffith, 83
  Griffydd, 80
  Hugh, 80, 83
  Isaac, 91, 95
  Isaiah, 90, 92, 96, 99
  Isaic, 87
  Jacob, 256
  Jane, 40
  Joel, 134
  John, 54, 92, 103, 134, 209
  Joseph, 252
  Kathrine, 41
  Kezia, 92
  Keziah, 251
  Mary, 15, 50, 51, 79, 81, 82, 88, 90, 148
  Philip, 249
  Rachel, 15
  Richard, 79, 85
  Richart, 83
  Richartt, 80

  Robert, 148
  Roderick, 257
  Sarah, 148, 248
  Stephen, 48, 103, 148
  Susana, 90
  Thomas, 252
  Timothy, 78
  William, 15, 85, 97
LIFTHALL, Lancaster, 60
LIGHTALL, Lancaster, 61
LIGHTFOOT, Ann, 202
  Catherine, 169
  Mary, 183
  Samuel, 151
  William, 151, 183
LIGHTFOOTT, Kathrine, 129
LINCH, James, 61
LINDSEY, Andrew, 258
  Ann, 219
  John, 234
  Robert, 43
LINGO, Katharine, 262
LISLE, Charles, 63
LISTER, John, 248
  Sorden, 248
LITLER, Sarah, 195
  Sidney, 211
LITTLE, Martha, 257
LITTLER, Deborah, 122, 132
  Hannah, 122, 132, 150
  John, 132, 150, 159, 177
  John Stapler, 132, 255
  Joshua, 122, 133, 149, 150, 151, 178
  Mary, 122, 190
  Minshall, 182
  Rachel, 122, 132
  Sarah, 122, 132, 151, 159, 173
  Sidney, 132
  Susannah, 149
  Thomas, 177
LITTON, Robert, 242
LIVINGSTON, Elizabeth, 20
  Magdalene, 17, 20
  Michael, 17, 20
LLOYD, John, 52
  Margaret, 6
  Mary Ann, 6
  Owen, 220
  Robert, 6
LOCKWOOD, Armwell, 244
  Thomas, 245
LOCKYER, George, 60
  Rebecca, 72
LODGE, Jozabad, 113
LOFTUS, John, 248
LOGAN, Elizabeth, 59
  Henry, 257
LOGU, Ruth, 206

LOGUE, Ruth, 173
LOHRA, Elizabeth, 61
LOLLAR, Thomas, 56
LONDON, ---, 57
LONG, Hugh, 243
  John, 50, 239
  Mary, 64, 260
LONGSTRETH, Benjamin, 200
LOVITT, Mary, 245
LOWBER, Peter, 251
LOWE, Joseph, 56
LOWMAN, Samuel, 5, 40
  William, 5
LOWNS, Caleb, 196
LOWTHER, Moses, 260
LUCAS, James, 246
LUDWICK, Jacob, 245
LUFF, George, 212
  Nathaniel, 213
  Susannah, 213
LUFFE, Caleb, 247
LUKENS, Jonathan, 197
LUKINS, Levi, 198
LUMMIS, Isabella, 56
LUNDEN, Ambrose, 39
LUNDY, Eleazer, 172
  Elizabeth, 172, 207
  Hannah, 172, 207, 208
  Rachel, 208
  Richard, 172
  Sarah, 172, 205
LUNDYS, Eliezar, 203
  Richard, 203
LUTTEN, James, 242
LUTTON, Ralph, 258
LUVENIGH, Philiip Vn., 231
LYNAM, John, 64
LYNCH, James, 226
  John, 250
LYON, John, 54, 240
LYONS, Hetty, 218
  John, 22
  Sarah, 22
  Thomas, 22

-M-

MCANNIS, Ann, 30
  James, 30
MCAVOY, Mary Ann, 57
MCBEATH, Alexander, 242
  Robert, 242
MCBRIDE, Barney, 61
  John, 8
  Margaet, 8
M'BRIDE, Martha, 257
MCBRIDE, Philip, 8
MCCABE, John, 243
MCCAFFDEED, Elizabeth, 51
MACCALL, George, 40
M'CALL, Robert, 260

MCCALLA, Elizabeth, 253
M'CALLA, Isabella, 258
  Mary, 257
MCCAMPBELL, Catharine, 8
  Philim, 8
M'CANLISS, David, 230
MCCART, Alexander, 49
MCCARTER, William, 53
MCCARTHY, Charles, 231, 233
MCCASKEY, William, 242
MCCAULEY, Catharine, 12
  Francis, 12
  John, 19
  Sarah, 19
  Susannah, 12
  William, 19
MCCAY, Elizabeth, 42
M'CAY, Mathew, 255
MCCELLAN, Francis, 31
MACCHESS, Archibald, 50
MCCLAY, Ann, 22
  Barney, 23, 26
  Henrietta Jane, 26
  Robert, 26
  Rosanna, 26
  Sarah, 23, 218
  Thomas, 23
MCCLINTOCK, Isabella, 48
MCCLURE, Catherine, 250
MCCOLLIAN, Jane, 35
  William, 35
MCCOLLOM, Abraham, 255
M'COLLOM, Samuel, 258
M'COLLOM (M'CHOLLOM),
Samuel, 258
MCCONNELL, James, 35
  Jane, 34
  Margaret, 32, 34
  Mary, 32, 35
  Penny, 64
  Richard, 32, 34
MCCONNISTER, John, 64
MCCONNOGHEE, James, 6
  Sicily, 6
MCCONOGEE, Cicely, 9
  James, 9
  John, 9
MCCONOLY, Cicily, 12, 14
  David, 12
  James, 12, 14
  Mary, 14
MCCOOMB, Elizabeth, 247
MCCORD, Ann, 241
  John, 241
MACCORDICE, Mary, 41
MCCORKLE, Thomas, 226
MCCORMACK, John, 99
MCCORMECK, Eliza, 48
MCCORMET, Mary, 49
MCCORMICK, Alice, 25

Elizabeth, 27
Hannah, 90
Jacob, 13
James, 27
John, 27, 87, 90
Margaret, 13
Mary, 25, 50, 58
Mrs., 27
Patrick, 25, 53
Sarah, 65
MCCOWAN, Martha, 241
MCCOWEN, Felix, 45
MCCOWN, Elizabeth, 242
MCCOY, Ephhraim, 45
M'COY, Martha, 258
MCCOY, Mary, 254
M'COY, Rachel, 255
MCCRACKIN, Jeremiah, 237
MCCREA, William, 235
MCCREDDEN, Morris, 44
MCCREDEN, Ann, 17
  Charles, 17
  Edward, 20, 22, 49, 50
  Elizabeth, 17, 20
  Jacob, 22
  Mary, 17
  Morris, 17
  Ruth, 20, 22
MCCRERY, Mr., 242
  Rebekah, 242
MCCUFFIN, Eliza, 54
MCCUGN, Bridget, 14
  Elizabeth, 14
  Felix, 14
MCCULLEY, Robert, 46
MCCULLOUGH, Eliza Jane, 30
  Elizabeth Eves, 60
  James, 30, 74
  Jane, 74
  Margaret, 48
MCCURDY, Jane, 53
MCCUTCHION, Mary, 100
M'DADE, Cornelius, 258
MCDADE, Mary, 217
  Rosanna, 58
MACDANIEL, Bryan, 40
  Daniel, 42
M'DANIEL, Elizabeth, 248
MACDANIEL, William, 3
MCDAVETT, Daniel, 232
MCDEAD, Mary, 46
MCDILL, Margaret, 50, 237
M'DONALD, Abigail, 230
MACDONALD, James, 48
  Mary, 48
M'DOWAL, Helen, 261
MCDOWEL, Esther, 253
M'DOWEL, John, 256
MCDOWELL, Eleanor, 28
  Ellen, 63

James, 28
Mary, 28, 62, 237
William, 239
MACELROY, Abia, 13
  Ann, 13
MCELROY, Frances, 241
MACELROY, John, 13
MCELWEE, Rebecca, 56
MCFARLAN, Mary, 65
MCFARLAND, Jennet, 19
  Martha, 19
  Mary, 44
  Robert, 19
MCFARLIN, John, 1
MCFEE, George, 49
MCFINLEY, Jane, 63
MCFUDGON, Patrick, 58
MCGEE, Eleanor, 60
M'GEE, Peggy, 256
MCGHEE, Elizabeth, 6
  John, 6
  Margaret, 6
  Mary, 16
  Robert, 16
  Sarah, 16
MCGILL, Elizbeth, 226
  John, 35
  Mary, 35
  Robert, 35
MCGINNIS, James, 15
  Margaret, 15
  Patrick, 58
  Samuel, 15, 46
  William, 241
MACGLATHRY, John, 59
MCGOWEN, Elizabeth, 38
  Hackey, 93, 100
  Mary, 38
  Nancy, 100
  Peter, 38
MCGOWIN, Ann, 100
  Hackey, 100
  Nancy, 93
MCGRANAHAN, Ann, 27
  George, 27
  James, 27
MCGREGOR, Samuel, 220
MCGUIRE, Ann, 27, 62
  Bartholomew, 11
  Bridget, 11
  Dennis, 27, 57
  Elizabeth, 38
  Frances Burrows, 38
  Jane, 11
  Margaretta, 226
  Thomas, 38
MCHANNAN, Benjm. C., 216
MCILHERAN, Robert, 236
MCILLHERAN, Robert, 49
M'ILVAIN, Mills, 261

M'INTIRE, Hanna, 263
  Jane, 259
MACK-SPARAN, Amilia, 100
MCKAY, John, 50
MACKAY, Mary, 104
  Robert, 104
MCKEAN, Mary, 71
  Thomas, 71, 236
MACKEE, John, 14
  Mary, 14
MCKEE, Mary, 55
MCKENNAN, William, 243
M'KENNON, Rebekah, 260
MCKIBBIN, Autre, 47
MCKIM, Alixander, 87
  Sarah, 89
  Thomas, 86
MCKINLEY, Ann, 62
  James, 28
  Jane, 165
  Margaret, 63
  Mary, 28
  Rebecca, 62
MCKINNAN, William, 245
MCKINNEY, William, 45, 238
MCKINSEY, Elizabeth, 62
M'KNIGHT, Andrew, 230
MCKNIGHT, John, 43
  Moses, 53
  William, 30
MCLALEE, Jane, 239
MCLANE, Allen, 63
MCLANNARD, Archibald, 61
MCLAUGHLIN, Ann, 21
  David, 6
  Elizabeth, 6, 8, 43, 47
  George, 52
  John, 21
  Mage, 48
  Mary, 16, 21
  Patrick, 16
  William, 16
MCLAUGHTLING, Samuel, 220
MCLEAN, Barkley, 253
  Benajamin, 58
  Eleanor, 24
  Elenor, 248
  Sarah, 24
MCLEER, Prudence, 255
MCLOGIN, Lydia, 46
MCLONEN, Daniel, 234, 235, 238
  Robert, 237, 239
MCLUM, Margaret, 51
MCMANAMY, Daniel, 55
MCMECHEN, Alexander, 234
  Dr., 59
  James, 235
  Rebecca, 235
  William, 237

MCMOLING, Thomas, 216
M'MULLAN, James, 259
MCMULLEN, Ann, 149
  Archibald, 62
  Benj., 248
  David, 149
  Jennet, 11
  Margaret, 56
MACMULLEN, Mary, 100
MCMULLEN, Mary, 11, 32, 57
  Patrick, 32
  Rebecca, 32
  Robert, 100, 239, 248
  Sarah, 32
MCMULLIN, Robert, 92, 101
MCMUN, Mary, 9, 17
  Robert, 9, 17, 238
MCNAMARA, Morris, 43
MCNAMEE, Ann, 15
  Elizabeth, 14
  Jane, 15
  John, 14, 15
  Martha, 14, 15
  William, 15
MCNAMME, John, 246
MCNATT, John, 248
MCNAUGHT, Malcum, 43
MCNEELIE, Mary, 51
MCNEIL, Laughlin, 46
MCNEMARA, Mary, 10
  Morris, 10
  William, 10
M'NIEL, Patrick, 260
MCNITT, Colin, 253
MCNULTY, Giles, 253
  James, 253
MACORMET, Susannah, 46
M'QUESTEN, Ann, 259
MCSPARRAN, Amelia, 100
MCSPAVEN, Amelia, 92
MCTOUCH, Ann, 24
  Elizabeth, 24
  Henry, 24
  Sarah, 24
MACUM, Ann, 50
  Catharine, 46
  Edward, 14
  John, 14
  Sarah, 14, 51
MCVEEY, Fergus, 52
MCWAY, Elizabeth, 22
  James, 22
  Sarah, 22
MCWHORTER, Agnes, 47
MCWILLIAM, Ann, 60
  Bankson, 36
  Elizabeth, 5, 65
  Hester, 5
  Hester Taylor, 36
  Louisa, 218

Margaret, 5
Rebecca, 67, 72
Richard, 1, 5, 36, 42, 65, 67, 230, 231, 232, 233, 235-241
Step., 242
Steph., 241
Stephen, 5
William, 5, 240
MCWILLIAMS, Elizabeth, 69
Esther, 24
Mary, 69
Rebecca, 24
Richard, 24, 69
Sarah, 59
MACWIRE, John, 97
M'WORTER, John, 258
Mary, 258
MADDOX, Ann, 43
MADICAR, Elizabeth, 61
MAFFETT, Rebecca, 21
MAGACHLIN, Hanah, 97
William, 91
MAGEE, David, 246
MAGENS, Eleanor, 32
Elizabeth, 26
Hester, 26
Maria, 64
Thomas, 26, 32, 66, 67
William, 32
MAGNER, Elizabeth, 33
Mary, 33
Stephen, 33
MAGUIRE, John, 91
MAHAN, Sarah, 39
MAINS, Catherine, 240
MALCOM, Barbara, 44
MALINGRE, Louis, 227
MALNE, Mary, 171
MANN, Ann, 261
MANSFIELD, Elizabeth, 218
William, 218
MANSON, Rachel, 250
MARDEN, Benjamin, 259
MARICE, Hugh, 94
MARICH, Joseph, 63
MARLEY, Adam, 4, 7
Ann, 7
Benjamin, 36, 37, 62
Hannah, 37
Louisa, 36, 37
Rebecca, 36
Robert, 4, 40
Rosanna, 7
Samuel, 7
MAROT, Ann, 132
Devenport, 132
Elizabeth, 132
Joseph, 132
Samuel, 132

William, 132
MARPOLE, Rebecca, 77
MARRIOT, Joseph, 154
Mary, 154
Thomas, 154
MARRIOTT, Martha, 132
Mary, 194
Sarah, 176
MARSH, Hetty, 262
MARSHAL, Nathaniel, 255
MARSHALL, Ann, 31, 34
Edward, 128, 205
Elisabeth, 139
Elizabeth, 51, 149
Henry, 31
James, 34, 128, 139, 152, 166, 177, 196, 199
Jane, 55, 139, 196
John, 30, 31, 34, 243
Joseph, 128
Margaret, 199
Martha, 166
Mary, 128, 177
Rebecca, 177
Samuel, 128, 139, 177, 196, 210
Sarah, 30, 184
Simon, 53
William, 30, 110, 128, 134, 139, 147, 152, 177, 196
MARTIN, Alice, 216
Ann, 22
Caleb, 258
David, 15
Eleanor, 47
Elisabeth, 136, 191
Elizabeth, 20, 51, 138
George, 136, 153, 191
Hannah, 138
Henry, 138
Hugh, 15, 50, 237, 243
Jacob, 230
James, 22, 57, 138, 212, 255
Jane, 15
John, 15, 20, 138, 153
Joseph, 200
Joseph Reynolds, 138
Josiah, 257
Lazarus, 200
Mary, 20
Mordecai, 200
Neal, 61
Rebecca, 138
Robert, 22
Sarah, 136, 191
Susanna, 200
MARTINS, Hellena, 59
MASH, Rachel, 172

MASON, Benjamin, 197
  Grace, 170, 196
  Joanna, 63
  John, 63
  Joseph, 255
MASSEY, Joseph Israel, 33
  Lydia, 33
  William, 33, 57
MASSY, Eleanor, 13
  James, 13
  Stephen, 242
MATHEAS, Margaret, 77
MATHER, Alcy, 261
MATHEW, Anthony, 78, 80, 84
  Jane, 84
  Simon, 78, 84
MATHEWS, Philip, 249
MATHOU, Simon, 80
MATHOW, Shan, 81
MATSON, Kittey, 260
  Rebekah, 260
MATTHEW, Antony, 99
MATTHEWS, Hugh, 41
  Johanna, 61
  Mary, 61
  Mr., 66
  Thomas, 241
  William, 241
MAUL, Content, 106
MAULE, Elizabeth, 146
  Hannah, 146
  Joshua, 146
  Martha, 146
  Mary, 146
  Rebecca, 146
MAULL, James, 262
MAURICE, Richard, 13
  Theodore, 13
MAXWELL, Bedwell, 245, 252
  Bidwell, 246
  Margaret, 230
  Mary, 4
  Robert, 216
MAXWILL, Francine, 222
  Margaret Bach, 222
  Robert, 222
MAY, William, 247
MAYBERY, Francis, 98
MEANS, Agnes, 42
MECAY, Angelica, 261
MEDFORD, George, 57
MEEK, Mary, 34
  Matthew, 34
MEERS, Catharine, 251
  Robert, 240
MEETEER, Thomas, 213
MEHOLLEN, Mary, 225
MELCHOR, Arthur, 78
  Elizabeth, 84
  Hannah, 78

MELONE, James, 197
  Mary, 197
MELSON, Lovey, 249
MENDENALL, Ann, 115
MENDENHALL, Benjamin, 62, 131
  Hannah, 113
  Isaac, 109, 194, 202
  Joseph, 109, 148
  Phebe, 110
  Rachel, 148
  Ruth, 109
  Sarah, 170
MENDINGHALL, Benjamin, 153, 156
  Eli, 156
  Hannah, 153, 156
  Lydia, 153
  Ruth, 156
MENDINHALL, Benjamin, 141
  Eli, 141, 142
  Hannah, 141
  Jesse, 141
  Joseph, 141
  Lydia, 141, 142
  Mary, 142
  Phebe, 141
  Rachel, 141
  Samuel, 142
MENOUGH, Isaac, 247
MEREDITH, Danniel, 244
  Joshua, 244
  Richard, 249
  Sarah, 246
MERRIDITH, Jesse, 213
MERRIE, James, 219
MERRIT, Mary, 63
MERRIWETHER, James, 1
MERSHALL, Moses, 195
MERYDITH, Jacob, 243
  Martha, 243
  Samuel, 244
MESSIC, Minus, 253
MESSICK, Job, 262
MICHEL, Marie, 227
MICKLEBRIGHT, George, 42
MIDDLETON, Isaac, 252
  Thomas, 63
MIFFLIN, Mary, 193
  William, 248
MIKELJOHN, Margaret, 259
MILBY, Arcada, 262
MILCHER, Arthur, 99
  Hanah, 99
MILCHOR, Arthyr, 82
  Elizabeth, 82
  Sara, 81
MILES, Alce, 78
  Dafydd, 82
  David, 78, 85, 233

Edward, 95, 100
Garlls, 83
James, 219
Jane, 81
John, 92
Laurance, 217
Margaret, 95
Mary, 88
Rachel, 83
Rebecca, 93
Samuel, 98
Sarah, 33, 95
Thomas, 33, 62
MILHOUSE, John, 129, 191
  Lidia, 191
  Margaret, 129
  Margarett, 191
  Ruth, 191
  Thomas, 129
MILLEN, David, 242
MILLER, David, 194
  Elizabeth, 93
  Flora, 14
  Hugh, 239
  Isaac, 140
  Isabella, 230
  Isaiah, 14
  Joana, 83
  Johanna, 79
  John, 52, 79, 225, 242
  Joseph, 45
  Lydia, 56
  Maria, 61
  Mary, 219
  Robert, 242
  William, 255
MILLES, David, 90
  Sarah, 90
MILLIGAN, James, 241
  Robert, 56
  William, 241
MILLIGIN, William, 217
MILLIKEN, James, 12
  Jane, 12
  William, 12
MILLIKIN, James, 10
  Jane, 10
  William, 10
MILLSON, Edward, 40
MILNER, Anna, 137
  Beulah, 137
  Catherine, 211
  Cyrus, 140, 212
  Daniel, 140, 212
  Elisabeth, 125
  Elizabeth, 131, 140, 212
  Esther, 137, 140
  Harriot, 137
  Isaac, 140, 212
  James, 112, 131

  Jehu, 140, 212
  John, 125, 137
  Joseph, 140, 212
  Larkin, 137, 212
  Lydia, 137
  Mary, 125, 137, 140, 212
  Nathan, 140, 212
  Phebe, 137, 169
  Rachel, 140, 212
  Samuel, 112, 125, 131, 137, 178
  Sarah, 125, 131
  Sidney, 137
  William, 125, 137, 178
MILOR, Garls, 80
  Joanna, 81
  Shon, 80
MILOS, Edward, 85
  Rachol, 81
MILS, Als, 81
MINAS, Mary, 248
MINOR, Elizabeth Polson, 7
  Jane, 47
  Susannah, 7, 43
  Thomas, 251
MINOUGH, Margaret, 93
MINSHALL, Griffith, 120, 136, 152, 154
  Isaac, 110
  Lydia, 176
  Mercy, 120
  Rebecca, 120
  Robert, 120
  Sarah, 120, 152
MIRICK, William, 82
MISKIMMON, David, 47
MITCHEL, Esther, 139
  John, 139
  Tacy, 139
MITCHELL, Ann, 57
  Elizabeth, 93, 247
  Hannah, 93
  John, 58, 197, 253
  Mary, 197
  Rudolph, 93
  Tacy, 197
MITCHER, Sarah, 98
MITTEN, James, 226
MOFFETT, Ann, 9
  James, 9
  Margaret, 9
MOHAER, Mary, 40
MOLESTON, Nancy, 245
MOLOSTON, Elizabeth, 243
MONEY, Thomas, 85, 98
MONRO, George, 232
MONROE, John, 4
  Rowland, 4
MONROW, George, 230

MONTGOMERY, Alexander, 236,
237, 238, 239
  Hugh, 243
  Sarah, 251
MOODY, Daniel, 235
  David, 46
  Lydia, 241
MOONEY, Patk., 241
MOONY, Mary, 101
MOOR, Martha, 166
MOORE, Alice, 179
  Charlotte, 63
  David, 179
  George, 57
  Jacob, 236, 246
  Jane, 49
  John, 47, 242, 254
  Jonathan, 179
  Joseph, 230
  Margaret, 51, 179
  Mary, 179, 225
  Mary Criston, 225
  Philip, 225
  Rebecca, 54
  Samuel, 43
  Sarah, 44
  Stephen, 179
  Thomas, 232
  William, 179
MORAN, Elizabeth, 232
  John, 49
MORE, Francis, 221
  James, 221
  Mary, 221
  William, 216
MORGAN, Abel, 79, 80, 85, 98
  Ann, 190
  Elizabeth, 91, 167
  Enoch, 77, 80, 85, 86, 91, 94, 99
  Hannah, 129, 167, 256
  James, 3
  Jesse, 191
  Joan, 99
  John, 86, 87, 90, 106, 242
  Judith, 84
  Lewis, 43, 90
  Magdalen, 77, 84, 89
  Martha, 246
  Mary, 90
  Morgan, 3
  Rachel, 91
  Rebecca, 193
  Samuel, 91
  Sarah, 91, 251
  Shuan (Jaen), 77
  Shunan, 81
  William, 167, 191, 242

MORING, Kathrine, 42
MORIS, Eleanor, 98
  Elinor, 81
  Margaret, 81
  Thomas, 80, 83
MORRIS, Anthony, 240
  Elinor, 99
  Hugh, 77, 99
  Janett, 84
  John, 250
  Mary, 47
  Matthew, 245
  Polly, 257
  Rebecah, 183
  Rebekah, 183
  Shannet (Jennet), 77
  Shonnet (Jennet), 77
  Thomas, 77, 84, 99
  William, 148
MORRISON, Catharine, 43
  Duglis, 219
  John, 61
  Patrick, 57
MORRISSON, Robert, 232
MORTON, A., 93
  Abigail, 92
  Agnes, 20
  Andrew, 19, 92, 241, 243
  Ann, 13, 15, 19, 57, 92
  Annie, 93
  Christina, 19
  David, 241, 263
  Dorcas, 18
  Ebenezer, 92, 100
  Elizabeth, 11, 55
  Grantham, 18
  Hannah, 9, 10
  Henry, 15, 19
  Jacob, 11, 20, 21, 45, 235, 258
  John, 10
  Margaret, 10
  Mary, 11, 19, 21
  Mathias, 15
  Matthias, 19
  Morton, 18, 52, 236
  Patience, 92
  Peter, 9, 10, 235
  Rachel, 92
  Rebecah, 249, 250
  Samuel, 178, 198
  Sarah, 10, 13, 18, 93, 99
  Susana, 92
  Thomas, 10, 13, 18
MORYS, Hugh, 80
MOSSMAN, Eleanor, 49
MOTT, Joshua, 211
  William, 252
MUCKLEHERRON, Margaret, 58
MUCKOVOY, Elliner, 256

MUKELHURON, Hugh, 14
  Mary, 14
  Robert, 14
MULLEN, Jane, 64
  Michael, 256
MULLICAN, William, 238
MULLIN, Hugh Alexander, 28
MUNCEY, John, 245
MUNDEL, James, 87, 99
  Margaret, 90
MURFEY, Margaret, 89
MURPHEY, Andrew, 19
  Barnabas, 19
  Bridget, 19
MURPHY, Daniel, 237
  Elizabeth, 222
  John, 57, 59, 222
  Jonathan, 248
  Thomas, 216, 222
  William, 244
MURRAIN, Ann, 91
MURROW, Charles, 222
  Mary, 222
  Thomas, 222
MUSGRAVE, Elizabeth, 130
MUSGRAVES, Aaron, 191
  Alice, 191
  Isarel, 191
  James, 191
  Mary, 191
MUSGROVE, Abraham, 195
  Ruth, 50
MUSTARD, John, 262
  Ruth, 258
MYERS, Ebenezer, 259

-N-

NAGEL, Michael, 248
NANNA, Abraham, 46
NAPIER, Thomas, 256
NASH, Sarah, 2
NEAL, Legor, 245
NEAL (NEILL), William, 231
NEBEKER, Elizabeth, 254
NEERING, Jacobus Williams, 40
NEIL, Andrew, 12
  John, 12
  Mary, 12
NEILL, Alexander, 233
NESBITT, ---, 65
NESSBITT, Deborah, 28
  Elizabeth, 28
  Hester, 28
  Mary, 28
  Mrs., 28
  Sarah, 28
NEWBERREY, Ann, 165
NEWCOMB, Elizabeth, 248
NEWEL, Elizabeth, 258

NEWELL, William, 242
NEWKIRK, Matthew, 64
NEWLAND, Ellis, 167
  Jain, 167
NEWLIN, Abigail, 145, 168
  Cyrus, 145, 146, 158, 168
  Edith, 126, 150
  Elisabeth, 126, 152
  Ellis, 126, 197
  Isaac, 145
  Joseph, 126, 152, 197
  Mary, 146, 193
  Nathaniel, 126, 253
  Nicholas, 154, 200
  Phebe, 126
  Robert, 145
  Samuel, 145
  Sarah, 145, 193
  Susanna, 188
  Thomas, 47, 154, 193
  Thomas Shipley, 146
NEWLIN (NEWTIN), Robert, 214
NEWMAN, Daniel, 247
NEWPHER, Benjamin, 253
NEWTON, Sarah, 59
NICHLAS, William, 94
NICHOLAS, Aboll, 83
  Elanor, 98
  Griffith, 83, 84, 99
  Griffyth, 81
  Lewis, 63
  Mary, 77, 82, 87, 98
  Philip, 93
  Sarah, 79
  William, 82
NICHOLS, Ann, 111
  Charity, 118
  Elisabeth, 157
  Elizabeth, 145
  Hannah, 145
  John, 104
  Joseph, 111, 145, 156
  Lydia, 145
  Margaret, 145
  Margarett, 156
  Margret, 173
  Martha, 157
  Mary, 104, 118
  Ruth, 145, 197
  Samuel, 145, 156, 157, 197
  Thomas, 104, 111
NICHOLSON, William, 54
NICKELS, Daniel, 108
NICKERSON, Joseph, 246
NICKOLS, Betty, 171
  Isaac, 108
  Martha, 171
NICOLAS, Griffith, 77

NICOLS, Mary, 105
NIGOLAS, Abel, 80
  Sarah, 81
NILES, Hezekiah, 150, 209
  Tobias, 150
NINBEY, Thomas, 219
NIXON, James, 257
NODES, Thomas, 53, 241
NOEL, Andr', 228
  Mario Zoe Marieanne, 228
NORRIS, William, 226
NORTH, William, 226
NOWELL, ---, 42
NOWLAND, Alfred C., 1
NOXON, Mary, 55
NULAND, Susannah, 166
NULIN, Ann, 252
NUMBERS, Rebekah, 260
NUTT, Elizabeth, 261

-O-

OBORN, J., 95
  John, 99
  Joseph, 94
  Mary, 94, 95
  Sarah, 90, 95
OBORNE, Hana, 89
  Rachel, 89
  Sarah, 90
O'CAIN, Francis, 233
OCHELTREE, James, 246
O'DANIEL, Francis, 260
OGDEN, Ann, 180
  David, 112, 180
  Sarah, 180
  Stephen, 136
  Zibiah, 180
OGLE, Benjamin, 3
  George, 237
  Howard, 63
  Margret, 243
  Mary, 41, 45
  Thomas, 3, 231
  William, 249
OGLEVEE, Judith, 243
OLDHAM, Edward, 243
  Elisha, 243
  Nathan, 50, 238
ORAM, Robert, 240
ORIM, William, 62
OSBORN, Ann, 175, 194
  Elizabeth, 194
  Hannah, 194
  Lidia, 81, 83
  Lydia, 194
  Sarah, 194
  Susanna, 194
OSBORNE, Ann, 169, 226
  Elizabeth, 169
  Hannah, 169
  Lydia, 150, 169
  Sarah, 90, 169
  Susannah, 169
OTWELL, Parker, 251
OVERTON, Ann, 22
  Matthew, 22
  Samuel, 22
OWEN, Catharine, 65
  Elizabeth, 89
  Jane, 41
  Richard, 99
  Susanna, 78
OWEN (THOMAS), Elizabeth, 88
OWENS, Aaron, 262
  Ann, 19
  Elenor, 129
  James, 129
  John, 129
  Sarah, 19
  William, 19
OZBURN, Elizabeth, 254
OZIER, Rebecca, 93

-P-

P..., Joseph, 199
PAGE, John, 167
  Rebecca, 167
PAIN, Elizabeth, 81, 94
  John, 80, 85
PAINE, John, 78, 83
  Nicolas, 86
PAINTER, Richard, 193
PALMER, Ann, 21
  John, 21, 46
  Lydia, 21
  Richard, 261
PANDER, James, 232
PARAMORE, Thomas, 249
PARK, Joseph, 47
PARKE, Thomas, 39
PARKER, Benjamin, 61
PARKINTON, John, 43
PARKS, Joseph, 45, 234
PARR, Stephen, 46
PARRADEE, Susanna, 39
PARRY, Catherine, 180
  Thomas, 148, 180
PARSON, Agnes, 230
  Simon, 81
  William, 80
PARVIN, Benjamin, 127, 167, 187
  Ephraim, 199
  Mary, 127, 187
  Sarah, 127, 167, 187
PASCHAL, Ann, 128
  Elizabeth, 128
  Frances, 128
  Hannah, 128

INDEX 309

Henry, 128
John, 128
Margarett, 128
Martha, 128
Mary, 128
Sarah, 128
Thomas, 128
PASCHALL, Ann, 188, 204
  Elizabeth, 204
  Frances, 204
  Francis, 188
  Hannah, 204
  Henry, 188
  John, 204
  Margaret, 188, 204
  Martha, 204
  Mary, 204
  Sarah, 147, 204
  Thomas, 204
  William, 147
PASEHALL, Ann, 170, 171
  Elizabeth, 171
  Francis, 170
  Hannah, 171
  John, 171
  Margaret, 170
  Mary, 170
PASMORE, John, 104
  Mary, 92
PASSMORE, John, 47, 239
  Sarah, 61
PASSONS, Ann, 250
PATTEN, Cornelius, 261
  George, 7
  Mary, 7
  William, 7
PATTERSBEY, James, 63
PATTERSON, Ann, 8
  Cathrine Margaret, 13
  Frances, 50
  Hester, 234
  John, 8, 9, 13, 56, 220
  Margaret, 8, 13, 52
  Mary, 9, 232
  Robert, 233
  William, 61
PATTON, John, 91
  Sarah, 91
PAULSON, Racheil, 253
PAYNE, John A., 49
  Jonathan, 237
PAYNTER, John, 226
  Samuel, 261
PEARCE, Anna Gertrude, 26
  Benjamin, 58, 241
  Gunning Bedford, 25
  Henry, 23, 29
  Margaret, 233
  Mary, 23, 25, 26, 27, 29

  Matthew, 1, 23, 25, 26, 27, 29
  Mrs., 66
  William, 29
PEARSON, Elijah, 211
  James, 86
PEDRICK, Elizabeth, 52, 175
PEERSON, William, 93
PEERY, James, 49, 237
PEG, John, 246
PEIRCE, Ann, 207
  Caleb, 114
  Hannah, 173
  Mariam, 173
  Martha, 173
  Miriam, 160
  Phebe, 207
PELHAM, E., 225
PELL, Elizabeth, 261
PEMBERTON, Joseph, 178
PENINGTON, James, 257
PENINTONG, John A., 218
PENLAND, William, 235, 236
PENNELL, Betsy, 247
  Mary, 167
  Thomas, 204
  William, 258
PENNEY, Edward, 250
PENNINGTON, Dealy, 221
  Margaret, 218
  Mary, 258
  Nimrod, 221
  Sarah, 221
PENNINTEN, Margaret, 221
PENNOCK, Allice, 117
  Joseph, 117
PENTON, Elizabeth, 59
  John, 35
PENYARD, Mary, 187
PERKINS, Catharine, 211
  Kathrine, 253
  Mary, 250
PERRY, Alexander, 217
  Ann, 221
  Eliphal, 121
  Elixander, 221
  Isick Lee, 221
  John, 121
  Margret, 121
  Mary, 121
  Nathan, 121
  Rest, 121
  Ruth, 121
  Sarah, 121
  William Elixander, 221
PERSON, Gidion, 176
  John, 244
PETEN, Malachi, 250
PETERMAN, Catharine, 250
PETERON, Richard, 6

Sarah, 6
William, 6
PETERS, Joseph, 107
Nancy, 247
Rebekah, 148
Thomas, 107
PETERSON, Abiah, 21
Alice, 5
Ann, 11
Catharine, 21
Cathrine, 44
Eleanor, 42
Elizabeth, 5
Ellis, 3
George, 3, 11
Hester, 240
Isaac, 11
Jacob, 66
Jacobus, 5
Jane, 5
Jesse, 244
Mary, 56
Peter, 21
Susanna, 5
PETTERSON, Sarah, 252
PETTIGREW, John, 246
William, 237
PHENIX, Mary, 49
PHEPOC, Richard, 62
PHILIP, Eleanor, 78
Hanah, 81
John, 78
Lewis, 78, 82, 99
Samuell, 80
PHILIPS, Betsey, 253
Cathrine, 157
Elenor, 263
Elinor, 83
Esther, 108
Hannah, 176, 253
John, 83, 99
Rebecca, 64
Robert, 157
Samuel, 83
PHILLIP, Lewis, 82
PHILLIPS, Ann, 161
Deborah, 172, 208
Eli, 198
George, 16
Hannah, 117, 172, 208
James, 108, 110, 157
Jane, 13, 15, 16
John, 15, 198
Lydia, 198
Mahlon, 198
Martha, 201
Mary, 13
Robert, 13, 15, 16, 117, 118, 161
Sarah, 110

Solomon, 157, 201
William, 108, 198
William Dixon, 161
PHILPOT, Erick, 51
PHILPS, Ashel Philo, 247
PHILZGERALD, Caty, 51
PHIPIPS, Elizabeth, 107
PHYLIP, Elonor, 81
PHYLIPS, Shon, 80
PICKEN, Samuel, 51
PICKIN, Joshua, 19
Margaret, 19
Samuel, 19
PIERCE, Aaron, 137
Benjamin, 241
Caleb, 204
Catherin, 40
Goshen, 137
Hannah, 137
James, 137, 153, 195
Joseph, 234
Josiah, 59
Lazarus, 260
Martha, 137
Mary, 137, 195
Miriam, 137, 195
Richard, 137, 195
Sarah, 93
PIERECE, Thomas, 257
PIGEON, Elizabeth, 247
PIKE, Stephen, 57
PILES, John, 234
PILKINTON, Rebecca, 186
Rebekah, 165
Richard, 186
Thomas, 186
Vincent, 165, 186
PINK, John, 63
PIPER, Peggy, 253
PIRCE, Ann, 81
PIRSONS, Simon, 98
PLATT, John, 242
Samuel, 230
PLEASANTON, David, 252
PLOWRIGHT, Eleanor, 46
POLK, Anna, 62, 256
Lucilla, 250
Wiliam, 254
POLLOCK, Polly Jane, 262
POLSON, Andrew, 18
Margaret, 18
Robinson, 18
POOL, Peery, 261
POOLE, Elisabeth, 129
Elizabeth, 129, 142
Hannah, 125, 142
Joseph, 125
Martha, 125
Mary, 142
Rebeckah, 142

INDEX

Rebekah, 125, 166
Samuel S., 142
Sarah, 142, 173
William, 125, 129, 142, 147, 148, 173
William Shipley, 142
POPPINS, Abigail, 49
PORTER, Agnes, 218
Alexander, 53
Amor, 249
Anthony, 93
David, 233
David Montgomery, 222
Eleanor, 241
Eliza, 221
Elizabeth, 208, 217
Jane, 44
John, 221, 222
Mary, 221
May, 222
Rebecca, 263
Sarah, 93
POST, Ann Catharine, 20, 21
Cathrine, 48
David, 16
Eleanor, 13, 56
John, 13, 16, 20, 21, 45, 233
Margaret, 249
Mary, 13, 16, 20, 21, 93, 242
Sarah, 18
Samuel, 48
William, 18
POTTS, Deborah Claypool, 158
Grace, 143, 158, 172, 208
Jonathan, 143, 158, 172
POULSON, Christiana, 41
Margaret, 64
Mary, 242
POWELL, Elizabeth, 246, 262
John, 255
Mark, 246
POYNTER, Elias, 244
Rattlife, 244
William, 244
PRATT, Frederick, 245
George, 245
Mary, 44
PRAYER, Sarah, 219
PRESTON, Ann, 49
Jonas, 167, 191
Mary, 167, 172, 191, 204, 250
William, 42
PRETTYMAN, Leah, 257
Robert, 246
Sally, 255
PREW, Caleb, 115

Sarah, 115
PRICE, Dorcas, 93
Elinor, 222
Hannah Ashburnham, 194
Isachar, 154
James, 220
John, 91, 92, 216, 258
Jonathan, 139, 154
Joseph (Jo's.), 87, 99, 154, 194
Mary, 88, 90, 97, 218
Roseannah, 194
Sarah, 64, 93, 154, 199, 222
Spencer, 218
Spenser, 62
William, 93, 222
PRICHARD, Lidia, 170
Mary, 261
PRICHETT, John, 133, 141, 156
Lydia, 156
PRINDLE, Thomas, 92
PRINGLE, Elizabeth, 92
James, 232
PRIOR, Joanna, 47
PRITCHARD, Ann, 219
Elizabeth, 97
John, 90
Mrs., 90
PRITCHET, Jesse, 210
PRITCHETT, John, 156
Phebe, 156
PROVOST, John, 252
PRYOR, Elizabeth, 115
James, 107, 115
Sarah, 115, 222
PRYS (Price), Mary, 79, 81
PUGH, Mary, 220
William, 114
PURSE, Alexander, 236
PUSEY, Abigail Israel, 25
Caleb, 115, 230, 231
David, 115
John, 178
Joshua, 25
Martha, 25
Mary, 25
Rebecca, 25
Sarah, 174
Thomas, 54
PYKE, William, 48
PYLE, John, 117
Ruth, 169, 196

-Q-
QUAINTANCE, Joseph, 194
Samuel, 194
Susannah, 194
William, 194

QUIGELY, William, 42
QUINN, Elizth, 93
　Nicholas, 93

-R-
RADLEY, Richard, 256
RAINY, Eleanor, 57
RALL, John, 42
RAMSAY, Mary, 45
RAMSEY, William, 234
RANDALL, Abraham, 195
　Ann, 195
　Elizabeth, 195
　Jane, 195
　Mary, 195
　Rachel, 195
RANDEL, Michael, 237
RANKIN, John, 232
　Robert, 48
　Surl John, 235
RASH, Andrew, 246
RASON, Sarah, 168
RAVIS, Benjamin, 220
RAWLINGS, Thomas, 52, 253
RAYFIELD, Betsy, 253
RAYSFORD, Ann, 24
　James, 24
REA, Elisabeth, 155
　Elizabeth, 171
　Isabell, 102
　John, 156
　Sarah, 235
　Sidney, 156
REABER, Sarah, 237
READ, Alexander, 25, 26
　Ann Catharine, 27
　Anne, 29
　Catharine, 63
　Charles, 30
　Elizabeth, 47
　George, 12, 23, 27, 29, 30, 32, 35, 37, 38, 39, 46, 57, 62, 74
　Gertrude, 12, 74
　Henry Meredith, 34
　James, 242
　Jane, 25, 68
　John, 12, 26, 29, 30, 34
　John Dickinson, 32
　John Meridth, 29
　Louisa, 37, 38, 39
　Louisa Gertrude, 39
　Lydia, 42
　Margaret, 25
　Margaret Meredith, 30, 34
　Mary, 23, 26, 27, 29, 30, 32, 34, 35, 47
　Mary Ann Murray, 37
　Mary Gertrude, 35
　Susanna, 5
　William, 1, 5, 29, 31, 67, 68
　William Archibald, 31
　William T., 1
　William Thompson, 27
READEN, Ann, 13
　Hannah, 13
　James, 13
READIN, Ann, 11
　Frances, 11
　James, 11, 44
READING, Philip, 55
READY, Benjamin, 256
REAPER, Jane, 19
　Joseph, 19
　Margaret, 19
RECHISSON, Sarah, 64
REDD, Adam, 113, 115
REDDEN, Sarah, 245
REDMAN, Thomas, 180
REECE, Jane, 13
　John, 13, 62, 238
　Joseph, 64
　Mary, 13, 56
　Rachel, 57
　Sarah, 62
REED, Ann, 248
　Elinor, 226
　George, 2, 3, 226
　John, 3
　Katharine, 5
　Lydia, 2, 39
　Sine, 248
　William, 4, 5
REES, Ann, 231
　Daniel, 78, 83
　David, 86, 253
　Elizabeth, 83, 84
　Evan, 85
　Feremia, 85
　Hanah, 89
　Hester, 89
　John, 86
　Lucretia, 56
　Mary, 85, 247
　Philip, 79, 94
　Thomas, 78, 84, 86
　William, 85
REESE, Catherine, 95
REID, Ezekiel, 245
REILY, Henry, 50
RELPH, James, 261
RENTFRO, John, 80
REREMANAND, John, 61
RESIR, Jacob, 258
REYNOLD, Elizabeth, 253
REYNOLDS, Abraham, 134, 197, 203
　Ann, 48, 126, 242, 250
　Anne, 230

INDEX 313

Benjamin, 117
Betty, 126
Daniel, 245
Eleanor, 7, 13
Elizabeth, 13, 47, 117,
126, 153, 165, 168
George, 230, 242
Hannah, 140, 201
Henry, 126, 130, 138,
140, 145, 153, 155, 159,
165, 181, 201
James, 140, 155, 201
Jane, 93, 134
Jennet, 7
John, 7, 13
Joseph, 126, 130
Margaret, 207
Margarett, 134
Mary, 74
Rebeccah, 168
Rebekah, 126
Richard, 126
Samuel, 134, 203
Sarah, 126, 130, 140,
145, 155, 168, 169, 192,
201, 209
Sarah Way, 140
Thomas, 117, 134, 193,
250
William, 254
RHICHART, Ann, 81
Shywan, 81
Thomas, 80
RHOADS, Thomas, 99
RHYDDARCH, Catherin, 82
Rees, 82
RHYS, Daniol, 80
Elizabeth, 81
Mary, 81
Philip, 80
Thomas, 80
Thomas Shonn, 80
RHYS(REES), Ann, 84
Daniel, 84
RICARDSON, John, 147
RICE, Ann, 34
Ann Ball, 34
Elizabeth, 243
Joseph Ball, 34
Philip, 49
Polly, 243
Rebekah, 217
Thomas, 34, 232
Veazey, 239
William, 256
RICH, James, 63
Sarah, 247
RICHARD, Joanna, 93
Thomas, 79, 93
RICHARDS, Ann, 63, 141

Betsey, 141
Catharine, 202
Dutton, 260
Isaac, 139, 141, 156, 157
Jacob, 259
Jesse, 141
John, 141
Lydia, 141
Martha, 88
Mary, 141, 157
Nathaniel, 141, 156
Rachel, 141
Samuel, 212
William, 141, 157, 202
RICHARDSON, Ann, 107, 123,
135
Ashton, 135
Daniel, 218
Eaesar, 93
Elisabeth, 123, 135, 153
Elizabeth, 158
John, 106, 107, 123, 135,
150
Joseph, 135
Mary, 100, 123, 184
Mary Ann, 258
Peter, 93
Rebecah, 107
Richard, 135, 150, 158,
176
Robert, 123, 147, 153,
232
Sarah, 123, 135, 158, 217
William, 41
RICHCHY, Mary, 91
RICKARDS, Hannah, 56
RICKETS, Grace, 45
RIDDLES, Ann, 240
RIDER, Andrew, 44
RIGGS, Eliza, 61
RIGHTER, Sarah, 256
RITCHIE, John, 63
RIVIERE, Claude, 227
Jeanne Louise Francoise,
227
Pierre Victor, 227
ROACH, Daniel, 258
ROBBINS, George, 18
Mary, 18
ROBERTS, Aaron, 200
Ann, 220
Martha, 147
Mary, 90, 108
ROBERTSON, Ann, 107
James, 108
Robert, 45
ROBESON, Francis, 103
Hugh, 51
Jamima, 169
Kathern, 102

ROBINET, Margaret, 84
  Mary, 79
ROBINETT, Margaret, 255
ROBINOT, Mary, 81
ROBINOTT, Margaret, 81
ROBINS, Mary, 256
ROBINSON, Ann, 41, 57, 89, 95, 168, 211
  Betty, 141
  Catharine, 114
  Charles, 125
  Edward, 4
  Elenor, 141, 155, 157
  Elinor, 122, 159
  Elisabeth, 123, 125, 129, 141, 183
  Elisha, 252
  Elizabeth, 89, 109, 112, 113, 145, 163, 166, 183, 259
  Ellinor, 141
  Francis, 113, 122, 123, 129, 145, 163
  George, 104, 184, 260
  Hannah, 184
  Hanson, 145
  Isobel, 253
  Jacob Wilson, 141
  James, 1, 122, 141, 155, 157, 159, 193, 202, 260
  Jane, 46
  Jemima, 155
  Joanna, 4
  John, 52, 103, 141, 220, 249
  Jonathan, 47
  Joseph, 109, 148
  Joshua, 41
  Martha, 109
  Mary, 105, 109, 122, 123, 141, 158, 159, 162, 236, 252
  Mary Ann, 64
  Matthew, 50, 237
  Nicholas, 113, 123, 145, 158, 162
  Rachel, 109, 122
  Rebecah, 107
  Rebecca, 164
  Rebekah, 123, 149, 178
  Samuel, 141
  Samuel Hanson, 145
  Sarah, 89, 254
  Thomas, 46, 87, 122, 125, 141, 157, 178
  Thomas Wilson, 141
  Valentine, 178
  Volentine, 125
  William, 54, 123, 141, 145, 162, 233, 252
ROBISON, Elinor, 226
  Elizaeth, 6
  Isarel, 40
  James, 3
  Jeroboam, 6
  Katherine, 40
  Mary, 6
  Priscilla, 3
ROCKHOLD, Elizabeth, 89
RODGERS, David, 44
  Margaret, 210
  Mary, 210
  Robert, 240
RODNEY, Caleb, 262
  George, 58
  George B., 1
  John, 253
  Phoebe, 224
ROGER, Elizabeth, 82
ROGERS, Enos, 160
  Hannah, 64
  Jacob, 3
  James, 1, 36, 62
  John, 216, 230
  Margaret, 3, 4, 173
  Marie, 36
  Martha, 31, 88, 99
  Mary, 90, 95, 173
  Rachel, 160, 173
  Robert, 31
  Sarah, 173, 210
  William Stewart, 31
RONTFRO, Margaret, 82
ROOS, Chathoring, 81
  Hannah, 88
ROS, Mary Weild, 81
ROSMIER, James, 246
ROSS, Aeneas, 5, 42, 67
  Andrew, 236, 237, 238
  Ann, 19, 36, 37, 38
  David, 64
  Eleanor, 19
  George, 67, 74, 231
  Georgius, 68
  Gertrude, 231
  Hester, 36
  Jacob, 6, 9
  James, 9, 19, 235
  Jane, 6, 9
  Joanna, 55
  John, 6
  Margaret, 55
  Mary, 72
  Mary Ann, 38
  Susannah, 37
  Thomas, 19, 36, 37, 38, 62
ROSSE, Anne, 5
  Eneas, 4
  George, 2, 4, 5

John, 2
Mr., 2
ROSTHILL, Richard, 64
ROSTON, Arthur, 44
ROTHARAM, Lydia, 172
ROTHERAM, Catherine, 163
ROTHERUM, Catharine, 134
Joseph, 134
ROTHWELL, Mary, 60, 88
ROWAN, Samuel, 48
ROWEL, Jeremiah, 98
Mary, 98
ROWELL, Jeremiah, 85
ROWEN, Adam, 63
Dorcas, 59
Elizabeth, 73
Henry, 32, 34, 66, 73
John, 32
Mary, 32, 34, 73
Robert, 60
Samuel, 56, 59, 73
ROWLAND, David, 89
Elizabeth, 261
Jane, 89
Jonathan, 189
Mary, 248
ROZELL, Joseph, 64
RUDDEN, James, 14
Jane, 14
Margaret, 14
RUDOLPH, John, 92
Mary, 93
RUDULPH, Mary, 175
RUMFORD, John, 259
Jonathan, 147
Sarah, 147
RUMSEY, Abraham, 59
Benjamin, 254
Charlotte Jane, 60
James Sykes, 30
Mary, 58
Robert, 225
RUMSFORD, Martha, 109
RUSSAM, Nathaniel, 262
RUSSEL, Elizabeth, 260
RUSSELL, Ann, 262
Fanny, 216
RUTH, George, 60, 262
Samuel, 237
RUTHE, Mary, 54
RUTHERFORD, William, 239
RUTTER, Mary, 93
RUZE, Mary, 93
RYALL, Mary, 42
RYAN, Ann, 262
Cornelius, 253
RYANS, Susanna, 252
RYDDARCH, Catharine, 77
Rees, 77
RYGAN, Lydia, 40

Morgan, 39
RYLAND, Jehu, 262
RYNHOLD, Jacob, 251

-S-

SADLER, Abraham, 18
Bridget, 18
William Sanky, 18
ST. MARTIN, Bernard, 227
SALMON, Benjamin, 255
SAMPLE, David, 62
SANDERS, Alice, 175
Ann, 157
Anne, 146, 175
Ellis, 146, 157, 174
Hannah, 146, 174
John, 157, 174, 207
Nathan, 175
Sarah, 174, 207
William, 46
SANDRESS, Mary, 249
SANKEY, Hannah, 241
SAPPINGTON, Cathrine, 18
Nathaniel, 18
Rebecca, 18
SAUCE, Johanna, 243
SAUNDERS, Amos, 199
Ann, 57
Charles, 146
Elizabeth, 146
Hannah, 146
Israel, 146
John, 146, 199, 208
Mary, 224
Mary Ann, 146
Nathan, 208
SAVILL, Jonathan, 260
SAXON, George, 245
SAXTON, Andrew, 246
SCANTLING, Mary, 240
SCHEER, Hance, 50
SCHOLFIELD, Andrew, 194
SCHOLIFIELD, David, 185
Enoch, 185
John, 185
Rachel, 185
Samuel, 185
SCOOLLEY, Robert, 260
SCOT, Ann, 51
Catharine, 45
Elizabeth, 217
Jesse, 249
SCOTHORN, Elioner, 246
Isaac, 243
Nathan, 246
SCOTT, Catharine, 232
Eleanor, 244
Elizabeth, 107, 241
John, 231
Mary, 8

Matthew, 47
Nathan, 244
Robert, 8
William, 242
SCOTTON, Rachel, 91
SEAL, Alice, 128
  Ann, 144, 163, 213
  Benjamin, 183
  Caleb, 114, 128, 139, 157, 163, 183
  Hannah, 128, 157, 183
  Isaac, 139
  John Polas, 201
  John Poles, 157
  Joseph, 183
  Joshua, 128, 139, 144, 171, 213
  Lydia, 128, 139, 171, 204
  Mary, 201
  Mary R., 139
  Rachel, 128, 165, 175, 183
  Rebecca, 62
  Sarah, 128
  Talor, 144
  Taylor, 213
  Thomas, 139, 183
  William, 114, 128, 139, 144, 157, 175, 183, 206, 213
SEARY, Richard, 85
SEATON, Allexander, 107
SEE, John, 233
  William, 216
SELL, Elizabeth, 111
SELLERS, Hannah, 123, 181
  Joseph, 123, 181
  Paschall, 123
  Sarah, 181
SENDIN, Mary Ann, 38
  Philip, 38
  Philip Fatio, 38
SERGEANT, Sarah, 54
SERMAN, Eunice, 255
SERREL, Alice, 201
SERRELL, Elizabeth, 158
  John, 130, 158
SERUY, Richard, 77
SEWALL, William E., 216
SHAFFER, Ruth, 251
SHAKESPEAR, Samuel, 216
SHAKISPER, Jain, 217
SHALCROSS, Catharine, 173
  Joseph, 173
SHALLCROSS, Betty, 142, 215
  Catherine, 210
  Deborah Claypool, 143
  Hannah, 142
  Isaac, 142
  John, 142, 143

Jonathan Potts, 143
Joseph, 142, 143, 158
Mary, 142
Orpah, 142, 143, 158, 163
Sarah, 143
Thomas, 142, 143, 158
William, 142
SHANNON, Hetty, 220
SHAPPON, Ann Mary, 4
  Mary, 42
  William, 4
SHARP, Ann, 257
  Caziah, 238
  Ehud, 216
  Lydia, 251
  Margaret, 45
  Mary, 175
  Samuel, 217
  Thomas, 216
SHARPLES, Benjamin, 130
  Edith, 130, 144
  Elizabeth, 144
  Joseph, 144
  Lydia, 144
  Nathan, 144
SHARPLESS, Benjamin, 142
  Caleb, 119
  Cathren, 163
  Eddith, 210
  Elizabeth, 210
  Isaac, 199
  Jonathan, 210
  Joseph, 194
  Martha, 142
  Nathan, 188
  Rebecca, 224
  Samuel, 210
SHARPLEY, Daniel, 140
  Esau, 256
  Rebekah, 256
  William, 256
SHAUGH, Barbara, 21
  John, 21
  Samuel, 21
SHAVER, Ruth, 251
SHAW, Deborah, 164
  George, 236
  Margaret, 42
  Mary, 50, 239
  Naomi, 247
  Rebecca, 163
  Susanna, 164
  William, 42
SHEARON, Ann, 223
SHEDFORD, William, 48
SHELEY, William, 63
SHELLEY, James, 251
SHEPHERD, Ann, 29
  Eleanor, 62
  Elizabeth, 16

John, 64
Margaret, 16, 21
Mary, 21
Thomas, 16
William, 21, 28
SHEPPERD, Hannah, 247
SHETFORD (THRETFORD),
  Walter, 231
SHEWARD, Benjamin, 133
  Caleb, 133, 144, 154,
  158, 207
  Hannah, 133, 154, 158
  Jane, 133
  Mary, 154
SHIELDS, Francina Bayard,
  216
  Robert, 60, 92, 96, 258
SHION, Elizabeth, 81
SHIPLEY, Ann, 129, 160
  Anna, 129, 136, 155
  Elisabeth, 129, 130, 147
  Elizabeth, 110, 136, 164,
  253
  Jane, 174
  John, 136
  Joseph, 129, 136, 168
  Margaret, 136
  Martha, 129
  Mary, 129, 136, 140, 151,
  155, 158, 160, 168
  Rebekah, 136
  Samuel, 129, 136
  Sarah, 129, 136, 147,
  158, 172, 193
  Thomas, 127, 129, 136,
  140, 151, 152, 155, 158,
  160, 211
  William, 129, 130, 147,
  197
SHIPON, Michael, 191
SHIRLEY, Elizabeth, 63
  Lydia, 168
SHIRLY, Lydia, 196
SHON, Dafydd, 80
  Ester, 81
  Hana, 81
  Shoncin, 80
SHONCINS, Mary, 81
SHONN, Ann, 81
  Robecca, 81
SHONN (CRYN), Thomas, 80
SHORT, Abraham, 54
  Araham, 12
  Elizabeth, 251
  John, 48
  Lovey, 256
  Mary, 12
  Polly, 257
  Rachel, 48
SHORTLEDGE, Abigail, 115

Hannah, 111
Isaac, 211
James, 115, 117
John, 117
SHUGAL, Eleanor, 8
  George, 8
  William, 8
SILSBEE, Mary, 53
  Nathaniel, 237
  Samuel, 230
SIMMONS, John, 255
  Nathan, 256
SIMONTON, Eleanor, 240
  John, 219, 240
SIMPERS, Margaret, 93, 101
SIMPSON, James, 242
  Jean, 242
SINCLAIR, Abraham, 195
  Ann, 45
  Hannah, 211
  Job, 195
SINGER, Morris, 51
SINGLETON, David McCormick,
  31
  John, 239
  Phoebe, 31
  Thomas, 31
SINKLEAR, Job, 195
  Keziah, 195
SINKLER, Abraham, 131
  Anne, 234
  Elizabeth, 131
  Hannah, 131
  Job, 131
  John, 131, 204, 206
  Kezia, 131
  Mary, 131
SIPPLE, Ann, 175, 209
  Catherine, 243
  Eliza Tatnall, 175
  Elizabeth, 161
  Garret, 160
  Silvia, 187
  Thomas, 160, 245
  Zadock, 245
  Zadok, 246
SKEER, Mary, 53
SKEGGS, Hetty, 216
SKELTON, Ann, 17
  Elizabeth, 13, 17
  Samuel, 13, 17, 47
SLATER, Eleanor, 53
  Mary, 108
  William, 263
SLAWTER, Rachel, 247
SLIZER, Samuel, 49
SLUBY, William, 1
SMALES, John, 55
SMALL, Elizabeth, 61
  John, 44

SMALLWOOD, John, 247
SMITH, Albin Gilpin, 212
  Alexander, 242, 250
  Andrew, 262
  Ann, 16, 18, 21, 220, 247
  Barbara, 54
  Benjamin, 250
  Christiana, 18
  Daniel, 21, 241
  Debora, 223
  Dorothy, 179, 182
  Elisabeth, 184
  Elizabeth, 12, 16, 28, 101, 222, 258
  Forgus, 42
  Francis, 222
  Gasper, 28
  George, 217, 252
  Gillis, 255
  Grace, 176
  James, 250, 251
  Jane, 114, 131, 175
  John, 2, 12, 41, 49, 179, 182, 184, 191, 251, 263
  Joshua, 184
  Lidia, 212
  Lydia, 219
  Margaret, 38, 93
  Marshall, 255
  Martha, 263
  Mary, 12, 27, 38, 42, 45, 88, 184, 247
  Mary Ann, 21
  Nancy, 251, 252
  Nelly, 262
  Pusey, 184
  Rachel, 226, 238
  Robert, 223, 239, 247
  Sally, 51
  Sampson, 16
  Samson, 18
  Samuel, 212
  Sarah, 90
  Thomas, 27, 92, 235, 244
  Widow, 89
  William, 2, 224, 226, 260
  Zacariah, 63
SMYTH, John, 244
SNOW, James, 249
SNOWDEN, John, 244
SNYVER, Adam, 37
  George Jackson, 37
  Jane, 37
  Teresa, 37
SOLLE'EL, Marie Francoise Clemintin, 227
SOLOMON, Jane, 234
SORENSEE, Mary, 77
SOWARD, George, 245
  Rebecca, 245

  Sarah 248
  Thomas, 245, 248
SPACKMAN, Ann, 136
  Anna, 145
  Deborah, 145, 175
  George, 136, 145, 161
  Hesther, 136
  Isaac, 136
  Joseph, 145
  Mary, 136, 161
  Samuel, 136, 145, 211
  Thomas, 145, 175
  Thomsin, 136
  Thomzin, 161
SPAIN, George, 253
SPEAKMAN, George, 168
  Tamzin, 168
SPEAR, John, 254
SPENCER, Ann, 59
  Elizabeth, 58
  George, 47
  Henry, 44
  Katherine, 246
  Mrs., 66
  Richard, 233, 241
  Stephen, 236, 238, 239
  Will, 236
  William, 233, 234, 235
SPENSER, William, 233
SPIRES, Jane, 47
SPOTSWOOD, Jane, 29
  Maria, 28
  Mary, 28
  William, 28, 29, 57
SPRINGER, Andrew, 33
  Ann, 12
  Benjamin, 33
  Caleb, 33
  Cathrine, 44, 46
  Charles, 12, 33, 243
  Christopher, 32
  Elizabeth, 59
  George, 33
  Hannah, 30, 32, 62
  Hannah Ball, 30
  Isabella Ann, 32
  Israel, 44
  Jacob, 46
  Jane, 33, 64
  Jeremiah, 31, 32, 56
  John, 67
  Joseph, 32
  Katherine, 231
  Lavinia, 63
  Lewis, 31
  Lydia, 14, 33
  Margaret, 14
  Maria, 64
  Mary, 30, 31, 32, 40, 60
  Peter, 30, 32, 246

Solomon, 14, 49
Thomas, 12, 61, 243
SPROAT, Rebecca, 219
SPROUL, Thomas, 235
SQUIB, Hannah, 175
SQUIBB, Hannah, 162
  Jacob Hewes, 144
  James Robinson, 144
  Margery, 162
  Mary, 144
  Nathaniel, 161, 162
  Robert, 144, 161
  Samuel, 144
  Thomas, 162
  Thomas Jefferson, 144
STAATS, Abraham, 240
  Ann, 216
STACKHOUS, Benjamin, 203
STACKHOUSE, William, 205
STAFFORD, James, 17
  John, 17
STALCOP, Agnus, 8
  Ann, 8
  Israel, 8, 42
STALCOPE, Bridget, 39
STALCUP, John, 51
STALFORD, Elizabeth, 176
STALLCOP, Mary, 231
STANDFIELD, John, 107
STANDLEY, Jane, 52
STANFIELD, Jean, 109
STAPLER, Esther, 146
  Hannah, 146
  Jemima, 124, 131
  John, 109, 124, 129, 146, 150
  John Littler, 124
  Joseph, 146
  Margaret, 146, 169
  Mary, 146, 170
  Rachel, 124, 129, 146
  Sarah, 124, 146, 150
  Stephen, 146
  Thomas, 146
  William, 146
STAPLES, John, 155
STAR, Rachel, 169
STARK, Susannah, 261
STARKEY, William, 86
STAROTS, Jacob, 261
STARR, Acquila, 133
  Caleb, 132, 200
  Elisabeth, 133
  Elisha, 133, 205, 213
  Elizabeth, 160, 161
  Elizabeth Tatnall, 175
  George, 186
  Hannah, 132, 154
  Isaac, 132, 133, 160, 161, 175, 209

Isaac H., 257
Jacob, 259
James, 258
Jane, 140, 154, 157
Joshua, 132
Margaret, 175, 183
Margarett, 132, 157
Mary, 184, 190, 209
Phebe, 161, 183
Rachel, 133
William, 132, 140, 154, 157, 193
William Lightfoot, 132
STAUTS, David, 261
STEANES, Mary, 254
STEDHAM, Honour, 260
STEEL, Hugh, 52
  Mary, 234
  Sarah, 234
  William, 51, 242
STEPHEN, Elanor, 82
  Elinor, 84
  Mary, 78, 82
  Nicholas, 78
  Nicolas, 82
STEPHENSON, David, 20
  George, 20
  James, 20
  John, 43
  Rebekah, 20
  Sally, 257
  Stephen, 20
STERRATT, Mary, 62
STETTS, Rachel, 243
STEUART, John, 237, 239
STEVENS, Priscilla, 54
STEVENSON, Mary, 255
STEWARD, Hannah, 131
  John, 131
STEWART, Agnes, 32
  Ann, 52, 131
  Anna, 259
  Charles, 55, 240
  Donald, 253
  Elisabeth, 131, 188
  Elizabeth, 54, 166, 169
  George Stuart, 131
  Hannah, 131, 166
  James, 218, 219, 221, 259
  Jane, 58, 220, 253
  John, 32, 131, 166, 237, 250
  Lydia, 221
  Martha, 131, 166, 188
  Mary, 93, 255
  Rachel, 245
  Robert, 46
  Sath, 219
  Stuart, 131
  William, 221, 251

STIDHAM, Ann, 60
　Elizabeth, 254
　Jonas, 254
　Peter, 58
　Sarah, 257
STILLEY, Sarah, 53
STOCKLEY, Polley, 261
STOCKLY, Patience, 258
　Woodman, 249
STOCKTON, Ann, 65, 74
　John, 1, 67, 74, 76
　Thomas, 76
STONE, Ann Jane, 30, 73
　Dorothea, 73
　Guy, 73
　Margaret, 63
　William, 39
STOOP, Alice, 6, 10
　Benjamin, 101
　Christopher, 10
　Cornelia, 10
　Eliakim, 10
　Elizabeth, 10
　Jeremiah, 10
　John, 1, 6, 10, 71
　Judith, 6, 10
　Leonard, 10
　Mary, 10
　Rebecca, 49
　Sarah, 10
STOOPS, Benjamin, 101
　Cornelia, 92
　Ephraim, 92
　John, 4
　Mary, 4
　Rachel, 192
　Sara, 93
　Sarah, 101
STORY, Beth, 173
　Joshua, 15, 49
　Lucretia, 15
　Rebecca, 15
STOUT, Martha, 250
STOUTT, John, 80
STOW, John, 92
STOWE, John, 42
STR..., Mary, 168
STRADLEY, Esther, 245
　Thomas, 245
STRAN, Deborah, 179
　Joseph, 179
　Mary, 179
　Rebekah, 179
STRANGE, Katharine, 113
STRATS (STREETS), Jacob, 221
　John Harmon, 221
STRATTON, Mary, 258
STREET, John, 254
　Robert, 41

STROUD, Ann, 146, 158
　Caleb, 138, 203
　Edward, 146, 202
　Elisabeth, 155
　Elizabeth, 138, 146, 196, 215
　George, 57
　Isaac, 138, 196
　James, 62, 138, 155, 158
　Jane, 166
　Jane R., 64
　John, 63
　Joshua, 138, 155, 203, 215
　Lydia, 138, 196
　Martha, 138, 203, 215
　Mary, 138, 146, 196, 203, 215, 252
　Rachel, 170
　Samuel, 138, 146, 158, 203
　Sarah Richardson, 146
　Thomas, 196, 199
STUARD, William, 255
STUART, Charles, 221
　Elisabeth, 181
　Hannnah, 181
　John, 147
　Martha, 181
　Mary, 221
　Robert, 147
STUBBS, Daniel, 133
　Sarah, 171, 200
　Thomas, 190
　Vincent, 191
STUBS, Addah, 172
STUCKEY, John, 58
STURGEON, Edward, 36, 37
　Margaret Letitia, 36
　Mary Ann, 36
　Susannah, 36, 37
　Thomas Knox, 37
STURGIS, John, 232
　Jonathan, 224, 225
　Lemuel Green, 224
　Maria, 224
　Mary, 224
　Rebecca, 224
SUGAR, Reuben, 217
SULIVAN, Mary, 226
SULLIVAN, Margaret, 62
　Mary, 252
SURMIZER, Catharine, 52
SUTHERLAND, Thomas, 239
SUTTON, ---, 66
　Alice, 11
　Ashberry, 260
　James, 248
　Jane, 11
　John, 11, 85, 91

INDEX

Mary, 11
Mrs., 66
Ruth, 91
Sarah, 11
Thomas, 234
William, 11
SWAIN, Betty, 190
SWAINEY, Edward, 239
SWANN, Esther, 61
SWANY, Joseph, 60
SWAYNE, William, 182
SWEANY, Timothy, 248
SWEENEY, Edward, 16
  Hugh, 16
  John, 46
  Judith, 16
SWETT, Ann, 149, 163
  Benjamin, 149, 178
  John, 106
  Susanna, 189
SWORD, Francis, 61
  John Ewer, 75
SYKES, James, 1, 3, 4
  Nathaniel, 3
  Stephen, 4
SYMMONDS, Catharine, 20
  Elizabeth, 20
  John, 20
SYNG, Mary, 241

-T-

TAGART, James, 255
TALLEY, Adam, 259
  Curtis, 251
  David, 257
  Hannah, 251
  Joseph, 251
TANNER, Catherin, 243
  John, 243
  Mary, 247
  Mrs., 66
TARNER, Sarah, 239
TATE, Ann, 173
  George, 113
  William, 113, 116, 200
TATLOW, Ann, 39
  Ann Cathrine, 19
  Elizabeth, 28, 43
  Hannah, 53
  John, 39, 60
  Joseph, 1, 14, 19, 28, 39, 66, 75
  Mary, 14, 19, 28
  Mary Janvier, 39
  Rachel, 14, 43
  Thomas Hyatt, 39
TATNALL, Ann, 135, 161
  Edward, 130, 135, 147, 150
  Elisabeth, 126, 135, 155
  Elizabeth, 159, 160, 161
  Esther, 135, 161
  Joseph, 126, 135, 139, 143, 150, 155, 159, 160, 161
  Margaret, 160
  Margarett, 135
  Mary, 147
  Sarah, 126, 135, 150, 155
  Thomas, 135
TAYLER, John, 91
TAYLOR, Abijah, 203
  Ambrose, 203
  Bankson, 62
  Benjamin, 217
  Benjamin Stuart, 216
  Ealenor, 242
  Elizabeth, 196
  George, 117
  Jacob, 66, 203
  Jane, 91
  Jesse, 119
  John, 56, 91, 174, 213, 242
  Joseph, 119
  Lydia, 255
  Margaret, 174, 213
  Mary, 203
  Minte, 252
  Mordecai, 203
  Peter, 203
  Ruth, 255
  Samuel, 201
  Stephen, 203
  Thomas, 242
  William, 45
TAYLOUR, Mary, 249
TEAT, James, 247
TEMPLE, Alice, 207
  Edward, 201
  Jane, 201
  Lydia, 114
  Mary, 207
  Thomas, 201, 207
  Timothy, 65
  William, 114, 207
TERNALL, Mary, 61, 263
TEST, John, 50
THACKREY, Stephen, 55
THAGER, Abigal, 81
THANE, Daniel, 235
  Mary, 235
THATCHER, Abigail, 85
  Amelia, 220
  Richard, 165
  Susanna, 188
  Susannah, 165
THELWELL, John, 259
THETFORD, Deborah, 49
THEVIN, Mrs., 66

THING (KING), Isaac, 220
  Johanna, 220
THOMAS, Ann, 79, 88
  Anthony, 240
  Asaneth, 217
  Catherine, 94
  Cathring, 81
  Charles, 58
  Dafydd, 80
  David, 77, 86, 93, 99
  Easther, 77
  Eleanor, 219
  Eles, 99
  Elias, 79, 80, 94
  Elinor, 81
  Elisabeth, 173
  Elisha, 83
  Elizabeth, 56, 81, 82, 206, 233
  Elizeus (Elisha), 77
  Elizous, 80
  Esther, 96
  Estor, 81
  Evan, 131, 159, 175, 233, 239, 252
  Evan H., 1
  Griffith, 45, 79
  Gryfyth, 80
  Jain, 217
  James, 79
  Jane, 90, 95, 131, 159, 175
  John, 78, 83, 85, 86, 94, 97, 173, 206, 244
  Joseph, 81, 159, 221, 231
  Lewis, 86, 94
  Martha, 78
  Mary, 77, 79, 81, 89, 94, 95, 219, 247
  Moris, 86
  Morris, 99
  Owen, 89
  Owon, 80
  Perry, 83
  Rachel, 78, 81, 240
  Richard, 45, 94
  Richart, 81
  Samuel, 263
  Sarah, 81, 88, 91, 221
  Sarah Hamly, 221
  Shonn, 80
  Thomas, 77, 88, 89, 90, 95, 233, 236
  Waine, 131
  William, 78, 80, 94, 95, 245
  Zachariah, 94
THOMASIS, Lewis, 95
THOMPSON, Ann, 224, 236
  David, 20, 237, 245
  Elizabeth, 20
  Esther, 236
  Hannah, 53
  Jane, 50, 237
  John, 224, 233, 235, 245, 261
  Martha, 53, 224
  Mary, 55, 60
  Matthew, 242
  Mordacai, 20
  Rachel, 224
  Ralph, 41
  Rebecca, 224
  Sarah, 66
  Stuart, 58
  Thomas, 59
  William, 44, 51, 61, 224, 245
THOMSON, Catharine Rebecca, 34
  Elisabeth, 174
  Elizabeth, 60
  James, 222
  Sarah, 34, 58
  Sarah Ann, 34
  William, 34
THORNBURY, Joseph, 180
  Mary, 180
  Robert, 180
  Sarah, 180
  Susanna, 180
  Thomas, 180
TIBBY, Elizabeth, 31
  Jane, 36
  John, 31, 36
  Martha, 31, 36
  William, 36
TILGHMAN, William G., 62
TILL, Gertrude, 46
  Jacob, 93
  Mrs., 66
  William, 1
TILTON, Elizabeth, 78, 81
  Lydia, 145
TITUS, Thomas, 59
TOBIN, Ann, 22
  Ashbury, 55
  Richard, 235
  Thomas, 238
TODD, Hannah, 250
  James, 250
TOLAND, James, 60
  John, 57
  Mary, 55
TOMBLINSON, Mary, 149, 164
  Othniel, 164
TOMLIN, John, 244
TOMPSON, Elizabeth, 91, 92
TOMSON, Agnes, 93
TOPPIN, Ann, 17

John, 17, 56
Rebecca, 17
Samuel, 60
TORTEN, Mary, 261
TOURSON, Fabius, 42
TOUSARD, Lewis, 258
TOWNLEY, Ann Jane, 253
TOWNSLEY, James, 237
TOWNSEND, Ann, 138, 202
  Brickers, 252
  Charles, 246
  David, 201
  Eleanor, 93
  Elizabeth, 202, 210
  Hannah, 138, 201, 210
  Isaac, 138, 202, 206, 213
  John, 87, 95, 202
  John Ferris, 138
  John Ferriss, 210
  Joseph, 138, 151, 210, 213
  Priscilla, 262
  Samuel, 196
  Sarah, 174, 202, 210, 211
  William, 183, 251
TOWNSLEY, James, 50
TOWSON, Magdalen, 89
TRAMPTON, Elizabeth, 226
TRAVERS, Matthew, 248
TREDWELL, Catherine, 248
TREVILLER, Jonathan, 252
TRIBET, Johun, 245
TRIBIT, Tyrell, 245
TRIMBLE, Rebekah, 132
TROTH, Elisabeth, 122
  Elizabeth, 181
  Hannah, 132, 181, 210
  Henry, 122, 140, 147, 154, 171, 181, 210
  Jane, 140, 210
  John, 122, 140, 181, 210
  Lydia, 181
  Margaret, 140, 210
  Samuel, 122, 181, 191
  Sarah, 122, 140, 154, 199, 210
  Sarah Pashill, 171
  William, 122, 140, 150, 181, 182, 210
TRUAX, Catharine, 250
  Cornelius, 83
  Cornolius, 80
  Elizabeth, 83
  Mary, 81, 235
  Philip, 78, 79, 85
  Rebecca, 57
  Rebekah, 81
  William, 80, 83
TRUITT, Solomon, 246
TRUMAN, Sarah, 254

TRUWAX, Elizabeth, 81
TRYON, Rebeckah, 250
TRYWAX, Phylip, 80
TUB, John, 6
TULL, Martha, 258
TURCHESS, Sarah, 251
TURNER, Araminta, 217
  Elizabeth, 243
  Lucretia, 18
  Margaret, 18
  Sidney, 250
  Thomas, 18, 46, 243
TURTLE, Anne, 230
TWEEDY, Elizabth, 219
  Mary, 230

-U-
UNDERHILL, Elizabeth, 194
  John, 148, 154, 194
  Thomas, 148, 154
UNDERLIN, William, 247
UNDERWOOD, Benjamin, 81, 94
  Joseph, 111, 115, 251
  Margaret, 57
  Mary, 82, 87
  Sarah, 94, 248
  Samuel, 249
  Thomas, 82, 111
  William, 115
UNSTER, Walbert, 39
USKER, Mathew, 70

-V-
VAIL, Elinor, 223
  Elixander, 223
  Elizabeth, 223
  Jan, 220
  Samuel, 236
VAN BEBBER, Mary, 71
VAN DEGRIFT, Mary, 233
VAN DIKE, James, 237
VAN HECKLIN (VANCECKLAN), Titus, 233
VAN LEU-ENIGH, Ann, 68
  Zach, 68
VAN LEURENIGH, Elizabeth, 75
VAN LUVENEIGH, Zachariah, 65
VAN SANT, Susanna, 217
VANDERSLICE, Barge, 64
VANDEVIR, Susannah, 45
VANDYKE, Grantham, 30
  Mary, 76, 30
  Nicholas, 75, 76, 30, 59, 67
VANGEZELL, Gertrude, 66
  John, 230, 1
  Susannah, 59
VANHOLAN, Sarah, 83

VANKIRK, David, 244
VANLEAR, Senna, 217
VANLEURENIGH, Mary, 8
  Philip, 8
  Zacharias, 8
VANNEMON, Abraham, 50
VANSANT, Asaph, 57
  Catharine, 23, 24
  Chambers, 22
  Cornelius, 79, 93
  George King, 24
  John, 23, 24
  Mary, 54
  Sarah, 23
VANZANT, George, 62
VAUBLANC, Marie Catherine
  Eliz. V., 228
VAUGHAN, John, 100
  William, 249
VEAIL, Arthur, 46
VEAL, Samuel, 48
VEAZEY, Samuel, 245
VENNEMAN, Abraham, 238
VERT, Rebecca, 93
  William, 93
VEZEY, Ann Elizabeth, 89
VICKERY, Judith, 230
VIDAL, Jean, 227
  Jean Francois Marie
  Felix, 227
VINEMAN, Rebekah, 255
VINING, James Rudolph, 29
VIRDIN, Jemima, 245
  John, 245, 246
  William, 245
VIRTUE, David, 33
  Margaret, 33
  Mary Ann, 33
VIZEY, Edward, 86
VNJOY, Robert, 58

-W-

WADE, William, 244
WAINSFORD, Jane, 40
WALIS, Mary, 81
WALKER, Andrew, 93, 96
  Cathrine, 16
  Elizabeth, 62, 63
  John, 247, 255
  Joseph, 243
  Margaret, 55, 63
  Mary, 93
  Matthew, 262
  Robert, 16
  Ruth, 225
  Samuel, 225
  Sarah, 256
  Susannah, 16
  Thomas, 58

  William, 46, 225, 243, 246
WALL, Edward, 238
  Sara, 55
WALLACE, James, 219
  Joseph, 242
  Mary, 99
  Rachel, 216
  Robert, 235
  Samuel, 203
  Sarah, 208
  William, 246
WALLIS, Mary, 78, 83
  Sarah, 172
WALRAVEN, John, 254
  Jonas, 54
  Rachel, 241
WALTER, James, 119
  Jane, 119
  Lydia, 109
  William, 116
WANN, Eliza Ann, 60
WANSFORD, Nicholas, 40
WAPLES, Catharine, 255
  Isaac, 256
  Joseph, 257
WARD, Elloner, 255
  George, 259
  Moses, 254
  Thomas, 260
WARDLOW, Elizabeth, 14
  James, 14
WAREN, Thomas, 191
WARING, Thomas, 195, 198
WARNER, Ann, 124, 143, 147
  Benjamin, 124, 180
  Daniel, 124, 180, 196
  David, 124
  Eleanor, 32
  Elisabeth, 147
  Elizabeth, 124
  Esther, 143
  Hesther, 137
  James, 124, 183
  Jesse, 137
  John, 124, 171, 178, 184
  Jonathan, 124
  Joseph, 60, 124, 137,
    143, 161, 166, 171, 178
  Joseph Tatnall, 143
  Levi, 171
  Lidia, 165
  Lydia, 171, 184
  Margery, 32
  Mary, 124, 137, 161, 166,
    171, 184
  Matthias, 32
  Nanny, 171
  Rachel, 171
  Samuel, 124, 180

Sarah, 32, 124, 180
Susanna, 137
Timcon, 198
William, 124, 137, 143, 147, 161, 180
WARNOCK, Eleanor, 262
  Elenor, 216
WARON, William, 193
WARREN, Elizabeth, 251
WARRING, Lowdman, 248
WARRINGTON, Agnew, 251
  Thomas, 251
WATERS, Savannah, 93
WATES, Jane, 93
WATKINS, Joseph, 100
  Rachel, 248
WATMOUGH, Anna, 22
  James Horatio, 22
  Maria Ellis, 22
WATSON, James, 217
  Jane, 18
  Jesse, 252
  John, 85, 94
  Mary, 88
  Mary Ann, 217
  Robert, 18
  Samuel, 48
WATT, Mary, 59
WATTSON, Cathrin, 89
  Sarah, 251
  Susana, 90
  Thomas, 236
WAXFORD, Gartwieth, 40
WAY, Ann, 128, 188
  Caleb, 139
  Edith, 110
  Elisabeth, 183
  Elizabeth, 122, 149
  Francis, 111, 150
  Hannah, 128, 188
  John, 128, 188
  Joseph, 59, 110, 166, 177
  Joshua, 122, 183
  Lidya, 188
  Martha, 128, 188
  Mary, 128, 150, 188
  Nicholas, 177
  Phebe, 128, 188
  Samuel, 177
  Sarah, 166, 177
  Shusanna, 177
  Thomas, 128, 188
WEARING, Thomas, 194
WEAVER, George, 258
WEB, Lydia, 131
WEBB, Ann, 51
  Ann Bond, 59
  Elizabeth, 41
  Hannah, 60
  Joseph, 110, 188

Joshua, 172
Lidia, 172
Roger, 102
Ruth, 102
Sarah, 119
WEBBS, Ann, 102
WEBSTER, Eliza, 146
  Hannah, 140, 153, 155, 170, 177
  John, 140, 146, 153, 155, 177
  Louissa, 146
  Lydia, 146
  Rebecca, 49, 236
WEEIR, William, 51
WEILD, Samuel, 80
  Thomas, 80
WELCH, Anne, 93
  Margaret, 93
WELDEN, Mary, 247
WELDON, Margaret, 130
WELL, Margaret, 61
WELLS, David, 246
  Edward, 151, 185
  Elizabeth, 252
  James, 250
  Sarah, 185
WELSH, Ann, 88
  Elizabeth, 21, 51
  Enoch, 186
  Hannah, 36
  Jacob, 67
  James, 21, 36, 54, 62
  Letice, 131
  Lettic, 175
  Margaret, 21
  Mary, 239
  Susanna, 39
  Thomas, 187
  William, 36
WESLEY, Ann, 261
WEST, Abigail, 131, 193
  Ann, 226
  Benjamin, 261
  Caleb, 131
  Charles, 131, 167
  Elenor, 108
  Elizabeth, 262
  George, 35, 257
  Hannah, 109
  John, 35
  Joseph, 112, 130
  Mary, 35, 129, 130, 131, 167, 180, 199
  Reuben, 253
  Sarah, 131, 177, 197
  Thomas, 129, 130, 257
  William, 35, 131, 177, 180
WETHERBEE, Ruth, 50

WETHERED, Harriet Cordelia, 25
  John, 1, 25
  Mary, 25
WETHERLEE, Ruth, 49
WHANN, Ann, 219
WHARTON, Charles, 153, 192
  Elisabeth, 192
  Joseph, 148, 153
  Samuel, 148
WHARUM, Milcay, 261
WHEALAND, William, 232
WHEELER, Lemuel, 244
WHITE, Alexander, 244
  Ann, 127, 142, 158
  Anna, 259
  Cathrine, 50
  Elisabeth, 127
  Eliza, 54
  Elizabeth, 142
  Esther, 127, 129
  George, 38
  Henry, 18, 21
  Jacob, 51, 261
  James, 10, 252
  Jane, 127, 249
  John, 18, 49, 104, 127, 142, 149, 158, 236
  Joseph, 127, 142
  Margaret, 56
  Mary, 10, 20, 38, 142, 249
  Mary Robinson, 142
  Nancy, 257
  Nicholas Robinson, 142
  Rebecca, 38, 142
  Rebekah, 21
  Robert, 61, 263
  Sarah, 18, 21
  Thomas, 18, 20
  William, 10, 20, 44, 104, 127, 142, 149, 158, 259
WHITEHEAD, Lamuel, 245
WHITELOCK, James, 220
  Martha, 174, 191
  Sarah, 130, 168
WHITELY, Mary, 235
WHITESIDE, Eleanor, 61
  William, 110
WHITIN, Rhichart, 80
WHITLEY, Abagail, 47
  Mary, 45
WHITSILL, Sarah, 226
WHITTEN, Benjamin, 50
  Rachel, 44
  Richard, 94
WHITTIM, Mary, 219
WHITTING, Benjamin, 239
  Thomas, 239
WICKERSHAM, Amos, 213

Elijah, 144
Isaac, 156
James, 144
John, 213
Mary, 156
Samuel, 144
Sarah, 144, 200
Thomas, 144, 156
WILD, John, 77, 82
  Nathaniel, 93
  Samuel, 77, 99
  Thomas, 77, 99
WILDERSON, Catharina, 19
  Catherine, 56
  Frederick, 19
  Sophia Catharina, 19
WILDS, Mary, 98
  Nathaniel, 80
WILENTS, William, 244
WILEY, Eleanor, 52
  Hugh, 236
  John, 62
  Margaret, 216
  Martha, 164
  Mary, 164
  Mrs., 93, 96
  Rebecca, 164
  Rebekah, 150
  Robert, 75
  Thomas, 164
  Vincent, 164, 183
WILIANA, Mary, 81
WILKINS, David, 235
  William, 255
WILKINSON, Alice, 144, 213
  Elizabeth, 144, 157, 213
  Hannah, 175
  Isaac, 175
  James, 144, 213
  Joseph, 144, 157, 189, 202, 213
  Margaret, 175
  Margret, 202
  Thomas, 144, 213
WILLCOX, Joseph, 256
WILLEN, Martha, 261
WILLET, Christopher, 242
WILLIAM, ---, 99
  James, 92, 96
  Jane, 96
  John, 83
  Margaret, 81, 98
  Martha, 87
  Mary, 78
  Shion, 80
  Susanah, 82
  Susannah, 96
  Thomas, 92
WILLIAMS, Andrew, 246
  Ann, 60, 216, 239

INDEX

Anne, 237
Charles, 34, 225
Christianna, 225
David, 95, 235
Edward, 34
Elizabeth, 58, 217
Ellenor, 41
Ennion, 190
George, 17
Griffith, 45
Hannah, 24, 190
Harding, 34
Isaac, 167, 190
Isabella, 61
James, 87, 90, 95, 101
Jane, 90, 234
John, 17, 24, 45, 256
Joseph, 235
Joshua, 237
Lydia, 167, 173, 190, 202
Margaret, 95
Martha, 43, 242
Mary, 17, 190
Matilda, 34
Owen, 179
Polly, 260
Rachel, 248
Rebecca, 34
Sarah, 23, 54, 56, 93, 240, 244
Thomas, 24, 44, 51
Thomas F., 61
Timothy, 43
WILLIAMSON, Adam, 119, 141, 168
  Alvina, 141
  George, 141
  Harriot, 141
  Harry Buckley, 141
  Henrietta, 141
  John, 119, 141
  Lydia, 141
  Margaret, 247
  Mary, 141, 168
  Mary Ann, 141
  Nicholas Gilpin, 141
WILLIN, Day, 247
WILLING, Eunice, 255
WILLIS, Benjamin, 64
  John, 49
  Robert, 262
WILLSON, Ann, 107
  Christopher, 106
  Thomas, 108
WILMER, James, 22
  Mary, 22
WILSON, Alexander, 200
  Alisanna, 137, 205
  Andrew, 235
  Ann, 118, 193
  Baynard, 205
  Benjamin, 139, 140, 212
  Bettey, 164
  Betty, 139, 141, 151, 155, 157, 167, 172, 212
  Charles, 255
  Christopher, 116
  Eleanor, 26
  Elizabeth, 216, 219, 259
  Esther, 110, 119, 187
  Ezekiel, 205
  George, 202
  Hannah, 112, 169, 181, 189, 202
  Isaac, 137, 139, 140, 205, 212
  Jacob, 116, 141, 151, 155, 157
  James, 9, 26, 116, 118, 119, 178, 242
  Jane, 117, 123, 187
  John, 111, 115, 137, 211, 256
  Jonathan, 53
  Joseph, 9, 119, 139, 187, 212
  Justis, 62
  Lowas, 43
  Margret, 169
  Mary, 116, 157, 172
  Mercy, 140, 212
  Mersey, 139
  Moore, 26
  Nicholas, 123
  Oliver, 139, 140, 212
  Peter, 205
  Rachel, 166, 205
  Robert, 123, 178
  Ruth, 181
  Samuel, 205, 239
  Sarah, 9, 123, 139, 173, 178, 181, 187, 207
  Stephen, 139, 140, 212
  Susana, 202
  Susanna, 137, 205
  Theodore, 258
  Thomas, 110, 116, 118, 123, 187, 202, 205, 255
  William, 118, 246
WILTBANK, Isaac, 255
WILTON, Jane, 179
  William, 179
WIN, Sarah, 41
WINDEMIRE, Elizabeth, 226
WINDER, Levin, 261
WINDLE, Lydia, 155, 170
  Mary, 155, 250
WINGATE, Lurena, 257
WINKLE, Ann Van, 218
WITSELL, Henry, 224, 225

James, 225
Rachel, 224, 225
William, 224
WITSILL, Henry, 226
WITTEN, Richard, 79
WOLASTON, Abigail, 134
  Allice, 134
  Deborah, 134
  Elisabeth, 134
  George, 134, 170
  Harmon, 170
  Jacob, 134
  Joanna, 134
  John Gregg, 170
  Joseph, 134
  Levy, 134
  Lydia, 134
  Mary, 134, 170
  William, 134
WOLESTON, Ann, 109
  Jereh., 109
WOLF, Jacob, 225
  Michael, 225
  Rebecca, 225
WOLINSWORTH, John, 83
WOLLASTON, Ann, 123
  Catherine, 123, 148
  Elisabeth, 134
  Hannah, 123
  James, 123, 208
  Jeremiah, 114, 123, 148
  Joseph, 134
  Joshua, 123
  Martha, 54
  Mary, 60, 150
  Sarah, 123
  Thomas, 123
  William, 208
WOLLESTON, James, 163
  Mary, 163
  William, 112
WOLLISTON, Catherine, 124, 179
  Deborah, 124
  Elisabeth, 124
  Elizabeth, 179
  Hannah, 164
  Jacob, 124, 178
  Jeremiah, 179
  Joseph, 124, 179
  William, 124
  Zabiah, 112
WOOD, Ann, 225
  E., 225
  Elizabeth, 151, 201, 238
  Enoch, 260
  Enos, 201
  Hannah, 125, 132
  Isaac, 176, 195
  Isable, 201
  Jacob, 201
  John, 47, 50, 201
  John Dickinson, 224
  Joseph, 132, 201
  Joshua, 201
  Judith, 112
  Letitia, 40
  Lewis, 201
  Maria Ervin, 225
  Martha, 60
  Mary, 112
  Nathan, 112, 125, 132
  Patience, 224
  Rachel, 132
  Rebekah, 132, 168
  Samuel, 224, 226
  Sarah, 165, 179
  Stephen, 255
  Thomas, 112
  William, 112, 132
WOOD..., Hannah, 192
WOODBRIDGE, Samuel, 91
  Sarah, 91
WOODCOCK, Anthony, 124
  Bancroft, 124, 125, 148, 156
  Deborah, 194
  Elisabeth, 125
  Isaac, 125
  Rachaell, 112
  Rachel, 124, 125, 156, 163
  Rebecca, 166
  Rebekah, 125
  Robert, 112, 124, 194
  Ruth, 124, 125, 156
  Samuel, 125
  William, 124, 125, 149
WOODCROFT, Bancroft, 211
  Ruth, 211
WOODDEN, Benjamin, 55
WOODLAND, Elizabeth, 220
  Rebecca, 220
  Sarah, 220
  William, 220
WOODLEY, Mary, 247
WOODNUT, Betty, 167
  Hannah, 167
  Mary, 167
WOODNUTT, Betty, 166, 185, 188
  Jonathan, 151, 185
  Mary, 185
WOODROW, Mary, 48
WOODS, Lettis, 92
  Robert, 53
WOODWARD, Alice, 204
  Ann, 231
  Esther, 106
  Jane, 164, 181

INDEX

Jesse, 164, 181, 185
Lydia, 53
Prudence, 164, 181
Richard, 107
Sarah, 108, 164, 181
WOOLASTON, Hannah, 156
  Jeremiah, 129
  Joanna, 215
  Joseph, 151
  Sarah, 156
  Thomas, 129, 156
  William, 151
WOOLSTON, Benjamin, 137, 208
  Elisabeth, 137
  Elizabeth, 175, 198
  Hannah, 137, 169, 193
  Jeremiah, 137
  Martha, 137
  Sarah, 137
WORKMAN, Polly, 254
WORMS, Daniel, 7, 12
  Elizabeth, 7
  Lena, 49
  Mary, 7, 12
  Peter, 7
WORRELL, Benjamin, 55
  Edward, 224
  George Washington, 224
  Rebecca, 224
  Thomas, 209
  William, 224
WORTH, Joseph, 121
WORTHINGTON, Benjamin, 55
WRIGHT, Ann, 206
  Anna, 174
  Catherine, 246
  Eleanor, 248
  Elijah, 262
  James, 188
  John, 216
  Joseph, 174
  Katherine, 246
  Marke, 102, 103
  Mary, 174
  Rebecca, 50, 239
WYNKOOP, Abram, 240
  James, 240

-Y-

YARNALL, Abner, 145
  Benjamin, 125, 149, 199
  David, 169
  Edith, 157
  Elisabeth, 125
  Elizabeth, 130, 145, 166
  Ephraim, 131, 157, 206, 214, 238
  Esther, 145, 166
  Holton, 206
  James, 185
  John, 133, 152

Jonathan, 125, 184
Joseph, 145, 190
Lydia, 169
Marib, 215
Mordecai, 145
Nathan, 152
Philip, 137
Phillip, 198
Rachel, 145
Sarah, 157, 162, 214
Stephen, 125, 191
YARNELL, Edith, 132
  Elisabeth, 132
  John, 132
  Phebe, 132
  Rachel, 132
YATES, Elizabeth, 45
YEARSLEY, Isaac, 141, 205
  James, 141, 205
  Mary, 141, 205
  Thomas, 141, 205
YEATES, Ann, 27, 40
  Ann Catharine, 70
  Donaldson, 241
  Elizabeth, 45
  John, 27, 57, 71, 238
YOUNG, Ann, 109
  Barnett, 84
  Barnott, 80
  Christopher, 2
  David, 245
  Deborah, 177
  Elizabeth, 2, 47
  Hercules, 110
  Jane, 46
  Jeany, 232
  John, 59
  Nathaniel, 244, 245
  Rhoda, 244
  Sylvester, 259
YOUNGER, Mary, 43
YOURASON, Giles, 51

-Z-

ZANE, Esther, 160
  Hester, 143
  Jess Shenton, 143
  Joel, 160
  Jonathan, 145, 153
  Mary, 145, 153
  Mary Hanson, 143
  Nathan Shenton, 143
  Richard Shenton, 160
  Susanah, 143
  Timothy Hanson, 143
  William, 153, 189
ZIMMERMAN, Elizabeth, 30
  John, 28, 30, 59
  Mary, 28, 30

www.ingramcontent.com/pod-product-compliance
Lightning Source LLC
Chambersburg PA
CBHW071954220426
43662CB00009B/1128